THE JOHN HARVARD LIBRARY

The Journal of John Winthrop, 1630–1649

GOVERNOR JOHN WINTHROP
(courtesy of the American Antiquarian Society)

The JOURNAL of
JOHN WINTHROP
1630–1649

Abridged Edition

EDITED BY

Richard S. Dunn and Laetitia Yeandle

JHL

The BELKNAP PRESS *of*
HARVARD UNIVERSITY PRESS

Cambridge, Massachusetts, and London, England
1996

J. M. HODGES LEARNING CENTER
WHARTON COUNTY JUNIOR COLLEGE
WHARTON, TEXAS 77488

For Bernard Bailyn

Copyright © 1996 by the President and Fellows of Harvard College
and the Massachusetts Historical Society
All rights reserved
Printed in the United States of America

Manuscript of Volume One Transcribed and Modernized by Laetitia Yeandle
Lost Manuscript of Volume Two Transcribed and Modernized by James Savage
Manuscript of Volume Three Transcribed and Modernized by Laetitia Yeandle
Abridgment, Introduction, and Annotations by Richard S. Dunn

Library of Congress Cataloging-in-Publication Data

Winthrop, John, 1588–1649.
[Journal of the transactions and occurrences in the settlement of
Massachusetts and the other New England Colonies. Selections]
The journal of John Winthrop, 1630–1649 / edited by Richard S.
Dunn and Laetitia Yeandle. — Abridged ed.
p. cm. — (The John Harvard library)
Includes bibliographical references (p.).
ISBN 0-674-48426-6 (cloth : alk. paper). — ISBN 0-674-48427-4
(pbk. : alk. paper)
1. Winthrop, John, 1588–1649—Diaries. 2. Massachusetts—History—
Colonial period, ca. 1600–1775. 3. New England—History—Colonial
period, ca. 1600–1775. I. Dunn, Richard S. II. Yeandle, Laetitia.
III. Title. IV. Series.
F67.W7842 1996
974'.02—dc20 96-20644

F
67
.W7842
1996
C.2

Contents

✧

Illustrations follow page 170

Acknowledgments

This abridged edition of Governor Winthrop's journal has had a long history. Many years ago, Bernard Bailyn invited us to produce a modernized, lightly annotated edition of John Winthrop's journal for the John Harvard Library. When we decided after much trial and error that we wanted to attempt something more ambitious—an edition that reproduced the governor's seventeenth-century spelling, punctuation, and capitalization as far as possible, buttressed by extensive annotations—Professor Bailyn remained strongly supportive, only urging us to get on with the job. Eventually we completed our full-scale scholarly edition. But the need for a more modest and accessible student edition remained. With the encouragement of Aida Donald at Harvard University Press and Louis Tucker at the Massachusetts Historical Society, we have produced a second version of Winthrop's journal. In the present volume, we incorporate about 40 percent of the governor's text, we modernize his spelling, punctuation, and capitalization throughout, and we provide trimmer annotations than in the full-scale edition.

The division of labor between the editors in this abridged edition is as follows: Laetitia Yeandle is responsible for transcribing and modernizing Governor Winthrop's text, while Richard Dunn is responsible for abridging it and elucidating what Winthrop wrote. But our collaboration is much closer than this, for we have both scrutinized every word in the text and every comment in the annotations. James Savage—though dead for more than a century—is the ghostly third partner in our enterprise, since his modernized transcription is our text for the lost middle volume of Winthrop's journal.

We are very grateful to a number of people for their help and encouragement: the late Louis B. Wright of the Folger Shakespeare Library; Malcolm Freiberg, Marjorie Gutheim, and Conrad Edick Wright of the Massachusetts Historical Society, who spent much time reviewing and correcting our work; Elizabeth Suttell of Harvard University Press; Allen Guelzo, Alison Games, and Ann Little, who labored extensively on the annotations; David Hall, Francis J. Bremer, and Philip Chadwick Foster Smith, who generously served as expert consultants; Mary Ellen Geer, who edited the text; Robert C. Forget, who drew the maps; and Gerald Aylmer, Hugh Dawson, Mary Maples Dunn, Rachelle Friedman, Michael McGiffert, Edmund Morgan, and Valerie Pearl, who also assisted us in various ways.

We thank the Folger Shakespeare Library and the University of Pennsylvania for essential institutional support and sabbatical leaves, and the Massachusetts Historical Society, the National Endowment for the Humanities, the American Council of Learned Societies, and the Center for Advanced Study in the Behavioral Sciences for invaluable fellowship support. Much material from Richard Dunn's article, "John Winthrop Writes His Journal," is incorporated into the Introduction to this edition with kind permission from the editor of *The William and Mary Quarterly*.

Numerous keyboarders at the Center for Advanced Study in the Behavioral Sciences and at Smith College have done much of the seemingly endless word processing. While hoping that all of these helpers will recognize their manifold contributions, we nevertheless take full responsibility for the final product.

RICHARD S. DUNN

LAETITIA YEANDLE

Introduction

For 350 years Governor John Winthrop's journal has been recognized as the central source for the history of Massachusetts in the 1630s and 1640s. Winthrop was both the chief actor and the chief recorder in New England for two crucial decades. He reported events—especially religious and political events—more fully and more candidly than any other contemporaneous observer, and his account of the founding of the colony has greatly influenced all subsequent interpretations of Puritan Massachusetts. The governor's journal has been edited and published three times previously—in 1790, in 1825–1826, and in 1908—but all of these editions have long been outmoded.[1] The present editors have prepared two new versions of the journal: a full-scale, unabridged, old-spelling edition,[2] and this abridged, modernized edition, which incorporates about 40 percent of the governor's text. We have added to the abridged edition Winthrop's celebrated statement of religious purpose, "A Model of Christian Charity," that articulates his hopes and

---

1. The 1790 edition, published by Noah Webster, is incomplete and full of textual errors. The 1825–1826 edition, prepared by James Savage and reissued in 1853, has a much sounder text but eccentric and outdated annotations. The 1908 edition, prepared by James Hosmer, reproduces Savage's text with a few expurgations, and has minimal annotations. The Massachusetts Historical Society began to publish an old-spelling fourth edition in 1931, but abandoned this project after printing the first year of the journal.

2. *The Journal of John Winthrop, 1630–1649*, ed. Richard S. Dunn, James Savage, and Laetitia Yeandle (Cambridge, Mass.: Harvard University Press, 1996).

fears as he set forth for America. The governor wrote his "Model" in 1630 just as he was beginning his journal, and the two texts are closely related.

Winthrop's journal is a challenging document to decipher and to edit. He recorded it in three notebooks, only two of which survive. The first notebook (spanning the dates 29 March 1630 to 14 September 1636) and the third notebook (spanning the dates 17 September 1644 to 11 January 1649)—both preserved at the Massachusetts Historical Society—are extremely hard to read because of the author's difficult handwriting and the worn condition of the volumes. The middle notebook (spanning the dates October 1636 to 8 December 1644) was accidentally destroyed by fire in 1825, and the only reliable transcription of its contents is a modernized version by James Savage, who was editing Winthrop's journal at the time of the fire. The present editors offer the reader two quite different modes of transcription. Our unabridged edition keeps the governor's seventeenth-century spelling, punctuation, and capitalization in the first and third volumes as closely as practicable, in combination with Savage's modernized text for the lost middle volume. This abridged edition modernizes the text throughout, combining Yeandle's 1990s-style modernization of the first and last parts with Savage's 1820s-style modernization of the middle part.

John Winthrop was born on 12 January 1588 in Edwardston, Suffolk, the son of a local lawyer. He attended Trinity College, Cambridge, for two years and then studied the law at Gray's Inn in London. In 1610 he bought the manor of Groton from his uncle, and he subsequently served as justice of the peace in Suffolk while also presiding over the manorial court at Groton. In 1627 he was appointed an attorney of the Court of Wards and Liveries in London. Thus he was a member of the English ruling elite, and had the habit of command—as is evident to any reader of his journal. Another fundamental feature of Winthrop's life is that he became a dedicated convert to Puritanism in his youth, and over the years formed a wide network of alliances with fellow Puritans. By 1630 he had a considerable family to provide for: he was married to his third wife, Margaret Tyndal, and had eight living children—seven sons and one daughter. Although he was a relatively wealthy man, he had fallen into debt in the late 1620s, and was disgusted by the corruption (as he saw it) of English life and by Charles I's religious and political policies. When the king broke with his critics in Parliament in March 1629, Winthrop decided to sell his English estate and emigrate to America. He joined the Massachusetts Bay Company, which had just received a royal charter granting broad powers of self-government. On 26 August 1629 he pledged with eleven other Puritan gentlemen to move with his family to Massachusetts if the seat of the Company's government and its charter were also transferred to America. The Company shareholders agreed to this, and on 20 October 1629 they chose Winthrop as their new governor. He was then forty-one years old. In the winter of 1629–1630 under his leadership the Company organized a migration of about a thousand persons who sailed to Massachusetts in seventeen ships during the following spring and summer.[3]

In March 1630, Winthrop came to Southampton and boarded the ship *Arbella* to sail for America; while still in port—on 29 March—he started to write his journal. It was very likely at just about this date that he composed his eloquent "Model of Christian Charity," in which he called upon his fellow migrants to join together in building a Christian commonwealth in America (see pp. 1–11 below). But his initial reason for keeping a journal was more prosaic: he wanted to record the day-to-day experience of crossing the ocean for the information of family and friends still in England who would be sailing in 1631 or after to join him in America. During the sea voyage he systematically

---

3. For further background, see Edmund S. Morgan, *The Puritan Dilemma: The Story of John Winthrop* (Boston: Little, Brown, 1958), ch. 1–4; Lee Schweninger, *John Winthrop* (Boston: Twayne, 1990), ch. 1–3; and James G. Moseley, *John Winthrop's World: History as a Story; the Story as History* (Madison: University of Wisconsin Press, 1992), ch. 1.

reported the events of every single day until the *Arbella* anchored at Salem on 14 June 1630.

After reaching Massachusetts, Winthrop sent an account of the Atlantic crossing based on his journal back to England. And he made the crucial decision to continue keeping his journal, so that when he had the leisure he could write a fuller account of the founding of the colony. Winthrop had a fully developed conceptual framework within which to work. As he explained in "A Model of Christian Charity," the Massachusetts colonists had a special vocation to love and support one another and to obey the Lord's commandments as they followed His injunction to build "a City upon a Hill." Should they serve the Lord faithfully, He would bless their efforts; should they deal falsely, He would destroy their plantation. However grand his sense of divine mission, Winthrop was so busy trying to keep the colony going during his initial months in Massachusetts—when many people died or returned to England—that his journal entries were exceedingly brief and irregular. By the winter of 1630–1631 he had a little more time to write. Surprised by the bitterly cold weather, he composed his first extended anecdote, about the harrowing adventures of six Bostonians shipwrecked and frozen on Cape Cod (pp. 33–34 below). Winthrop saw this episode as evidence that God was testing the colonists' corrupt hearts, and he became openly jubilant in February 1631 when the *Lyon* returned from England with emergency provisions, because he sensed that the survival crisis was ending. During 1631 and 1632 he settled into a new form of record keeping, in which he took up his notebook several times a month, and wrote at greater length than in 1630. By the mid-1630s he was averaging nearly a full page every time he put pen to paper. There is almost no evidence in the first notebook that he wrote retrospectively. At most, he discussed incidents a month or two after they occurred.

Having filled up his first notebook in September 1636, Winthrop continued his journal in a (lost) second notebook. And he gradually changed his format, until by the early 1640s his narrative became less segmented and more continuous. His journal was turning into a history. Furthermore, during the course of his second notebook Winthrop began to write lengthy sections of his narrative well after the events described had taken place. This point cannot be proved incontrovertibly, since the original manuscript is destroyed, but close examination of his wording discloses solid evidence of a change from frequent writing sessions and contemporaneous reporting in 1636–1637 to irregular writing sessions and retrospective reporting by 1643–1644. Sometime in mid-1644, Winthrop seems to have stopped keeping his journal altogether for three or four years, and then finished the second notebook in 1647 or 1648.[4]

Winthrop probably took up his third notebook, which carries the narrative from 17 September 1644 to 11 January 1649, no earlier than mid-1648, and so he wrote most of the entries in this volume well after the events described. Inspection of Winthrop's handwriting indicates that he was working fast. He appears to have written twenty pages at one stretch, and fifteen pages on three other occasions. He made many more slips and errors than previously, writing up ten entries twice over and sometimes getting his dates wrong. His style also betrays haste; he has lost the compact precision characteristic of the entries from the 1630s. He seems to have composed most if not all of his final volume during the last few months of his life, between May 1648 and early March 1649, when he became too ill to write. He died on 26 March 1649.[5]

As he gradually changed his mode of composition between 1630 and 1649, Winthrop also gradually altered his perception of his own role

4. For a fuller discussion of Winthrop's changing method of composition, see the Introduction to the unabridged edition.

5. Winthrop's terminal date of composition cannot be established, except that the final entry is dated 11 Jan. 1649. Winthrop became bedridden in early Feb., and by 14 Mar. he was too weak to write. See *WP*, 5:311–312, 319, 325.

as author-actor. At first he narrated as anonymously as possible, presenting the *Arbella* passengers and the Massachusetts colonists collectively as "we," while seldom referring to his own leadership role as governor and rarely disclosing his personal opinions. But after he landed in Massachusetts, Winthrop could no longer keep himself out of the story, and soon he was reporting controversial matters that are not mentioned in the official colony records. Only through his journal do we learn that in April 1631 the magistrates reprimanded the Salem church for choosing Roger Williams as its minister, or that in 1632 Winthrop had a series of ugly confrontations with the deputy governor, Thomas Dudley. The portrait that Winthrop sketched of Dudley as a jealous, irascible colleague is bound to linger in the reader's consciousness. It is the first of a long series of unflattering vignettes. Winthrop was not a real portraitist; he never described people in three-dimensional detail. But like Benjamin Franklin in his *Autobiography*, he was adept at thrusting a few barbs into most of the personages who figure prominently in his story. Naturally he found little good to say about such outright adversaries as Thomas Morton, Roger Williams, Anne Hutchinson, Mary Dyer, John Underhill, Samuel Gorton, Peter Hobart, and Robert Child. But he was seldom unequivocally positive about his fellow magistrates. John Endecott was rash and blundering, Henry Vane was a spoiled youth, Richard Saltonstall was a dangerous incendiary, John Humfrey was a deserter. Likewise among the clergy, John Cotton was unsound, John Eliot was naive, Thomas Hooker was aggressive, Nathaniel Ward was meddlesome. To be sure, Winthrop freely admitted his own defects on occasion. Yet the reader who accepts his presentation will certainly conclude that the author of the journal was much the best and wisest public man in early Massachusetts.

Winthrop was the governor of his colony for twelve of the nineteen years he kept the journal: he was in charge in 1630–1634, 1637–1640, 1642–1644, and 1646–1649, and was continuously a magistrate. Once his administration came under attack, he began to explain and defend his actions. For example, on 17 February 1632 he tells how he convinced the people of Watertown—who had refused to pay taxes levied by the magistrates because they had no representatives at the General Court— that they were in error, "so their submission was accepted and their offence pardoned" (p. 45). But actually the Watertowners were the winners in this dispute. The May 1632 General Court voted that two representatives from every town should advise the magistrates on taxation, and in the spring of 1634 the freemen agitated for a larger share of power. Winthrop tells us that when the town representatives read the company charter, they discovered that the freemen were authorized to meet four times a year to make laws. Winthrop explained to them that the freemen were too numerous to legislate, nor were they qualified to establish a representative assembly. Nevertheless, on 14 May 1634 the General Court voted that deputies from each town were henceforth to meet with the magistrates four times a year to tax and legislate. Voting by secret ballot for the first time, the freemen in May 1634 chose Dudley as governor in place of Winthrop.

The General Court of May 1634 was Winthrop's worst defeat. The constitutional change was a greater blow than the electoral change, because he never could accept the new deputies from the towns as in any way equal to the magistrates; for the rest of his life he fought to restore the magistrates' independence and supremacy. But the electoral rebuff was also hard. For three years, from 1634 to 1637, other men took over the governorship and Winthrop was not always in agreement with their policy. This section of his journal is especially informative and interesting, because he supplies some inside details about the controversial issues of the day. These were difficult years for the Bay Colony. In England, Archbishop Laud was attacking the Massachusetts Bay Company, and in America, many of the Massachusetts colonists moved to Connecticut, Roger Williams was banished and fled to Narragansett Bay, the colonists plunged into a bloody war with the Pequot Indians, and in October 1636 the Antinomian controversy exploded in

Boston. Winthrop hints (and sometimes openly states) that matters in 1634–1637 could have been much better handled.

Yet Winthrop at this time was neither as full nor as frank a writer as he later became. For example, his reports on Roger Williams from 1631 to 1636 raise questions about what really happened and why. Winthrop presents Williams's rebellion against the Massachusetts church-state system as the work of a rigid and isolated fanatic who enjoyed no support outside of Salem. In January 1636 Winthrop seems to have been quite as eager as any of his fellow magistrates to ship the banished man back to England. Yet Williams later claimed that Winthrop encouraged him to flee to Narragansett Bay, and the Bay magistrates and clergy charged Winthrop with "overmuch lenity and remissness" immediately after Williams's flight, very likely because they suspected him of giving covert aid to the Salem rebel (pp. 87–89).

The journal reaches its most dramatic point in 1636–1637 with the Pequot War and the Antinomian controversy (pp. 96–135). Winthrop's interpretation of the Pequot War is somewhat equivocal. He hints, without quite saying so, that the Bay government blundered into the war, then briskly describes the virtual extermination of the Pequots in May–August 1637. But he was in no way equivocal about Anne Hutchinson. He saw this "woman of a ready wit and bold spirit" as a very dangerous adversary, since her stronghold was Winthrop's own Boston church, and her supporters included John Cotton and Governor Vane. Winthrop presents himself in the journal as the Antinomians' chief opponent. And at the May 1637 General Court, he scored the most satisfying triumph of his career when the freemen in a tense and stormy meeting elected him governor and dropped Vane and two other Antinomian magistrates from office (p. 119). In November 1637 the General Court consolidated this victory by banishing Hutchinson and Wheelwright and disarming or disenfranchising seventy-five of their supporters (pp. 132–133). In March 1638 the Boston church was finally persuaded to excommunicate Anne Hutchinson (pp. 139).

Once restored to power, Winthrop used his journal more aggressively than in the early 1630s to denigrate his opponents. In January 1638 he made a list of the "foul errors" and "secret opinions" of the Antinomians. In March 1638 he discovered that Mary Dyer, one of Hutchinson's supporters, had been delivered of a deformed stillborn fetus, and in September 1638 he heard that Hutchinson herself had a somewhat similar stillbirth after she was exiled to Rhode Island, whereupon Winthrop entered full descriptions of both "monstrous births" into his journal as proof positive that God had turned against the Antinomians (pp. 141–142, 146–147). By this time, Winthrop was clearly drafting the official history of his administration. He began to make notes on where to add further documentation when he got around to expanding his narrative, and he sometimes pointed out controversial issues, as when in 1641 he wrote: "Query, whether the following be fit to be published"—and then reported how Governor Bellingham improperly pursued and married a young lady who was pledged to another man (p. 192). Winthrop consulted with Thomas Shepard about how to present topics such as this, and Shepard—who told Winthrop that "you will have the hearts and prayers of many in the compiling of the History"—urged him to be completely candid: "Surely Sir," he wrote, "the work is of God."[6]

As Winthrop composed his narrative, he not only changed his mode of composition, and his perception of his personal role as author-actor, but also revised his understanding of God's design in bringing His chosen people to New England. Initially, he believed—as he stated in "A Model of Christian Charity"—that God intended the colonists to build a united covenanted community in Massachusetts, knitted together by bonds of brotherly affection. Through the first two years of his journal he played up the external challenges that the colonists faced, and played down the internal divisions among them. But by the mid-

6. Shepard to Winthrop, 27 Jan. 1640, *WP*, 4:182–183.

1630s he was focusing on Puritan troublemakers like Roger Williams, and when the Pequot War and the Antinomian controversy broke out simultaneously in 1636–1637, he saw that Satan was trying hard to destroy Christ's kingdom in New England. The Pequot War sharpened his hostility toward the Indians, and led him to conclude that the English could never live in settled peace with the natives unless they expunged their aboriginal culture. Much more important to Winthrop, the emergence of Puritan fanatics such as Roger Williams and Anne Hutchinson forced him to abandon his hope that the English colonists could live together in loving harmony. Williams and Hutchinson (in his view) were so utterly self-deluded that they not only rebelled against sound Christian policy but entered into active alliance with Satan. From 1638 onward, Winthrop viewed developments in Rhode Island (where most of the banished Puritan fanatics had gone) or in New Hampshire and Maine (where most of the anti-Puritan colonists were clustered) with the deepest suspicion. His reports on events from beyond the Massachusetts borders became news bulletins of abominable crimes and miserable disorders. Even within Massachusetts, "the devil would never cease to disturb our peace, and to raise up instruments one after another" (p. 149).

This sense of perpetual contest between the forces of good and evil was sharpened after 1640 when Charles I was forced to summon Parliament. Naturally Winthrop sided with the king's parliamentary critics, but he was greatly distressed when the expectation of reform at home stopped the Puritan migration to New England and persuaded many colonists to return to old England. And as civil war broke out between Parliament and the king, Winthrop discovered to his horror that the Puritans in London were entertaining radical ideas that had been banned in Boston in the 1630s, and that Parliament in 1644 and 1646 actually protected his Rhode Island adversaries Roger Williams and Samuel Gorton when they went to England and complained of being harassed by Massachusetts. Thus the revolutionary crisis at home deepened his conviction that Massachusetts must be ever vigilant in dealing with so-called friends as well as enemies. And as he interpreted the troublesome events of the 1640s, he found a powerful model in the historical books of the Old Testament, most particularly Exodus, Deuteronomy, and Judges. Here Winthrop could find a story line exactly to his purpose, recounting how God's chosen people—despite plentiful evidence of human backsliding and divine wrath—escaped from captivity and came to the promised land.

As Winthrop changed from a journalist to a historian, he not only wrote more belligerently but more voluminously: his treatment of the years 1643–1646 is more than twice the length of his treatment of the years 1633–1636. He explained his support for the wily French commander La Tour and for the grasping Boston merchant Robert Keayne in 1643 very fully (pp. 224–231), because he was criticized for mishandling both situations. And in his third volume, he deliberately magnified the Hingham mutiny of 1645 (pp. 274–284) and the Remonstrants' protest of 1646 (pp. 306–318) in order to demonstrate the baseness of his critics. He wrote up his impeachment trial of 1645 as a personal ordeal and vindication, and included the full text of his masterful "little speech" in which he lectured the court on the meaning of liberty and authority. Winthrop's electoral defeat in 1634 had been at least as important, both to him and to the colony, as his victory over the Hingham petitioners in 1645, yet he wrote up the 1634 episode in two pages and the 1645 episode in seventeen. And he was even more circumstantial in denouncing Dr. Robert Child and his fellow Remonstrants, who tried to subvert the colony government by appealing to Parliament.

Winthrop devoted much attention in his second and third volumes to sexual scandal—to cases of rape, fornication, adultery, sodomy, and buggery—but of course his purpose was not to titillate. When he reported that William Hatchet was executed for copulating with a cow or that George Spencer of New Haven was executed for siring a piglet with human resemblances, he was exhibiting these specimens of human depravity as proof that even in godly New England the Devil was continually at work. He dwelt as much on the penitential scaffold scenes as on the crimes, for God always searched out these sex offenders and punished them justly. Winthrop also reported on the punishments that God meted out to the political and religious rebels who rejected the Massachusetts church-state system. Anne Hutchinson, the greatest rebel, received the harshest judgment: first her monstrous childbirth in 1638 and then her murder by Indians in 1643. John Humfrey, who deserted Massachusetts for the West Indies and took many colonists with him, was punished by a fire that destroyed his barn and his stored crops, while his little daughter was raped by child molesters. Dr. Child was publicly humiliated on the streets of London, "and besides God had so blasted his estate as he was quite broken, etc." (p. 338). Winthrop might have observed that his own estate had also been blasted; in 1639 his bailiff contracted debts in his name totaling £2,500, forcing Winthrop to sell much of his property. The Massachusetts freemen dropped him from the governorship for two years after this happened, and in 1641 one of the deputies wanted to drop him from office altogether because he was "grown poor." Yet Winthrop barely mentioned his financial troubles, and then mainly to grumble that the colonists only raised £500 in a voluntary contribution to help him, for he categorically refused to interpret his own property loss as a providential sign.

It is striking to follow our author, who had been silent or evasive on controversial issues in the early 1630s, as he pursued such topics with special zest during the later 1640s. One of the great features of his journal/history, especially in the second and third volumes, is that Winthrop reveals so many of the friction points in his society. Surely few writers have adopted a more pugilistic mode of conflict resolution. Taking pains to identify the issues causing conflict, and to report the public debate over these issues, Winthrop argued for the correctness of his own position and then showed how his adversaries were deservedly punished for their sins. Writing in this aggressive fashion, he built lasting significance into the seemingly small-scale actions of a few thousand colonists in early New England. Which is why his journal will always remain the central source for the history of Massachusetts in the 1630s and 1640s. And why readers of today, as in past generations, will find themselves engaged—and sometimes repelled—by John Winthrop's militant view of his world.

Editorial Method

Our objective in this abridged edition is to present the essential features of Winthrop's journal while excising 60 percent of his text. We have made our cuts pretty evenly throughout the text, so as to preserve the overall shape of the journal and to illustrate the striking changes in Winthrop's style and interpretation as he turned from a journalist into a historian and as he turned from themes of communal brotherhood to themes of contest between good and evil. We have retained what appear to us to be the most interesting and colorful passages from the journal. Thus we keep Winthrop's account of the storms his ship passed through in sailing to America, most of his sparse commentary on the first months in Massachusetts, and much of his reportage throughout the journal on the chief political and religious controversies of the 1630s and 1640s, as well as most of his observations on the Indians and on such key oppositional figures as Roger Williams, Anne Hutchinson, and Samuel Gorton. We also provide a representative sample of Winthrop's comments on the weather and crop conditions, on the formation of new towns and the social life of the early settlers, and on Massachusetts' relations with the other New England colonies and with the French and Dutch. Finally, we keep many of his providential stories about the people in New England who were punished by God for their evil behavior. We have followed the same principles in our abridgment of Winthrop's "Model of Christian Charity."

Deletions of entire journal entries or of lengthy passages within entries are indicated by three ellipses: . . . Deletions of a single word, a phrase, or a sentence within journal entries are not noted.

Laetitia Yeandle has modernized the text for volumes one and three of the journal in a somewhat different fashion from James Savage's modernization of the text for the lost middle volume. These differences reflect changes in editorial practice between the 1820s and the 1990s. In the first and last parts of the journal, Yeandle keeps Winthrop's initial spelling of personal, place, and ship names in order to retain something of his seventeenth-century style, but modernizes the spelling of names in subsequent references. Similarly, she keeps the initial spelling of Indian words (such as "pawawes"). She also retains numerals and some abbreviations, and notes the most significant erasures and corrections. In the middle part of the text, Savage generally modernizes the spelling of personal, place, and ship names, as well as Indian words. He expands all abbreviations, usually spells out numerals, and only occasionally notes Winthrop's compositional changes. We have changed his spelling of several names to conform to our spelling in volumes one and three.

In all three parts of the journal, deleted words are placed ⟨within angle brackets⟩, inserted words are placed ∧within carets∧, and conjectural readings and editorial insertions are presented [within square brackets]. When Winthrop refers to a month by number, the name of the month is added [within square brackets].

The footnotes are designed to identify persons and places mentioned in the text, to clarify obscure words, to clarify Winthrop's references to dates, to supply Biblical citations, to translate Latin phrases, to supply cross-references to corresponding entries, and to provide interpretive commentary on substantive issues raised in the governor's narrative.

A MODEL OF
CHRISTIAN CHARITY
✥

Christian Charity: A Model Hereof [1]

God Almighty in His most holy and wise providence hath so disposed of the condition of mankind, as in all times some must be rich, some poor, some high and eminent in power and dignity, others mean and in subjection.[2]

The Reason hereof.

1. Reas: First, to hold conformity with the rest of His works, being delighted to show forth the glory of His wisdom in the variety and difference of the creatures, and the glory of His power in ordering all these differences for the preservation and good of the whole and the

---

1. Modernized and abridged from the text of the "Model" as printed in *WP*, 2:282–295. While no one doubts that JW is the author of this work, the only known seventeenth-century manuscript (owned by the New-York Historical Society) is not in his hand. This ur-copy of the "Model" has a cover note, obviously added later, which reads: "Written On Boarde the Arrabella, On the Atlantick Ocean. By the Honorable John Winthrop Esquire. In His passage, (with the great Company of Religious people, of which Christian Tribes he was the Brave Leader and famous Governor;) from the Island of Great Brittaine, to New-England in the North America. Anno 1630" (*WP*, 2:282). But Hugh J. Dawson argues that JW actually wrote and delivered this discourse before embarking for America, and that his friends circulated the piece in manuscript in England after he left; see Dawson's article, "John Winthrop's Rite of Passage: The Origins of the 'Christian Charitie' Discourse," *Early American Literature* 26 (1991): 219–231. Whichever view is correct, JW wrote the "Model" just as he was beginning to keep his journal.

2. JW was completely committed to this hierarchical view of society. In his day, England was governed by the king, the nobility, and a few thousand landed gentlemen (JW being one of these). And JW always assumed that the magistrates of the MBC, being high and

glory of His greatness; that as it is the glory of princes to have many officers, so this great King will have many Stewards, counting Himself more honored in dispensing His gifts to man by man then if He did it by His own immediate hand.

2. Reas: Secondly, that He might have the more occasion to manifest the work of His Spirit: first, upon the wicked in moderating and restraining them, so that the rich and mighty should not eat up the poor, nor the poor and despised rise up against their superiors and shake off their yoke. 2ly, in the regenerate in exercising His graces in them, as in the great ones, their love, mercy, gentleness, temperance, etc.; in the poor and inferior sort, their faith, patience, obedience, etc.

3. Reas: Thirdly, that every man might have need of other, and from hence it appears plainly that no man is made more honorable than another or more wealthy, etc., out of any particular and singular respect to himself, but for the glory of his Creator and the Common good of the Creature, Man. All men being thus (by Divine Providence) ranked into two sorts—rich and poor—under the first are comprehended all such as are able to live comfortably by their own means duly improved, and all others are poor according to the former distribution.[3]

There are two rules whereby we are to walk one towards another: Justice and Mercy. There is likewise a double law by which we are

---

eminent, were fully entitled to power and dignity in New England; see his statement on the magistrates' large authority and the people's small liberty, delivered on 3 July 1645, below. But JW also believed that the leaders of society have a divine mission to protect the poor from oppression, and to achieve communal unity through the practice of charity—meaning love. This is the central theme of his "Model."

3. In seventeenth-century England, there was a fundamental social and economic division between the propertied upper half of the population and the propertyless lower half of the population—who were permanently "poor," without education or hope of advancement, and who were barely able to survive as wage laborers. JW did not expect this situation to change in New England. Hence his invocation of "a City upon a Hill" is not a call for social transformation in America, but for spiritual transformation and Christian community.

regulated in our conversation one towards another: the Law of Nature and the Law of Grace, or the moral law [and] the law of the gospel. By the first of these laws, man [is] commanded to love his neighbor as himself; upon this ground stands all the precepts of the moral law, which concerns our dealings with men. To apply this to the works of Mercy, this law requires that every man afford his help to another in every want or distress. Secondly, that he perform this out of the same affection which makes him careful of his own good according to that of our Saviour, Math: [7:12], whatsoever ye would that men should do to you. This was practiced by Abraham and Lott in entertaining the Angels and the old man of Gibea.[4]

The Law of Grace or the Gospel hath some difference from the former as in these respects: first, the law of nature was given to man in the estate of innocency, this of the gospel in the estate of regeneracy. 2dly, the former propounds one man to another, as the same flesh and image of God, [but the law of grace] teacheth us to put a difference between Christians and others. 3dly, the law of nature could give no rules for dealing with enemies, for all are to be considered as friends in the estate of innocency, but the Gospel commands love to an enemy. If thine enemy hunger, feed him; love your enemies, do good to them that hate you, Math. 5.44.

This Law of the Gospel propounds likewise a difference of seasons and occasions. There is a time when a Christian must sell all and give to the poor, as they did in the Apostles' times. There is a time also when a Christian must give beyond their ability. Community of perils calls for extraordinary liberality, and so doth community in some special service for the Church . . .

Quest. What rule shall a man observe in giving in respect of the measure?

4. See Gen. 18–19; and Judg. 19:16–21.

Ans. If the time and occasion be ordinary, he is to give out of his abundance—let him lay aside, as god hath blessed him. If the time and occasion be extraordinary, then a man cannot likely do too much.

Objection. A man must lay up for posterity. The fathers lay up for posterity and children, and he is worse than an Infidel that provideth not for his own.[5]

Ans: [This is] meant of the ordinary and usual course of fathers, and cannot extend to times and occasions extraordinary. And it is without question that he is worse than an Infidel who through his own sloth and voluptuousness shall neglect to provide for his family.

Objection. The wise man's eyes are in his head (saieth Salomon)[6] and forseeth the plague; therefore we must forecast and lay up against evil times when he or his may stand in need of all he can gather.

Ans. This very argument Salomon useth to persude to liberality. Eccle: [11.1], cast thy bread upon the waters, etc. For first, he that gives to the poor lends to the Lord, and he will repay him even in this life an hundred fold to him or his. And I would know of those who plead so much for laying up for time to come, whether they hold that to be Gospel, Math: 16. 19, Lay not up for yourselves Treasures upon Earth, etc. When Elisha comes to the widow of Sareptah[7] and finds her preparing to make ready her pittance for herself and family, he bids her first provide for him; he challengeth first God's part which she must first give before she must serve her own family. These teach us that the Lord looks that when He is pleased to call for His right in anything we have, our own interest must stand aside till His turn be served . . .

Quest: What rule must we observe and walk by in cause of community of peril?

Ans: With more enlargement towards others, and less respect to-

5. 1 Tim. 5:8.
6. Eccl. 2:14.
7. 1 Kings 17:8–24.

wards our selves and our own right. Hence it was that in the primitive church they sold all, had all things in common, neither did any man say that that which he possessed was his own.[8] Likewise in the [Hebrews'] return out of the Captivity, because the work was great for the restoring of the church and the danger of enemies was common to all, Nehemiah exhorts the Jews to liberality and readiness in remitting their debts to their brethren. Thus did some of our forefathers in times of persecution here in England,[9] and so did many of the faithful in other churches, and it is to be observed that both in Scriptures and later stories of the Churches that such as have been most bountiful to the poor Saints, especially in these extraordinary times and occasions, God hath left them highly commended to posterity . . .

Having already set forth the practice of Mercy according to the rule of God's law, it will be useful to lay open the grounds of it also, being the other part of the commandment. And that is the affection from which this exercise of Mercy must arise. The Apostle tells us that this Love is the fulfilling of the law,[10] not that it is enough to love our brother and so no further. The way to draw men to the works of mercy is not by force of argument from the goodness or necessity of the work, but by framing these affections of love in the heart . . .

The definition which the Scripture gives us of Love is this: Love is the bond of perfection.[11] First, it is a bond, or ligament. 2ly, it makes the work perfect. There is no body but consists of parts, and that which knits these parts together gives the body its perfection, because it makes

8. See Acts 2:44–45; 4:32–35. JW jotted down this reference—along with several other Biblical citations that he drew upon in composing the "Model"—in an end page of the notebook he used for the first volume of his journal. See *The Journal of John Winthrop, 1630–1649*, ed. Richard S. Dunn, James Savage, and Laetitia Yeandle (Cambridge, Mass.: Harvard University Press, 1996), Appendix A.

9. JW's use of this phrase indicates to Hugh J. Dawson that he had not yet embarked for America when he wrote this discourse.

10. Rom. 13:10.

11. Col. 3:14.

each part so contiguous to other as thereby they do mutually participate with each other, both in strength and infirmity, in pleasure and pain. To instance in the most perfect of all bodies, Christ and His Church make one body. The several parts of this body, considered apart before they were united, were as disproportionate and as much disordering as so many contrary qualities or elements, but when Christ comes and by His Spirit and Love knits all these parts to Himself and each to other, it is become the most perfect and best proportioned body in the world, Eph: 4. 16.

From hence we may frame these conclusions.

1. First, all true Christians are of one body in Christ.

2ly. The ligaments of this body which knit together are Love.

3ly. No body can be perfect which wants its proper ligaments.

4ly. All the parts of this body being thus united are made so contiguous in a special relation as they must needs partake of each other's strength and infirmity, joy and sorrow, weal and woe. 1 Cor: 12. 26. If one member suffers, all suffer with it; if one be in honor, all rejoice with it.

5ly. This sensibleness and sympathy of each other's conditions will necessarily infuse into each part a native desire and endeavor to strengthen, defend, preserve, and comfort the other.

To insist a little on this conclusion being the product of all the former, the truth hereof will appear both by precept and pattern. 1 John 3:10,[12] ye ought to lay down your lives for the brethren. Gal: 6.2, bear ye one another's burdens and so fulfill the law of Christ.

For patterns, we have that first of our Saviour, who out of His good will in obedience to His father, becoming a part of this body, and being knit with it in the bond of love, found such a native sensibleness of our infirmities and sorrows as He willingly yielded Himself to death, to ease the infirmities of the rest of His body and so heal their sorrows.

12. Actually, 1 John 3:16.

From the like sympathy of parts did the Apostles and many thousands of the Saints lay down their lives for Christ again. The like we shall find in the histories of the church in all ages, the sweet sympathy of affections which was in the members of this body one towards another, their cheerfulness in serving and suffering together, how liberal they were without repining, and helpful without reproaching, which only makes the practice of Mercy constant and easy.

The next consideration is how this Love comes to be wrought. Adam in his first estate was a perfect model of mankind. But Adam, rent in himself from his Creator, rent all his posterity also one from another, whence it comes that every man is born with this principle in him, to love and seek himself only, and thus a man continueth until Christ comes and takes possession of the soul, and infuseth another principle: Love to God and our brother. Love cometh of God and every one that loveth is born of God, so that this Love is the fruit of the new birth, and none can have it but the new Creature. Now when this quality is thus formed in the souls of men, it works like the Spirit upon the dry bones, Ezek. 37 [7]. Bone came to bone, it gathers together the scattered bones or perfect old Adam and knits them into one body again in Christ, whereby a man is become again a living soul . . .

Thus it is between the members of Christ, each discerns by the work of the Spirit his own image and resemblance in another, and therefore cannot but love him as he loves himself . . . If any should object that it is not possible that Love should be bred or upheld without hope of requital, it is granted, but that is not our cause, for this Love is always under reward. It never gives, but it always receives with advantage . . . Nothing yields more pleasure and content to the soul than when it finds that which it may love fervently, for to love and live beloved is the Soul's paradise, both here and in Heaven. In the state of wedlock there be many comforts to bear out the troubles of that condition, but let such as have tried the most say if there be any sweetness in that condition comparable to the exercise of mutual Love . . .

It rests now to make some application of this discourse by the present design,[13] which gave the occasion of writing it. Herein are 4 things to be propounded: first the persons; 2ly, the work; 3ly, the end; 4ly, the means.

1. For the persons, we are a company professing ourselves fellow members of Christ. Though we were absent from each other many miles, and had our employments as far distant,[14] yet we ought to account ourselves knit together by this bond of Love, and live in the exercise of it, if we would have comfort of our being in Christ.

2ly. For the work we have in hand, it is by a mutual consent through a special overruling providence, and a more than an ordinary approbation of the Churches of Christ to seek out a place of cohabitation and consortship under a due form of government both civil and ecclesiastical. In such cases as this, the care of the public must oversway all private respects.

3ly. The end is to improve our lives, to do more service to the Lord, the comfort and increase of the body of Christ whereof we are members, that ourselves and posterity may be the better preserved from the common corruptions of this evil world to serve the Lord and work out our Salvation under the power and purity of His holy Ordinances.

4ly. For the means whereby this must be effected, we must not content ourselves with usual ordinary means. Whatsoever we did or ought to have done when we lived in England,[15] the same must we do and more also where we go. That which the most in their Churches maintain as a truth in profession only, we must bring into familiar and

---

13. The plan to create a Christian commonwealth in Massachusetts.

14. JW is noting that the Puritan migrants to Massachusetts in 1630 came from all over England. But in fact the large majority came from JW's neighborhood in SE England: the counties of Suffolk and Essex, and the city of London.

15. JW's wording here seems to support the traditional view that he had departed from England before he wrote the "Model," and that this discourse was composed during the Atlantic voyage.

constant practice, as in this duty of Love we must love brotherly without dissimulation,[16] we must love one another with a pure heart fervently,[17] we must bear one another's burdens.[18]

Neither must we think that the Lord will bear with such failings at our hands as He doth from those among whom we have lived. He hath taken us to be His after a most strict and peculiar manner, which will make Him the more jealous of our love and obedience. So He tells the people of Israel: you only have I known of all the families of the Earth, therefore will I punish you for your transgressions.[19]

When God gives a special commission, He looks to have it strictly observed in every article. Thus stands the cause between God and us. We are entered into Covenant with Him for this work, we have taken out a Commission, the Lord hath given us leave to draw our own Articles. Now if the Lord shall please to hear us, and bring us in peace to the place we desire, then hath He ratified this Covenant and sealed our Commission, [and] will expect a strict performance of the Articles contained in it. But if we shall neglect the observation of these Articles which are the ends we have propounded, and dissembling with our God, shall fall to embrace this present world and prosecute our carnal intentions, seeking great things for ourselves and our posterity, the Lord will surely break out in wrath against us, be revenged of such a perjured people, and make us know the price of the breach of such a Covenant.

Now the only way to avoid this shipwreck and to provide for our posterity is to follow the Counsel of Micah: to do justly, to love mercy, to walk humbly with our God.[20] We must be knit together in this work as one man, we must entertain each other in brotherly affection, we

16. Rom. 12:9–10.
17. 1 Pet. 1:22.
18. Gal. 6:2.
19. Amos 3:2.
20. Micah 6:8.

must be willing to abridge ourselves of our superfluities for the supply of others' necessities, we must delight in each other, mourn together, labor and suffer together, always having before our eyes our Commission and Community in the work. So shall we keep the unity of the Spirit in the bond of peace.[21] The Lord will be our God and delight to dwell among us, so that we shall see much more of His wisdom, power, goodness, and truth than formerly we have been acquainted with. We shall find that the God of Israel is among us, when ten of us shall be able to resist a thousand of our enemies, when He shall make us a praise and glory, that men shall say of succeeding plantations: the Lord make it like that of New England. For we must consider that we shall be as a City upon a Hill,[22] the eyes of all people are upon us; so that if we shall deal falsely with our God in this work we have undertaken, and so cause Him to withdraw His present help from us, we shall be made a story and a by-word through the world. We shall open the mouths of enemies to speak evil of the ways of God and all professors[23] for God's sake; we shall shame the faces of many of God's worthy servants, and cause their prayers to be turned into Curses upon us till we be consumed out of the good land where we are going. And to shut up this discourse with that exhortation of Moses, that faithful servant of the Lord in his last farewell to Israel, Deut. 30, Beloved, there is now set before us life and good, death and evil, in that we are commanded this day to love the Lord our God, and to love one another, to walk in His ways and to keep His Commandments and His Ordinance and His laws, and the Articles of our Covenant with Him that we may live and be multiplied, and that the Lord our God may bless us in the land where we go to possess it. But if our hearts shall turn away so that we will not obey, but shall be seduced and worship ⟨serve⟩ other Gods,

21. Eph. 4:3.
22. Matt. 5:14.
23. Professing Christians; in this context, church members.

our pleasures, and profits, and serve them; it is propounded unto us this day, we shall surely perish out of the good land whither we pass over this vast Sea to possess it:

> Therefore let us choose life,
> that we, and our seed,
> may live; by obeying His
> voice, and cleaving to Him,
> for He is our life, and
> our prosperity.

THE JOURNAL OF
JOHN WINTHROP

❧

Anno Domini 1630, March 29, Monday.

Easter Monday.[1] Riding at the Cowes near the Isle of Wight in the *Arbella*,[2] a ship of 350 tons whereof Captain Peter Milborne was master, being manned with 52 seamen and 28 pieces of ordnance (the wind coming to the N. and by W. the evening before), in the morning there came aboard us Mr. Cradocke,[3] the late governor, and the masters of his 2 ships, Captain John Lowe master of the *Ambrose* and Mr. Nicholas Hurlston master of the *Jewell*, and Mr. Thomas Beecher master of the *Talbott*, which 3 ships rode then by us—the *Charles*, the *Mayflower*, ∧the *William and Francis*∧, the *Hopewell*, the *Whale*, the *Success*, and the *Tryall* being still at Hampton[4] and not ready—when upon conference it was agreed that (in regard it was uncertain when the rest [of]

---

1. JW had boarded ship at Southampton about 20 March and reached Cowes, a port on the Isle of Wight, by 22 March. He began his journal on 29 March because he expected the fleet to sail that morning. But continual SW winds and stormy seas blocked his departure for ten days, until 8 April.

2. Named for Lady Arbella Johnson, sister of the earl of Lincoln and the highest born passenger in the fleet of 1630. The MBC had made a down payment of £750 for this ship, previously named the *Eagle*.

3. Matthew Cradock (d. 1641) was a wealthy London merchant, member of the East India and Virginia companies, and governor of the MBC from March 1629 until JW was elected his successor in Oct. 1629.

4. Southampton.

the fleet would be ready)[5] these 4 ships should consort together: the *Arbella* to be admiral, the *Talbot* vice-admiral, the *Ambrose* rear admiral, and the *Jewel* a captain. And accordingly articles of consortship were drawn between the said captain and masters, whereupon [Mr.] Cradock took leave of us and our captain gave [him] a farewell with 4 or 5 shot.[6]

About 10 of the clock we weighed anchor and set sail with the wind at N. and came to an anchor again over against Yarmouthe, and the *Talbot* weighed likewise and came and anchored by us. Here we met with a ship of [Hampton] called the *Plantation*, newly come from Virginia. Our captain saluted her and she us again, and the master, one Mr. Gueres, came aboard our ship and stayed with us about 2 or 3 hours, and in the meantime his ship came to an anchor by us.

Tuesday, [March] 30. In the morning about 10 of the clock, the wind being come to the W. with fair weather, we weighed and rode nearer Yarmouth. When we came before the town, the castle put forth a flag. Our captain saluted them and they answered us again . . .

Thursday, April 1, and 2. The wind continued very strong at W. and by S. with much rain. We kept a fast aboard our ship. In the time of our fast 2 of our landmen prized a rundlet of strong water[7] and stole some of it, for which we laid them in bolts[8] all the night, and the next morning the principal was openly whipped, and both kept with bread and water that day . . .

Monday, 5 April. The wind still W. and S. with fair weather. A maid of Sir R. Saltonstall[9] [fell] down at the grating by the cook room, but the carpenter's man (who occasioned her fall unwittingly) caught hold

---

5. The seven ships still at Southampton set sail in May and arrived in Massachusetts in early July, about three weeks after the *Arbella*. Altogether, 17 ships carried about 1,000 passengers to Massachusetts in 1630.

6. Cradock may have taken with him a copy of JW's lay sermon, "A Model of Christian Charity"; see p. 1 above.

7. Forced open a cask of liquor.

8. Leg irons.

9. Sir Richard Saltonstall (1586–1661) of Kellingley Manor, Yorkshire, an assistant and

of her with incredible nimbleness and saved her. Otherwise, she had fallen into the hold.

Tuesday, 6 [April]. Captain Burleigh, captain of Yarmouth Castle, a grave, comely gentleman and of great age, came aboard us and stayed breakfast, and offering us much courtesy he departed, our captain giving him 4 shot out of the forecastle for his farewell. He was an old sea captain in Q. Eliz. time and, being taken prisoner at sea, was kept prisoner in Spain 3 years. Himself and 3 of his sons were captains in Roe's voyage.[10] . . . Our captain called over our landmen and tried them at their muskets, and such as were good shot among them were enrolled to serve in the ship, if occasion should be. The lady Arbella and the gentlewomen and Mr. Johnson[11] and some others went on shore to refresh themselves . . .

Thursday, 8 [April]. About 6 in the morning, the wind being E. and N. ∧(fair weather)∧, we weighed anchor and set sail, and before 10 we gat through the Needles,[12] having so little wind as we had much to do to stem the tide, so as the rest of our fleet (we [being] 9 in all), ∧whereof∧ some ∧were∧ small ships which were bound for Newf: lande, could not get [out] all [of] them till the ebb. In the afternoon the wind came S. and W. and we were becalmed, but before 10 at night the wind came about to the N. a good gale, so ∧we∧ put up a light in the poop and weighed and set sail, and by daylight, *Friday, 9 April,* we were come to Portland, but the ⟨*Talbot* and some of⟩ the other ships being not able to hold up with us, we were forced to spare our mainsail and went on with a merry gale. In the morning we descried from the top 8 sail astern of us, whom Captain Lowe told us he had seen at

one of the most prominent members of the MBC, was sailing on the *Arbella* with five of his children.

10. Sir Thomas Roe had led an expedition to Guiana in 1610–1611.

11. Isaac Johnson (1601–1630), the husband of Lady Arbella and the richest passenger in the fleet of 1630, was the largest stockholder in the MBC.

12. Chalk pinnacles at the western tip of the Isle of Wight.

∧Dunne∧ nose[13] in the evening. We supposing they might be Dian-kerks,[14] our captain causes the gun room and gun deck to be cleared, all the hamackoes[15] were taken down, our ordnance laded, and our powder chests and fireworks made ready, and our landmen quartered among the seamen, and 25 of them appointed for muskets, and every man written down for his quarter.

The wind continued N. with fair weather, and after noon it calmed and we still saw these 8 ships to stand towards us, and having more wind than we they came up apace, so as our captain and the masters of our consorts were more occasioned to think they might be Dunkirks (for we were told at Yarmouth that there were 10 sail of them waiting for us). Whereupon we all prepared to fight with them, and took down some cabins which were in the way of our ordnance,[16] and out of every ship were thrown such bed mats as were subject to take fire, and we heaved out our longboats and put up our waist cloths[17] and drew forth our men and armed them with muskets and other weapons and instruments for fireworks; and for an experiment our captain shot a ball of wildfire fastened to an arrow out of a crossbow which burnt in the water a good time. The lady Arbella and the other women and children were removed into the ⟨quarter⟩ ∧lower∧ deck that they might be out of danger. All things being thus fitted, we went to prayer upon the upper deck. It was much to see how cheerful and comfortable all the company appeared, not a woman or child that showed any fear, though all did apprehend the danger to have been great if things had proved as might well be expected (for there had been 8 against 4 and the least

13. Dunnose, the headland on the SE coast of the Isle of Wight.

14. Privateers from Dunkirk, a port on the French coast held by Spain, which was at war with England in 1630.

15. Hammocks.

16. As JW explains on 17 April below, many of the *Arbella*'s passengers lodged on the gun deck; the cabins installed for them to sleep in were now dismantled.

17. Canvas cloths hung along a ship's waist, the exposed upper deck between the forecastle and the poop, to screen the crew during combat.

of the enemy's ships were reported to carry 30 brass pieces). But our trust was in the Lord of Hosts and the courage of our captain, and his care and diligence did much encourage us. It was now about one of the clock and the fleet seemed to be within a league[18] of us; therefore our captain (because he would show he was not afraid of them, and that he might see the issue before night should overtake us) tacked about and stood to meet them. And when we came near we perceived them to be our friends: the *Litle Neptune,* a ship of some 20 pieces of ordnance, and her 2 consorts bound for the Streightes,[19] a ship of Flushing and a Frenchman and three other English ships bound for Canada and Newfoundland. So when we drew near every ship (as they met) saluted each other, and the musketeers discharged their small shot. And so (God be praised) our fear and danger was turned into mirth and friendly entertainment. Our danger being thus over, we espied 2 boats on-fishing in the Channell, so every of our 4 ships manned out a skiff and we bought of them great store of excellent fresh fish of divers sorts.

Saturday, 10 April. The wind at E. and by N., a handsome gale with fair weather. By 7 in the morning we were over against Plimmouthe. About noon the wind slacked, and we were come within sight of the Lizard,[20] and towards night it grew very calm and a great fog, so as our ships made no way . . . This day 2 young men falling at odds and fighting, contrary to the orders which we had published and set up in the ship, were adjudged to walk upon the deck till night with their hands bound behind them, which accordingly was executed; and another man, for using contemptuous speeches in our presence, was laid in bolts till he submitted himself and promised open confession of his offense . . . And upon this occasion I must add here one observation, that we have many young gentlemen in our ship who behave themselves well and are conformable to all good orders . . .

18. Three nautical miles.
19. The Strait of Gibraltar.
20. The southernmost tip of Cornwall, and JW's last sight of England.

Sunday, April 11. The wind at N. and by W., a very stiff gale . . . The sickness of our minister[21] and people put us all out of order this day, so as we could have no sermons.

Monday, April 12. In the afternoon less wind, and our people began to grow well again. Our children and others that were sick and lay groaning in the cabins we fetched out, and having stretched a rope from the steerage to the mainmast, we made them stand, some of one side and some of the other, and sway it up and down till they were warm, and by this means they soon grew well and merry . . .

Thursday, [April] 15. At noon our captain made observation by the cross-staff[22] and found we were in 47° ∧37′∧ N. latitude. About 10 at night the wind grew so high and rain withal that we were forced to take in our topsail, and having lowed our mainsail and foresail the storm was so great as it split our foresail and tore it in pieces, and a knot[23] of the sea washed our tub overboard wherein our fish was awatering. The storm still grew and it was dark with clouds (though otherwise moonlight), so as (though it was the *Jewel*'s turn to carry the light this night, yet) lest we should lose or go foul one of another, we hanged out a light upon our mizzen shrouds. Before midnight we lost sight of our vice-admiral.[24] Our captain, so soon as he had set the watch at 8 in the evening, called his men and told them he feared we should have a storm and therefore commanded them to be ready upon the deck if occasion should be, and himself was up and down the decks ⟨most⟩ ∧all∧ times of the night.

Friday, [April] 16. About 4 in the morning the wind slacked a little,

---

21. The Rev. George Phillips; see 27 April below.

22. A simple instrument for measuring the altitude of the sun, moon, or stars above the horizon; it could determine latitude with some accuracy but not longitude, hence JW's precise estimates (as here) of his N-S positions and rougher estimates of his E-W positions.

23. Swelling.

24. The *Talbot* was not seen again until 2 July when it straggled into Charlestown 20 days after the *Arbella* had reached Salem.

yet it continued a great storm still, and though in the afternoon it blew not much wind, yet the sea went so high as it tossed us more than before, and we carried no more but our mainsail, yet our ship steered well with it, which few such ships could have done. All the time of the storm few of our people were sick (except the women who kept under hatches), and there appeared no fear or dismayedness among them.

Saturday, [April] 17. The wind SW., very ⟨strong⟩ ∧stormy∧ and boisterous. This day our captain told me that our landmen were very nasty and slovenly, and that the gun deck where they lodged was so beastly and noisome with their victuals and beastliness as would much endanger the health of the ship. Hereupon, after prayer we took order and appointed 4 men to see to it and to keep that room clean for 3 days, and then 4 other should succeed them, and so forth on. We were this evening (by our account) about 90 leagues from Sille,[25] W. and by S. At this place there came a swallow and lighted upon our ship . . .

Monday, [April] 19. This day, by observation and account, we found ourselves to be in 48° N. latitude and 220 leagues W. from the meridian of London. Here I think good to note that all this time, since we came from the Wight, we had cold weather, so as we could well endure our warmest clothes . . .

Friday, [April] 23. The wind still WNW., a small gale with fair weather. About 11 of the clock our captain sent his skiff and fetched aboard us the masters of the other 2 ships and Mr. Pincheon,[26] and they dined with us in the round house, for the Lady and gentlewomen dined in the great cabin. This day and the night following we had little wind, so as the sea was very smooth and the ship made little way . . .

Sunday, [April] 25. The wind northerly, fair weather but still calm.

25. The Scilly Isles, SW of Cornwall.
26. William Pynchon (1590–1662) of Springfield, Essex, was an assistant in the MBC and the future founder of Springfield, Mass.

We stood W. and by S. and saw 2 ships ahead of us as far as we could descry . . .

Monday, [April] 26. The 2 ships which we saw yesterday were bound for Canada. They bare up with us and, falling close under our lee, we saluted each other and conferred together so long till his vice-admiral was becalmed by our sails and we were foul one of another, but there being little wind and the sea calm, we kept them asunder with oars, etc., till they heaved out their boat and so towed their ship away . . .

Tuesday, [April] 27. The wind still westerly, a stiff gale with close weather. We steered WNW. About noon ∧some∧ rain, and all the day very cold. We appointed Tuesdays and Wednesdays to catechize our people, and this day Mr. Philipes[27] began it . . .

Thursday, [April] 29. We had been now 3 weeks at sea and were not come above 300 leagues, being about $\frac{1}{3}$ part of our way, viz., about 46 N. latitude and near the meridian of the Terceras[28] . . .

May 1, Saturday. It grew a very great tempest all the night, with fierce showers of rain intermixed and very cold.

Lord's day, May 2. The tempest continued all the day with the wind W. and by N., and the sea raged and tossed us exceedingly; yet through God's mercy we were very comfortable, and few or none sick, but had opportunity to keep the Sabbath, and Mr. Phillips preached twice that day. The *Ambrose* and *Jewel* were separated far from us the first night, but this day we saw them again.

Monday, [May] 3. In the night the wind abated. But all the time of the tempest we could make no way, but were driven to the leeward, and the *Ambrose* struck all her sails but her mizzen and lay a hull.[29] She

27. The Rev. George Phillips (1593–1644), previously vicar at Boxted, Essex, settled at Watertown, Mass. in 1630 and served as minister there until his death.

28. Terceira is an island in the Azores. JW's fleet continued at about the same rate of speed, taking another six weeks to reach the Massachusetts coast.

29. With the sails (except on the mizzenmast) furled and the helm lashed to the lee side.

brake her main yard. This day we made observation and found we were in 43 $\frac{1}{2}$ N. latitude.[30] We set 2 fighters in the bolts till night, with their hands bound behind them. A maidservant in the ship, being stomach sick, drunk so much strong water that she was senseless and had near killed herself. We observed it a common fault in our young people that they gave themselves to drink hot waters very immoderately . . .

Thursday, [May] 6. The wind at N., a good gale and fair weather. So we stood full west and ⟨went⟩ ∧ran∧ in 24 hours about 30 leagues. ⟨Three⟩ ∧Four∧ things I observed here: 1. That the declination of the polestar[31] was much, even to the view, beneath that it is in England; 2. That the new moon when it first appeared was much smaller than at any time I had seen it in England; 3. That all the way we came we saw fowls flying and swimming, when we had no land near by 200 leagues; 4. That wheresoever the wind blew, we had still cold weather, and the sun did ⟨not warm us⟩ not give so much heat as in England . . .

Saturday, [May] 8. About 4 of the clock we saw a whale who lay just in our ship's way (the bunch of his back about a yard above water). He would not shun us, so we passed within a stone's cast of him as he lay spouting up water . . .

Monday, [May] 10. The wind increased and was a great storm all the night. About midnight our rear admiral put forth 2 lights, whereby we knew that some mischance had befallen her. We answered her with 2 lights again and bare up to her so near as we durst (for the sea went very high and she lay ⟨abackstays⟩ ∧by the lee∧), and having hailed her we ⟨found⟩ ∧thought∧ she had sprung a leak; ∧but she had broken some of her shrouds∧, so we went a little ahead of her and, bringing our foresail abackstays, we stayed for her. And about 2 hours after she filled her sails and we stood our course together. But our captain went

---

30. They had now worked their way 6° S since leaving Southampton, to the latitude of the Maine coast. For the rest of the voyage they tried to hold to a due westerly course, which was difficult because they had to fight a prevailing W wind.

31. Polaris or the North Star.

not to rest till 4 of the clock, and some others of us slept but little that night.

Tuesday, [May] 11. The storm continued all this day till 3 in the afternoon, and the sea went very high, so as our ship could make no way, being able to bear no more but our mainsail about mid mast high. At 3 there fell a great shower of rain which laid the wind, and the wind shifting into the W. we tacked and stood into the head sea to avoid the rolling of our ship, and by that means we made no way, the sea beating us back as much as the wind put us forward . . .

Wednesday, [May] 12. Complaint was made to our captain of some injury that one of the under officers of the ship had done to one of our landmen. He called him and examined the cause, and commanded him to be tied up by the hands and a weight to be hanged about his neck, but at the intercession of the governor[32] (with some difficulty) he remitted his punishment . . .

Monday, [May] 17. The wind at S., a fine gale ∧and fair weather∧. We stood W. and by S. We saw a great drift, so we heaved out our skiff, and it proved a fir log which seemed to have been many years in the water, for it was all overgrown with barnacles and other trash. We sounded here and found no ground at 100 fathoms and more.[33] We saw 2 whales.

Tuesday, [May] 18. About 9 at night the wind grew very strong at SW. In this storm we were forced to take in all our sails, save our mainsail, and to low that so much as we could . . .

Wednesday, [May] 19. We were now in 44 12$'$ and by our account in the midway between the False Banke and the Maine Bancke.[34] All this night a great storm at W. by N.

---

32. That is, JW.

33. They were now approaching the longitude of the Grand Bank off Newfoundland. Had they found ground here, they would have known that they were too close to Newfoundland and too northerly.

34. The False Bank or Flemish Cap is the easternmost shoal of the Grand (or Main) Bank. By JW's account, the *Arbella* was now about 300 miles SE of Newfoundland.

Thursday, [May] 20. The storm continued all this day. Fast in the great cabin at 9 at night, etc., and the next day again etc. The storm continued all this night.

Friday, [May] 21. The wind still NW., little wind and close weather. We stood SW. with all our sails, but made little way and at night it was a still calm. A servant [of] one of our company had bargained with a child to sell him a box worth 3d. for 3 biscuits a day all the voyage, and had received about 40 and had sold them and many more to some other servants. We caused his hands to be tied up to a bar and hanged a basket with stones about his neck, and so he stood 2 hours.

Saturday, [May] 22. The wind SSW., much wind and rain. Our spritsail[35] laid so deep in as it was split in pieces with a head sea at the instant as our captain was going forth of his cabin very early in the morning to give order to take it in. It was a great mercy of God that it did split, for otherwise it had endangered the breaking of our bowsprit and topmasts at least, and then we had had no other way but to have returned for England, except the wind had come east. About 10 in the morning in a very great fret of wind it chopt suddenly into the W. as it had done divers times before, and so continued with a small gale and stood N. and by W. About 4 in the afternoon there arose a sudden storm of wind and rain, so violent as we had not a greater. It continued thick and boisterous ⟨till well in⟩ all the night. This day at 12 we made observation and were about 43[o], but the storm put us far to the N. again. Still cold weather . . .

Monday, [May] 24. We stood SW. About noon we had occasion to lie by the lee to straight our mizzen shrouds and the rear admiral and *Jewel,* being both to windward of us, bore up and came under our lee to inquire if anything were amiss with us. So we heard the company was in health in ⟨both the ships⟩ the *Jewel,* but that 2 passengers were dead in the *Ambrose* and one other cow . . .

35. A sail slung under the bowsprit.

Thursday, [May] 27. This day our skiff went aboard the *Jewel* for a hogshead of meal which we borrowed because we could not come by our own, and there came back in the skiff the master of the *Jewel* and Mr. Revell,[36] so our captain stayed them dinner and sent for Captain Lowe. We understood now that the 2 which died in the *Ambrose* were Mr. Cradock's servants, who were sick when they came to sea, and one of them should have been left at Cowes if any house would have received him. In the *Jewel* also one of the seamen died, a most profane fellow, and one who was very injurious to the passengers . . .

Lord's day, [May] 30. The wind N. by E., a handsome gale, but close, misty weather and very cold; so our ship made good way in a smooth sea, and our 3 ships kept close together. By our account we were in the same meridian with Isle Sable and $42\frac{1}{2}$[37] . . .

June 1, Tuesday. We stood W. by N. A woman in our ship fell in travail, and we sent and had a midwife out of the *Jewel*. She was so far ahead of us at this time (though usually we could spare her some sail), as we shot off a piece and lowed our topsails, and then she brailed[38] her sails and stayed for us. This evening we saw the new moon more than half an hour after sunset, being much smaller than it is at any time in England.

Wednesday, [June] 2. In the evening a great fog. Our captain, supposing us now to be near the N. coast[39] and knowing that to the S. there were dangerous shoals,[40] fitted on a new mainsail that was very strong ∧and∧ double, and would not adventure with his old sails as before when he had sea room enough.

Thursday, [June] 3. The wind S. by W., a good steady gale, and we

---

36. John Revell, an assistant in the MBC and part owner of the *Arbella;* he stayed only a few weeks in Massachusetts before returning to England.

37. Sable Island is 100 miles SE of Nova Scotia. By JW's reckoning they were passing 100 miles S of this island and were about 550 miles from their destination.

38. Hauled up.

39. Nova Scotia.

40. Georges Bank, E of Cape Cod.

stood W. and by N. The fog continued very thick and some rain withal. We sounded in the morning and again at noon and had no ground. We sounded again about 2 after noon, and had ground about ⟨63⟩ ∧80∧ fathoms, a fine gray sand.[41] So we presently tacked and stood SSE., and shot off a piece of ordnance to give notice to our consorts whom we saw not since last evening.[42] The fog continued all this night and a steady gale at SW.

Friday, [June] 4. The fog continued all this day. We sounded every 2 hours, but had no ground.

Saturday, [June] 5. In the morning the wind came to NE., a handsome gale, and the fog was dispersed; so we stood before the wind W. and by N. all the afternoon, being rainy. At night we sounded, but had no ground.

In the great cabin thanksgiving.

It rained most part of this night, yet our captain kept abroad and was forced to come in in the night to shift his clothes. We sounded every half watch, but had no ground.

Lord's day, [June] 6. The wind NE. and after N., a good gale, but still foggy at times and cold. We stood WNW., both to make Cape Sable[43] if we might and also because of the current, which near the west shore sets to the S., that we might be the more clear from the southern shoals, viz. of Cape Cod. About 2 in the afternoon we sounded and had ground at about 80 ∧fathoms∧, and the mist then breaking up, we saw the shore to the N. about 5 or 6 leagues off, and were (as we suppose) ∧to∧ the ⟨W⟩SW. of Cape Sable, and in 43 ¼. We tacked and stood W. and by N., intending to make land at Aquamenticus,[44] being to the N. of the Isles of Shoales.

41. The base of the *Arbella*'s sounding lead was coated with tallow, to which bottom samples adhered. JW's ship was now entering the shoals off the Nova Scotia coast.

42. The three ships separated at this point. JW did not see the *Jewel* again until it reached Salem on 13 June, nor the *Ambrose* until 19 June.

43. At the southern tip of Nova Scotia.

44. Now York, Me. Having made landfall at Cape Sable, Capt. Milborne planned to

Monday, [June] 7. The wind S. About 4 in the morning we sounded and had ground at 30 fathoms and was somewhat calm, so we put our ship astays and took, in less than 2 hours with a few hooks, ⟨55⟩ ∧67∧ codfish, most of them very great fish, ∧some 1 yard and $\frac{1}{2}$ long and a yard in compass∧. This came very seasonably, for our salt fish was now spent . . . A woman was delivered of a child in our ship, stillborn. The woman had divers children before but none lived, and she had some mischance now which caused her to come near a month before her time; but she did very well . . .

Tuesday, [June] 8. About 3 in the afternoon we had sight of land to the NW about ⟨8⟩ ∧15∧ leagues, which we ∧supposed∧ was the Isles of Monthegen, ∧but it proved ⟨otherwise⟩ Mounte Mansell.∧[45] Then we tacked and stood WSW. We had now fair sunshine weather and so pleasant a sweet ether as did much refresh us, and there came a smell off the shore ⟨which was⟩ like the smell of a garden. There came a wild pigeon into our ship and another small land bird.

Wednesday, [June] 9. Now we had very fair weather and warm. About noon the wind came to SW., so we stood WNW. with a handsome gale, and had the mainland upon our starboard all that day about ∧8 or∧ 10 leagues off. It is very high land, lying in many hills, very unequal.[46] At night we saw many small islands, being low land, between us and the main about 5 or 6 leagues off us; and about 3 leagues from us towards the main a small rock a little above water.[47] At night we sounded and had soft oozy ground at 60 fathoms, so the wind being

---

sail due W toward the southern Maine coast, fearing if he sailed SW more directly toward Massachusetts that the Arctic current would carry him onto Georges Bank. In fact, he sailed NW and touched the Maine coast at Mt. Desert Island instead of at York.

45. The *Arbella* was sighting Mt. Desert Island, known to JW as Mt. Mansell (named for an English admiral, Sir Robert Mansell). Mt. Desert is 65 miles further up the Maine coast than Monhegan Island.

46. The Camden Hills. The *Arbella* was now passing Penobscot Bay.

47. Matinicus Rock, 20 miles off the mouth of Penobscot Bay.

now scant at W., we tacked again and stood SSW. We were now in 43 $\frac{1}{2}$.

Thursday, [June] 10. In the morning a thick fog. Then it cleared up with fair weather, but somewhat close. After we had run some 10 leagues W. and by S., we lost sight of the former land but made other high land on our starboard as far off as we could descry.[48] About 4 in the afternoon we made land on our starboard bow, called the 3 Turks Heades,[49] being ∧a∧ ridge of 3 hills upon the main whereof the southmost is the greatest. Towards night we might see the trees in all places very plainly and a small hill to the southward of the Turks Heads. All the rest of the land to the S. was plain low land. Here we had a fine fresh smell from shore.

Friday, [June] 11. The wind still SW., close weather. We stood to and again all this day within sight of Cape ∧Anne∧. The Isles of Shoals were now within 2 leagues of us, and we saw a ship lie there at anchor, and 5 or 6 shallops under sail up and down. We took many mackerels, and met a shallop which stood from Cape Ann towards the Isles of Shoals, which belonged to some English fishermen.

Saturday, [June] 12. About 4 in the morning we were near our port. We shot off 2 pieces of ordnance and sent our skiff to Mr. Peirce his ship which lay in the [Salem] harbor.[50] About an hour after, Mr. Allerton came aboard us in a shallop as he was sailing to Pemaquid.[51] As we stood towards the harbor, we passed through the narrow strait between Bakers Isle and Kettle Isle[52] and came to an anchor a little within the islands.

48. Perhaps the White Mountains.

49. Mt. Agamenticus, near York, Me.

50. The *Lion*, captained by William Peirce, had left Bristol in Feb. with 80 passengers and reached Salem in May.

51. Isaac Allerton (1586?-1659) of Plymouth Colony was engaged in fur trading ventures along the Maine coast.

52. JW seems to have mixed up the names of two islands. He had passed Kettle Island

After Mr. Peirce came aboard us, and returned to fetch Mr. Endicutt,[53] who came to us about 2 of the clock, and with him ∧a Mr. Skelton[54] and∧ Captain Levett.[55] We that were of the assistants and some other gentlemen, and some of the women and our captain, returned with them to Nahumkeeke,[56] where we supped with a good venison pasty and good beer, and at night we returned to our ship, but some of the women stayed behind.[57] In the meantime most of our people went on shore upon the land of Cape Ann which lay very near us, and gathered store of ∧strawberries∧. An Indian came aboard us and lay there all night.[58]

Lord's day, [June] 13. In the morning the Sagamore ∧of Agawame∧[59] and one of his men came aboard our ship and stayed with us all day. About 2 in the afternoon we descried the *Jewel,* so we manned out our skiff and wafted[60] them in, and they went as near the harbor as the tide and wind would suffer.

---

while rounding Cape Ann, but was now passing between Little Misery Island and Baker's Island to enter Salem harbor.

53. John Endecott (1589?-1659) had been governor of the MBC's advance settlement at Salem from 1628 until JW's arrival. He continued to serve in the colony government as an assistant, and was eventually elected governor numerous times, starting in 1644.

54. The Rev. Samuel Skelton (d. 1634), formerly chaplain to the earl of Lincoln, had arrived in 1629 and was pastor of the Salem church.

55. Christopher Levett (1586–1630), a pioneer settler in Casco, Me.

56. Naumkeag, the Indian name for Salem.

57. JW returned to his ship and stayed there all the next day (Sunday) because, not yet having subscribed to the covenant of a gathered church, he was excluded from communion at Skelton's Salem church—a striking testimonial to the differences between religious practices in England and New England.

58. Notwithstanding this cheerful account of his arrival, JW found a distressing state of affairs at Salem. Eighty of the 300 colonists sent over by the MBC in 1628–1629 were dead, the others were sick and nearly out of food, and little preparation had been made for the 1,000 new arrivals of 1630. By mid-June, when the *Arbella* landed, the New England growing season was already well advanced. Since the MBC settlement at Salem could not possibly accommodate all the newcomers, JW and his colleagues had to decide quickly where else to settle, in order to clear fields and build lodgings before winter.

59. Masconomo was the sachem of the Pawtucket Indians who lived N of Salem. His base at Agawam ("fish curing place") was soon renamed Ipswich by the colonists.

60. Guided.

Monday, [June] 14. In the morning early we weighed anchor and, the wind being against us and the channel so narrow as we could not well turn in, we warped in our ship[61] and came to anchor in the inward harbor. In the afternoon we went with most of our company on shore, and our captain gave us 5 pieces.[62]

Thursday, [June] 17. We went to Mattachusettes to find out a place for our sitting down. We went up Misticke River about 6 miles.[63]

We lay at Mr. Mauerocke's[64] and returned home on Saturday. As we came home, we came by Nataskott, and sent for Captain Squibb ashore (he had brought the ⟨Plymouth⟩ west country people, viz. Mr. Ludlowe, Mr. Rossiter, Mr. Maverocke, etc., to the Bay, who were set down at Mattapan) and ended a difference between him and the passengers.[65]

61. Hurling the *Arbella*'s anchor well in advance, they moved the ship forward by hauling in the anchor cable.

62. A volley in salute. Here ends the first phase of JW's journal, his daily shipboard record, with 24 MS pages of entries meticulously covering the events of two and a half months (29 March–14 June). From now on the entries become much more irregular and brief, with only three MS pages of notes for JW's first six months in America (14 June–14 Dec. 1630). As he remarked in hurried letters to his family in England, JW was too busy during these crisis months to describe events adequately. But cryptic as these entries are, they supply more information about the initial settlement process than other contemporary records.

63. These two sentences are among the most tantalizing in the whole journal. By "Mattachusettes" JW means the environs of Boston harbor, inhabited at this time by only a handful of Englishmen. Five days after arrival, JW and the other newcomers were clearly bent on finding "a place" in this vicinity for their settlement. Possibly they were planning to build a single community for all the incoming colonists, but more likely they were looking for a site for the *Arbella* passengers, expecting that the other newly arriving groups would plant elsewhere. A small settlement had already been started at Charlestown, and a shipload of people from SW England was starting to plant at Mattapan on the S side of Boston harbor. Among the *Arbella* passengers there was disagreement as to the best site: JW seems to have favored the Mystic River, while Dep. Gov. Thomas Dudley preferred the Charles River.

64. Samuel Maverick (1602?–1676?) had been living for about six years on Noddle's Island, now East Boston. He was no Puritan, and gradually came into conflict with the MBC government.

65. Capt. Squib, master of the *Mary and John*, had embarked from Plymouth, Devon, on 20 March with 140 emigrants from the West of England; he landed them on 30 May at Nantasket at the southern entrance to Boston harbor, refusing to bring them into the

Whereupon, he sent his boat to his ship (the ⟨*Margett*⟩ ∧*Marye*∧ and *John*) and at our parting gave us 5 pieces. At our return we found the *Ambrose* in the harbor at Salem.

July 1, Thursday. The *Mayflower* and the *Whale* arrived safe in Charlton[66] harbor. Their passengers were all in health, but most of their cattle dead.

July 2, Friday. The *Talbot* arrived there. She had lost 14 passengers. My son H. W. was drowned at Salem.[67]

Saturday, [July] 3. The *Hopewell* and *William and Francis* arrived.

Monday, [July] 5. The *Trial* arrived at Charlestown, and the *Charles* at Salem.

Tuesday, [July] 6. The *Success* arrived. Many of her passengers were near starved . . .

Thursday, [July] 8. We kept a day of thanksgiving in all the plantations[68] . . .

[August 23,] Monday. We kept a court.[69]

Friday, [August] 27. We of the congregation kept a fast and chose Mr. Wilson our teacher, and Mr. Nowell an elder, and Mr. Gagar and Mr. Aspenall deacons. We used imposition of hands, but with this pro-

---

Charles River where they wanted to go. The three west country leaders mentioned by JW were Roger Ludlow (1590–1664?) and Edward Rossiter (d. 1630), both assistants in the MBC, and the Rev. John Maverick (1578–1636), who was Samuel Maverick's father. They all settled at Mattapan, soon rechristened Dorchester.

66. JW's abbreviation for "Charlestown." During late June, JW and the other new arrivals had been ferrying their goods from Salem to Charlestown. By 14 July JW was living in Charlestown, occupying a "great house" built by MBC servants the previous year.

67. Henry Winthrop, JW's second son, had just arrived in Massachusetts; he was swimming across a river to fetch a canoe when he caught a cramp and drowned, age 22. Writing to his wife on 16 July, JW displayed more emotion: "My son Henry, my son Henry, ah poor child" (*WP*, 2:302).

68. For the safe arrival of the ships from England. But on 30 July they held a fast day because so many of the colonists were sick and dying.

69. The first MBC Court of Assistants in Massachusetts met at Charlestown on 23 Aug. to discuss maintenance for the colony clergy, the judicial powers of the assistants, and the regulation of housebuilders' wages and prices.

testation by all, that it was only as a sign of election and confirmation, not ∧of∧ any intent that Mr. Wilson should renounce his ministry he received in England.[70]

September 20. Mr. Gager died.

September 30. About 2 in the morning Mr. Isack Johnson died, his wife the Lady Arbella of the house of Lincoln being dead about 1 month before. He was a holy man and wise and died in sweet peace, leaving ⟨a good⟩ ∧some∧ part of his substance to the colony.[71]

The wolves killed 6 calves at Salem, and they killed one wolf.

Thomas Morton adjudged to be imprisoned till he were sent into England, and his house burnt down, for his many injuries offered to the Indians and other misdemeanors.[72]

Finche ∧of Waterton∧ had his wigwam burnt and all his goods . . .

October 23. Mr. Rossiter, one of the assistants, died[73] . . .

70. Here JW describes the organization of his covenanted church, where—despite his disclaimers—the founders were rejecting Anglican forms and adopting Congregational practices. This church was started in Charlestown and soon transferred to Boston. The Rev. John Wilson (1588–1667) had formerly been a Puritan lecturer at Sudbury, Suffolk; he was starting a 37-year pastorate at Boston. As for the other officers, Increase Nowell (1590–1655) of London was an assistant in the MBC, William Gager was a Suffolk surgeon who died less than a month after his election, and William Aspinwall was a notary who later joined the Antinomians.

71. Two of the 14 officers of the MBC died in 1630 (Johnson and Rossiter), and another five returned to England (Revell, Vassall, Saltonstall, Sharpe, and Coddington), which left only seven magistrates to manage the colony by the spring of 1631. Among the colonists at large, the loss was almost as severe: some 200 of the 1,000 immigrants died within the first year and another 200 returned home.

72. Morton was the first of many dissidents to be expelled by the MBC. He was a bacchanalian character who had built a house called Merry Mount in present Quincy where he set up a maypole and sold liquor and firearms to the Indians. His punishment was ordered by the Court of Assistants on 7 Sept.

73. JW omits mention of the important General Court of 19 Oct., the first open meeting of the MBC in America. At this meeting, the magistrates proposed that the company freemen should elect the assistants, and the assistants should choose the governor and deputy governor. This proposal, which greatly curtailed the chartered rights of the MBC freemen, was accepted "by the general vote of the people." The magistrates then enrolled 108 men—probably just about every male household head in the colony—as freemen (*MR*, 1:79–80).

[November] 10. Firmin of Watertown had his wigwam burnt. Divers had their haystacks burnt by burning the grass.[74]

[November] 27. Three of the governor's servants were from this day to the 1 of December abroad in his skiff among the islands in bitter frost and snow (being kept from home by the NW. wind), and without victuals. At length they gat to Mount Woollaston and left their boat there and came home by land. Laus Deo.[75]

December 6. The governor and most of the assistants and other met at Rockesburie, and there agreed to build a town fortified upon the neck between this and Boston, and a committee was appointed to consider of all things requisite, etc.

[December] 14. The committee met at Roxbury and it was concluded that we could not have a town in the place aforesaid: 1. Because men would be forced to keep 2 families; 2. There was no running water, and if there were any springs they would not suffice the town; 3. The most part of the people had built already and would not be able to build again. So we agreed to meet at Watertown that day sennight and in the meantime other places should be viewed . . .

December 21. We met again at Watertown, and there, upon view of a place a mile beneath the town, all agreed it a fit place for a fortified town, and we took time to consider further about it.[76]

[December] 24. Till this time there was (for the most part) fair open weather with gentle frosts in the night. But this day the wind came NW., very strong, and some snow withal, but so cold as some had their

---

74. Many of the colonists were living in highly flammable Indian-style temporary housing during these early months, and they were also setting brush fires in order to clear their land preparatory to planting corn.

75. By this date JW was living in Boston; he moved from Charlestown in Oct. His servants had left their skiff near the site of Morton's Merry Mount.

76. The place agreed upon was Newtown (later renamed Cambridge). JW and Dep. Gov. Dudley were continuing the tug of war they started in June over where the colony leaders should live. JW saw Boston as the best site for the chief town, while Dudley wanted all the magistrates to move to Newtown, where he himself built a house in 1631.

fingers frozen and in danger to be lost. 3 of the governor's servants coming in a shallop from Mystic were driven by the wind upon Noddle's Island and forced to stay there all that night without fire or food; yet, through God's mercy, they came safe to Boston next day, but the fingers of 2 of them were blistered with cold, and one swooned when he came to the fire.

[December] 26. The rivers were frozen up, and they of Charlestown could not come to the sermon at Boston till the afternoon at high water. Many of our cows and goats were forced to be still abroad for want of houses.

[December] 22. Richard Garrard, a shoemaker of Boston and one of the congregation there, with one of his daughters, a young maid, and 4 others, went towards Plymouth in a shallop against the advice of his friends, and about the Gurnettes Nose[77] the wind overblew so much at NW. as they were forced to come to a killick[78] at 20 fathoms; but their boat drave and shaked out the stone, and they were put to sea, and the boat took in much water which did freeze so hard as they could not free her. So they gave themselves for lost and, commending themselves to God, they disposed themselves to die; but one of their company espying land near Cape Cod, they made shift to hoise up part of their sail, and by God's special providence were carried through the rocks to the shore, where some gat on land but some had their legs frozen into the ice so as they were forced to be cut out. Being come on shore they kindled a fire, but having no hatchet they could get little wood, and were forced to lie in the open air all night, being extremely cold. In the morning 2 of their company went towards Plymouth (supposing it had been within 7 or 8 miles, whereas it was near 50 miles from them). By the way they met with 2 Indian squaws, who coming home told their husbands that they had met 2 Englishmen. They thinking (as

77. The spit at the N entrance to Plymouth harbor.
78. Throw out an anchor made of a stone encased in a wooden frame.

it was) that they had been shipwrecked, made after them and brought them back to their wigwam and entertained them kindly; and one of them went with them the next day to Plymouth and the other went to find out their boat and the rest of their company, which were 7 miles off, and having found them he holpt them what he could, and returned to his wigwam and fetched a hatchet, and built them a wigwam and covered it, and gat them wood (for they were so weak and frozen as they could not stir). And Garrard died about 2 days after his landing, and the ground being so frozen as they could not dig his grave, the Indian hewed a hole about $\frac{1}{2}$ yard deep with his hatchet, and having laid the corpse in it he laid over it a great heap of wood to keep it from the wolves. By this time the governor of Plymouth had sent 3 men to them with provisions . . . [but] another of their company died (his flesh being mortified with the frost), and the 2 who went towards Plymouth died also, one of them being not able to get thither and the other had his feet so frozen as he died of it after. The girl escaped best; and one Harwood, a godly man of the congregation of Boston, lay long under the surgeon's hands[79] . . .

January. A house at Dorchester was burned down.

February 11. Mr. Freeman's house at Watertown was burned down, but being in the daytime his goods were saved.

February 5. The ship *Lyon,* Mr. William Peirce master, arrived at Nantasket. She brought Mr. Williams (a godly m⟨inister⟩an)[80] with his wife, Mr. Throgmorton, Perkins, Onge, and others with their wives and children, about 20 passengers, and about 200 ton of goods. She set sail from Bristow, December 1. She had a very tempestuous passage,

---

79. Garrett's daughter and Henry Harwood (d. 1637) were the only survivors among the six people in this party.

80. Roger Williams (1603–1683), the future founder of Rhode Island, had been a private chaplain at Otes, Essex. As JW soon discovered, he was a radical Puritan who believed in total separation from the Church of England.

yet through God's mercy all her people came safe, except Waye his son,[81] who fell from the spritsail yard in a tempest and could not be recovered, though he kept in sight near $\frac{1}{4}$ of an hour. Her goods also came all in good condition[82] . . .

[February] *10.* The frost brake up and after that, though we had many snows and sharp frosts, yet they continued not, neither were the waters frozen up as before. It hath been observed, ever since this bay was planted by Englishmen, viz. 7 years, that at this day the frost hath broke up every year.

The poorer sort of people (who lay long in tents, etc.) were much afflicted with the scurvy and many died, especially at Boston and Charlestown, but when this ship came and brought store of juice of lemons many recovered speedily. It hath been always observed here that such as fell into discontent and lingered after their former conditions in England fell into the scurvy and died.

[February] *18.* Of those which went back in the ships this summer for fear of death or famine, etc., many died by the way and after they were landed, and others fell very sick and low, etc. . . . The provisions which came to us this year came at excessive rates, in regard of the dearness of corn in England, so as every bushel of wheat meal stood us in 14s., peas ⟨8⟩11s. etc.

[February] *22.* We held a day of thanksgiving for this ship's arrival by order from the Governor and Council directed to all the plantations.

March *16.* About noon the chimney of Mr. Sharpe's house in Boston took fire (the splints being not clayed at the top),[83] and taking the thatch

---

81. Probably a son of Henry Way, a Devonshire man who had come to Dorchester, Mass. in 1630.

82. Peirce had hurried to Bristol for provisions in July 1630. His freight bill to JW shows that he spent £281 for wheat, peas, oatmeal, beef, pork, cheese, butter, suet, barley seed, and rye seed (*WP*, 2:318). By Feb. 1631 these goods were desperately needed.

83. Splints were laths, used here to build a chimney of wattle and daub (plaster-coated lattice) rather than of brick or stone.

burned it down, and the wind being NW. drive the fire to Mr. Colburne's house, and burnt that down also, yet they saved most of their goods.[84]

[March] 23. Chickatabot[85] came with his sanopps[86] and squaws and presented the governor with a hogshead of Indian corn. After they had all dined and had ∧each∧ a small cup of sack ∧and beads∧, and the men tobacco, he sent away all his men and women (though the governor would have stayed them in regard of the rain and thunder). Himself and one squaw and one sannup stayed all night, and, being in English clothes, the governor set him at his own table, where he behaved himself as soberly, etc., as an Englishman. The next day after dinner he returned home, the governor giving him cheese and peas and ∧a rug and∧ some other small things.

[March] 26. John Sagamore and James his brother[87] with divers sannups came to the governor to desire his letter for recovery of 20 beaver skins which one Wattes in England had cozened him of. The governor entertained them kindly and gave him his letter with directions to Mr. Downing in England, etc.[88]

The night before alarm was given in divers of the plantations. It arose through the shooting off some pieces at Watertown by occasion of a calf which Sir Richard S[altonstall] had lost, and the soldiers were sent out with their pieces to fright the wolves from thence till they might find it[89] . . .

---

84. Thomas Sharpe, an assistant in the MBC, sailed for England two weeks after this disaster. But William Colbron, who was the deacon of the Boston church, stayed on.

85. Sagamore of the Massachusett Indians who lived immediately S of Boston.

86. Sannups were married males or warriors.

87. Sagamore John on the Mystic River and Sagamore James on the Saugus River led the Pawtucket Indians who lived immediately N of Boston.

88. Emmanuel Downing (1585–1659?) was JW's brother-in-law and a London attorney who handled many of his English business affairs.

89. This reading is highly conjectural, since the bottom edge of the page is damaged and several words are almost impossible to decipher. Thomas Dudley reported the same event as follows: "Upon the twenty-fifth of this March, one of Waterton having lost a calf

April 12. At a court holden at Boston (upon information to the governor that they of Salem had called Mr. Williams to the office of a teacher)[90] a letter was written from the court to Mr. Endecott to this effect, that whereas Mr. Williams had refused to join with the congregation at Boston because they would not make a public declaration of their repentance for having communion with the churches of England while they lived there, and besides had declared his opinion that the magistrate might not punish the breach of the Sabbath nor any other offence, as it was a breach of the First Table,[91] therefore they marveled they would choose him without advising with the Council, and withal desiring him that they would forbear to proceed till they had conferred about it.[92]

[April] 13. Chickatabot came to the governor and desired to buy some English clothes for himself. The governor told him that English sagamores did not use to truck, but he called his tailor and gave him order to make him a suit of clothes; whereupon he gave the governor 2 large skins of coat beaver . . .

[April] 15. Chickatabot came to the governor again, and he put him into a very good new suit from head to foot; and after he set meat before them, but he would not eat till the governor had given thanks, and after meat he desired him to do the like and so departed . . .

---

and about ten of the clock at night hearing the howling of some wolves not far off, raised many of his neighbors out of their beds, that by discharging their muskets near about the place where he heard the wolves, he might so put the wolves to flight and save his calf" (Everett Emerson, ed., *Letters from New England: The Massachusetts Bay Colony, 1629–1638* [Amherst: University of Massachusetts Press, 1976], p. 82).

90. In New England churches with two ministers, one was generally appointed as the pastor and the other as the teacher. At Salem, Samuel Skelton was the pastor.

91. The tablet on which the first four of the Ten Commandments were engraved (Exod. 20:2–11); in Williams's interpretation the Lord was here requiring separation of church from state.

92. This letter to Endecott (unrecorded in the court minutes) opened a public breach between Roger Williams, with his insistence on total separation from the Church of England, and the Boston church with its policy of nominal allegiance to the mother church. The magistrates were intervening for the first time in the affairs of a covenanted church.

One ⟨Mr. Gardiner, calling himself⟩ Sir Christopher G., knight of the golden melice,[93] being accused to have 2 wives in England, was sent for, but he had intelligence and escaped and traveled up and down among the Indians about a month, but by news of the governor of Plymouth he was taken by the Indians and brought, *May 4,* to Boston[94] . . .

[May] 17. A General Court at Boston. The former governor was chosen again and all the freemen of the Commons were sworn to the government[95] . . .

June 14. At a Court, John Sagamore and Chickatabot being told at last Court of some injuries that their men did to our cattle and giving consent to make satisfaction, etc., now one of their men was complained of for shooting a pig, etc., for which Chickatabot was ordered to pay a small skin of beaver, which he presently paid.

At this Court one Philip Ratlife, a servant of Mr. Cradock's, being convict ore tenus[96] of most foul, scandalous invectives against our churches and government, was censured to be whipped, lose his ears, and be banished the plantation; which was presently executed.[97]

[June] 25. Captain Neale, governor of P[ascatawye][98], sent a packet of letters to the governor, directed to Sir Ch. Gardiner; which when the governor had opened, he found it came from Sir Ferdin. Gorges

93. A knighthood conferred by the Pope.

94. Sir Christopher Gardiner had come to Massachusetts shortly before JW arrived, apparently sent by Sir Ferdinando Gorges (see below) to spy on the MBC. He settled near Boston with "a comely young woman whom he called his cousin" (Bradford, 247). JW considered him a wicked Catholic as well as a bigamist; on 1 March the Court of Assistants ordered him sent as a prisoner to England.

95. This court was the second public MBC meeting convened in New England. The company officers gave the freeman's oath to 116 colonists, and secured an agreement that in the future only church members could become freemen (*MR*, 1:87).

96. By word of mouth.

97. This action stirred quick complaint against the MBC government in England; see p. 54 below.

98. Piscataqua, now Portsmouth, N.H.

(who claims a great part of the bay of Massachusetts).[99] In the packet was one letter to Thomas Morton (sent prisoner before into England). By both which letters it appeared that he had some secret design to recover his pretended right, and that he reposed much trust in Sir Christopher Gardiner[1] . . .

July 4. The governor built a bark at Mystic, which was launched this day and called *The Blessinge of the Baye* . . .

July 13. Canonicus's son, the great sachem of Naragansett, came to the governor's house with John Sagamore.[2] After they had dined he gave the governor a skin, and the governor requited him with a fair pewter pot which he took very thankfully, and stayed all night . . .

[July] 21. The governor and deputy and ∧Mr. Noell∧, the elder of the congregation at Boston, went to Watertown to confer with Mr. Phillips, the pastor, and Mr. Browne,[3] the elder of the congregation there, about an opinion which they had published that the churches of Rome were true churches. The matter was debated before many of both congregations, and by the approbation of all the assembly except 3 was concluded an error . . .

July] 30. Mr. Ludlow in digging the foundation of his house at Dorchester found 2 pieces of French money. One was coined 1596. They were in several places and above a foot within the firm ground.[4]

---

99. Sir Ferdinando Gorges (1588–1647) had obtained in 1620 a royal charter for his Council for New England, with title to a vast tract in America from the latitude of Philadelphia N to the St. Lawrence River; in the 1620s he started his own colony at Piscataqua. The Council for New England had issued a land patent to the newly formed MBC in 1628, but Gorges was hostile to the Puritan migration of 1630.

1. JW here added the following marginal comment: "These letters we opened because they were directed to one who was our prisoner, and had declared himself an ill willer to our government."

2. JW probably entertained Canonicus's nephew Miantonomi; this sachem shared command of the Narragansett Indians, who lived on the western shore of Narragansett Bay.

3. Richard Brown (1576?–1660) of Hawkedon, Suffolk, was formerly a member of a separatist congregation in London.

4. These French coins document the trading between Native Americans and Europeans that predated Puritan settlement in Massachusetts.

August 8. The Tarentines to the number of 100 came in 3 canoes, and in the night assaulted the wigwam of the Sagamore of Agawam by Merimak, and slew 7 men and wounded John Sagamore and James and some others (whereof some died after), and rifled a wigwam where Mr. Cradock's men kept to catch sturgeon, took away their nets and biscuit, etc.[5] . . .

[August] 31. The governor's bark called *The Blessing of the Bay,* being of 30 ton, went to sea.

September 6. . . . At the last Court a young fellow[6] was whipped for soliciting an Indian squaw to incontinency; her husband and she complained of the wrong, and were present at the execution and very well satisfied. At the same Court one Henry Linne was whipped and banished for writing letters into England full of slander against our government and orders of our churches . . .

[October] 11. The governor, being at his farm house at Mystic, walked out after supper, and took a piece in his hand supposing he might see a wolf (for they came daily about the house and killed swine and calves, etc.), and being about $\frac{1}{2}$ a mile off it grew suddenly dark, so as in coming home he mistook his path and went till he came to a little house of Sagamore John, which stood empty. There he stayed, and having a piece of match[7] in his pocket (for he always carried about him match and a compass, and in summertime snake-weed[8]), he made a good fire near the house, and lay down upon some old mats which he found there, and so spent the night, sometimes walking by the fire, sometimes singing psalms, and sometimes getting wood, but could not sleep. It was (through God's mercy) a warm night, but a little before day it began to rain, and having no cloak he made shift by a long pole

5. The Tarentines were Abnaki Indians from the Maine coast. The Sagamore of Agawam had killed some Tarentines, and this raid was in retaliation.

6. John Dawe, who was probably a servant.

7. Cord or cloth dipped in sulphur.

8. The root of this plant was used as a remedy against snake bites.

to climb up into the house. In the morning there came thither an Indian squaw, but perceiving her before she had opened the door he barred her out, yet she stayed there a great while assaying to get in, and at last she went away and he returned safe home, his servants having been much perplexed for him, and having walked about and shot off pieces and hallooed in the night, but he heard them not . . .

October 30. The governor having erected a building of stone at Mystic, there came so violent a storm of rain for 24 hours from the NE. and SE. as (it being not finished and laid with clay for want of lime) 2 sides of it were washed down to the ground, and much harm was done to other houses by that storm . . .

November 2. The ship *Lion,* William Peirce master, arrived at Nantasket. There came in her the governor's wife,[9] his eldest son and his wife,[10] and other of his children,[11] and Mr. Eliot a minister,[12] and other families, being in all about 60 persons who all arrived in good health, having been 10 weeks at sea and lost none of their company but 2 children, whereof one was the governor's daughter Anne, about one year and half old, which died about a week after they came to sea.

[November] 3. That night the governor went to the ship, and lay aboard all night, and the next morning the wind coming fair, she came to an anchor before Boston.

[November] 4. The governor, his wife, and children went on shore

9. Margaret Winthrop (1591–1647), JW's third wife, married him in 1618 and by 1631 had borne him six children, four of whom were living. Upon arrival, she immediately joined the Boston church.

10. John Winthrop, Jr. (1606–1676), identified hereafter as JW2, was the future founder of three New England towns and governor of Connecticut. Before coming to New England he had attended Trinity College in Dublin, traveled for a year in the Mediterranean, and married his cousin Martha Fones of London.

11. Mary (age 19) and Samuel (4). Two other sons, Stephen (12) and Adam (11), had come over with their father in 1630, and Deane (8) was left in England.

12. John Eliot (1604–1690) had taught school at Little Baddow, Essex; in New England he served as pastor to the Roxbury church for nearly 60 years and became the most notable Massachusetts missionary to the Indians.

with Mr. Peirce in his ship boat. The ship gave them 6 or 7 pieces. At their landing the captains with their companies in arms entertained them with a guard, and divers volleys of shot, and 3 drakes. And divers of the assistants and most of the people of the near plantations came to welcome them, and brought and sent for divers days great store of provisions, as fat hogs, kids, venison, poultry, goose, partridge, etc., so as the like joy and manifestation of love had never been seen in N.E. It was a great marvel that so much people and such store of provisions could be gathered together at so few hours' warning.

[November] *11.* We kept a day of thanksgiving at Boston.

[November] *17.* The governor of Plymouth[13] came to Boston and lodged in the ship . . .

[November] *23.* The congregation at Watertown (whereof Mr. George Phillips was pastor) had chosen one Richard Brown for their elder, before named, who persisting in his opinion of the truth of the Rom[ish] church and maintaining other errors withal, and being a man of a very violent spirit, the Court wrote a letter to the congregation directed to the pastor and brethren to advise them to take into consideration whether Mr. Brown were fit to be continued their elder or not. To which after some weeks they ⟨made⟩ returned answer to this effect, that if we would take the pains to prove such things as were objected against him, they would endeavor to redress them.

December 8. The said congregation being much divided about their elder, both parts repaired to the governor for assistance, etc. Whereupon he went to Watertown with the deputy governor and Mr. Nowell, and the congregation being assembled, the governor told them that being come to settle peace, etc., they might proceed in 3 distinct respects: 1. as the magistrates (their assistance being desired); 2. as mem-

---

13. William Bradford (1590–1657), who had been governor of Plymouth since 1621, was paying his first visit to Boston. It would be interesting to know if JW showed him the journal he was keeping, since Bradford says that he began to write his history of Plymouth plantation about 1630.

bers of a neighbor congregation; 3. upon the answer which we received of our letter, which did no way satisfy us. But the pastor, Mr. Phillips, desired us to sit with them as members of a neighbor congregation only, whereto the governor, etc., consented.[14] Then the one side were moved to open their grievances which they did to this effect, that they could not communicate with their elder, being guilty of errors both in judgment and conversation. After much debate of these things, at length they were reconciled and agreed to seek God in a day of humiliation, and so to have a solemn uniting, each party promising to refer what had been amiss, etc. And the pastor gave thanks to God and the assembly broke up.

January 27. The governor and some company with him went up by Charles River about 8 miles above Watertown, and named the 1 brook on the north side of the river (being a fair stream and coming from a pond a mile from the river) Beauer Brooke,[15] because the beavers had shorn down divers great trees there and made divers dams across the brook. Thence they went to a great rock upon which stood a high stone cleft in sunder that 4 men might go through it, which they called Adams Chaire because the youngest of their company was Adam Winthrop.[16] Thence they came to another brook, greater than the former, which they called Masters Brook because the eldest of their company was one John Masters.[17] Thence they came to another high ∧pointed∧ rock having a fair assent on the west side, which they called Mount Feake, from one Robert Feake who had married the governor's daughter-in-law.[18] On the west side of Mount Feake they went up a very high rock,

14. Phillips was trying to avoid a confrontation such as the Salem church had had with the magistrates in April 1631. By restricting JW, Dudley, and Nowell to the role of visitors from another congregation, he could turn the meeting to reconciling the two Watertown factions and sidestep the court's directive to dismiss Brown as elder.

15. This brook, still so named, rises in Waltham.

16. JW's 11-year-old son.

17. Masters was about 57 years old; he lived in Watertown and died in 1639.

18. Feake, a Londoner who settled in Watertown, had married Elizabeth Fones, the widow of JW's son Henry. His "mount" is in Waltham.

from whence they might see all over Neipnett[19] and a very high hill due west about 40 miles off, and to the NW. the high hills by Merrimack above 60 miles off[20].

February 7. The governor, Mr. Nowell, Mr. Eliot, and others went over Mystic River at Medford, and going about 2 or 3 miles they came to a very great pond which they called Spott Ponde. They went all about it upon the ice. From thence they came to the top of a very high rock. This place they called Cheese Rocke, because when they went to eat somewhat, they had only cheese (the governor's man forgetting for haste to put up some bread) . . .

February 17. The governor and assistants called before them at Boston divers of Watertown, the pastor and elder by letter, and the others by warrant. The occasion was for that a warrant being sent to Watertown for levying of £8, part of a rate of £60 ordered for the fortifying of the new town,[21] the pastor and elder, etc., assembled the people and delivered their opinions that it was not safe to pay moneys after that sort, for fear of bringing themselves and posterity into bondage. Being come before the governor and council, after much debate they acknowledged their fault, confessing freely that they were in an error, and made a retractation and submission under their hands, and were enjoined to read it in the assembly[22] the next Lord's day. The ground of their error was for that they took this government to be no other but as of a mayor and aldermen, who have not power to make laws or raise taxations without the people. But understanding that this government was rather in the nature of a Parliament, and that no assistant could be chosen but by the freemen who had power likewise to remove

19. Possibly the estuary of the Neponset River, S and W of Dorchester.

20. They were viewing Wachusett Mountain, a 2,000 ft. peak in Worcester County, and also the spurs of Mt. Monadnock in SW New Hampshire.

21. Newtown was renamed Cambridge in 1638.

22. At the Watertown church service.

the assistants and put in others, and therefore at every General Court (which was to be held once every year) they had free liberty to confer and propound anything concerning the same, and to declare their grievances with∧out∧ being subject to question, or etc., they were fully satisfied, and so their submission was accepted and their offence pardoned[23] . . .

1632, April 3.[24] At a Court at Boston, the deputy Mr. Dudly[25] went away before the Court was ended, and then the secretary[26] delivered the governor a letter from him, directed to the governor and assistants, wherein he declared a resignation of his deputyship and place of assistant. But it was not allowed . . .

May 1. The governor and assistants met at Boston to consider of the deputy his deserting his place. The points discussed were 2: the 1. upon what grounds he did it; 2., whether it were good ∧or void∧. For the 1., his main reason was for public peace, because he must needs discharge his conscience in speaking freely and he saw that bred disturbance, etc. For the 2., it was maintained by all that he could not leave his place except by the same power which put him in. Yet he would not be put from his contrary opinion, nor would be persuaded to continue till the General Court which was to be the 9th of this month.

23. Although JW claims victory in this controversy, the Watertown agitators had effectively challenged the executive independence of the MBC magistrates. The General Court on 8 May 1632 (see below) acceded to Watertown's complaint by ordering that two delegates from every town should advise the magistrates on taxation—a clear step toward the formation of a legislative assembly, made up of deputies from every town, in 1634.

24. JW employed the Julian, or Old Style, calendar, which was ten days behind the Gregorian, or New Style, calendar finally adopted by Englishmen and Americans in 1752. The Old Style calendar started the new year on 25 March rather than 1 Jan., and since this is JW's first entry after that date, he notes the new year at this point.

25. Thomas Dudley (1576–1653), the flinty deputy governor of the MBC, was a Northampton man who had served under Henry IV of France in his youth, and was the earl of Lincoln's steward in the 1620s before sailing with JW on the *Arbella.*

26. Simon Bradstreet (1603–1697), the most junior magistrate at this date, eventually became governor of the colony; his wife was the poet Anne Bradstreet.

Another question fell out with him about some bargains he had made with some poor men, members of the same congregation, to whom he had sold 7 bushels and $\frac{1}{2}$ of corn to receive 10 for it after harvest, which the governor and some others held to be oppressing usury and within compass of the statute; but he persisted to maintain it to be lawful and there arose hot words about it, he telling the governor that if he had thought he had sent for him to his house to give him such usage he would not have come there, and that he never knew any man of understanding of other opinion, and that the governor thought otherwise of it, it was his weakness. The governor took notice of these speeches and bare them with more patience than he had done upon a like occasion at another time. Upon this there arose another question about his house, the governor having formerly told him that he did not well to bestow such cost about wainscotting and adorning his house in the beginning of a plantation, both in regard of the necessity of public charges and for example, etc. His answer now was that it was for the warmth of his house and the charge was little, being but clapboards nailed to the walls in the form of wainscot. These and other speeches passed before dinner. After dinner the governor told them that he had heard that the people intended at next General Court to desire that the assistants might be chosen anew every year, and that the governor might be chosen by the whole Court and not by the assistants only. Upon this Mr. Ludlow grew into passion and said that then we should have no government, but there would be an interim wherein every man might do what he pleased, etc. This was answered and cleared in the judgment of the rest of the assistants, but he continued stiff in his opinion and protested he would then return back into England . . .

Thus the day was spent and no good done, which was the more uncomfortable to most of them because they had commended this meeting to God in more earnest manner than ordinary at other meetings.

May 8. A General Court at Boston. Whereas it was (at our first coming) agreed that the freemen should choose the assistants and they the governor, the whole court agreed now that the governor and assistants should all be new chosen every year by the General Court (the governor to be always chosen out of the assistants), and accordingly the old governor Jo. W. was chosen over all the rest as before, and Mr. Humfrye and Mr. Coddington also, because they were daily expected.[27]

The deputy governor, Thomas Dudley, Esq., having submitted the validity of his resignation to the vote of the Court, it was adjudged a nullity, and he accepted of his place again, and the governor and he being reconciled the day before, all things were carried very lovingly amongst all, etc., and the people carried themselves with much silence and modesty.

John Winthrop, the governor's son, was chosen an assistant.

A proposition was made by the people that every company of trained men might choose their own captain and officers, but the governor giving them reasons to the contrary, they were satisfied without it.

Every town choose 2 men to be at the next Court to advise with the governor and assistants about the raising of a public stock, so as what they should agree upon should bind all, etc.

The governor (among other things) used this speech to the people after he had taken his oath, that he had received gratuities from divers towns, which he received with much comfort and content; he had also received many kindnesses from particular persons, which he would not refuse lest he should be accounted uncourteous, etc., but he professed that he received them with a trembling heart in regard of God's rule and the consciousness of his own infirmity. And therefore desired them that hereafter they would not take it ill if he did refuse presents from particular persons except they were from the assistants or from some special friends. To which no answer was made, but he was told after

27. Both John Humfrey and William Coddington had previously been assistants. Coddington, having gone back to England in 1631, returned to Massachusetts in 1633; Humfrey arrived for the first time in 1634.

that many good people were much grieved at it, for that he never had any allowance towards the charge of his place.[28]

[May] 24. The fortification upon the Corne Hill[29] at Boston was begun.

[May] 25. Charlestown men came and wrought upon the fortification; Roxbury the next, and Dorchester the next . . .

[June] 13. A day of thanksgiving in all the plantations by public authority, for the good success of the King of Sweden and Protestants in Germany against the Emperor, etc.,[30] and for the safe arrival of all the ships, they having not lost one person nor one sick among them[31] . . .

[July]. At Watertown there was (in the view of divers witnesses) a great combat between a mouse and a snake, and after a long fight the mouse prevailed and killed the snake. The pastor of Boston, Mr. Wilson, a very sincere, holy man, hearing of it gave this interpretation: that the snake was the devil, the mouse was a poor contemptible people which God had brought hither, which should overcome Satan here and dispossess him of his kingdom. Upon the same occasion he told the governor that before he was resolved to come into this country he dreamed he was here, and that he saw a church arise out of the earth, which grew up and became a marvelous goodly church . . .

August 3. The deputy Mr. Thomas Dudley being still discontented with the governor, partly for that the governor had removed the frame of his house which he had set up at Newe towne, and partly for that

---

28. JW did receive a stipend of £150 in July 1633. But he claimed in 1634 that the governorship had cost him over £1,200 (*WP*, 3:173–174).

29. A promontory soon renamed Fort Hill on the SE shore of Boston peninsula, commanding the ship channel to the town.

30. In Sept. 1631 and April 1632 Gustavus Adolphus twice beat the imperial army under Count von Tilly, a turning point in the Thirty Years' War, because the Swedish victories prevented the Hapsburgs from establishing absolute political control and the Catholics from gaining total religious control in Germany.

31. JW reported that five ships arrived from England in 1632—the same number as in 1631—but they carried 245 passengers, an increase of 155.

he took too much authority upon him (as he conceived), renewed his complaints to Mr. Wilson and Mr. Welde,[32] who acquainting the governor therewith, a meeting was agreed upon at Charlestown, where were present the governor and deputy, Mr. Nowell, Mr. Wilson, Mr. Weld, Mr. Maverick, and Mr. Warham.[33] The conference being begun with calling upon the Lord, the deputy began to complain of the breach of promise, both in the governor and others, in not building at Newtown. The governor answered that he had performed the words of the promise, for he had a house up and 7 or 8 servants abiding in it by the day appointed. And for the removing of his house, he alleged that seeing that the rest of the assistants went not about to build, and that his neighbors of Boston had been discouraged from removing thither by Mr. Deputy himself, and thereupon had (under all their hands) petitioned him that he would not leave them, ⟨which⟩ ∧this∧ was the occasion that he removed his house. Upon these and other speeches to this purpose, the ministers went apart for one hour; then returning, they delivered their opinion that the governor was in fault for removing of his house so suddenly without conferring with the deputy and the rest of the assistants, but if the deputy were the occasion of discouraging Boston men from removing, it would excuse the governor a tanto but not a toto.[34] The governor, professing himself willing to submit his own opinion to the judgment of so many wise and godly friends, acknowledged himself faulty.

After dinner the deputy then demanded of him the ground and limits of his authority, whether by the patent or otherwise. The governor answered that he would challenge no greater authority than he might by the patent. The deputy replied that then he had no more authority than every assistant (except power to call courts and precedency for

32. The Rev. Thomas Weld (1595–1661), of Terling, Essex, had just arrived in Massachusetts; he became pastor at Roxbury.

33. The Rev. John Warham (1595–1670) was Maverick's colleague at Dorchester church.

34. From much, but not from all.

honor and order). The governor answered he had more, for the patent making him a governor gave him whatsoever power belonged to a governor by common law or the statutes, and desired him to show wherein he had exceeded, etc. In speaking this somewhat apprehensively, the deputy began to be in passion and told the governor that if he were so round he would be round too. The governor bade him be round if he would. So the deputy rose up in great fury and passion and the governor grew very hot also, so as they both fell into bitterness, but by mediation of the mediators they were soon pacified . . .

August 5. . . . The congregation of Boston and Charlestown began the meeting house at Boston for which and Mr. Wilson's house they had made a voluntary contribution of about £120.

[August] 14. This summer was very wet and cold (except now and then a hot day or 2), which caused great store of musketoes and rattlesnakes. The corn in the dry sandy grounds was much better than other years, but in the fatter grounds much worse, and in Boston, etc., much shorn down close by the ground with worms . . .

September 4. One Hopkins of Watertown was convicted for selling a piece and pistol with powder and shot to James Sagamore, for which he had sentence to be whipped and branded in the cheek. It was discovered by an Indian, one of James's men, upon promise of concealing him (for otherwise he was sure to be killed) . . .

There was much suspicion that the Indians had some plot against the English, both for that many Narragansett men, etc., gathered together, and divers insolent speeches were used by some of them; and they did not frequent our houses as they were wont, and one of their pawawes[35] told us that there was a conspiracy to cut us off to get our victuals and other substance. Upon this there was a camp pitched at Boston in the night to exercise the soldiers against need might be, and Captain Underhill (to try how they would behave themselves) caused

---

35. Priests or medicine men.

an alarm to be given upon the quarters, which discovered the weakness of our people who, like men amazed, knew not how to behave themselves, so as the officers could not draw them into any order. All the rest of the plantations took the alarm and answered it; but it caused much fear and distraction among the common sort, so as some which knew of it before, yet through fear had forgotten and believed the Indians had been upon us. We doubled our guards and kept watch day and night.

[September] 14. The rumors still increasing, the 3 next sagamores were sent for, who came ∧presently∧ to the governor . . .

[October] 25. The governor, with Mr. Wilson, pastor of Boston, went [by] shallop to Wessaguscus.[36] The next morning the governor and his company went on foot to Plymouth and came thither within the evening. The governor of Plymouth, Mr. ⟨John⟩ ∧William∧ Bradforde (a very discreet and grave man), with Mr. Brewster the elder,[37] and some others came forth and met them without the town, and conducted them to the governor's house where they were very kindly entertained, and feasted every day at several houses. On the Lord's day there was a sacrament which they did partake in, and in the afternoon Mr. Roger Williams[38] (according to their custom) propounded a question to which the pastor, Mr. Smith,[39] spake briefly. Then Mr. Williams prophesied, and after, the governor of Plymouth spake to the question; after him the elder, then some 2 or 3 more of the congregation. Then the elder desired the governor of Massachusetts and Mr. Wilson to speak to it, which they did. When this was ended, the deacon Mr. Fuller[40] put the

---

36. Wessagusset is the Indian name for Weymouth, Mass.

37. William Brewster (1567–1644) had been the elder of the Pilgrim's church, first in Holland and then in Plymouth, since about 1609.

38. Having been blocked from the Salem pulpit (see 12 April 1631, above), Williams came to Plymouth where he stayed about two years; he then quarreled with the Pilgrims and returned to Salem in 1633.

39. The Rev. Ralph Smith was pastor at Plymouth from 1629 to about 1636.

40. Samuel Fuller had visited Salem in 1629–1630, and urged the Pilgrim form of worship upon the Massachusetts colonists.

congregation in mind of their duty of contribution; whereupon the governor and all the rest went down to the deacon's seat and put it into the box, and then returned . . .

[October] 31. Being Wednesday about 5 in the morning, the governor and his company came out of Plymouth, the governor of Plymouth with the pastor and elder, etc., accompanying them near $\frac{1}{2}$ a mile out of town in the dark. When they came to the great river,[41] they were carried over by one Luddam their guide (as they had been when they came, the stream being very strong and up to the crotch), so the governor called that passage Luddham Forde. Thence they came to a place called Hues Crosse; the governor being displeased at the name, in respect that such things might hereafter give the papists occasion to say that their religion was first planted in these parts, changed the name and called it Hues Follye. So they came that evening to Wessaguscus, where they were bountifully entertained as before with store of turkeys, geese, ducks, etc., and the next day came safe to Boston . . .

[November] 22. A fast was held by the congregation of Boston, and Mr. Wilson (formerly their teacher) was chosen pastor and Oliver a ruling elder,[42] and both were ordained by imposition of hands, first by the teacher and the 2 deacons (in the name of the congregation) upon the elder, and then by the elder and the deacons upon the pastor . . .

January 9. Mr. Oliver, a right godly man and elder of the Church of Boston, having 3 or 4 of his sons, all very young, cutting down wood upon the Necke,[43] one of them being about 15 years old had his brains beaten out with the fall of a tree which he had felled. The good

41. The North River between Marshfield and Scituate.
42. Thomas Oliver, a surgeon from Bristol, had joined the Boston church in 1630; he supported the Antinomians in 1636–1637.
43. Boston Neck, the narrow isthmus connecting the town of Boston to Roxbury. In the nineteenth century the colonial town's topography was totally reconfigured—and Boston Neck was obliterated—by extensive landfill on both the Charles River side and the Boston harbor side of the isthmus.

old father (having the news of it in as fearful a manner as might be by another boy, his brother) called his wife (being also a very godly woman) and went to prayer and bore it with much patience and honor.

[January] *17.* The governor, having intelligence from the east that the French had bought the Scottish plantation near Cape Sable and that the fort and all the ammunition were delivered to them, and that the cardinal[44] having the managing thereof had sent some commands already and preparation was made to send many more the next year and divers priests and Jesuits among them, called the assistants to Boston and the ministers and captains and some other chief men to advise what was fit to be done for our safety in regard the French were like to prove ill neighbors (being papists). At which meeting it was agreed that a plantation and a fort should forthwith be begun at Nantasket. And also, that the fort begun at Boston should be finished. Also, that a plantation should be begun at Agawam (being the best place in the land for tillage and cattle), lest an enemy finding it void should possess and take it from us. The governor's son, being one of the assistants, was to undertake this and to take no more out of the Bay than 12 men, the rest to be supplied at the coming of the next ships . . .

February 21. The governor and 4 of the assistants with 3 of the ministers and others, about 26 in all, went in 3 boats to view Nantasket, the wind W., fair weather; but the wind arose at NW. so strong, and extreme cold, that they were kept there 2 nights, being forced to lodge upon the ground in an open cottage upon a little old straw which they pulled from the thatch. Their victuals also grew short so as they were forced to eat mussels. Yet they were very merry and came all safe home the 3 day after through the Lord's special providence. Upon view of

---

44. Cardinal Richelieu, chief minister of France, had made peace with England in 1629, and in 1631 Charles I ordered Sir William Alexander, who had a charter to Nova Scotia and a settlement at Port Royal, to hand over his colony to the French.

the place it was agreed by all that to build a fort there would be of too great charge and of little use. Whereupon the planting of that place was deferred[45] . . .

[February] 26. Two little girls of the governor's family were sitting under a great heap of logs, plucking of birds, and the wind driving the feathers into the house, the governor's wife caused them to remove away. They were no sooner gone but the whole heap of logs fell down in the place and had crushed them to death if the Lord in his special providence had not delivered them.

1633, March. The governor's son, John Winthrop, went with 12 more to begin a plantation at Agawam, after called Ipswch. . . .

May. By [two] ships [from London] we understood that Sir Christopher Gardiner and Thomas Morton and Philip Ratcliffe (who had been punished here for their misdemeanors) had petitioned to the King and Council against us (being set on by Sir Ferdinando Gorges and Captain Mason who had begun a plantation at Pascataquack and aimed at the general government of New England for their agent there, Captain Neale). The petition was of ∧many∧ sheets of paper and contained many false accusations (and among some truths misreported), accusing us to intend rebellion, to have cast off our allegiance, and to be wholly separate from the church and laws of England; that our ministers and people did continually rail against the state, church, and bishops there, etc. Upon which such of our company as were then in England, viz. Sir Richard Saltonstall, Mr. Humfrey, and Mr. Cradock, were called before a ∧committee of the∧ Council to whom they delivered in an answer in writing. Upon reading whereof it pleased the Lord our gracious God and protector so to work with the lords and after with the King's Majesty that he said he would have them severely punished who did abuse his governor and the plantation, that the defendants were

45. The town of Hull on Nantasket neck was eventually founded in the 1640s.

dismissed with a favorable order for their encouragement, being assured from some of the Council that his Majesty did not intend to impose the ceremonies of the Church of England upon us, for that it was considered that it was the freedom from such things that made people come over to us. And it was credibly informed to the Council that this country would in time be very beneficial to England for masts, cordage, etc. . . .

July 2. At a court it was agreed that the governor, John Winthrop, should have towards his charges this year £⟨130⟩150, and the ⟨debt⟩ money which he had disbursed in public businesses, as officers' wages, etc., being between £200 and £300, should be forthwith paid . . .

September 4. The *Griffin*, a ship of 300 ∧ton∧, arrived. She brought about ∧200∧ passengers, having lost some 4, whereof one was drowned 2 days before as he was casting forth a line to take mackerel. In this ship came Mr. Cotton,[46] Mr. Hooker, and Mr. Stone, ministers,[47] and Mr. Peirce, Mr. Haynes (a gentleman of great estate), Mr. Hoffe, and many other men of good estates.[48] They gat out of England with much difficulty, all places being belayed[49] to have taken Mr. Cotton and Mr. Hooker who had been long sought for to have been brought into the High Commission,[50] but the master being bound to touch at the Wight, the pursuivants attended there, and in the meantime the said ministers

46. Heading the passenger list, in by far the most impressive boatload of immigrants since the *Arbella* in 1630, was the eminent Puritan preacher John Cotton (1584–1652), who had been vicar of St. Botolph's Church, Boston, Lincs. for 21 years until he was forced to resign in 1633.

47. Thomas Hooker (1586–1647) and Samuel Stone (1602–1633) had been Puritan lecturers in Essex and Northamptonshire respectively, both being too radical to secure regular parishes. Since 1630 Hooker had lived in exile at Delft and Rotterdam.

48. John Haynes (1588?–1654) of Copford Hall, Essex, was elected governor of the MBC in 1635 and governor of Connecticut in 1639. Atherton Hough (1580?–1650) was a prominent merchant in Boston, Lincs.

49. Watched by guards.

50. The Court of High Commission, one of the Crown's prerogative courts devoted to ecclesiastical causes, sought in the 1630s to suppress opposition to the Anglican establish-

were taken in at ∧the∧ Downes.[51] Mr. Hooker and Mr. Stone went presently to Newtown, where they were to be entertained, and Mr. Cotton stayed at Boston.

On Saturday evening the congregation met in their ordinary exercise, and Mr. Cotton being desired to speak to the question (which was of the Church), he showed out of the Canticles 6[52] that some churches were as queens, some as concubines, some as damosels, and some as doves, etc. He was then (with his wife) propounded to be admitted a member. The Lord's day following he exercised in the afternoon, and being to be admitted he signified his desire and readiness to make his confession according to order, which he said might be sufficient in declaring his faith about baptism (which he then desired for his child born in their passage and therefore named Seaborne).[53] He gave 2 reasons why he did not baptize it at sea (not for want of fresh water, for he held sea water would have served): 1. because they had no settled congregation there; 2. because a minister hath no power to give the seals[54] but in his own congregation. He desired his wife might also be admitted a member and gave a modest testimony of her, but withal requested that she might not be put to make open confession, etc., which he said was against the Apostle's Rule and not fit for women's modesty, but that the elders might examine her in private. So she was asked if she did consent in the Confession of Faith made by her husband and if she did desire to be admitted, etc.; whereto she answered affirmatively. And so both were admitted and their child baptized, the father presenting it . . .

---

ment by censuring, fining, or imprisoning clergy suspected of being Puritans. It was abolished by the Long Parliament in 1641.

51. After leaving London, the *Griffin* paused at this roadstead along the coast of Kent en route to the Isle of Wight, where the pursuivants or royal warrant officers were watching.

52. Song of Sol. 6:8–9.

53. This was the 48-year-old Cotton's first child; he went on to graduate from Harvard College (1651), and became a minister.

54. The symbols of the church covenant.

[September] *7.* The governor and Council met at Boston and called the ministers and elders of all the Churches to consider about Mr. Cotton his sitting down. He was desired to divers places, and those who came with him desired he might sit down where they might keep store of cattle, but it was agreed by full consent that the fittest place for him was Boston, and in that respect those of Boston might take farms in any part of the Bay not belonging to other towns . . .

October *2.* The bark *Blessing* which was sent to the southward returned. She had been ∧at∧ an island over against Conectecot called Longe Iland because it is near 50 leagues long; the E. part about 10 leagues from the main, but the W. end not one mile. There they had store of the best wamponp[ea]k,[55] both white and blue. The Indians there are a very treacherous people; they have many canoes so great as one will carry 80 men. They were also in the river of Connecticut which is barred at the entrance, so as they could not find above one fathom water. They were also at the Dutch plantation upon Hudsons River (called New Netherlandes) where they were very kindly entertained and had some beaver and other things for such commodities as they put off. They showed the governor (called Gwalter Van Twilly)[56] their commission, which was to signify to them that the King of England had granted the river and country of Connecticut to his own subjects, and therefore desired them to forbear to build there, etc. The Dutch governor wrote back to our governor (his letter was very courteous and respectful, as it had been to a very honorable person), whereby he signified that the Lords the States had also granted the same parts to the W. Indye Company,[57] and therefore requested that we would forbear the same till the matter were decided between the King of England and the said Lords . . .

55. Wampum.

56. Wouter van Twiller, governor of New Netherland from 1633 to 1638.

57. In 1621 the Estates General of the Dutch Republic had chartered the Dutch West India Company, which operated all Dutch colonies and trading posts in America.

[October] 10. A fast was kept at Boston, and Mr. Leverett, an ancient, sincere professor of Mr. Cotton's congregation in England, was chosen a ruling elder, and Mr. Firmin, a godly man, an apothecary of Sudburye in England, was chosen deacon by imposition of hands, and Mr. Cotton was then chosen teacher of the congregation of Boston and ordained by imposition of the hands of the Presbytery in this manner. First, he was chosen by all the congregation testifying their consent by erection of hands. Then Mr. Wilson the pastor demanded of him if he did accept of that call. He paused, and then spake to this effect, that howsoever he knew himself unworthy and unsufficient for that place, yet having observed all the passages of God's providence (which he reckoned up in particular) in calling him to it, he could not but accept it. Then the pastor and the 2 elders laid their hands upon his head, and the pastor prayed; and then taking off their hands laid them on again, and speaking to him by his name they did thereby design him to the said office in the name of the Holy Ghost, and did give him the charge of the congregation, and did thereby (as by a sign from God) indue[58] him with the gifts fit for his office; and lastly did bless him. Then the neighbor ministers which were present did (at the pastor's motion) give him the right hands of fellowship, and the pastor made a stipulation between him and the congregation.[59] When Mr. Cotton accepted of the office, he commended to the congregation such as were to come over who were of his charge in England, that they might be comfortably provided for . . .

November. A great mortality among the Indians. Chickatabot, the sagamore of Naponsett, died and many of his people. The disease was the smallpox. ⟨Many⟩ ∧Some∧ of them were cured by such means as

---

58. Endow.

59. This circumstantial account of Cotton's installation expresses the covenant between minister and congregation far more explicitly than JW's guarded account of Wilson's installation on 27 Aug. 1630, above.

they had from us. Many of their children escaped and were kept by the English . . .

The scarcity of workmen had caused them to raise their wages to an excessive rate, so as a carpenter would have 3s. the day, a laborer 2s. 6d., etc. And accordingly, those who had commodities to sell advanced their prices sometimes double to that they cost in England, so as it grew to a general complaint; which the Court taking knowledge of, as also of some further evils which were springing out of the excessive rates of wages, they made an order that carpenters, masons, etc., should take but 2s. the day and laborers but 18d., and that no commodity should be sold at above 4d. in the shilling more than it cost for ready money in England; oil, wine, etc., and cheese [excepted], in regard of the hazard of bringing, etc. The evils which were springing, etc., were: 1. many spent much time idly, etc., because they could get as much in 4 days as would keep them a week. 2. They spent much in tobacco and strong waters, etc., which was a great waste to the commonwealth, which by reason of so many foreign commodities expended could not have subsisted to this time but that it was supplied by the cattle and corn which were sold to newcomers at very dear rates, viz., corn at 6s. the bushel, a cow at £20, yea, some at £24, some £26, a mare at £35, an ewe goat at £3 or £4 . . .

[November] 12. News of the taking of Machias[60] by the French. Mr. Allerton of Plymouth and some others had set up a trading wigwam there, and left in it 5 men and store of commodities. La Tour,[61] governor of the French in those parts, making claim to the place came to displant them, and finding resistance killed 2 of the men and carried away the other 3 and the goods . . .

[November] 11. The congregation of Boston met to take order for

60. On the northern Maine coast.
61. Charles de Saint-Étienne de la Tour, governor of Acadia.

Mr. Cotton's passage and house, and his and Mr. Wilson's maintenance. Mr. Cotton had disbursed £80 for his passage and towards his house, which he would not have again, so there was ∧about∧ £60 raised (by voluntary contribution) towards the finishing of his house and about £100 towards their maintenance . . .

[December] 5. John Sagamore died of the smallpox, and almost all his people (above 30 buried by Mr. Maverick of Winesementt in one day). The towns in the Bay took away many of the children, but most of them died soon after. James Sagamore of Saugus died also, and most of his folk. John Sagamore desired to ∧be∧ brought among the English (so he was) and promised (if he recovered) to live with the English and serve their God. He left one son which he disposed to Mr. Wilson, the pastor of Boston, to be brought up by him. He gave to the governor a good quantity of wampumpeag, and to divers others of the English he gave gifts and took order for the payment of his own debts and his men's. He died in a persuasion that he should go to the Englishmen's God. Divers of them in their sickness confessed that the Englishmen's God was a good God and that if they recovered they would serve him.

It wrought much with them that when their own people forsook them yet the English came daily and ministered to them, and yet ∧few∧ ⟨only 2 families⟩ took any infection by it. Among others, Mr. Maverick of Winnissimet is worthy of a perpetual remembrance. Himself, his wife, and servants went daily to them, ministered to their necessities, and buried their dead, and took home many of their children. So did other of the neighbors[62] . . .

---

62. Modern commentators believe that European diseases, against which the Indians had no acquired immunity, killed 75 to 90 percent of the native population during the seventeenth century. In 1616–1619, before the Pilgrims and Puritans arrived, an epidemic introduced by European traders had wiped out most of the villages along the Massachusetts coast. The smallpox epidemic of 1633, described here by JW, killed thousands more, ravaging the Narragansetts and tribes further west.

December. It pleased the Lord to give special testimony of his presence in the Church of Boston, after Mr. Cotton was called to office there. More were converted and added to that Church than to all the other churches in the Bay.[63] Divers profane and notorious evil persons came and confessed their sins and were comfortably received into the bosom of the Church. Yea, the Lord gave witness to the exercise of prophesy, so as thereby some were converted and others much edified. Also, the Lord pleased greatly to bless the practice of discipline wherein he gave the pastor Mr. Wilson a singular gift to the great benefit of the Church. After much deliberation and serious advice the Lord directed the teacher Mr. Cotton to make it clear by the Scripture that the ministers' maintenance, as well as all other charges of the Church, should be defrayed out of a stock or treasury which was to be raised out of the weekly contribution; which accordingly was agreed upon.

December 27. The governor and assistants met at Boston and took into consideration a treatise which Mr. Williams (then of Salem) had sent to them, and which he had formerly written to the governor and Council of Plymouth, wherein among other things he ⟨questions⟩ ∧disputes∧ their right to the lands they possessed here, and concluded that claiming by the King's grant they could have no title, nor otherwise except they compounded with the natives. For this, taking advice with some of the most judicious ministers (who much condemned Mr. Williams's error and ⟨over⟩ presumption), they gave order that he should be convented at the next Court to be censured, etc. There were 3 passages chiefly whereat they were much offended: 1. For that he chargeth King James to have told a solemn public lie, because in his patent he blessed God that he was the first Christian prince that had discovered

63. The Boston church records show that the church had about 80 members at Cotton's arrival, and that 44 new members joined between Sept. and Dec. 1633. The revival continued in 1634 with 93 additional new members.

this land; 2. For that he chargeth him and others with blasphemy for calling Europe Christendom or the Christian world; 3. For that he did personally apply to our present King Charles these 3 places in the Revelation, viz.[64]

Mr. Endecott being absent, the governor wrote to him to let him know what was done, and withal added divers arguments to confute the said errors, wishing him to deal with Mr. Williams to retract the same, etc. Whereunto he returned a very modest and discreet answer. Mr. Williams also wrote very submissively, professing his intent to have been only to have written for ∧the private∧ satisfaction of the governor, etc., of Plymouth without any purpose to have stirred any further in it if the governor here had not required a copy of him; withal offering his book or any part of it to be burnt, etc. So it was left and nothing done in it.

January 21. News came from Plymouth that Captain Stone, who this last summer went out of the Bay, putting in at the mouth of Connecticut in his way to Virginia, where the Pequins inhabit, was there cut off by them with all his company, being ⟨10 or 12⟩ ∧8∧. The manner was thus: ⟨3 of his men, being gone ashore to kill fowl, were cut off. Then the sachem with some of his men came aboard, and stayed with Captain Stone in his cabin till Captain Stone (being alone with him) fell on sleep. Then he knocked him on the head, and all the rest of the English being in the cook room, the Indians took such pieces as they found there ready charged, and bent them at the English. Whereupon one took a ⟨fire stick⟩ ∧piece∧, and ∧by accident∧ gave fire to the powder, which blew up the deck. But most of the Indians, perceiving what they went about, shifted overboard, and after they returned, and killed such as remained and burned the pinnace. We agreed to write to the gov-

---

64. According to *WP*, 3:147–148, Williams's three applications were Rev. 16:13–14 (the spirits of devils go forth unto the kings of the earth); Rev. 17:12–14 (ten kings give their power and strength to the beast to make war with the lamb); and Rev. 18:9 (the kings of the earth have committed fornication with the whore).

ernor of Virginia (because Stone was one of that colony) to move him to revenge it, and upon his answer to take further counsel.)[65]

[January] 20. Hall and the 2 other who went to Connecticut November 3 came now home, having lost themselves and endured much misery. They informed us that the smallpox was gone as far as any Indian plantation was known to the W., and much people dead of it, by reason whereof they could have no trade. At Narragansett by the Indians' report there died 700, but beyond Pascataquack none to the E . . .

[February]. This winter was very mild, little wind, and most S. and SW.; but oft snows and great. One snow the 15 of this month was near 2 foot deep all over.

Such of the Indians' children as were left were taken by the English, most whereof did die of the pox soon after; 3 only remaining, whereof one which the governor kept was called Knowe God (the Indians' usual answer being, when they were put in mind of God, Me no know God) . . .

March 4. By order of Court a mercate[66] was erected at Boston to be kept upon Thursday the 5 day of the week, being the Lecture Day. Samuell Cole set up the first house for common entertainment, and John Cogan, merchant, the first shop . . .

[March] 7. At the lecture at Boston a question was propounded about veils. Mr. Cotton concluded that where (by the custom of the place) they were not a sign of the women's subjection they were not commanded by the Apostle. Mr. Endecott opposed and did maintain it by the general arguments brought by the Apostle.[67] After some debate, the governor perceiving it to grow to some earnestness interposed, and so it brake off.

---

65. JW deleted this description of Stone's murder after writing a second account under the date 6 Nov. 1634, below.

66. Market.

67. Paul in 1 Cor. 11:5–16.

Among other testimonies of the Lord's gracious presence with his own ordinances, there was a youth of 14 years of age (being the son of one of the magistrates)[68] so wrought upon by the ministry of the word as for divers months he was held under such affliction of mind as he could not be brought to apprehend any comfort in God, being much humbled and broken for his sins (though he had been a dutiful child and not given up to the lusts of youth), and especially for his blasphemous and wicked thoughts wherewith Satan buffeted him, so as he went mourning and languishing daily. Yet he came at length to be freed from his temptations and to find comfort in God's promises, and so, being received into the congregation upon good proof of his understanding in the things of God, he went on cheerfully in a Christian course, falling daily to labor as a servant, and as a younger brother of his did, who was no whit short of him in the knowledge of God's will, though his youth kept him from daring to offer himself to the congregation[69] . . .

April 1. Order was taken for ministering an oath to all housekeepers and sojourners being 20 years of age and not freemen,[70] and for making a survey of the houses and lands of all freemen.

Notice being sent out of the General Court to be held the 14 day of the (3) month called May, the freemen deputed 2 of each town to meet and consider of such matters as they were to take order in at the same General Court; who having met, desired a sight of the patent,[71] and

68. JW's son Stephen Winthrop (1619–1658), who was almost 15 at this date, had come over on the *Arbella* and joined the Boston church in March 1634.

69. Probably Adam Winthrop (1620–1652), who was 13 years old at this time; he joined the Boston church in 1640.

70. This oath, printed in *MR*, 1:115–116, stipulates loyalty to the colony government but makes no mention of allegiance to the king.

71. The royal charter of March 1629. Up to this point the officers of the MBC had kept the terms of the charter a secret and had freely ignored many of its provisions. They had altered the definition of freeman from shareholder in the company to adult male church member in the colony and had circumscribed the freemen's powers. The charter authorized the MBC freemen to elect their officers annually, which they did not do until 1632; the

conceiving thereby that all their laws should be made at the General Court, repaired to the governor to advise with him about it and about the abrogating of some orders formerly made, as for killing of swine in corn, etc. He told them that when the patent was granted the number of freemen was supposed to be (as in like corporations) so few as they might well join in making laws, but now they were grown to so great a body as it was not possible for them to make or execute laws, but they must choose others for that purpose. And that howsoever it would be necessary hereafter to have a select company to intend that work, yet for the present they were not furnished with a sufficient number of men qualified for such a business, neither could the commonwealth bear the loss of time of so many as must intend it. Yet this they might do at present, viz., they might at the General Court make an order that once in the year a certain number should be appointed (upon summons from the governor) to review all laws, etc., and to refer what they found amiss therein, but not to make any new laws, but prefer their grievances to the Court of Assistants, and that no assessment should be laid upon the country without the consent of such a committee, nor any lands disposed of[72] . . .

[May]. By this time the fort at Boston was in defence and divers pieces of ordnance mounted in it.

Those of Newtown complained of straitness for want of land, especially meadow, and desired leave of the Court to look out either for enlargement or removal, which was granted. Whereupon, they sent men to see Agawam and Merrimack, and gave out they would remove, etc.

[May] 14. At the General Court Mr. Cotton preached and delivered this doctrine, that a magistrate ought not to be turned into the condition

---

charter authorized them to meet four times a year in a General Court to make laws, but the freemen met only once a year and had no legislative role.

72. JW's concessions were too limited to satisfy the freemen. See 14 May 1634, below.

of a private man without just cause and to be publicly convict, no more than the magistrates may not turn a private man out of his freehold, etc., without like public trial, etc. This falling in question in the Court, and the opinion of the rest of the ministers being asked, it was referred to further consideration.[73]

The Court chose a new governor,[74] viz., Thomas Dudley, Esq., the former deputy, and Mr. Ludlow was chosen deputy, and John Haines, Esq., an assistant, and all the rest of the assistants chosen again.[75]

At this Court it was ordered that 4 General Courts should be kept every year, and that the whole body of the freemen should be present only at the court of election of magistrates, etc., that at the other 3 every town should send them deputies who should assist in making laws, disposing lands, etc.[76] Many good orders were made this Court. It held 3 days and all things were carried very peaceably, notwithstanding that some of the assistants were questioned by the freemen for some errors in their government, and some fines imposed, but remitted again before the Court brake up. The Court was kept in the meeting house at Boston, ⟨and the new governor and assistants were together entertained at the house of the old governor, as before⟩ . . .

June 1. The *Thunder,* which went to Bermuda the October 17, now returned bringing corn and goats from Virginia [and] brought news also of a great ship arrived in Patomack River in Virginia with a gov-

73. Cotton was trying to restrain those freemen who wanted to remove JW from office because he had overstepped his powers during his five years as governor; and he won his essential point. In 1634 JW was demoted from governor but kept his place as a magistrate.

74. JW added in the margin: "chosen by papers." The freemen voted for the first time by secret ballot.

75. JW added in the margin: "Mr. Cottington chosen treasurer." The freemen rotated their officers in 1634, but the only new assistant was Haynes. The new leaders they chose—Dudley and Ludlow—were at least as autocratic as JW.

76. Eight towns—Boston, Charlestown, Dorchester, Newtown, Roxbury, Salem, Saugus, and Watertown—sent three delegates apiece to legislate with the assistants at the 14 May court session (*MR,* 1:116–119). JW was undoubtedly distressed by this decision to broaden the legislature, though he concealed his displeasure in this journal entry.

ernor and colony sent by the Lord Bartimore, who was expected there shortly himself.[77] It appeared after that the King had written to Sir John Harvey, ∧knight∧, governor of Virginia, to give all assistance to that new plantation which was called Mary land by the Queen of England; and those which came over were many of them papists and did set up Mass openly.

July. The last month arrived here 14 great ships, and one at Salem. Mr. Humfrey ∧and the Lady Susan∧ his wife, ∧one∧ of the earl of Lincoln's sisters, arrived here.[78] He brought more ordnance, muskets, and powder, bought for the public by moneys given to that end, for godly people in England began now to apprehend a special hand of God in raising this plantation, and their hearts were generally stirred to come over. Mr. Humfrey brought certain propositions from some persons of great quality and estate (and of special note for piety), whereby they discovered their intentions to join with us if they might receive satisfaction therein.[79] It appeared further by many private letters that the departure of so many of the best, both ministers and Christians, had bred sad thoughts in those behind of the Lord's intentions in this work and an apprehension of some evil days to come upon England. Then it began now to be apprehended by the archbishops and others of the Council as a matter of state, so as they sent out warrant to stay the ships and to call in our patent.[80] But upon petition of the shipmas-

77. A Catholic nobleman, Cecilius Calvert, second Lord Baltimore, was lord proprietor of the new colony of Maryland (named in honor of Charles I's consort, Queen Henrietta Maria). The first colonists reached Maryland in March 1634, led by Leonard Calvert, the proprietor's brother. Baltimore himself never came to America.

78. John Humfrey (1596–1653), from Chaldon, Dorset, was one of the founders of the MBC and had been chosen deputy governor in 1629, when it was expected that he would join JW in the migration of 1630. His wife was sister to Lady Arbella Johnson, who had come over in 1630 and quickly died. The Humfreys settled at Salem.

79. Viscount Saye and Sele, Lord Brooke, and other leading Puritans proposed to come over on condition that Massachusetts establish a hereditary aristocracy with its own legislative chamber, equivalent to the House of Lords.

80. The Privy Council had formed a Committee for New England, headed by the anti-

ters, alleging how beneficial this plantation was to England, in regard of the Newfoundland fishing which they took in their way homeward, the ships were at that time released. But Mr. Cradock (who had been governor in England before the governor was sent over) had strict charge to deliver in the patent; whereupon he wrote to us to send it home upon receipt of his letter. The governor and Council consulted about it and resolved to answer Mr. Cradock's letter, but not to return any answer or excuse to the Council at that time . . .

6 of Newtown went in the *Blessing* (being bound to the Dutch plantation) to discover Connecticut River, intending to remove their town thither[81] . . .

[July] 29. The governor and Council and divers of the ministers and others met at Castle Island, and there agreed upon erecting 2 platforms and one small fortification to secure them both, and for the present furtherance of it they agreed to lay out £5 a man till a rate might be made at the next General Court. The deputy, Roger Ludlow, was chosen overseer of this work[82] . . .

August 4. At the Court the new town at Agawam was named Ipswich in acknowledgment of the great honor and kindness done to our people which took shipping there, etc.,[83] and a day of thanksgiving appointed a fortnight after for the prosperous arrival of them there, etc.

A letter was delivered to Mr. Winthrop by Mr. Jefferye, an old

---

Puritan Archbishop Laud. In Feb. 1634 this committee temporarily stayed 12 ships bound for New England.

81. The people of Newtown, bolstered by the arrival of Hooker and his followers, were feeling hemmed in by Boston, Charlestown, Dorchester, Roxbury, and Watertown. In May they had sent a search party to the Merrimack River to explore a move to the northern frontier of the MBC patent. Now they are contemplating a much bolder move to the Connecticut River, beyond the MBC limits, where in 1635–1636 they would found Hartford, the chief town in a new colony.

82. Castle Island, strategically located in the center of Boston harbor, commanded the ship channel to Boston.

83. Two ships, the *Elizabeth* and the *Francis,* had sailed from Ipswich, Suffolk, in April 1634, carrying 186 passengers to Massachusetts.

planter, written to him from Morton, wherein he related how he had obtained his long suit, and that a commission was granted for a General Governor to be sent over, with many railing speeches and threats against this plantation, and Mr. Winthrop in particular.[84] Mr. Winthrop acquainted the governor and Council with it, and some of the ministers.

This summer was hotter than many before . . .

Our neighbors of Plymouth and we had oft trade with the Dutch at Hudson's River, called by them New Netherlands. We had from them about 40 sheep, and beaver, and brass pans, and sugar, etc., for sack, strong waters, linen cloth, and other commodities. They have a great trade of beaver, about 9 or 10,000 skins in a year. Our neighbors of Plymouth had great trade also this year at Kenebecke, so as Mr. Wins-lowe carried with him into England this year about 20 hogsheads of beaver, the greatest part whereof was traded for wampumpeag.[85]

One pleasant passage happened which was acted by the Indians. Mr. Winslow coming in his bark from Connecticut to Narragansett, and he left her there, and intending to return by land, he went to Osamekin the sagamore, his old ally, who offered to conduct him home to Plymouth. But before they took their journey, Osamekin sent one of his men to Plymouth to tell them that Mr. Winslow was dead, and directed him to show how and where he was killed. Whereupon there was much fear and sorrow at Plymouth. The next day when Osamekin brought him home, they asked him why he sent such word, etc. He answered that it was their manner to do so, that they might be more welcome when they came home . . .

September 4. The General Court began at Newtown and continued

---

84. Thomas Morton wrote this letter on 1 May 1634. His recipient, William Jeffrey, had come to Massachusetts Bay in the 1620s, settled at Wessagusset (Weymouth), and was admitted freeman to the MBC in 1631. JW later entered Morton's letter into his journal; see 9 Sept. 1644, below.

85. Edward Winslow (1595-1655) was one of the chief leaders of Plymouth Colony, and a vigorous entrepreneur.

a week, and then was adjourned 14 days. The main business, which spent the most time and caused the adjourning of the Court, was about the removal of Newtown. They had leave the last General Court to look out some place for enlargement or removal, with promise of having it confirmed to them if it were not prejudicial to any other plantation. And now they moved that they might have leave to remove to Connecticut. This matter was debated divers days, and many reasons alleged pro and con. The principal reasons for their removal were: 1. their want of accomodation for their cattle, so as they were not able to maintain their ministers, nor could receive any more of their friends to help them; and here it was alleged by Mr. Hooker as a fundamental error that towns were set so near each to other.[86] 2. The fruitfulness and commodiousness of Connecticut, and the danger of having it possessed by other, Dutch or English. 3. The strong bent of their spirits to remove thither.

Against these it was said: 1. that in point of conscience they ought not to depart from us, being knit to us in one body, and bound by oath to seek the welfare of this commonwealth. 2. That in point of state and civil policy we ought not to give them leave to depart: (1.) because we were now weak and in danger to be assailed; (2.) the departure of Mr. Hooker would not only draw many from us, but also divert other friends that would come to us; (3.) we should expose them to evident peril both from the Dutch (who made claim to the same river and had already built a fort there) and from the Indians, and also from our own state at home, who would not endure they should sit down without a patent in any place which our king lays claim unto. 3. They might be

---

86. Hooker's participation in the projected move to Connecticut gave the new colony a clerical leader equal to Cotton in stature. JW does not fully present Hooker's reasons for wanting to leave, but probably—in addition to wanting more space for settlement—Hooker thought he would be safer from English royal intervention on the Connecticut River, and since his followers had not yet invested much time or labor on settlement at Newtown they could readily begin again at a new site which would be independent of JW's and Cotton's Boston.

accommodated at home by some enlargement, which other towns offered. 4. They might remove to Merrimack or any other place within our patent. 5. The removing of a candlestick is a great judgment, which is ⟨only⟩ to be avoided.

Upon these and other arguments, the Court being divided, it was put to vote, and of the deputies 15 were for their departure and 10 against it. The governor and 2 assistants were for it, and the deputy and all the rest of the assistants were against it (except the secretary who gave no vote). Whereupon no record was entered, because there were not 6 assistants in the vote as the patent requires.[87] Upon this grew a great difference between the governor and assistants, and the deputies. They would not yield the assistants a negative voice, and the other (considering how dangerous it might be to the commonwealth if they should not keep that strength to balance the greater number of the deputies) thought it safe to stand upon it.[88] So, when they could proceed no further, the whole Court agreed to keep a day of humiliation to seek the Lord, which accordingly was done in all the congregations the 18 day of this month; and the 24 the Court met again. Before they began, Mr. Cotton preached (being desired by all the Court upon Mr. Hooker's instant excuse of his unfitness for that occasion). He took his text out of Hag. 2:4, etc., out of which he laid down the nature or strength (as he termed it) of the magistracy, ministry, and people; viz., the strength of the magistracy to be their authority, of the people their liberty, and of the ministry their purity, and showed how all of them

87. Only three of the eleven magistrates voted in favor, whereas the charter required a majority—in this case six votes—for approval of any measure. Gov. Dudley, a resident of Newtown, favored the removal even though it weakened his own town, whereas Deputy Gov. Ludlow, who himself moved to Connecticut in 1635, voted against it. JW was clearly opposed.

88. If the votes of deputies and magistrates were counted collectively, the removal to Connecticut was approved 18–17, with one abstention. But if—as JW desired—the votes of deputies and magistrates were counted separately, the magistrates could exercise a "negative voice" or veto over the deputies' decision.

had a negative voice, etc.; and that yet the ultimate resolution, etc., ought to be in the whole body of the people, etc., which answered to all objections, and a declaration of the people's duty and right to maintain their true liberties against any unjust violence, etc., which gave great satisfaction to the company. And it pleased the Lord so to assist him and to bless his own ordinance that the affairs of the Court went on cheerfully; and although all were not satisfied about the negative voice to be left to the magistrates, yet no man moved aught about it, and the congregation of Newtown came and accepted of such enlargement as had formerly been offered them by Boston and Watertown, and so the fear of their removal to Connecticut was removed[89] . . .

September 18. At this Court were many laws made against tobacco, and immodest fashions, and costly apparel, etc., as appears by the records. And £600 raised towards fortifications and other charges, which were the more hastened because the *Griffin* and another ship now arriving with about 200 passengers and 100 cattle (Mr. Lothrop and Mr. Simmes, 2 godly ministers, coming in the same ship),[90] there came over a copy of the commission granted to the 2 archbishops and 10 other of the Council to regulate all plantations, and power given them or any 5 of them to call in all patents, to make laws, to raise tithes and portions for ministers, to remove and punish governors, and to hear and determine all causes, and inflict all punishments, even death itself, etc.[91] This being advised from our friends to be intended specially for us, and that

89. JW was too optimistic. The Newtown people started their removal to Connecticut in 1635.

90. John Lothrop, pastor of a gathered church in Southwark, London, had been imprisoned for two years; he went to Scituate church in Plymouth Colony. Zachariah Symmes, rector at Dunstable, Bedforshire, went to Charlestown church and served there until his death in 1672. Another passenger on this ship—soon noticed by JW—was Anne Hutchinson.

91. Charles I constituted this Royal Commission for Regulating Plantations, headed by Archbishop Laud, on 28 April 1634.

there were ships and soldiers provided to compel us by force to receive a new governor, and the discipline of the Church of England, and the laws of the Commissioners, occasioned the magistrates and deputies to hasten our fortifications and to discover our minds each to other . . .

November 6. At the Court of Assistants[92] complaint was made by some of the country (viz. Richard Brown of Watertown in the name of the rest) that the ensign at Salem was defaced, viz., one part of the red cross taken out.[93] Upon this an attachment was ⟨granted⟩ awarded against Rich: Davenport, ensign bearer, to appear at the next Court to answer. Much matter was made of this as fearing it would be taken as an act of rebellion or of like high nature in defacing the King's colors, though the truth were it was done upon this opinion, that the red cross was given to the kings of England by the Pope as an ensign of victory, and so a superstitious thing and a relic of Antichrist . . .

The *Rebecka* came from Narragansett with 500 bushels of corn given to Mr. John Oldham. The Indians had promised him 1000 bushels, but their store fell out less than they expected. They gave him also an island in the Narragansett Bay called Chippacuesett,[94] containing about ⟨1000 acres⟩ ∧6 miles long and 2 miles broad.∧ This is a very fair bay, being above 12 leagues square with divers great islands in it, a deep channel close to the shore, being rocky. The country on the W. of the Bay of Narragansett is all champion[95] for many miles, but very stony and full of Indians. [Capt. Peirce] saw there above 1000 men, women, and children, yet the men were many abroad on hunting. Nantucket is an island full of Indians about 10 leagues in length E. and W.

92. This court actually met on 7 Nov. (*MR*, 1:133).

93. Although the exact design of the ensign used by the Massachusetts colonists in 1634 is unclear, it was a flag that displayed the red St. George's cross of England on a white ground. John Endecott, the Salem magistrate, had defaced the St. George's cross, possibly at Roger Williams's instigation.

94. Chibachuwese or Prudence Island in Narragansett Bay.

95. Level open country.

November 6. There came to the deputy governor about 14 days since a messenger from the Pequot sachem to desire our friendship.[96] He brought 2 bundles of sticks whereby he signified how many beaver and otter skins he would give us for that end, and great store of wampumpeag, about 2 bushels by his description. He brought a small present with him, which the deputy received, and returned a moose coat of as good value, and withal told him that he must send persons of greater quality, and then our governor would treat with them. And now there came 2 men who brought another present of wampumpeag. The deputy brought them to Boston where most of the assistants were assembled by occasion of the lecture, who calling to them some of the ministers grew to this treaty with him: that we were willing to have friendship, etc., but because they had killed some Englishmen, viz. Captain Stone, etc., they must first deliver up those who were guilty of his death, etc. They answered that the sachem who then lived was slain by the Dutch and all the men who were guilty, etc., were dead of the pox except 2, and that if they were worthy of death they would move their sachem to have them delivered (for they had no commission to do it). But they excused the fact, saying that Captain Stone coming into their river took 2 of their men and bound them and made them show him the way up the river, which when they had done, he with 2 other and the 2 Indians (their hands still bound) went on shore, and 9 of their men watched them, and when they were on sleep in the night they killed them. Then going towards the pinnace to have taken that, it suddenly blew up into the air. This was related with such confidence and gravity as having no means to contradict it we inclined to believe it.[97]

The reason why [the Pequots] desired so much our friendship was

96. JW's account of the Pequot peace initiative is especially interesting because the English soon went to war against these Indians; see August 1636, below.

97. Compare JW's earlier version (21 Jan. 1634, above) of this episode, in which the Indian attack is unprovoked.

because they were now in war with the Narragansett whom till this year they had kept under, and likewise with the Dutch who had killed their old sachem and some other of their men, for that the Pequots had killed some Indians who came to trade with the Dutch at Connecticut; and by these occasions they could not trade safely anywhere. Therefore they desired us to send a pinnace with cloth and we should have all their trade. They offered us also all their right at Connecticut, and to further us what they could if we would settle a plantation there.

When they came to the governor they agreed according to the former treaty, viz., to ⟨give⟩ deliver us the 2 men who were guilty of Captain Stone's death when we would send for them, to yield up Connecticut, to give us 400 fathom of wampumpeag and 40 beaver and 30 otter skins,[98] and that we should presently send a pinnace with cloth to trade with them, and so should be at peace with them and as friends to trade with them, but not to defend them, etc.

The next morning news came that 2 or 300 of the Narragansetts were come to Cohannet, viz. Naponsett,[99] to kill the Pequot ambassadors, etc. Presently we met at Roxbury and raised some few men in arms, and sent to the Narragansett men to come to us. When they came, there were no more but 2 of their sachems and about 20 more who had been on hunting thereabouts and came to lodge with the Indians at Cohannet as their manner is. So we treated with them about the Pequots, and at our request they promised they should go and come to and from us in peace, and they were also content to enter further treaty of peace with them, and in all things showed themselves very

98. The wampum and pelts were worth about £250. Some historians argue that the MBC was exacting stiff compensation for Capt. Stone's death in order to discourage further Pequot attacks on white traders, while others see this Pequot treaty as a device for justifying future intrusion into the Connecticut River valley.

99. Cohannet was the Indian name for Taunton, which was settled around 1640 by Plymouth Colony. But JW may be referring here to Cohasset, on the coast at the Massachusetts-Plymouth border, which is closer to the Neponset river and estuary.

ready to gratify us. So the Pequots returned home, and the Narragansett departed well satisfied. Only they were told in private that if they did make peace with the Pequot we would give them part of that wampumpeag which they should give us, for the Pequot held it dishonorable to offer them anything as of themselves, yet were willing we should give it them, and indeed did offer us so much for that end.

The agreement they made with us was put in writing, and the 2 ambassadors set to their marks: one a bow with an arrow in it, and the other a hand[1] . . .

[November] *27.* The assistants met at the governor's to advise about the defacing of the cross in the ensign at Salem, where (taking advice with some of the ministers) we agreed to write to Mr. Downing in England of the truth of the matter under all our hands, that if occasion were he might show it in our excuse, for therein we expressed our dislike of the thing and our purpose to punish the offenders, yet with as much wariness as we might, being doubtful of the lawful use of the cross in an ensign, though we were clear that ∧fact[2] as concerning∧ the manner was very unlawful.

It was then informed us how Mr. Eliot, the teacher of the Church of Roxbury, had taken occasion in a sermon to speak of the peace made with the Pequots and to lay some blame upon the magistrates for proceeding therein without consent of the people, and for other failings (as he conceived). We took order that he should be dealt with by Mr. Cotton, Mr. Hooker, and Mr. Weld to be brought to see his error, and to heal it by some public explanation of his meaning, for the people began to take occasion to murmur against us for it.

It was likewise informed that Mr. Williams of Salem had broken his promise to us in teaching publicly against the King's patent and our great sin in claiming right thereby to this country, etc., and for usual

1. This treaty has not survived.
2. The thing done.

terming the churches of England Antichristian. We granted summons to him for his appearance at the next Court.

The aforesaid 3 ministers, upon conference with the said Mr. Eliot, brought him to acknowledge his error in that he had mistaken the ground of his doctrine, and that he did acknowledge that for a peace only (whereby the people were not to be engaged in a war) the magistrates might conclude plebe inconsulto,[3] and so promised to express himself in public next Lord's day . . .

December 4. Was an extraordinary tempest of wind and snow at NNE. which continued 24 hours, and after that such frost as within 2 days the whole Bay was frozen over, but free again before night . . .

[December] 22. By a letter from Plymouth it was certified that the Dutch of Hudson's River had been at Connecticut and came in warlike manner to put the Plymouth men out of their house there, but when they stood upon their defense they departed without offering any violence . . .

[January] 19. All the ministers except Mr. Ward of Ipswich[4] met at Boston, being requested by the governor and assistants to consider of these 2 cases: 1. What we ought to do if a General Governor should be sent out of England. 2. Whether it be lawful for us to carry the cross in our banners. In the 1. case, they all agreed that if a General Governor were sent we ought not to accept him but defend our lawful possessions (if we were able); otherwise to avoid or protract. For the matter of the cross they were divided, and so deferred it to another meeting.

Month 11th [January]. About the middle of this month Mr. Allerton's pinnace came from the French about Porte Royall. They went to fetch

---

3. Without consulting the people.

4. The Rev. Nathaniel Ward (1578–1652) had been suspended by Laud as rector of Stondon Massey, Essex, and emigrated in 1634 at the advanced age of 56. He settled at Ipswich, drafted the MBC Body of Liberties of 1641, and published *The Simple Cobler of Aggawam in America* (London, 1647).

the 2 men which had been carried by the French from Machias and to demand the goods taken, etc.,[5] but Mr. La Tour made the answer that he took them as lawful prize, and that he had authority from the King of France who challenged all from Cape Sable to Cape Cod, wishing them to take notice and to certify the rest of the English that if they traded to the east of Pemaquid he would make prize of them. Being desired to show his commission, he answered that his sword was commission sufficient, where he had strength to overcome. Where that wanted he would show his commissions . . .

Month 1 [March], 4. A General Court at Newtown. One of the deputies, ⟨Mr. Israell St⟩[6] was questioned for denying the magistracy among us, affirming that the power of the governor was but ministerial, etc. He had also much opposed the magistrates and slighted them, and used many weak arguments against the negative voice, as himself acknowledged upon record. He was adjudged by all the Court to be disabled for 3 years from bearing any public office.[7]

One of the assistants[8] was called to the lower end of the table to answer for refusing to pay towards a rate made by the Court, and was fined £5, which was after released.

Mr. Endecott was called to answer for defacing the cross in the ensign, but because the Court could not agree about the thing, whether the ensigns should be laid by in regard that many refused to follow them, the whole cause was deferred till the next General Court, and

5. See 12 Nov. 1633, above.

6. Israel Stoughton of Dorchester had fought for a legislative role for the deputies in the General Court of April–May 1634, and had led the deputies' attack upon the magistrates' negative voice in Sept. 1634. He then circulated a treatise boldly questioning the powers of the MBC magistracy.

7. Stoughton's offending treatise was also burned. Two years later he was permitted to resume office, and was promptly chosen deputy and then assistant (*MR*, 1:135, 136, 175, 185, 195).

8. William Pynchon had complained that his town of Roxbury was taxed too heavily (*MR*, 1:136).

the commissioners for military affairs gave order in the meantime that all the ensigns should be laid aside, etc. . . . .

Month 2 [April]. Some of our people went to Cape Cod and made some oil of a whale which was cast on shore. There were 3 or 4 cast up, as it seems there is almost every year . . .

[April] 30. The governor and assistants sent for Mr. Williams. The occasion was for that he had taught publicly that a magistrate ought not to tender an oath to an unregenerate man, for that we thereby have communion with a wicked man in the worship of God, and cause him to take the name of God in vain.[9] He was heard before all the ministers and very clearly confuted. Mr. Endecott was at first of the same opinion, but he gave place to the truth.

Month 3 [May], 6. A General Court was held at Newtown, where John Haynes, Esq. was chosen governor, Rich: Bellingham, Esq. deputy governor, and Mr. Hough and Mr. Dummer chosen assistants to the former, and Mr. Ludlow, the late deputy, left out of the magistracy. The reason was partly because the people would exercise their absolute power, etc., and partly upon some speeches of the deputy who protested against the election of the governor as void, for that the deputies of the several towns had agreed upon the election before they came, etc. But this was generally distrusted, and the election adjudged good.[10]

Mr. Endecott was also left out, and called into question about the defacing the cross in the ensign, and a committee was chosen; viz., every town chose one (which yet were voted by all the people) and the magistrates chose 4, who made report to the Court, that they found

9. Williams was here challenging the MBC's requirement that all adult males—including non-freemen and non-church members—take an oath of allegiance. He contended that this application of sacred discipline to profane persons polluted the Massachusetts ecclesiastical system.

10. In this election, the freemen chose nine of the eleven magistrates from 1634 (Haynes, Dudley, JW, Humfrey, Coddington, Pynchon, Nowell, Bradstreet, and JW2); dropped two (Ludlow and Endecott); and added three (Bellingham, Hough, and Dummer).

his offence to be great, viz., rash and without discretion, taking upon him more authority than he had ∧and not seeking advice of the Court, etc.∧; uncharitable in that he, judging the cross, etc., to be a sin, did content himself to have reformed it at Salem, not taking care that others might be brought out of it also, laying a blemish also upon the rest of the magistrates as if they would suffer idolatry, etc.; and giving occasion to the state of England to think ill of us. For which they adjudged him worthy admonition and to be disabled for one year from bearing any public office, declining any heavier sentence because they were persuaded he did it out of tenderness of conscience and not of any evil intent . . .

The governor and deputy were elected by papers wherein their names were written, but the assistants were chosen by papers without names; viz., the governor propounded one to the people, then they all went out and came in at one door and every man delivered a paper into a hat. Such as gave their vote for the party named gave in a paper with some figures or scroll in it; others gave in a blank.

The new governor in his speech to the people declared his purpose to spare their charge towards his allowance this year, partly in respect of their love showed towards him, and partly for that he observed how much the people had been pressed lately with public charges which the poorer sort did much groan under.[11]

A petition was preferred by many of Dorchester, etc., for releasing the sentence against Mr. Stoughton the last General Court, but it was rejected and the sentence affirmed by the country to be just.

The matter of altering the cross in the ensign was referred to the next meeting (the Court being adjourned for 3 weeks), it being pro-

---

11. The General Court had levied £412 upon the towns in 1633 and £600 in 1634. In 1635, despite Haynes's refusal of salary, public charges increased to £700 (*MR*, 1:110, 129, 138, 149, 158).

pounded to turn it to the red and white rose, etc.,[12] and every man was to deal with his neighbors to still their minds who stood so stiff for the cross until we should fully agree about it, which was expected, because the ministers had promised to take pains about it and to write into England to have the judgments of the most wise and godly there.

The deputies having conceived great danger to our state in regard that our magistrates, for want of positive laws in many cases, might proceed according to their discretions, it was agreed that some men should be appointed to frame a body of grounds of laws in resemblance to a Magna Carta, which being allowed by ∧some of∧ the ministers and the General Court should be received for fundamental laws.[13]

At this General Court some of the chief of Ipswich desired leave to remove to Quascacunquen[14] to begin a town there, which was granted them and it was named Nueberrye. Also, Watertown and Roxbury had leave to remove whither they pleased so as they continued under this governor. The occasion of their desire to remove was for that all towns in the Bay began to be much straitened by their o'er nearness one to another, and their cattle being so much increased . . .

16 June. By a letter from the Lord Saye[15] and report of divers passengers it was certified to us that Captain Mason[16] and other, the adversaries of this colony, had built a great ship to send over the General

12. The emblems of the royal houses of Lancaster and York, from which Charles I traced his English ancestry; this design betokened allegiance to England and avoided the popish St. George's cross.

13. The court deputed Haynes, Bellingham, JW, and Dudley "to make a draft of such laws as they shall judge needful for the well ordering of this plantation" (*MR*, 1:147).

14. This was the Abnaki Indian name for the town site of Newbury, meaning "the long ridge."

15. William Fiennes, Viscount Saye and Sele (1582–1662), was a Puritan nobleman who was actively interested in American colonization.

16. John Mason (1586–1635), an anti-Puritan ally of Sir Ferdinando Gorges, had been trying to establish a colony just N of Massachusetts along what is now the New Hampshire coast.

Governor, etc., which being launched fell in sunder in the middest. It appeared likewise by a copy of a petition sent over to us that they had divided all this country of N. E., viz., between St. Croix[17] in the east and that ∧of∧ Lord Baltimore called Maryland, into 12 provinces disposed to 12 in England who should find each 10 men to attend the General Governor coming over.[18] But the project not [taking] effect, the Lord frustrated their design . . .

June 24. Mr. Graves in the *James* and Mr. Hodges in the *Rebecca* set sail for the Isle of Sable for sea horse[19] (which are there in great number) and wild cows . . .

August 26. They returned from their voyage. They found there upon the island 16 Frenchmen who had wintered there and built a little fort, and had killed some black foxes. They had killed also many of the cattle, so as they found not above 140, and but 2 or 3 calves. They could kill but few sea horse by reason they were forced to travel so far in the sand as they were too weak to strike them, and they came away at such time as they use to go up highest to eat green pease. The winter there is very cold and the snow above knee-deep.

Month 5 [July], 8. At the General Court, Mr. Williams of Salem was summoned and did appear. It was laid to his charge that being under question before the magistrates and churches for divers dangerous opinions, viz., 1. that the magistrate ought not to punish the breach of the First Table otherwise than in such cases as did disturb the civil peace; 2. that he ought not to tender an oath to an unregenerate man; 3. that a man ought not to pray with such, though wife, child, etc.; 4. that a man ought not to give thanks after the sacrament nor after meat, etc.;

---

17. The river marking the present boundary between Maine and New Brunswick.

18. The Council for New England had met in Feb. 1635 and divided its land into shares, the largest going to Sir Ferdinando Gorges and John Mason. The Council then resigned its charter to Charles I, expecting him to confirm these land patents and appoint Gorges as governor general.

19. Walruses.

and that the other Churches were about to write to the Church of Salem to admonish him of these errors. Notwithstanding, the church had since called him to affirm of a teacher. Much debate was about these things. The said opinions were adjudged by all magistrates and ministers (who were desired to be present) to be erroneous and very dangerous, and the calling of him to office at that time was judged a great contempt of authority. So, in fine, time was given to him and the Church of Salem to consider of these things till the next General Court, and then either to give satisfaction to the Court or else to expect the sentence. It being professedly declared by the ministers (at the request of the Court to give their advice) that he who should obstinately maintain such opinions (whereby ⟨he⟩ ∧a∧ church might run into heresy, apostacy, or tyranny, and yet the civil magistrate could not intermeddle) were to be removed, and that the other churches ought to request the magistrate so to do[20] . . .

Salem men had preferred a petition at the last General Court for some land in Marble Head necke which they did challenge as belonging to their town, but because they had chosen Mr. Williams their teacher while he stood under question of authority and so offered contempt to the magistrates, etc., their petition was refused till, etc. Upon this the Church of Salem wrote to other churches to admonish the magistrates of this as a heinous sin, and likewise the deputies, for which at the next General Court their deputies were not received until they should give satisfaction about the letter . . .

Month 6, August. Mr. Williams, ∧pastor∧ of Salem, being sick and not able to speak, wrote to his church a protestation that he could not communicate with the churches in the Bay, neither would he communicate with them except they would refuse communion with the rest. But the whole church was grieved herewith . . .

20. This important decision, by which the MBC asserted its regulatory power over refractory clergymen and churches, was not entered into the court records.

8th Month [October], 6. Here arrived 2 great ships, the *Defence* and
the *Abigaill,* with Mr. Wilson, pastor of Boston, Mr. Shepheard, Mr.
Jones, and other ministers, amongst others Mr. Peter, pastor of the
∧English∧ Church in Rottordam.[21] The special goodness of the Lord
appeared in this that the passengers came safe and hale in all ships,
though some of them long passages, the *Abigail* 10 weeks from Plymouth with 220 persons and many cattle, infected also with the smallpox, yet, etc.

There came also John Winthrop the younger with commission from
the Lord Saye, Lord Brooke, and divers other great persons in England
to begin a plantation at Connecticut and to be governor there. They
sent also men and ammunition and £2000 in money to begin a fortification at the mouth of the river.[22]

Here came also one Mr. Henry Vane,[23] son and heir to Sir Henry
Vane, Controller of the King's house, who being a young gentleman
of excellent parts and had been employed by his father (when he was
ambassador) in foreign affairs, yet being called to the obedience of the
Gospel, forsook the honors and preferments of the Court to enjoy the
ordinances of Christ in their purity here. This noble gentleman, having
order from the said Lords and others, treated with the magistrates here

21. Thomas Shepard (1605–1649) had been pursued by Laud and was in hiding in
England in 1634–1635; he succeeded Hooker as pastor of the Newtown (Cambridge)
church, and became one of the principal preachers and authors in early New England. John
Jones (1592?–1665) had been deprived of his English living; he settled at Concord before
moving on to Connecticut in 1644. Hugh Peter (1598–1660) had preached in London before
fleeing to the Netherlands; he succeeded Williams as pastor of the Salem church until he
returned home in 1641 to join the English civil war.

22. This was Saybrook plantation at the mouth of the Connecticut River, begun in
Nov. 1635, and named for Viscount Saye and Sele and his partner Baron Brooke. JW2
(who had visited England in 1634–1635) left Saybrook in 1636, and his sponsors never
came over to settle.

23. Henry Vane (1613–1662), though only 22 years old on arrival, was elected governor
of the MBC in 1636; he returned to England in 1637, shortly after JW replaced him as
governor. Ironically, Vane and Peter, arriving together in 1635, also ended their lives in
the same way, executed for treason after the restoration of Charles II.

and those who were to go to Connecticut about the said design of the Lords to this issue: that either the 3 towns gone thither[24] should give place, upon full satisfaction, or else sufficient room must be found therein for the Lords and their companies, etc., or else they would divert their thoughts and preparations some other ways.

November 1. Mr. Vane was admitted a member of the Church of Boston.

October. At this General Court Mr. Williams, the teacher of Salem, was again convented, and all the ministers in the Bay being desired to be present he was charged with the said 2 letters: that to the churches, to complaining of the magistrates for injustice, extreme oppression, etc., and the other to his own church, to persuade them to renounce communion with all the churches in the Bay as full of Antichristian pollution, etc. He justified both these letters and maintained all his opinions, and being offered further conference or disputation and a month's respite, he chose to dispute presently. So Mr. Hooker was appointed to dispute with him, but could not reduce him from any of his errors. So the next morning the Court sentenced him to depart out of our jurisdiction within 6 weeks, all the ministers save one approving the sentence. And his own church had him under question also for the same cause, and he at his return home refused communion with his own church, who openly disclaimed his errors and wrote an humble submission to the magistrates acknowledging their fault in joining with Mr. Williams in that letter to the churches against them, etc.

October 15. About 60 men, women, and little children went by land towards Connecticut with their cows, horses, and swine, and after a tedious and difficult journey arrived safe there[25] . . .

24. Migrants from Newtown were beginning to settle Hartford, Conn.; migrants from Dorchester were beginning to settle Windsor, Conn.; and migrants from Watertown were beginning to settle Wethersfield, Conn. Vane was trying to negotiate with these three groups on behalf of the Saybrook proprietors.

25. This was a party from Newtown, who went to lay out the first homesteads at Hartford.

It is useful to observe, as we go along, such especial providences of God as were manifested for the good of these plantations . . . [One] providence was in ∧the∧ voyage of Mr. Winthrop the younger and Mr. Wilson into England, who returning in the wintertime,[26] in a small and weak ship bound for Barnstaple, were driven by foul weather upon the coast of Ireland, not known by any in the ship, and were brought through many desperate dangers into Gallowaye, where they parted, Mr. Winthrop taking his journey overland to Dublin, and Mr. Wilson by sea. And being come within sight of Lundaye in the mouth of Seaverne, they were forced back by tempest to Kinsale where some ships perished in their view.[27] Mr. Wilson being in Ireland gave much satisfaction to the Christians there about New England. Mr. Winthrop went to Dublin and from thence to Antrim in the north. From thence he passed over into Scotland, and so through the north of England, and all the way he met with persons of quality whose thoughts were towards N. E., who observed his coming among them as a special providence of God . . .

November 3. Mr. Winthrop, junior, the governor appointed by the Lords for Connecticut, sent a bark of 30 ton and about 20 men with all needful provisions to take possession of the mouth of Connecticut and to begin some building . . .

[November] 26. There came 13 men from Connecticut. They had been 10 days upon their journey and had lost one of their company, drowned in the ice by the way, and had been all starved but that by God's providence they lighted upon an Indian wigwam. Connecticut River was frozen up the 15 of this month . . .

---

26. JW2 and Wilson had sailed for England in the fall of 1634.

27. Lundy is an island at the entrance to the Bristol Channel, the mouth of the River Severn. At this point, they were within 35 miles of the Devon port of Barnstaple, but the storm forced them back to the southern Irish port of Kinsale and on to the western Irish port of Galway, where they landed.

[December]. The 2 and 3 of this month fell a snow about knee-deep with much wind from the N. and NE . . .

11th Month, January. The governor and assistants met at Boston to consult about Mr. Williams, for that they were credibly informed that notwithstanding the injunction laid upon him (upon the liberty granted him to stay till the spring) not to go about to draw others to his opinions, he did use to entertain company in his house and to preach to them, even of such points as he had been censured for; and it was agreed to send him into England by a ship then ready to depart. The reason was because he had drawn above 20 persons to his opinion and they were intended to erect a plantation about the Narragansett Bay, from whence the infection would easily spread into these churches (the people being many of them much taken with the apprehension of his godliness). Whereupon a warrant was sent to him to come presently to Boston to be shipped, etc. He returned answer (and divers of Salem came with it) that he could not come without hazard of his life, etc., whereupon a pinnace was sent with commission to Captain Underhill, etc., to apprehend him and carry him aboard the ship (which then rode at Nantasket), but when they came at his house they found he had been gone 3 days before, but whither they could not learn.[28]

He had so far prevailed at Salem as ⟨divers⟩ ∧many∧ there (especially of devout women) did embrace his opinions and separated from the churches for this cause, that some of their members going into

___

28. In this account, JW appears to be quite as eager as any of his fellow MBC magistrates to ship Williams back to England. But Williams himself claimed (many years later, in 1670) "that ever honored governor Mr. Winthrop privately wrote to me to steer my course to Narragansett Bay and Indians, for many high and heavenly and public ends, encouraging me, from the freeness of the place from any English claims or patents" (Edmund S. Morgan, *The Puritan Dilemma: The Story of John Winthrop* [Boston: Little, Brown, 1958], p. 129). Williams's numerous letters to JW in 1636–1637 (see especially *WP*, 3:296–298, 314–318, 455–456) also indicate that he saw JW as his secret benefactor and continuing friend.

England did hear the ministers there, and when they came home the churches here held communion with them . . .

January, Month 11, 18. Mr. Vane and Mr. Peter, finding some distraction in the commonwealth arising from some difference in judgment, and withal some alienation of affection among the magistrates and some other persons of quality, and that hereby factions began to grow among the people, some adhering more to the old governor Mr. Winthrop, and others to the late governor Mr. Dudley, the former carrying matters with more lenity and the latter with more severity, they procured a meeting at Boston of the governor, deputy, Mr. Cotton, Mr. Hooker, Mr. Wilson, and there was present Mr. Winthrop, Mr. Dudley, and themselves. Where, after the Lord had been sought, Mr. Vane desired all present to take up a resolution to deal freely and openly with the parties and they each with other, that nothing might be left in their breasts which might break out to any jar or difference hereafter (which they promised to do).[29] Then Mr. Winthrop spake to this effect: that when it pleased Mr. Vane to acquaint him with what he had observed of the dispositions of men's minds inclining to the said faction, etc., it was very strange to him, professing solemnly that he knew not of any breach between his brother Dudley and himself since they were reconciled long since. Neither did he suspect any alienation of affection in him or others from himself, save that of late he had observed that some newcomers had estranged themselves from him since they went to dwell at Newtown, and so desired all the company that if they had seen anything amiss in his government or otherwise they would deal freely and faithfully with him, and for his part he promised to take it in good part and would endeavor by God's grace to amend it. Then

---

29. JW presents this conference as meddlesome interference by the newcomers Vane and Peter, but in fact the colony leaders were not in harmony. In addition to the friction between JW and Dudley, the founding magistrates of 1630 were at odds with the new arrivals of 1633–1636, and the Boston leaders were upset that Hooker and Haynes of Newtown were migrating to Connecticut.

Mr. Dudley spake to this effect: that for his part he came thither a mere patient,[30] not with any intent to charge his brother Winthrop with anything, for though there had been formerly some differences and breaches between them, yet they had been healed, and so left it to others to utter their own complaints. Whereupon the governor, Mr. Haynes, spake to this effect: that Mr. Winthrop and himself had been always in good terms, etc.; therefore he was loath to give any offence to him, and he hoped that considering what the end of this meeting was he would take it in good part if he did deal openly and freely as his manner ever was. Then he spake of one or 2 passages wherein he conceived that [Mr. Winthrop] dealt too remissly in point of justice. To which Mr. Winthrop answered that it was his judgment that in the infancy of plantations justice should be administered with more lenity than in a settled state, because people were then more apt to transgress, partly of ignorance of new laws and orders, partly through oppression of business and other straits. But if it might be made clear to him that it was an error, he would be ready to take up a stricter course. Then the ministers were desired to consider of the question by the next morning and to set down a rule in the case. The next morning they delivered their several reasons, which all sorted to this conclusion: that strict discipline both in criminal offences and in martial affairs was more needful in plantations than in a settled state, as tending to the honor and safety of the Gospel. Whereupon, Mr. Winthrop acknowledged that he was convinced that he had failed in overmuch lenity and remissness, and would endeavor (by God's assistance) to take a more strict course hereafter.[31] Whereupon there was a renewal of love amongst them and articles drawn to this effect:

30. Passive bystander.

31. JW's colleagues probably suspected that he had given covert aid to Roger Williams; they perhaps also found him too indulgent to Endecott when the Salem flag was defaced; and they may have blamed him for surrendering too many charter privileges to the freemen and their deputies in April–May 1634.

1. That there should be more strictness used in civil government and military discipline.

2. That the magistrates should (as far as might be) ripen their consultations beforehand, that their vote in public might be one (as the voice of God).

3. That in meetings out of court the magistrates should not discuss the business of parties in their presence, nor deliver their opinions, etc.

4. That trivial things, etc., should be ended in towns, etc.

5. If differences fall out among them in public meetings, they shall observe these rules: 1. not to touch any person differing, but speak to the cause; 2. to express their difference in all modesty and due respect to the court and such as differ, etc.; 3. or to propound their difference by way of question; 4. or to desire a deferring of the cause to further time; 5. after sentence (if all have agreed) none shall intimate his dislike privately, or if one dissent he shall sit down without showing any further distaste, publicly or privately.

6. The magistrates shall be more familiar and open each to other, and more frequent in visitations, and shall in tenderness and love admonish one another (without reserving any secret grudge), and shall avoid all jealousies and suspicions, each seeking the honor of another and all of the Court, not opening the nakedness of one another to private persons, in all things seeking the safety and credit of the Gospel.

7. To honor the governor in submitting to him the main direction and ordering the business of the Court.

8. One assistant shall not seem to gratify any man in undoing or crossing another's proceedings, without due advice with him.

9. They shall grace and strengthen their under officers in their places, etc.

10. All contempts against the Court or any of the magistrates shall be specially noted and punished, and the magistrates shall appear more

solemnly in public with attendance, apparel, and open notice of their entrance into the Court.[32]

Month 12 [February], *1*. Mr. Shepard, a godly minister come lately out of England, and divers other good Christians intending to raise a church body came and acquainted the magistrates therewith, who gave their approbation.[33] They also sent to all the neighbor churches for their elders to give their assistance at a certain day at Newtown, when they should constitute their body. Accordingly, at this day there met a great assembly where the proceeding was as followeth:

Mr. Shepard and 2 others (who were after to be chosen to office) sat together in the elders' seat. Then the elder of them began with prayer. After this Mr. Shepard ∧prayed with deep confession of sin, etc.∧ Then the elder desired to know of the churches assembled what number were needful to make a church, and how they ought to proceed in this action. Whereupon some of the ancient ministers conferring shortly together gave answer, that the Scripture did not set down any certain rule, but that 7 might be a fit number. And for their proceeding, they advised that such as were to join should make confession of their faith and declare what work of grace the Lord had wrought in them, which accordingly they did, Mr. Shepard first, then 4 others, then the elder, and one who was to be a deacon (who had also prayed), and another member. Then the covenant was read and they all gave a solemn assent to it. Then the elder desired of the churches that if they did approve them to be a church they would give them the right hand of fellowship. Whereupon Mr. Cotton (upon short speech with some

32. The thrust of these 10 articles was to discipline the MBC magistracy—like the ministry—into a unified leadership stance. Very likely Vane was trying to foster an elitist ambiance satisfactory to Puritan aristocrats like Lords Saye and Brooke. Instead, Vane helped to set the rules for the MBC's demolition of the Antinomian movement and his own political defeat in 1637.

33. This new church of Shepard's in Newtown replaced Hooker's church, whose members were almost all moving to Hartford.

other near him) in the name of the churches gave his hand to the elder, with a short speech of their assent and desired the peace of the Lord Jesus to be ⟨upon⟩ with them. Then Mr. Shepard made an exhortation to the rest of this body about the nature of their covenant and to stand firm to it, and commended them to the Lord in a most heavenly prayer. Then the elder told the assembly that they were intended to choose Mr. Shepard for their pastor, and desired the churches that if they had anything to except against him they would impart it to them before the day of ordination. Then he gave the churches thanks for their assistance and so left them to the Lord.

At the last General Court it was referred to the military commissioners to appoint colors for every company, who did accordingly and left out the cross in all of them, appointing the King's arms to be put into that of Castle Island, and Boston to be the 1 company . . .

[February] 25. The distractions about the churches of Salem and Saugus and the removal of other churches and the great scarcity of corn, etc., occasioned a general fast to [be] proclaimed, which because the Court was not at hand was moved by the elders of the churches, and assented unto by the ministers. The Church of Boston renewed their covenant this day, and made a large explanation of that which they had first entered into, and acknowledged such failings as had fallen out, etc. . . .

Month 2 [April], 1. Mr. Mather[34] and other of Dorchester intending to begin a new Church there (a great part of the old one being gone to Connecticut) desired the approbation of ∧the∧ other churches and of the magistrates. And accordingly they assembled this day, and after some of them had given proof of their gifts, they made confession of their faith, which was approved of. But proceeding to manifest the

---

34. Richard Mather (1596–1669) had arrived in 1635, having been suspended by the Archbishop of York from the parish of Toxteth Park, Lancs. He was the father of Increase Mather and the grandfather of Cotton Mather.

work of God's grace in themselves, the churches by their elders and the magistrates, etc., thought them not meet at present to be the foundation of a Church. And thereupon they were content to forbear to join till further consideration. The reason was for that most of them (Mr. Mather and one more excepted) had builded their comfort of salvation upon unsound grounds, viz., some upon dreams and ravishments of spirit by fits, other upon the reformation of their lives, others upon duties and performances, etc., wherein they discovered 3 special errors: 1. that they had not come to hate sin because it was filthy, but only left it because it was hurtful; 2. that by reason of this they had never truly closed with Christ (or rather Christ with them) but had made use of him only to help the imperfection of their sanctification and duties, and not made him their sanctification, wisdom, etc.; 3. they expected to believe by some power of their own and not only and wholly from Christ[35] . . .

[April] 7. At a General Court it was ordered that a certain number of the magistrates should be chosen for life (the reason was for that it was showed from the word of God, etc., that the principal magistracy ought to be for life). Accordingly the 25 of the 3 month [May] John Winthrop and Thomas Dudley were chosen to this place, and Henry Vane, by his place of governor, was president of this Council for his year.[36] It was likewise ordered that quarter courts should be kept in several places for ease of the people, and in regard of the scarcity of victuals the remote towns should send their votes by proxy to the Court of Elections, and that no church, etc., should be allowed, etc., that was gathered without consent of the churches and the magistrates . . .

35. Some of the would-be church founders of Dorchester betray an Antinomian tendency to rely on inspiration, others an opposite Arminian tendency to rely on external good behavior. But Mather soon got his people to make a better presentation of their case; on 23 Aug. 1636 the Dorchester church was gathered with the approval of the MBC magistrates and ministry.

36. This Standing Council was much criticized and soon effectually abolished; see pp. 159, 202, 217 below.

[May]. Here arrived a ship called the *St. Patricke*, belonging to Sir Tho: Wentworth, deputy of Ireland,[37] one Palmer master. When she came near Castle Island the lieutenant of the fort went aboard her and made her strike her flag, which the master took as a great injury and complained of it to the magistrates, who calling the lieutenant before them heard the cause and declared to the master that he had no commission so to do. And because he had made them strike to the fort (which had then no colors abroad) they tendered the master such satisfaction as he desired, which was only this: that the lieutenant aboard their ship should acknowledge his error, that so all the ship's company might receive satisfaction, lest the lord deputy should have been informed that we had offered that discourtesy to his ship which we had never offered to any before.

[May] 25. Henry Vane, Esq. before mentioned was chosen governor,[38] and because he was son and heir to a privy councillor in England, the ships congratulated his election with a volley of great shot. The next week he invited all the masters (there were then 15 great ships, etc.) to dinner. After they had dined he propounded 3 things to them: 1. that all ships which should come after this year should come to an anchor before they came at the fort, except they did send their boat before and did satisfy the commander that they were friends; 2. that before they offered any goods to sale they would deliver an invoice, etc., and give the governor, etc., 24 hours' liberty to refuse, etc; 3. that their men might not stay on shore (except upon necessary business) after sunset. These things they all willingly condescended unto.[39]

---

37. Wentworth (1593–1641), the future Earl of Strafford, had been Charles I's Lord Deputy of Ireland since 1633. He was—in partnership with Laud—the king's most vigorous and authoritarian minister.

38. JW was elected deputy governor (*MR*, 1:174).

39. The problem Gov. Vane tried to solve was that every May a large number of ships arrived in Massachusetts almost simultaneously, having left England in early spring. This posed a security problem for the MBC and opened Boston to a glut of high-priced consumer goods and a horde of non-Puritan sailors.

[May] *31.* Mr. Hooker, pastor of the Church of Newtown, and the most of his congregation went to Connecticut. His wife was carried in a horse litter, and they drove 160 cattle and fed of their milk by the way.

The last winter Captain Mason died. He was the chief mover in all attempts against us and was to have sent the General Governor, and for this end was providing shipping. But the Lord in mercy taking him away, all the business fell on sleep, so as ships came and brought what and whom they would without any question or control.

Divers of the ships this spring, both out of the Downs and from Holland, came in 5 weeks, and Mr. Babb his ship went from hence to England the 16 of January and saw land there in 18 days.

One Miller, master's mate in the *Hecter,* spake to some of our people aboard his ship that because we had not the king's colors at our fort we were all traitors and rebels, etc. The governor sent for the master, Mr. Ferne, and acquainted him with it, who promised to deliver him to us. Whereupon we sent the marshall and 4 sergeants to the ship for him, but the master not being aboard they would not deliver him. Whereupon the master went himself and brought him to the court, and the words being proved against him by 2 witnesses he was committed. The next day the master, to pacify his men (who were in a great tumult), requested he might be delivered to him and did undertake to bring him before us again the day after, which was granted him, and he brought him to us at the time appointed. Then in the presence of all the rest of the masters he acknowledged his offence and set his hand to a submission and was discharged. Then the governor desired the masters that they would deal freely and tell us if they did take any offense and what they required of us. They answered that in regard they should be examined upon their return what colors they saw here, they did desire that the king's colors might be spread at our fort. It was answered that we had not the king's colors. Thereupon 2 of them did offer them freely to us. We replied that for our parts we were fully persuaded that the cross in the ensign was idolatrous, and therefore might not set it in our ensign, but because the fort was the king's and maintained in his name, we thought that his own colors might be spread there. So the governor accepted the colors of Captain Palmer and promised they should be set up at Castle Island. We had conferred overnight with Mr. Cotton, etc., about the point. The governor and Mr. Dudley and Mr. Cotton were of opinion that they might be set up at the fort upon that distinction that it was maintained in the king's name. Others not being so persuaded answered that the governor and Mr. Dudley, being 2 of the Council[40] and being persuaded of the lawfulness, etc., might use their power to set them up. Some other being not so persuaded could not join in that act, yet would not oppose as being doubtful, etc.[41] . . .

Month 5 [July], 20. John Gallop, with one man more and 2 little boys, coming from Connecticut in a bark of 20 ton, intending to put in at Long Island to trade, ⟨were⟩ ∧and∧ being at the mouth of the harbor, were forced by a sudden change of the wind to bear up for Blocke Island, or Fishers Island,[42] lying before Narragansett, where they espied a small pinnace, which drawing near unto they found to be Mr. Oldham's (an old planter and a member of Watertown congregation, who had been long out atrading, having with him only 2 English boys and 2 Indians of Narragansett). So they hailed him but had no answer, and the deck was full of Indians (14 in all) and a canoe was gone from her full of Indians and goods. Whereupon they suspected they had killed John Oldham, and the rather because the Indians let slip and set up sail, being 2 miles from shore and the wind and tide being off the shore of the island, whereby they drove towards the main at Narragansett. Whereupon they went ahead of them, and having but

40. The Standing Council created on 25 May 1636.

41. JW himself was clearly opposed to the use of the popish cross, even at Castle Island.

42. Gallop sailed past Fishers Island at the E entrance to Long Island Sound and proceeded to Block Island, 20 miles further E, where he found Oldham's pinnace.

2 pieces and 2 pistols and nothing but duck shot, they bear up near the Indians (who stood ready armed with guns, pikes, and swords) and let fly among them and so galled[43] them as they all gat under hatches. Then they stood off again and returning with a good gale they stemmed her upon the quarter[44] and almost overset her, which so frighted the Indians as 6 of them leaped overboard and were drowned. Yet they durst not board her, but stood off again and fitted their anchor so as, stemming her the 2 time, they bored her bow through with their anchor, and so sticking fast to her they made divers shot through her (being but inch board) and so raked her fore-and-aft as they must needs kill or hurt some of the Indians. But seeing none of them come forth, they gat loose from her and stood off again. Then 4 or 5 more of the Indians leaped into the sea and were likewise drowned. So there being now but 4 left in her they boarded her, whereupon one Indian came up and yielded. Him they bound and put into hold. Then another yielded whom they bound, but John Gallop being well acquainted with their skill to untie themselves if 2 of them be together, and having no place to keep them asunder, he threw him bound into [the] sea. And looking about they found John Oldham under an old seine, stark naked, his head cleft to the brains and his hands and legs cut as if they had been cutting them off, and yet warm. So they put him into the sea, but could not get to the other 2 Indians who were in a little room underneath with their swords. So they took the goods which were left and the sails, etc., and towed the bark away, but night coming on and the wind rising they were forced to heave her off, and the wind carried her to the Narragansett shore.

[July] 26. The 2 Indians which were with Mr. Oldham and one other came from Canonicus, the chief sachem of Narragansett, with a letter from Mr. Williams to the governor to certify him what had befallen

43. Harassed.
44. Rammed the pinnace along its side.

Mr. Oldham, and how grievously they were offended, and that Muntunommoh[45] was gone with 17 canoes and 200 men to take revenge, etc. But upon examination of the Indian who was brought prisoner to us, we found that all the sachems of the Narragansett except Canonicus and Miantonomi were the contrivers of Mr. Oldham's death, and the occasion was, because he went to make peace and trade with the Pequots last year. The prisoner said also that Mr. Oldham's 2 Indians were acquainted with it, but because they were sent as messengers from Canonicus we would not imprison them. But the governor wrote back to Mr. Williams to let the Narragansetts know that we expected they should send us the 2 boys and take revenge upon the islands, and withal gave Mr. Williams a caution to look to himself if we should have occasion to make war upon the Narragansetts, for Block Island was under them.[46] And the next day, ⟨27⟩28, he wrote to Canonicus by one of those 2 Indians, and that he had suspicion of him, etc., yet he had sent him back because he was a messenger, but did expect that if he should send ⟨for⟩ the said 2 Indians he should send them to us to clear themselves.

[July] 30. Mr. Oldham's 2 boys were sent home by one of Miantonomi his men with a letter from Mr. Williams signifying that Miantonomi had caused the sachem of Nianticke[47] to send to Block Island for them, and that he had near 100 fathom of wampum and other goods of Mr. Oldham's which should be reserved for us, and that 3 of the 7 which were drowned were sachems, and one of the 2 which were hired by the sachem of Niantic was dead also. So we wrote back to have the rest of these which were accessary to be sent to us, and the rest of the

---

45. The name of this Narragansett sachem in modern spelling is Miantonomi.

46. In fact, the English decided to make peace with the Narragansetts, even though they had murdered Oldham, and to fight the Pequots instead.

47. This was Ninigret, sachem of the Eastern Niantics who were allies of the Narragansetts. The Eastern Niantics lived on the present Rhode Island–Connecticut border, with the Narragansetts to the E of them and the Pequots to the W.

goods, and that he should tell Canonicus and Miantonomi that we held them innocent, but that 6 other under-sachems were guilty, etc. . . .

[August] 8. Leutt. Edwd. Gibbons and Jo: Higginson[48] with Cut-sh'ammekin,[49] the sagamore of Massachusetts, were sent to Canonicus to treat with him about the murder of John Oldham.

[August] 13. They returned, being very well accepted and good success in their business. They observed in the sachem much state, great command over his men, and marvellous wisdom in his answers and the carriage of the whole treaty, clearing himself and his neighbors of the murder and offering assistance for revenge of it, yet upon very safe and wary conditions.[50]

Month 6 [August], 25. The governor and Council having lately assembled the rest of the magistrates and ministers to advise with them about doing justice upon the Indians for the death of Mr. Oldham, and all agreeing that it should be attempted with expedition, did this day send forth 90 men distributed to 4 commanders: Captain John Underhill, Captain Nathl. Turner, Ensign Jenyson, and Ensign Davenport; and over them all as general, John Endecott, Esq., one of the assistants, was sent. They were embarked in 3 pinnaces and carried 2 shallops and 2 Indians with them. They had commission to put to death the men of Block Island, but to spare the women and children and to bring them away, and to take possession of the island, and from thence to go to the Pequots to demand the murders of Captain Stone and other English, and 1000 fathom of wampum for damages, etc., and some of their

48. Gibbons was a Boston merchant and military officer; Higginson was the son of the Rev. Francis Higginson, and eventually became the minister of the Salem church.

49. This sachem succeeded Chickatabot as spokesman for the Massachusett Indians after the smallpox epidemic of 1633. He was frequently used by the MBC as a messenger and interpreter.

50. Canonicus and his nephew Miantonomi, the two chief Narragansett sachems, had adopted a clever strategy. By pursuing Oldham's killers they had driven the remaining suspects in this crime into taking refuge with the Pequots, which shifted the MBC's vengeance from the Narragansetts to the Pequots.

children as hostages. Which if they should refuse, they were to obtain it by force . . .

August 24. John Endecott, Esq. and 4 captains under him with 20 men apiece set sail. They arrived at Block Island the last of the same, the wind blowing hard at NE. There went so great a surf as they had much to do to land, and about 40 Indians were ready upon the shore to entertain them with their arrows which they shot oft at our men, but being armed with corslets[51] they had no hurt, only one man was lightly hurt upon his neck and another near his foot. So soon as one man leaped on shore they all fled. The island is about 10 miles long and 4 broad, full of small hills and all overgrown with brushwood of oak, no good timber in it, so as they could not march but in one file and in the narrow paths. There were about 2 plantations 3 miles in sunder,[52] and about 60 wigwams, some very large and fair, and above 200 acres of corn, some gathered and laid on heaps and the rest standing. When they had spent 2 days in searching the island and could not find the Indians, they burnt their wigwams and all their mats and some corn, and staved 7 canoes and departed. They could not tell what men they killed, but some were wounded and carried away by their fellows.

Thence they went to the mouth of Connecticut where they lay windbound 4 days, and taking thence 20 men and 2 shallops they sailed to the Pequot harbor[53] where an Indian came to them in a canoe and demanded what they were and what they would have. The general told him he came from the governor of Massachusetts to speak with their sachems. He told him Sasacoos was gone to Long Island. Then he bade him go tell the other sachem,[54] etc. So he departed, and in the meantime our men landed but with much danger if the Indians had made use of

51. Body armor.

52. Asunder or apart.

53. The mouth of the Pequot (later Thames) River; now Groton, Conn.

54. Probably Uncas, sachem of the Mohegans, who lived upstream from the Pequots and had been contending with Sassacus for the leadership of the Pequots.

their advantage, for all the shore was high ragged rocks, etc. Then the messenger returned and the Indians began to gather together about our men till there were about 300 of them, and some 4 hours passed while the messenger went to and fro, bringing still excuses for the sachem's not coming. At last the general told the messenger and the rest of the Indians near the particulars of his commission, and sent him to tell the sachem that if he would not come to him, nor yield to these demands, he would fight with them. The messenger told him that the sachem would meet him if our men would lay down their arms as his men should do their bows, etc. When the general saw they did but dally to gain time, he bade them be gone and shift for themselves, for they had dared the English to come fight with them and now they were come for that purpose. Thereupon they all withdrew. Some of our men would have made a shot at them, but the general would not suffer them, but when they were gone out of musket shot he marched after them, supposing they would have stood to it awhile as they did to the Dutch, but they all fled and shot at our men from the thickets and rocks, but did us no harm. 2 of them our men killed, and hurt others. So they marched up to their town and burnt all their wigwams and mats, but their corn being standing they could not spoil it. At night they returned to their vessels, and the next day they went ashore on the west side of the river and burnt all their wigwams and spoiled their canoes, and so set sail and came to the Narragansett where they landed their men, and the 14 of September they came all safe to Boston, which was a marvelous providence of God that not a hair fell from the head of any of them, nor any sick or feeble person among them. As they came by Narragansett, Cutshamekin, an Indian who went with them for an interpreter, who being armed with a corslet and a piece had crept into a swamp and killed a Pequot, and having flayed off the skin of his head,[55] he sent it to Canonicus, who presently sent it to all the sachems about

---

55. Scalping was not widely practiced among the southern New England Indians.

him and returned many thanks to the English, and sent 4 fathom of wampum to Cutshamekin.

The soldiers who went were all voluntaries and had only their victuals provided, but demanded no pay. The whole charge of the voyage came to above £200. The seamen had all wages.

The Narragansett men told us after that 13 of the Pequots were killed and 40 wounded, and but one of Block Island killed . . . Canonicus sent us word of some English whom the Pequots had killed at Saybrooke, and Mr. Williams wrote that the Pequots and Narragansetts were at truce, and that Miantonomi told him that the Pequots had labored to persuade them that the English were minded to destroy all Indians. Whereupon we sent for Miantonomi to come to us.[56]

A Continuation of the History of New England [57]

1636 8ber [October]. After Mr. Endecott and our men were departed from the Pequod, the twenty men of Saybrook lay wind-bound there, and went to fetch some of the Indians' corn;[58] and having fetched every man one sackful to their boat, they returned for more, and having loaded themselves, the Indians set upon them. So they laid down their corn and gave fire upon them, and the Indians shot arrows at them. The place was open for the distance of musket shot, and the Indians kept the covert, save when they came forth, about ten at a time, and discharged their arrows. The English put themselves into a single file, and some ten only (who had pieces which could reach them) shot; the

56. This is the last entry selected from the first volume of JW's journal.

57. This second volume of JW's journal was accidentally destroyed in 1825; see p. ix above. The heading seems to have been in JW's hand, and he kept to this wording when he entitled the third volume; see p. 263 below.

58. These 20 Saybrook men were commanded by Lion Gardiner, who was furious at Endecott and the MBC for stirring up the Pequots and leaving him to face the consequences.

others stood ready to keep them from breaking in upon our men. So they continued the most part of the afternoon. Our men killed some of them, as they supposed, and hurt others; and they shot only one of ours through the leg. Their arrows were all shot compass,[59] so as our men, standing single, could easily see and avoid them; and one was employed to gather up their arrows. At last they emptied their sacks, and retired safe to their boat.

About two days after, five men of Saybrook went up the river about four miles, to fetch hay in a meadow on Pequot side. The grass was so high as some Pequots, being hid in it, set upon our men, and one, that had hay on his back, they took; the others fled to their boat, one of them having five arrows in him (but yet recovered). About fourteen days after, three of them went forth on fowling, (which the lieutenant[60] had strictly forbidden them). Two had pieces, and the third only a sword. Suddenly about one hundred Indians came out of the covert, and set upon them. He who had the sword brake through them (and received only two shot, not dangerous) and escaped to the house, which was not a bow-shot off, and persuaded[61] the other two to follow him; but they stood still till the Indians came and took them, and carried them away with their pieces.

[October] 21. Miantonomi, the sachem of Narragansett, (being sent for by the governor), came to Boston with two of Canonicus's sons, and another sachem, and near twenty sanaps. The governor sent twenty musketeers to meet him at Roxbury. He came to Boston about noon. The governor had called together most of the magistrates and ministers, to give countenance to our proceedings and to advise with them about the terms of peace. It was dinner time, and the sachems and their

59. In a curving projectory.
60. Lion Gardiner.
61. Pleaded with.

council dined by themselves in the same room where the governor dined, and their sanaps were sent to the inn. After dinner, Miantonomi declared that they would continue in war with the Pequots and their confederates, till they were subdued; and desired we should so do: They would deliver our enemies to us, or kill them: That if any of theirs should kill our cattle, that we would not kill them, but cause them to make satisfaction: That they would now make a firm peace, and two months hence they would send us a present.

The governor told them they should have answer the next morning.

In the morning we met again, and concluded the peace upon the articles underwritten, which the governor subscribed, and they also subscribed with their marks, and Cutshamekin also. But because we could not well make them understand the articles perfectly, we agreed to send a copy of them to Mr. Williams, who could best interpret them to them. So, after dinner, they took leave, and were conveyed out of town by some musketeers, and dismissed with a volley of shot.

The Articles.

1. A firm peace between us and our friends of other plantations (if they consent) and their confederates (if they will observe the articles, etc.), and our posterities.

2. Neither party to make peace with the Pequots without the other's consent.

3. Not to harbor, etc., the Pequots, etc.

4. To put to death or deliver over murderers, etc.

5. To return our fugitive servants, etc.[62]

6. We to give them notice when we go against the Pequots, and they to send us some guides.

7. Free trade between us.

---

62. Throughout the seventeenth century considerable numbers of Massachusetts servants ran away to join the Indians. See James Axtell, "The White Indians of Colonial America," *WMQ*, 3d ser., 32 (1975): 55–88.

8. None of them to come near our plantations during the wars with the Pequots, without some Englishman or known Indian.

9. To continue to the posterity of both parties.

The governor of Plymouth wrote to the deputy,[63] that we had occasioned a war, etc., by provoking the Pequots. The deputy took it ill (as there was reason), and returned answer accordingly, and made it appear, 1. That there was as much done as could be expected, considering they fled from us, and we could not follow them in our armor, neither had any to guide us in their country. 2. We went not to make war upon them, but to do justice, etc., and having killed thirteen of them for four or five, which they had murdered of ours, and destroyed sixty wigwams, etc., we were not much behind with them . . .

About the middle of this month, John Tilley, master of a bark, coming down Connecticut River, went on shore in a canoe three miles above the fort to kill fowl; and having shot off his piece, many Indians arose out of the covert and took him, and killed one other, who was in the canoe. This Tilley was a very stout[64] man, and of great understanding. They cut off his hands, and sent them before, and after cut off his feet. He lived three days after his hands were cut off; and themselves confessed, that he was a stout man, because he cried not in his torture . . .

One Mrs. Hutchinson,[65] a member of the church of Boston, a woman of a ready wit and bold spirit, brought over with her two dangerous errors: 1. That the person of the Holy Ghost dwells in a justified person. 2. That no sanctification can help to evidence to us our justification.— From these two grew many branches; as, 1, Our union with the Holy

---

63. JW.

64. Valiant.

65. Anne Hutchinson (1591–1643) was the daughter of the Rev. Francis Marbury, a silenced Lincolnshire minister, and the wife of a merchant, William Hutchinson of Alford, Lincs. She had come to Boston with her husband and eleven children in 1634, and settled in a house across the street from JW.

Ghost, so as a Christian remains dead to every spiritual action, and hath no gifts nor graces, other than such as are in hypocrites, nor any other sanctification but the Holy Ghost himself.[66]

There joined with her in these opinions a brother of hers, one Mr. Wheelwright,[67] a silenced minister sometimes in England.

[October] 25. The other ministers in the bay, hearing of these things, came to Boston at the time of a general court, and entered conference in private with them, to the end they might know the certainty of these things; that if need were, they might write to the church of Boston about them, to prevent (if it were possible) the dangers which seemed hereby to hang over that and the rest of the churches. At this conference, Mr. Cotton was present, and gave satisfaction to them,[68] so as he agreed with them all in the point of sanctification, and so did Mr. Wheelwright; so as they all did hold that sanctification did help to evidence justification. The same he had delivered plainly in public, divers times; but, for the indwelling of the person of the Holy Ghost, he held that still ⟨as some others of the ministers did⟩, but not union with the person of the Holy Ghost ⟨⟨as Mrs. Hutchinson and others did⟩⟩, so as to amount to a personal union.

Mr. Cotton, being requested by the general court, with some other

66. With this paragraph JW introduces the most dramatic chapter in his narrative, the Antinomian controversy that wracked Massachusetts from Oct. 1636 to March 1638. Like Roger Williams, Anne Hutchinson was a religious radical who found JW's brand of Puritan orthodoxy to be spiritually dead, but she posed a more serious challenge to JW, because her stronghold was his Boston church, her supporters included Cotton and Vane, and she held religious meetings in her house that rivaled in influence the clerical conferences of ministers and elders. By Oct. 1636 Hutchinson's weekly religious exercises had generated a public crisis, and JW doubtless realized that if he could not defeat her, he might well be forced out of the colony himself.

67. John Wheelwright (1592?–1679) had been vicar of Bilsby, Lincs., a village near Alford where the Hutchinsons lived. He had married William Hutchinson's sister. Removed from the ministry at Bilsby in 1632, he arrived at Boston in May 1636.

68. Cotton's fellow ministers were worried by the sermons he had been preaching, admired by Hutchinson and her followers, in which he seemed to deny that "sanctification"—man's obedience to God's moral law and works—offered satisfactory evidence of a prior act of "justification" or redemptive grace.

ministers, to assist some of the magistrates in compiling a body of fundamental laws, did this court present a model of Moses his judicials, compiled in an exact method, which were taken into further consideration till the next general court.[69]

[October] 30. Some of the church of Boston, being of the opinion of Mrs. Hutchinson, had labored to have Mr. Wheelwright to be called to be a teacher there. It was propounded the last Lord's day, and was moved again this day for resolution. One of the church[70] stood up and said he could not consent, etc. His reason was, because the church being well furnished already with able ministers, whose spirits they knew, and whose labors God had blessed in much love and sweet peace, he thought it not fit (no necessity urging) to put the welfare of the church to the least hazard, as he feared they should do by calling in one whose spirit they knew not, and one who seemed to dissent in judgment, and instanced in two points, which he delivered in a late exercise there; 1. That a believer was more than a creature. 2. That the person of the Holy Ghost and a believer were united. Hereupon the governor[71] spake, that he marvelled at this, seeing Mr. Cotton had lately approved his doctrine. To this Mr. Cotton answered, that he did not remember the first, and desired Mr. Wheelwright to explain his meaning. He denied not the points, but showed upon what occasion he delivered them. Whereupon, there being an endeavor to make a reconciliation, the first replied that, although Mr. Wheelwright and himself might likely agree about the point, and though he thought reverendly of his godliness and abilities so as he could be content to live under such a ministry, yet seeing he was apt to raise doubtful dispu-

---

69. Cotton's Old Testament law code—which prescribed the death penalty for profanation of the Sabbath and reviling the magistracy as well as for fornication, incest, sodomy, and buggery—was not adopted in Massachusetts, but supplied the framework for the legal code of New Haven Colony.

70. JW.

71. Henry Vane.

tations, he could not consent to choose him to that place. Whereupon the church gave way, that he might be called to a new church to be gathered at Mount Woollaston, ∧now Braintree∧.

Divers of the brethren took offence at the said speech against Mr. Wheelwright; whereupon the same brother spake in the congregation the next day to this effect: That he was desirous to give satisfaction. 1. For that he had charged the brother in public, and for a thing so long since delivered, and had not first dealt with him privately. For this he acknowledged it was a failing; but the occasion was that when he heard the points delivered, he took them in a good sense, as spoken figuratively, but hearing very lately that he was suspected to hold such opinions, it caused him to think he spake as he meant. The 2d cause of offence was, that in his speech appeared some bitterness. For that he answered, that they well knew his manner of speech was always earnest in things which he conceived to be serious; and professed that he did love that brother's person, and did honor the gifts and graces of God in him. The 3d was, that he had charged him to have held things which he did not. For this he answered, that he had spoken since with the said brother; and for the two points,—that a believer should be more than a creature, and that there should be a personal union between the Holy Ghost and a believer,—he had denied to hold either of them; but by necessary consequence, he doth hold them both; for he holds (said he) that there is a real union with the person of the Holy Ghost, and then of necessity it must be personal, and so a believer must be more than a creature, viz., God-man, even Christ Jesus. Now, whether this were agreeable to the doctrine of the church or not, he left to the church to judge; hoping that the Lord would direct our teacher[72] to clear these points fully, as he had well done in good measure already, and concluded, that he did not intend to dispute the matter (as not having place or calling thereunto then); yet, if any brother desired to see what light

72. John Cotton.

he walked by, he would be ready to impart it to him. How this was taken by the congregation did not appear, for no man spake to it.

A day or two after, the same brother wrote his mind fully, with such scriptures and arguments as came to hand, and sent it to Mr. Cotton[73] . . .

[November]. The governor, Mr. Vane, a wise and godly gentleman, held, with Mr. Cotton and many others, the indwelling of the person of the Holy Ghost in a believer, and went so far beyond the rest as to maintain a personal union with the Holy Ghost; but the deputy, with the pastor[74] and divers others, denied both; and the question proceeded so far by disputation (in writing, for the peace sake of the church, which all were tender of,) as at length they could not find the person of the Holy Ghost in scripture, nor in the primitive churches three hundred years after Christ. So that, all agreeing in the chief matter of substance, viz. that the Holy Ghost is God, and that he doth dwell in the believers, it was earnestly desired, that the word person might be forborn, being a term of human invention, and tending to doubtful disputation in this case.[75]

10ber [December]. The governor, receiving letters from his friends in England, which necessarily required his presence there,[76] imparted the same to the council and some others; and, being thereupon resolved of his return into England, called a court of deputies to the end he might have free leave of the country, etc. They, being assembled in

73. JW's statement to Cotton is lost. JW also wrote two "papers" (also lost) against the Antinomian position that he showed to Wilson; one was a declaration on justification, and the other a plea for pacification within the Massachusetts church. When Shepard saw these papers, he urged JW not to circulate them further, for he found JW's arguments to be dangerously close to conceding man an initiative in the quest for salvation. See *WP*, 3:326–332.

74. JW with John Wilson.

75. When JW wrote this paragraph in Nov. 1636, he seems to have hoped that the Antinomian controversy was blowing over.

76. Vane's father was at this time busily acquiring landed property, and he may have wanted his son home so as to arrange a marriage settlement.

court, and himself declaring the necessity of his departure, and those
of the council affirming the reasons to be very urgent, though not fit
to be imparted to the whole court, they desired respite to consider
thereof till the morning; when one of the assistants[77] using some pa-
thetical passages of the loss of such a governor in a time of such danger
as did hang over us from the Indians and French, the governor brake
forth into tears, and professed that howsoever the causes propounded
for his departure were such as did concern the utter ruin of his outward
estate, yet he would rather have hazarded all than have gone from them
at this time, if something else had not pressed him more, viz. the
inevitable danger he saw of God's judgments to come upon us for these
differences and dissensions which he saw amongst us, and the scandalous imputations brought upon himself, as if he should be the cause of
all; and therefore he thought it best for him to give place for a time,
etc. Upon this the court concluded that it would not be fit to give way
to his departure upon these grounds. Whereupon he recalled himself,
and professed that the reasons concerning his own estate were sufficient
to his own satisfaction for his departure, and therefore desired the court
he might have leave to go; as for the other passage, it slipped him out
of his passion and not out of judgment. Upon this the court consented,
silently, to his departure. Then the question was about supply of his
place. Some were of opinion, that it should be executed by the deputy;
but this scruple being cast in, that if the deputy should die then the
government would be vacant, and none have power to call any court,
or to preside therein, etc., it was agreed to call a court of elections for
a new governor and deputy, in case the present deputy should be chose
governor; and an order was made (in regard of the season) that such
as would might send their votes by proxy, in papers sealed up and

77. Probably William Coddington or Richard Dummer, who were Vane's allies in the
Antinomian controversy.

delivered to the deputies. And so this court was adjourned four days, and two days after the court of elections was to assemble.[78] These things thus passed, divers of the congregation of Boston met together, and agreed that they did not apprehend the necessity of the governor's departure upon the reasons alleged, and sent some of them to declare the same to the court; whereupon the governor expressed himself to be an obedient child to the church, and therefore, notwithstanding the license of the court, yet, without the leave of the church, he durst not go away.

Whereupon a great part of the court and country, who understood hereof, declared their purpose to continue him still in his place, and therefore, so soon as the day of election came, and the country were assembled, it was thought the best way for avoiding trouble, etc., not to proceed to election, but to adjourn the court to the great general court in May.

[December 7]. At this court the elders of the churches were called, to advise with them about discovering and pacifying the differences among the churches in point of opinion. The ministers had met a little before, and had drawn into heads all the points wherein they suspected Mr. Cotton did differ from them, and had propounded them to him, and pressed him to a direct answer, affirmative or negative, to every one; which he had promised, and taken time for. This meeting being spoke of in the court the day before, the governor took great offence at it, as being without his privity, etc., which this day Mr. Peter told him as plainly of (with all due reverence), and how it had sadded[79] the ministers' spirits that he should be jealous of their meetings, or seem to restrain their liberty, etc. The governor excused his speech, as sudden

78. The general court, having met on 7 Dec., adjourned to 13 Dec. in order to hold a special election to replace Vane on 15 Dec.

79. Saddened.

and upon a mistake. Mr. Peter told him also that ⟨before he came,⟩ within less than two years since, the churches were in peace, etc. The governor answered, that the light of the gospel brings a sword, and the children of the bondwoman would persecute those of the freewoman.[80] Mr. Peter also besought him humbly to consider his youth and short experience in the things of God, and to beware of peremptory conclusions, which he perceived him to be very apt unto.

Mr. Wilson made a very sad speech of the condition of our churches, and the inevitable danger of separation if these differences and alienations among brethren were not speedily remedied; and laid the blame upon these new opinions risen up amongst us, which all the magistrates, except the governor and two others, did confirm, and all the ministers but two[81] . . .

The speech of Mr. Wilson was taken very ill by Mr. Cotton and others of the same church, so as he and divers of them went to admonish him. But Mr. Wilson and some others could see no breach of rule, seeing he was called by the court about the same matter with the rest of the elders, and exhorted to deliver their minds freely and faithfully, both for discovering the danger and the means to help. But this would not satisfy, but they called him to answer publicly, [December] 31; and there the governor pressed it violently against him, and all the congregation except the deputy and one or two more, and many of them with much bitterness and reproaches; but he answered them all with words of truth and soberness, and with marvellous wisdom. It was strange to see, how the common people were led, by example, to condemn him in that, which (it was very probable) divers of them did not

80. The reference is to Abraham's natural son Ishmael by his slave Hagar and his lawful son Isaac by his wife Sarah. See Gen. 21:9 and Paul's interpretation in Gal. 4:29–31.

81. Wilson, having lost almost all support within his own church, was here appealing openly to the MBC and to the colony ministers for help against Vane, Coddington, Dummer, Cotton, and Wheelwright.

understand, nor the rule which he was supposed to have broken. The teacher[82] joined with the church in their judgment of him (not without some appearance of prejudice) yet with much wisdom and moderation. They were eager to proceed to present censure, but the teacher staid them from that, but gave him a grave exhortation. The next day Mr. Wilson preached notwithstanding, and the Lord so assisted him as gave great satisfaction, and the governor himself gave public witness to him . . .

Upon these public occasions, other opinions brake out publicly in the church of Boston,—as that the Holy Ghost dwelt in a believer as he is in heaven; that a man is justified before he believes; and that faith is no cause of justification. And others spread more secretly,—as that the letter of the scripture holds forth nothing but a covenant of works; and that the covenant of grace was the spirit of the scripture, which was known only to believers; and that this covenant of works was given by Moses in the ten commandments; that there was a seed (viz., Abraham's carnal seed) went along in this, and there was a spirit and life in it, by virtue whereof a man might attain to any sanctification in gifts and graces, and might have spiritual and continual communion with Jesus Christ, and yet be damned. After, it was granted that faith was before justification, but it was only passive, an empty vessel, etc.; but in conclusion, the ground of all was found to be assurance by immediate revelation.

All the congregation of Boston, except four or five, closed with these opinions or the most of them; but one of the brethren wrote against them, and bore witness to the truth, together with the pastor, and very few others joined with them.

About this time the rest of the ministers, taking offence at some doctrines delivered by Mr. Cotton, and especially at some opinions

82. John Cotton.

which some of his church did broach, drew out sixteen points and gave them to him, entreating him to deliver his judgment directly in them, which accordingly he did, and many copies thereof were dispersed about.[83] Some doubts he well cleared, but in some things he gave not satisfaction. The rest of the ministers replied to these answers, and at large showed their dissent, and the grounds thereof;[84] and at the next general court, held 9th of the 1st,[85] they all assembled at Boston, and agreed to put off all lectures for three weeks, that they might bring things to some issue . . .

12 mo. [February] 22. The lieutenant of Saybrook,[86] at the mouth of Connecticut, going out with nine men armed with swords and pieces, they started three Indians whom they pursued till they were brought into an ambush of fifty, who came upon them and slew four of their men, and had they not drawn their swords and retired, they had been all slain. The Indians were so hardy as they came close up to them, notwithstanding their pieces . . .

[January] 20. A general fast was kept in all the churches. The occasion was the miserable estate of the churches in Germany; the calamities upon our native country, the bishops making havock in the churches, putting down the faithful ministers, and advancing popish ceremonies and doctrines, the plague raging exceedingly, and famine and sword threatening them; the dangers of those at Connecticut, and of ourselves also, by the Indians; and the dissensions in our churches.

The differences in the said points of religion increased more and more, and the ministers of both sides (there being only Mr. Cotton of

---

83. These 16 questions, together with Cotton's replies, were later published in England in 1644. JW tucked a MS copy of the 16 questions into the second volume of his journal, where Ezra Stiles found it when he read the journal in 1771; JW's copy is now in the Belknap Papers, MHS. Both the published version of the 16 questions and JW's copy are printed in Hall, pp. 44–59.

84. The ministers' reply and Cotton's lengthy rejoinder are printed in Hall, pp. 60–151.

85. 9 March 1637.

86. Lion Gardiner.

one party) did publicly declare their judgments in some of them, so as all men's mouths were full of them. And there being, 12 mo. 3 [February 3], a ship ready to go for England and many passengers in it, Mr. Cotton took occasion to speak to them about the differences, etc., and willed them to tell our countrymen that all the strife amongst us was about magnifying the grace of God; one party seeking to advance the grace of God within us, and the other to advance the grace of God towards us (meaning by the one justification, and by the other sanctification); and so bade them tell them that, if there were any among them that would strive for grace, they should come hither; and so declared some particulars. Mr. Wilson spake after him, and declared that he knew none of the elders or brethren of the churches but did labor to advance the free grace of God in justification, so far as the word of God required; and spake also about the doctrine of sanctification, and the use and necessity, etc., of it; by occasion whereof no man could tell (except some few, who knew the bottom of the matter) where any difference was: which speech, though it offended those of Mr. Cotton's party, yet it was very seasonable to clear the rest, who otherwise should have been reputed to have opposed free grace. Thus every occasion increased the contention, and caused great alienation of minds; and the members of Boston (frequenting the lectures of other ministers) did make much disturbance by public questions, and objections to their doctrines which did any way disagree from their opinions; and it began to be as common here to distinguish between men, by being under a covenant of grace or a covenant of works, as in other countries between Protestants and Papists.[87]

February 6. A man of Weymouth (but not of the church) fell into some trouble of mind, and in the night cried out, "Art thou come, Lord

87. One consequence of the controversy was that the Boston church, which had admitted 206 members between Sept. 1633 (when Cotton arrived) and the close of 1636, admitted only two members in 1637 and three in 1638.

Jesus?" and with that leaped out of his bed in his shirt, and breaking from his wife, leaped out at a high window into the snow and ran about seven miles off, and being traced in the snow was found dead next morning. They might perceive, that he had kneeled down to prayer in divers places.

(1.) [March] 9. The general court began. When any matter about these new opinions was mentioned, the court was divided; yet the greater number far were sound. They questioned the proceeding against Mr. Wilson for his speech in the last court, but could not fasten upon such as had prejudiced[88] him, etc.; but by the vote of the greater party his speech was approved, and declared to have been a seasonable advice, and no charge or accusation.

The ministers, being called to give advice about the authority of the court in things concerning the churches, etc., did all agree of these two things: 1. That no member of the court ought to be publicly questioned by a church for any speech in the court, without the license of the court.[89] The reason was, because the court may have sufficient reason that may excuse the sin, which yet may not be fit to acquaint the church with, being a secret of state. The second thing was, that in all such heresies or errors of any church members as are manifest and dangerous to the state, the court may proceed without tarrying for the church; but if the opinions be doubtful, etc., they are first to refer them to the church, etc.

At this court, when Mr. Wheelwright was to be questioned for a sermon which seemed to tend to sedition, etc.,[90] near all the church of

88. Injured.

89. Wilson, while neither a magistrate nor a deputy, was considered a "member of the court" when called upon by the MBC for advice in Dec. 1636. The other clergy wanted to protect him from public questioning by the Boston church for his sad speech.

90. Wheelwright had preached this sermon on 19 Jan. in the Boston church. JW found the sermon seditious because Wheelwright identified the Boston church with Jesus and the rest of Massachusetts with Herod and Pontius Pilate, and rallied his followers to fight "those under a covenant of works" and to "kill them with the word of the Lord."

Boston presented a petition to the court for two things: 1. That as freemen they might be present in cases of judicature. 2. That the court would declare if they might deal in cases of conscience before the church, etc. This was taken as a groundless and presumptuous act, especially at this season, and was rejected with this answer: That the court had never used to proceed judicially but it was openly; but for matter of consultation and preparation in causes, they might and would be private.

One Stephen Greensmith, for saying that all the ministers, except A. B. C., did teach a covenant of works, was censured to acknowledge his fault in every church, and fined £40.[91]

Mr. Wheelwright, one of the members of Boston, preaching at the last fast, inveighed against all that walked in a covenant of works, as he described it ⟨to be⟩, ∧viz., such as maintain sanctification as an evidence of justification, etc.∧ and called them antichrists, and stirred up the people against them with much bitterness and vehemency. For this he was called into the court, and his sermon being produced, he justified it, and confessed he did mean all that walk in such a way. Whereupon the elders of the rest of the churches were called, and asked whether they, in their ministry, did walk in such a way. They all acknowledged they did. So, after much debate, the court adjudged him guilty of sedition and also of contempt, for that the court had appointed the fast as a means of reconciliation of the differences, etc., and he purposely set himself to kindle and increase them. The governor and some few more (who dissented) tendered a protestation, which, because it wholly justified Mr. Wheelwright and condemned the proceedings of the court, was rejected. The church of Boston also tendered a petition in his behalf, justifying Mr. Wheelwright's sermon. The court deferred

91. Greensmith was a Boston lumber merchant who eventually paid his £40 fine, but moved to New Hampshire. According to the court records, his three exceptions were "Mr. Cotton, Mr. Wheelwright, and he thought Mr. Hooker" (*MR*, 1:189).

sentence till the next court. Much heat of contention was this court between the opposite parties; so as it was moved, that the next court might be kept at Newtown.[92] The governor refused to put it to the vote; the deputy was loath to do it except the court would require him, because he dwelt in Boston, etc. So the court put it to Mr. Endecott . . .

Mo. 2. [April] 1. Those of Connecticut returned answer to our public letters, wherein they showed themselves unsatisfied about our former expedition against the Pequots, and their expectations of a further prosecution of the war, to which they offer to send men, and signify their unpreparedness to declare themselves in the matter of government, in regard of their engagement to attend the answer of the gentlemen of Saybrook about the same matter[93] . . .

[May] 12. We received a letter from [Mr. Haynes] and others, being then at Saybrook, that the Pequots had been up the river at Weathersfield and had killed six men, being at their work, and twenty cows and a mare, and had killed three women, and carried away two maids[94] . . .

[May] 17. Our court of elections was at Newtown. So soon as the court was set, being about one of the clock, a petition was preferred by those of Boston. The governor would have read it, but the deputy said it was out of order; it was a court for elections, and those must first be despatched, and then their petitions should be heard. Divers

92. Another defeat for the Boston church. By moving the May court of election from Boston to Newtown, the orthodox party improved its chances of unseating Vane as governor.

93. It was still unsettled whether the new Connecticut River towns were to be governed by the MBC, or by the Saybrook proprietors, or were to be independent of both. In March 1636 the Connecticut migrants had accepted a one-year commission of government from the MBC and the absentee Saybrook proprietors (*MR,* 1:170–171), but that commission had now expired. Although the Connecticut people lacked an English title to their land and claimed "unpreparedness," they were effectually forming an independent government of their own.

94. Since Endecott's raid of Aug.-Sept. 1636, the Pequots had killed or captured 20 English colonists, 8 at Saybrook and 12 elsewhere on the Connecticut River.

others also opposed that course, as an ill precedent, etc.; and the petition, being about pretence of liberty, etc. (though intended chiefly for revoking the sentence given against Mr. Wheelwright), would have spent all the day in debate, etc.; but yet the governor and those of that party would not proceed to election, except the petition was read. Much time was already spent about this debate, and the people crying out for election, it was moved by the deputy that the people should divide themselves, and the greater number must carry it. And so it was done, and the greater number by many were for election.[95] But the governor and that side kept their place still, and would not proceed. Whereupon the deputy told him, that if he would not go to election, he and the rest of that side would proceed. Upon that, he came from his company, and they went to election; and Mr. Winthrop was chosen governor, Mr. Dudley deputy, and Mr. Endecott of the standing council; and Mr. Israel Stoughton and Mr. Richard Saltonstall were called in to be assistants; and Mr. Vane, Mr. Coddington, and Mr. Dummer (being all of that faction) were left quite out.[96]

There was great danger of a tumult that day; for those of that side grew into fierce speeches and some laid hands on others; but seeing themselves too weak, they grew quiet. They expected a great advantage that day, because the remote towns were allowed to come in by proxy; but it fell out that there were enough beside. But if it had been otherwise, they must have put in their deputies, as other towns had done, for all matters beside elections.[97] Boston, having deferred to choose

95. At this point JW's supporters left the meetinghouse and went outdoors; the Rev. John Wilson is said to have climbed a tree and urged them to proceed to election.

96. This election, the most hotly contested in early Massachusetts, returned JW to the colony leadership after a three-year eclipse. With several of the MBC leaders of 1634–1637 having left for Connecticut, and others purged in the Antinomian controversy, management of the colony reverted to the men who had dominated the scene in 1630–1633.

97. Even if the Antinomian minority had been able to muster more individual voters for the election of officers than the orthodox majority, they would still have been defeated on all other issues, because in General Court the towns acted by deputy, with the three Boston deputies pitted against the 29 deputies from the other towns.

deputies till the election was passed, went home that night and the next morning they sent Mr. Vane, the late governor, and Mr. Coddington, and Mr. Hough, for their deputies; but the court, being grieved at it, found a means to send them home again, for that two of the freemen of Boston had not notice of the election. So they went all home, and the next morning they returned the same gentlemen again upon a new choice; and the court not finding how they might reject them, they were admitted.

Upon the election of the new governor, the serjeants who had attended the old governor to the court (being all Boston men, where the new governor also dwelt) laid down their halberds[98] and went home; and whereas they had been wont to attend the former governor to and from the meetings on the Lord's days, they gave over now, so as the new governor was fain to use his own servants to carry two halberds before him; whereas the former governor had never less than four.

Divers writings were now published about these differences. Among the rest, the magistrates set forth an apology to justify the sentence of the court against Mr. Wheelwright, which the adverse party had much opposed and spoken evil of, and did also set forth a remonstrance to that end, in which they did not deal fairly; for, in abbreviating Mr. Wheelwright his sermon, they clear altered both the words and meaning of such passages in it whereat the offence was taken, and which were the ground of the court's sentence . . .

Mr. Cotton stated the differences in a very narrow scantling;[99] and Mr. Shepard, preaching at the day of election, brought them yet nearer, so as, except men of good understanding and such as knew the bottom of the tenents of those of the other party, few could see where the difference was; and indeed it seemed so small as (if men's affections

98. A halberd was a late medieval military weapon, combining a spear with a battle-ax; in seventeenth-century New England it was used for ceremonial purposes only, not for fighting the Indians.

99. Measure or limit.

had not been formerly alienated, when the differences were formerly stated as fundamental) they might easily have come to reconciliation. For in these particulars they agreed: 1. That justification and sanctification were both together in time; 2. That a man must know himself to be justified before he can know himself to be sanctified; 3. That the spirit never witnesseth justification without a word and a work.

The difference was, whether the first assurance be by an absolute promise always, and not by a conditional also, and whether a man could have any true assurance, without sight of some such work in his soul as no hypocrite could attain unto.[1]

At the court Mr. Wheelwright, according as he was enjoined, did appear; but the court gave him respite to the next session (which was appointed the first Tuesday in August) to bethink himself that, retracting and reforming his error, etc., the court might show him favor, which otherwise he must not expect. His answer was, that if he had committed sedition, then he ought to be put to death; and if we did mean to proceed against him, he meant to appeal to the king's court; for he could retract nothing . . .

Having received intelligence from Miantonomi that the Pequots had sent their women and children to an island for their safety, we presently sent away forty men by land to the Narragansetts, and there to take in Miantonomi (and he offered to send sixteen men with ours) and so, in the night, to set upon them.

We also provided to send one hundred and sixty more after them to prosecute the war; and Mr. Stoughton, one of the magistrates, was sent with them, and Mr. Wilson, the pastor of Boston . . .

---

1. This statement has helped to persuade some readers of JW's journal that the Antinomian controversy was an absurdly pointless dispute. In fact, however, issues of fundamental theological importance for Cotton and Shepard were at stake. And in May 1637, when Cotton was seemingly reducing the conflict to zero, he was actually being forced to choose between continued alliance with Hutchinson and Wheelwright or alliance with JW and the orthodox majority.

[May] *24*. By letters from Mr. Williams we were certified (which the next day was confirmed by some who came from Saybrook) that Capt. Mason[2] was come to Saybrook with eighty English and one hundred Indians; and that the Indians had gone out there and met with seven Pequots; five they killed; one they took alive, whom the English put to torture; and set all their heads upon the fort. The reason was, because they had tortured such of our men as they took alive . . .

The former governor and Mr. Coddington, being discontented that the people had left them out of all public service, gave further proof of it in the congregation; for they refused to sit in the magistrate's seat (where Mr. Vane had always sitten from his first arrival) and went and sate with the deacons, although the governor sent to desire them to come in to him. And upon the day of the general fast, they went from Boston to keep the day at the Mount with Mr. Wheelwright.

Another occasion of their discontent, and of the rest of that party, was an order which the court had made to keep out all such persons as might be dangerous to the commonwealth, by imposing a penalty upon all such as should retain any, etc., above three weeks which should not be allowed by some of the magistrates; for it was very probable that they expected many of their opinion to come out of England from Mr. Brierly his church, etc.[3] . . .

[May] *25*. Our English from Connecticut, with their Indians, and many of the Narragansetts, marched in the night to a fort of the Pequots at Mystic, and besetting the same about break of the day, after two hours' fight they took it (by firing it) and slew therein two chief sachems, and one hundred and fifty fighting men, and about one hundred and fifty old men, women, and children, with the loss of two English

---

2. John Mason (1600–1672), a veteran of the Dutch wars, had been a militia captain in Massachusetts and a resident of Dorchester before moving to Windsor, Conn.

3. Roger Brereley was the curate of Grindleton Chapel in Yorkshire; his followers were known as Grindletonians and were accused of having Antinomian tendencies. None of them came to New England.

⟨whereof but one was⟩ killed by the enemy. Divers of the Indian friends were hurt by the ⟨English⟩ Pequots ⟨because they had not some mark to distinguish them from the Pequots, as some of them had⟩[4] . . . The general defeat of the Pequots at Mystic happened the day after our general fast.

Mo. 4 [June] 3. Upon the news from Mr. Williams, that the Pequots were dispersed, and some come in and submitted to the Narragansetts (who would not receive them before he had sent to know our mind), the governor and council thought it needless to send so many men, and therefore sent out warrants only for one half of the two hundred; but some of the people liked not of it, and came to the governor to have all sent. He took it ill; and though three of the ministers came with them to debate the matter, he told them that if any one, discerning an error in the proceedings of the council, had come in a private manner to acquaint him therewith, etc., it had been well done; but to come, so many of them, in a public and popular way was not well, and would bring authority into contempt. This they took well at his hands, and excused their intentions. So it was thought fit to send about forty men more, which was yielded rather to satisfy the people than for any need that appeared.

[June] 15. There was a day of thanksgiving kept in all the churches for the victory obtained against the Pequots, and for other mercies . . .

[June] 26. There arrived two ships from London, the *Hector* and the [blank]. In these came Mr. Davenport and another minister, and Mr. Eaton and Mr. Hopkins, two merchants of London, men of fair estate and of great esteem for religion, and wisdom in outward affairs.[5] In

---

4. It is not clear why JW altered this sentence to make it appear that the Pequots, rather than the English, had injured the "Indian friends." Roger Williams told him (*WP*, 3:427) that many Narragansetts had been hurt by the English because they didn't have distinguishing yellow or red paint marks on their heads.

5. The Rev. John Davenport (1597–1670), the Rev. Samuel Eaton (1596?–1665), and his brother Theophilus Eaton (1590–1658) were the principal founders of New Haven

the *Hector* came also the Lord Ley,[6] son and heir of the Earl of Marlborough, being about nineteen years of age, who came only to see the country . . .

We had news of a commission granted in England to divers gentlemen here for the governing of New England, etc.; but instead thereof we received a commission from Sir Ferdinando Gorges to govern his province of New Somersetshire, which is from Cape Elizabeth to Sagadahoc,[7] and withal to oversee his servants and private affairs; which was observed as a matter of no good discretion, but passed in silence. As for the commission from the king, we received only a copy of it, but the commission itself staid at the seal[8] for want of paying the fees . . .

Mo. 5 [July]. Capt. Stoughton and his company, having pursued the Pequots beyond Connecticut, and missing of them, returned to Pequot River, where they were advertised[9] that one hundred of them were newly come back to a place some twelve miles off. So they marched thither by night and surprised them all. They put to death twenty-two men, and reserved two sachems, hoping by them to get Sassacus[10] (which they promised). All the rest were women and children, of whom they gave the Narragansetts thirty, and our Massachusetts Indians three, and the rest they sent hither.

Colony in 1638. Davenport had been vicar of St. Stephen's in Coleman Street, London, until he was driven into exile in Holland in 1633; Theophilus Eaton had been a Baltic merchant in London and a charter member of the MBC. Edward Hopkins (1600–1657), who married Theophilus Eaton's stepdaughter Ann Yale, had been a Turkey merchant in London; he migrated to Hartford and shared with John Haynes the political leadership of Connecticut Colony.

6. James Ley (1618–1665) succeeded his father as the third Earl of Marlborough in 1638, immediately after his visit to Massachusetts. He became a royalist in the English Civil War.

7. Gorges's province, which he obtained from the Council for New England in 1635, encompassed the southern Maine coast from the Piscataqua River to the Kennebec River.

8. Remained unsealed by the royal clerks.

9. Informed.

10. The leading Pequot sachem.

The differences grew so much here as tended fast to a separation; so as Mr. Vane, being among others invited by the governor to accompany the Lord Ley at dinner, ⟨not only⟩ refused to come (alleging by letter that his conscience withheld him) ⟨but also, at the same hour, he went over to Nottle's Island to dine with Mr. Maverick and carried the Lord Ley with him⟩.

[July] 6. There were sent to Boston forty-eight women and children. There were eighty taken, as before is expressed. These were disposed of to particular persons in the country. Some of them ran away and were brought again by the Indians our neighbors, and those we branded on the shoulder . . .

[July] 13. Mr. Stoughton, with about eighty of the English, sailed to the west in pursuit of Sassacus, etc. At Quinepiack,[11] they killed six and took two. At a head of land a little short they beheaded two sachems; whereupon they called the place Sachem's Head.[12] About this time they had given a Pequot his life to go find out Sassacus. He went and found him not far off; but Sassacus, suspecting him, intended to kill him, which the fellow perceiving, escaped in the night, and came to the English. Whereupon Sassacus and Mononotto, their two chief sachems, and some twenty more, fled to the Mohawks. But eighty of their stoutest men, and two hundred others, women and children, were at a place within twenty or thirty miles of the Dutch, whither our men marched, and being guided by a Divine Providence, came upon them where they had twenty wigwams hard by a most hideous swamp, so thick with bushes and so quagmiry as men could hardly crowd into it. Into this swamp they were all gotten. Lieut. Davenport and two or three more that entered the swamp were dangerously wounded by the Indian arrows, and with much difficulty were fetched out. Then our men surrounded the swamp, being a mile about, and shot at the Indians,

11. The site of New Haven, where Eaton and Davenport would settle in 1638.
12. Now in Guilford, Conn.

and they at them, from three of the clock in the afternoon till they desired parley and offered to yield, and life was offered to all that had not shed English blood. So they began to come forth, now some and then some, till about two hundred women and children were come out, and amongst them the sachem of that place, and thus they kept us two hours till night was come on, and then the men told us they would fight it out; and so they did all the night, coming up behind the bushes very near our men, and shot many arrows into their hats, sleeves, and stocks,[13] yet (which was a very miracle) not one of ours wounded. When it was near morning it grew very dark, so as such of them as were left crept out at one place and escaped, being (as was judged) not above twenty at most, and those like to be wounded; for in the pursuit they found some of them dead of their wounds. Here our men gat some booty of kettles, trays, wampom, etc., and the women and children were divided, and sent some to Connecticut, and some to the Massachusetts. The sachem of the place, having yielded, had his life and his wife and children, etc. The women which were brought home reported that we had slain in all thirteen sachems, and that there were thirteen more left. We had now slain and taken, in all, about seven hundred. We sent fifteen of the boys and two women to Bermuda, by Mr. Peirce; but he, missing it, carried them to Providence Isle.[14]

Mo. 6 [August]. Mr. Stoughton sailed, with some of his company, from Pequot to Block Island. They came thither in the night, yet were discovered, and our men having killed one or two of them and burnt some of their wigwams, etc., they came to parley, and submitting themselves to become tributaries in one hundred fathom wampompeague, and to deliver any that should be found to have any hand in Mr.

13. Neckcloths.

14. A Caribbean island off the Nicaraguan coast, colonized by Lord Brooke, Viscount Saye and Sele, and other English Puritans, until the Spanish captured it in 1641. The island is now called Santa Catalina.

Oldham's death, they were all received and no more harm done them . . .

[August] 3. The Lord Ley and Mr. Vane went from Boston to the ship riding at Long Island,[15] to go for England. At their departure, those of Mr. Vane's party were gathered together and did accompany him to the boat (and many to the ship); and the men, being in their arms, gave him divers vollies of shot and five pieces of ordnance, and he had five more at the castle. But the governor was not come from the court, but had left order with the captain for their honorable dismission . . .

[August] 5. Mr. Hooker and Mr. Stone came with Mr. Wilson from Connecticut by Providence;[16] and the same day Mr. Ludlow, Mr. Pynchon, and about twelve more came the ordinary way by land, and brought with them a part of the skin and lock of hair of Sassacus and his brother and five other Pequot sachems, who, being fled to the Mohawks for shelter with their wampom, being to the value of £500, were by them surprised and slain, with twenty of their best men. Mononottoh was also taken, but escaped wounded. They brought news also of divers other Pequots which had been slain by other Indians, and their heads brought to the English; so that now there had been slain and taken between eight and nine hundred. Whereupon letters were sent to Mr. Stoughton and the rest, to call them all home . . .

Mr. Hooker and the rest of the elders, meeting divers days, they agreed (with consent of the magistrates) upon a day of humiliation to be kept in all the churches the 24th of this month; the day for the conference to be the 30th day. At their private meetings some reconciliation was made between Mr. Cotton and Mr. Wheelwright and Mr. Wilson, he professing that by his speech in the court[17] he did not intend

15. In Boston harbor.
16. Roger Williams's town in Rhode Island.
17. In Dec. 1636.

the doctrine of Mr. Cotton or Mr. Wheelwright delivered in the public congregation, but some opinions (naming three or four) which were privately carried in Boston and other parts of the country; and accordingly Mr. Cotton declared so much in the congregation the Lord's day following. This sudden change[18] was much observed by some, who were privy that Mr. Wilson had professed as much before . . .

[August] 31. The Narragansetts sent us the hands of three Pequots,—one the chief of those who murdered Capt. Stone . . .

Mr. Eaton, and some others of Mr. Davenport's company, went to view Quinepiack, with intent to begin a plantation there. They had many offers here and at Plymouth, and they had viewed many places, but none could content . . .

[August] 30. The synod, called the assembly, began at Newtown. There were all the teaching elders through the country, and some new come out of England, not yet called to any place here, as Mr. Davenport, etc.

The assembly began with prayer made by Mr. Shepard, the pastor of Newtown. Then the erroneous opinions which were spread in the country were read (being eighty in all);[19] next the unwholesome expressions;[20] then the scriptures abused. There were about eighty opinions, some blasphemous, others erroneous, and all unsafe, condemned by the whole assembly; whereto near all the elders and others sent by the churches subscribed their names; but some few liked not subscription, though they consented to the condemning of them.

---

18. On the part of John Cotton, who had led the outcry against Wilson's speech.

19. JW assembled a catalog of 82 (not 80) erroneous Antinomian opinions, with the ministers' refutation of each error; this catalog was the first document in JW's *A Short Story of the Rise, reign, and ruine of the Antinomians, Familists & Libertines* (London, 1644), and is reprinted in Hall, pp. 219–243.

20. JW assembled a catalog of nine Antinomian "Unsavoury speeches," with the ministers' refutation of each speech; this was the second document in his *Short Story* and is reprinted in Hall, pp. 243–247.

Some of the church of Boston, and some others, were offended at the producing of so many errors, as if it were a reproach laid upon the country without cause; and called to have the persons named which held those errors. To which it was answered and affirmed by many, both elders and others, that all those opinions could be proved by sufficient testimony to be held by some in the country; but it was not thought fit to name the parties, because this assembly had not to do with persons, but doctrines only. Upon this some of Boston departed from the assembly, and came no more.

After the errors condemned, there were five points in question between Mr. Cotton and Mr. Wheelwright on the one part, and the rest of the elders on the other part, ⟨which were after reduced to three,⟩ and those after put into such expressions as Mr. Cotton and they agreed, but Mr. Wheelwright did not:—

1. The first was about our union with Christ. The question was whether we were united before we had active faith. The consent was that there was no marriage union with Christ before actual faith, which is more than habitual.

2. The second was about evidencing justification by sanctification. The consent was that some saving sanctifications (as faith, etc.) were coexistent, concurrent, and coapparent (or at least might be) with the witness of the Spirit always.

3. That the new creature is not the person of a believer, but a body of saving graces in such a one; and that Christ, as a head, doth enliven or quicken, preserve and act the same, but Christ himself is no part of this new creature.

4. That though, in effectual calling (in which the answer of the soul is by active faith wrought at the same instant by the Spirit), justification and sanctification be all together in them, yet God doth not justify a man before he be effectually called, and so a believer.

5. That Christ and his benefits may be offered and exhibited to a

man under a covenant of works, but not in or by a covenant of works[21] . . .

Mo. 7 [September]. The last day of the assembly other questions were debated and resolved:—

1. That though women might meet (some few together) to pray and edify one another, yet such a set assembly (as was then in practice at Boston) where sixty or more did meet every week, and one woman[22] (in a prophetical way, by resolving questions of doctrine and expounding scripture) took upon her the whole exercise, was agreed to be disorderly and without rule.

2. Though a private member might ask a question publicly after sermon, for information, yet this ought to be very wisely and sparingly done, and that with leave of the elders: but questions of reference (then in use), whereby the doctrines delivered were reproved and the elders reproached, and that with bitterness, etc., was utterly condemned.

3. That a person, refusing to come to the assembly to abide the censure of the church, might be proceeded against, though absent; yet it was held better, that the magistrates' help were called for, to compel him to be present.

4. That a member, differing from the rest of the church in any opinion which was not fundamental, ought not for that to forsake the ordinances there; and if such did desire dismission to any other church which was of his opinion, and did it for that end, the church whereof he was ought to deny it for the same end . . .

[October] 12. A day of thanksgiving kept in all the churches for our

---

21. John Cotton presented his version of this theological dispute in *A Conference Mr. John Cotton Held at Boston with the Elders of New-England* (London, 1646), where he reduced the debate to three questions, and somewhat differently in *The Way of the Congregational Churches Cleared* (London, 1648), where he treated all five of the points listed by JW. Hall reprints these tracts, pp. 175–198, 397–437.

22. Anne Hutchinson.

victories against the Pequots, and for the success of the assembly; but by reason of this latter, some of Boston would not be present at the public exercises. The captains and soldiers who had been in the late service were feasted, and after the sermon the magistrates and elders accompanied them to the door of the house where they dined.

(9.) [November] 1. Miantonomi, the Narragansett sachem, came to Boston. The governor, deputy, and treasurer[23] treated with him, and they parted upon fair terms. He acknowledged that all the Pequot country and Block Island were ours, and promised that he would not meddle with them but by our leave. We gave him leave to right himself for the wrongs which Janemoh and Wequash Cook[24] had done him; and for the wrong they had done us, we would right ourselves in our own time . . .

There was great hope that the late general assembly would have had some good effect in pacifying the troubles and dissensions about matters of religion; but it fell out otherwise. For though Mr. Wheelwright and those of his party had been clearly confuted and confounded in the assembly, yet they persisted in their opinions, and were as busy in nourishing contentions (the principal of them) as before. Whereupon the general court, being assembled in the 2 of the 9th month,[25] and finding upon consultation that two so opposite parties could not contain in the same body without apparent hazard of ruin to the whole, agreed to send away some of the principal; and for this a fair opportunity was offered by the remonstrance or petition which they preferred to the court the 9th of the 1st month, wherein they affirm Mr. Wheelwright to be innocent and that the court had condemned the truth of Christ,

23. JW, Thomas Dudley, and Richard Bellingham.

24. Juanemo (also called Ninigret) was sachem of the Eastern Niantics, and had refused to deliver the Pequots who had surrendered to him. Wequash Cook was a Mohegan who lived near Saybrook; see 28 July 1642, below.

25. 2 Nov. 1637.

with divers other scandalous and seditious speeches, subscribed by more than sixty of that faction,[26] whereof one William Aspinwall, being one and he that drew the said petition, being then sent as a deputy for Boston, was for the same dismissed and after called to the court and disfranchised and banished. John Coggeshall was another deputy who, though his hand were not to the petition, yet professing himself to approve it, etc., was also dismissed and after disfranchised.[27] Then the court sent for Mr. Wheelwright, and he persisting to justify his sermon and his whole practice and opinions, and refusing to leave either the place or his public exercisings, he was disfranchised and banished.[28] Upon which he appealed to the king, but neither called witnesses nor desired any act to be made of it. The court told him that an appeal did not lie; for by the king's grant we had power to hear and determine without any reservation, etc. So he relinquished his appeal, and the court gave him leave to go to his house upon his promise that, if he were not gone out of our jurisdiction within fourteen days, he would render himself to one of the magistrates.

The court also sent for Mrs. Hutchinson, and charged her with divers matters,[29] as her keeping two public lectures every week in her house, whereto sixty or eighty persons did usually resort, and for reproaching most of the ministers (viz., all except Mr. Cotton) for not preaching a covenant of free grace, and that they had not the seal of the spirit, nor were able ministers of the New Testament; which were clearly proved

26. JW included a copy of this Boston petition of 9 March 1637 in his *Short Story;* it is reprinted in Hall, pp. 249–250.

27. Aspinwall, a notary, had been a founding member of the Boston church in 1630; Coggeshall, a silk mercer, had joined the Boston church in 1634. They both moved to Rhode Island after being banished.

28. After his banishment Wheelwright moved to Exeter, N.H.

29. Anne Hutchinson's court examination is reported in two versions, a dramatically detailed stenographic account that recreates the battle of words and wits between this redoubtable woman and her magisterial and ministerial adversaries, and JW's more generalized account in his *Short Story*. In the stenographic account, JW's role as chief prosecutor is very prominent. Both trial reports are printed in Hall, pp. 262–276, 311–348.

against her, though she sought to shift it off. And after many speeches to and fro, at last she was so full as she could not contain, but vented her revelations; amongst which this was one, that she had it revealed to her that she should come into New England, and she should here be persecuted, and that God would ruin us and our posterity and the whole state for the same. So the court proceeded and banished her;[30] but because it was winter, they committed her to a private house where she was well provided, and her own friends and the elders permitted to go to her, but none else.

The court called also Capt. Underhill and some five or six more of the principal, whose hands were to the said petition; and because they stood to justify it they were disfranchised, and such as had public places were put from them.[31]

The court also ordered, that the rest, who had subscribed the petition, (and would not acknowledge their fault, and which near twenty[32] of them did,) and some others, who had been chief stirrers in these contentions, etc., should be disarmed.[33] This troubled some of them very much, especially because they were to bring them in themselves; but at last, when they saw no remedy, they obeyed.[34]

---

30. When JW delivered the court sentence, Mrs. Hutchinson asked, "I desire to know wherefore I am banished?" and he replied, "Say no more, the court knows wherefore and is satisfied" (Hall, p. 348).

31. In addition to banishing three of the leading Antinomians—Aspinwall, Wheelwright, and Anne Hutchinson—the court disfranchised eight others: Coggeshall, John Underhill, William Balston, Edward Hutchinson, Thomas Marshall, Richard Gridley, William Dinely, and William Dyer (*MR*, 1:207–208).

32. Only 10 subscribers acknowledged their fault in court, according to the records (*MR*, 1:208–209); their names were crossed off the remonstrance.

33. The court ordered 75 persons disarmed—58 from Boston and 17 from Salem, Newbury, Roxbury, Ipswich, and Charlestown. Their names are recorded in *MR*, 1:211–212. This was a very severe punishment. Only a few months before, during the Pequot War, the court had ordered all persons over 18 to carry muskets and ammunition whenever they traveled or came to public assemblies (*MR*, 1:190).

34. The disarmament order helped to persuade 35 additional Antinomians to acknowledge their fault in signing the petition supporting Wheelwright. See the lists of their names in *WP*, 3:513–516.

All the proceedings of this court against these persons were set down at large, with the reasons and other observations, and were sent into England to be published there, to the end that ⟨all⟩ our godly friends might not be discouraged from coming to us, etc.[35]

After this, many of the church of Boston, being highly offended with the governor for this proceeding, were earnest with the elders to have him called to account for it; but they were not forward in it, and himself, understanding their intent, thought fit to prevent such a public disorder and so took occasion to speak to the congregation to this effect . . . He showed that, though Christ's kingly power be in his church, yet that is not that kingly power whereby he is King of kings and Lord of lords, for by that kings reign and princes, etc. It is true, indeed, that magistrates, as they are church members, are accountable to the church for their failings, but that is when they are out of their calling. If a magistrate shall in a private way take away a man's goods or his servants, etc., the church may call him to account for it; but if he doth thus in pursuing a course of justice (though the thing be unjust), yet he is not accountable, etc.

For himself, he did nothing in the cases of the brethren but by the advice and direction of our teacher and other of the elders. For in the oath which was administered to him and the rest, etc., there was inserted, by his advice, this clause,—In all causes wherein you are to give your vote, etc., you are to give your vote as in your judgment and conscience you shall see to be most for the public good, etc.; and so

---

35. JW himself seems to have assembled the documents on the Antinomian controversy; but if JW's collection was sent to England in 1637, it was not published in London until 1644, when it appeared anonymously under the title *Antinomians and Familists Condemned By the Synod of Elders in New-England: with the Proceedings of the Magistrates against them, and their Apology for the same* (London, 1644). Thomas Weld, then in England, found this book in print and immediately issued a second edition. He supplied a new preface and a new title: *A Short Story of the Rise, reign, and ruine of the Antinomians, Familists & Libertines, that infected the Churches of New-England* (London, 1644).

for his part he was persuaded that it would be most for the glory of God, and the public good, to pass sentence as they did.

He would give them one reason which was a ground for his judgment, and that was for that he saw that those brethren, etc., were so divided from the rest of the country in their judgment and practice as it could not stand with the public peace that they should continue amongst us. So, by the example of Lot in Abraham's family, and after Hagar and Ishmael, he saw they must be sent away[36] . . .

[January]. Upon occasion of the censures of the court upon Mrs. Hutchinson and others, divers other foul errors were discovered which had been secretly carried by way of inquiry but after were maintained by Mrs. Hutchinson and others; and so many of Boston were tainted with them, as Mr. Cotton, finding how he had been abused and made (as himself said) their stalking horse, (for they pretended to hold nothing but what Mr. Cotton held, and himself did think the same,) did spend most of his time both publicly and privately to discover those errors, and to reduce such as were gone astray. And also the magistrates, calling together such of the elders as were near, did spend two days in consulting with them about the way to help the growing evils.

Some of the secret opinions were these:—

That there is no inherent righteousness in a child of God.

That neither absolute nor conditional promises belong to a Christian.

That we are not bound to the law, not as a rule, etc.

That the Sabbath is but as other days.

That the soul is mortal till it be united to Christ, and then it is annihilated and the body also, and a new given by Christ.

That there is no resurrection of the body.

Mo. 12 [February]. Divers gentlemen and others, being joined in a military company, desired to be made a corporation, etc. But the coun-

---

36. Gen. 13:5–9; 21:9–14.

cil, considering (from the example of the Pretorian band among the Romans, and the Templars in Europe)[37] how dangerous it might be to erect a standing authority of military men, which might easily in time overthrow the civil power, thought fit to stop it betimes. Yet they were allowed to be a company, but subordinate to all authority.[38]

About this time the Indians which were in our families were much frightened with Hobbamock (as they call the devil) appearing to them in divers shapes, and persuading them to forsake the English, and not to come at the assemblies, nor to learn to read, etc.

[February] 26. Mr. Peirce in the Salem ship, the *Desire,* returned from the West Indies after seven months. He had been at Providence, and brought some cotton, and tobacco, and negroes,[39] etc., from thence, and salt from Tertugos.[40] Dry fish and strong liquors are the only commodities for those parts. He met there two men-of-war, set forth by the lords, etc., of Providence[41] with letters of mart,[42] who had taken divers prizes from the Spaniard, and many negroes.

Mo. 1 [March]. While Mrs. Hutchinson continued at Roxbury, divers of the elders and others resorted to her, and finding her to persist in maintaining those gross errors beforementioned and many others to the number of thirty or thereabout, some of them wrote to the church at Boston, offering to make proof of the same before the church, etc., [March] 15; whereupon she was called, (the magistrates being desired

37. The Praetorians, originally bodyguards to magistrates in the Roman Republic, became corrupt power-brokers in the Roman Empire. The Knights Templars, founded in 1119 to protect pilgrims to the Holy Land at the time of the crusades, became rich and powerful before they were suppressed by the Papacy in 1312.

38. The Ancient and Honorable Artillery Company was founded in 1638, with Robert Keayne as the first captain.

39. This is the earliest evidence of African slaves being shipped to New England.

40. Tortuga, off the NW coast of Hispaniola.

41. The Providence Company, chartered in 1630 to colonize Providence Island, had among its shareholders the Earl of Warwick, Lord Brooke, Viscount Saye and Sele, and John Pym.

42. Letters of marque, or licenses for privateering: in this case to attack the Spanish.

to give her license to come,) and the lecture was appointed to begin at ten. (The general court being then at Newtown, the governor and the treasurer, being members of Boston, were permitted to come down, but the rest of the court continued at Newtown.) When she appeared, the errors were read to her.[43] The first was that the souls of men are mortal by generation, but after made immortal by Christ's purchase. This she maintained a long time; but at length she was so clearly convinced by reason and scripture, and the whole church agreeing that sufficient had been delivered for her conviction, that she yielded she had been in an error. Then they proceeded to three other errors: That there was no resurrection of these bodies, and that these bodies were not united to Christ, but every person united hath a new body, etc. These were also clearly confuted, but yet she held her own; so as the church (all but two of her sons)[44] agreed she should be admonished, and because her sons would not agree to it, they were admonished also.

Mr. Cotton pronounced the sentence of admonition with great solemnity, and with much zeal and detestation of her errors and pride of spirit.[45] The assembly continued till eight at night, and all did acknowledge the special presence of God's spirit therein; and she was appointed to appear again the next lecture day . . .

At this court, divers of our chief military officers, who had declared themselves favorers of the familistical persons and opinions, were sent for,[46] and being told that the court having some jealousy of them for the same, and therefore did desire some good satisfaction from them, they did ingenuously acknowledge how they had been deceived and

43. A full transcript of Mrs. Hutchinson's trial in Boston Church was taken by Robert Keayne and is printed in Hall, pp. 350–388.

44. Her son Edward Hutchinson and her son-in-law Thomas Savage, both of whom soon moved to Portsmouth, R.I.

45. For the text of Cotton's admonition, see Hall, pp. 368–373.

46. The court records show that four military officers were called upon: Capt. William Jenyson, Ens. Thomas Cakebread, Lt. Edward Gibbon, and Ens. Robert Harding (*MR*, 1:224–226).

misled by the pretence which was held forth of advancing Christ, and debasing the creature,[47] etc., which since they have found to be otherwise, and that their opinions and practices tended to disturbance and delusions; and so blessed God that had so timely discovered their error and danger to them.

At this court, a committee was appointed of some magistrates, some ministers, and some others, to compile a body of fundamental laws[48] . . .

[March] 22. Mrs. Hutchinson appeared again; (she had been licensed by the court, in regard she had given hope of her repentance, to be at Mr. Cotton's house that both he and Mr. Davenport might have the more opportunity to deal with her;) and the articles being again read to her, and her answer required, she delivered it in writing, wherein she made a retractation of near all, but with such explanations and circumstances as gave no satisfaction to the church; so as she was required to speak further to them. Then she declared that it was just with God to leave her to herself, as he had done, for her slighting his ordinances, both magistracy and ministry; and confessed that what she had spoken against the magistrates at the court (by way of revelation) was rash and ungrounded; and desired the church to pray for her. This gave the church good hope of her repentance; but when she was examined about some particulars, as that she had denied inherent righteousness, etc., she affirmed that it was never her judgment; and though it was proved by many testimonies that she had been of that judgment, and so had persisted and maintained it by argument against divers, yet she impudently persisted in her affirmation, to the astonishment of all the assembly. So that after much time and many ar-

---

47. The created order of things, including the ministry, and all human means of obtaining grace.

48. Eleven persons were appointed to this committee, headed by JW. John Cotton, who had previously compiled a body of laws (see 25 Oct. 1636, above), was not among the five clergymen.

guments had been spent to bring her to see her sin, but all in vain, the church with one consent cast her out. Some moved to have her admonished once more;[49] but, it being for manifest evil in matter of conversation, it was agreed otherwise; and for that reason also the sentence was denounced[50] by the pastor,[51] matter of manners belonging properly to his place.

After she was excommunicated, her spirits which seemed before to be somewhat dejected revived again, and she gloried in her sufferings, saying that it was the greatest happiness next to Christ that ever befell her. Indeed it was a happy day to the churches of Christ here, and to many poor souls who had been seduced by her, who by what they heard and saw that day were (through the grace of God) brought off quite from her errors, and settled again in the truth.

At this time the good providence of God so disposed, divers of the congregation (being the chief men of the party, her husband[52] being one) were gone to Narragansett to seek out a new place for plantation, and taking liking of one in Plymouth patent, they went thither to have it granted them; but the magistrates there, knowing their spirit, gave them a denial, but consented they might buy of the Indians an island in the Narragansett Bay.[53]

After two or three days the governor sent a warrant to Mrs. Hutchinson to depart this jurisdiction before the last of this month, according to the order of court, and for that end set her at liberty from her former constraint, so as she was not to go forth of her own house till her departure; and upon the 28th she went by water to her farm at the

49. According to the trial record, these were the two Boston elders, Thomas Oliver and Thomas Leverett, Hutchinson's brother-in-law Richard Scott, and a "Straynger" unknown to recorder Robert Keayne (Hall, pp. 385–387).

50. Proclaimed.

51. John Wilson.

52. William Hutchinson.

53. Aquidneck Island (now known as Rhode Island). Toward the N end of this island, Coddington, Hutchinson, and others laid out the town of Portsmouth.

Mount, where she was to take water with Mr. Wheelwright's wife and family to go to Pascataquack; but she changed her mind, and went by land to Providence, and so to the island in the Narragansett Bay which her husband and the rest of that sect had purchased of the Indians, and prepared with all speed to remove unto. For the court had ordered, that except they were gone with their families by such a time they should be summoned to the general court, etc.

[March] 30. Mr. Davenport and Mr. Prudden,[54] and a brother of Mr. Eaton (being ministers also) went by water to Quinepiack; and with them many families removed out of this jurisdiction to plant in those parts, being much taken with the opinion of the fruitfulness of that place, and more safety (as they conceived) from danger of a general governor, who was feared to be sent this summer; which, though it were a great weakening to these parts, yet we expected to see a good providence of God in it, both for possessing those parts which lay open for an enemy and for strengthening our friends at Connecticut, and for making room here for many who were expected out of England this year, and for diverting the thoughts and intentions of such in England as intended evil against us, whose designs might be frustrate by our scatterings so far . . .

The wife of one William Dyer,[55] a milliner in the New Exchange, a very proper and fair woman, and both of them notoriously infected with Mrs. Hutchinson's errors, and very censorious and troublesome

54. The Rev. Peter Prudden came to Massachusetts in 1637 with a group of associates from Hertfordshire. They settled at Milford in New Haven Colony, where Prudden as pastor of the church was soon clashing with Davenport, the pastor at New Haven.

55. Mary Dyer had married William in 1633; they came to Massachusetts soon after and joined the Boston church in 1635. When William was disfranchised and disarmed, and Mary publicly disgraced, they moved to Portsmouth, R.I. in 1638. One of their sons had the formidable Old Testament name of Mahershalalhashbaz. Mary became a Quaker in the 1650s and returned as a missionary to Boston, where she was arrested four times and executed in 1660.

(she being of a very proud spirit, and much addicted to revelations), had been delivered of [a] child some few months before, October 17 [1637], and the child buried (being stillborn) and viewed of none but Mrs. Hutchinson and the midwife, one Hawkins's wife,[56] a rank familist also; and another woman had a glimpse of it, who not being able to keep counsel as the other two did, some rumor began to spread that the child was a monster. One of the elders, hearing of it, asked Mrs. Hutchinson, when she was ready to depart; whereupon she told him how it was, and said she meant to have it chronicled,[57] but excused her concealing of it till then (by advice, as she said, of Mr. Cotton), which coming to the governor's knowledge, he sent for the midwife, and examined her about it. At first she confessed only that the head was defective and misplaced, but being told that Mrs. Hutchinson had revealed all, and that he intended to have it taken up and viewed, she made this report of it, viz.: It was a woman child, stillborn about two months before the just time, having life a few hours before; it came hiplings[58] till she turned it; it was of ordinary bigness; it had a face, but no head, and the ears stood upon the shoulders and were like an ape's; it had no forehead, but over the eyes four horns, hard and sharp; two of them were above one inch long, the other two shorter; the eyes standing out, and the mouth also; the nose hooked upward; all over the breast and back full of sharp pricks and scales, like a thornback;[59] the navel and all the belly, with the distinction of the sex, were where the back should be, and the back and hips before, where the belly should have been; behind between the shoulders it had two mouths, and in

56. Jane Hawkins, wife of Richard, came from St. Ives, Cornwall, and lived in Boston. In 1638, after she was prohibited from practicing midwifery and banished, she and her husband moved to Portsmouth, R.I.

57. The birth recorded.

58. With the hips foremost.

59. Ray or skate.

each of them a piece of red flesh sticking out; it had arms and legs as other children; but instead of toes, it had on each foot three claws like a young fowl, with sharp talons.[60]

The governor speaking with Mr. Cotton about it, he told him the reason why he advised them to conceal it. He considered that, if it had been his own case, he should have desired to have had it concealed, and that he thought God might intend only the instruction of the parents, and such other to whom it was known, etc. The like apology he made for himself in public, which was well accepted.

(2.) [April]. The governor, with advice of some other of the magistrates and of the elders of Boston, caused the said monster to be taken up, and though it were much corrupted yet most of those things were to be seen, as the horns and claws, the scales, etc. When it died in the mother's body (which was about two hours before the birth), the bed whereon the mother lay did shake, and withal there was such a noisome savor[61] as most of the women were taken with extreme vomiting and purging, so as they were forced to depart; and others of them their children were taken with convulsions (which they never had before nor after) and so were sent for home, so as by these occasions it came to be concealed.

The midwife, presently after this discovery, went out of the jurisdiction; and indeed it was time for her to be gone, for it was known that she used to give young women oil of mandrakes and other stuff to cause conception; and she grew into great suspicion to be a witch,

---

60. JW seized upon Dyer's monstrous birth as proof positive that God had turned against the Antinomians. He quickly sent descriptions to William Bradford and Roger Williams, and likewise to friends in England, together with a drawing of the monster (now lost). In 1642, an account based on JW's report entitled *Newes from New-England: of A most strange and prodigious Birth* was published in London. And JW's *Short Story*, belatedly published in 1644, included yet another lurid description of Dyer's monster, very similar in wording to the account in his journal; see Hall, pp. 280–282.

61. Signs that a devil was within her.

for it was credibly reported that, when she gave any medicines, (for she practised physic,) she would ask the party, if she did believe, she could help her, etc. . . .

[April] 12. A general fast was kept through all the churches, by advice from the court, for seeking the Lord to prevent evil that we feared to be intended against us from England by a general governor; for the safe arrival of our friends from thence (very many being expected); and for establishment of peace and truth amongst us . . .

[April] 24. The governor and deputy went to Concord to view some land for farms, and going down the river about four miles, they made choice of a place for one thousand acres for each of them.[62] So, at the place where the deputy's land was to begin, there were two great stones, which they called the Two Brothers, in remembrance that they were brothers by their children's marriage,[63] and did so brotherly agree, and for that a little creek near those stones was to part their lands. At the court in the 4th month after, two hundred acres were added to the governor's part.

[April] 26. Mr. Coddington (who had been an assistant from the first coming over of the government, being, with his wife, taken with the familistical opinions) removed to Aquiday Island in the Narragansett Bay.

(3.) [May] 2. At the court of elections, the former governor, John Winthrop, was chosen again.[64] The same day, at night, he was taken with a sharp fever which brought him near death; but many prayers were put up to the Lord for him, and he was restored again after one month.

---

62. In Nov. 1637 the General Court had awarded JW and Dudley 1,000 acres apiece (*MR*, 1:206).

63. JW's daughter Mary had married Dudley's son Samuel.

64. Thomas Dudley was reelected deputy governor, and eight of the nine assistants from 1637 (all except Endecott) were also reelected. *MR*, 1:227–228.

This court the name of Newtown was altered, and it was called Cambridge[65] . . .

Many ships arrived this year with people of good quality and estate, notwithstanding the council's order that none such should come without the king's license; but God so wrought that some obtained license, and others came away without. The troubles which arose in Scotland about the book of common prayer, and the canons which the king would have forced upon the Scotch churches, did so take up the king and council that they had neither heart nor leisure to look after the affairs of New England[66] . . .

Many of Boston and others who were of Mrs. Hutchinson's judgment and party removed to the Isle of Aquiday; and others, who were of the rigid separation[67] and savored anabaptism, removed to Providence, so as those parts began to be well peopled.

There came over this summer twenty ships, and at least three thousand persons, so as they were forced to look out new plantations. One was begun at Merrimack, and another four or five miles above Concord, and another at Winicowett[68] . . .

(7.) [September]. The general court was assembled, in which it was agreed that whereas a very strict order was sent from the lords commissioners for plantations for the sending home our patent, upon pretence that judgment had passed against it upon a quo warranto,[69] a

---

65. Because of the new college which was soon to open in this town. The great majority of university men in Massachusetts had attended Cambridge rather than Oxford.

66. In July 1637 the Scots in Edinburgh had rioted against the new prayer book and canons which Archbishop Laud had imposed on the Scottish church; by 1638 the Scots were organizing armed resistance against Laud and Charles I.

67. Rigid separatists from the Church of England, who were therefore compatible with Roger Williams.

68. These new towns were Colechester, Mass. (renamed Salisbury in 1640), Sudbury, Mass., and Hampton, N.H.

69. In 1635 the English government had served a writ of *quo warranto* on the charter members of the MBC, requiring them to answer by what right they governed Massachu-

letter should be written by the governor in the name of the court to excuse our not sending of it; for it was resolved to be best not to send it, because then such of our friends and others in England would conceive it to be surrendered, and that thereupon we should be bound to receive such a governor and such orders as should be sent to us, and many bad minds, yea, and some weak ones among ourselves would think it lawful if not necessary to accept a general governor . . .

At this court also, Capt. Underhill (being about to remove to Mr. Wheelwright)[70] petitioned for three hundred acres of land promised him formerly; by occasion whereof he was questioned about some speeches he had used in the ship lately in his return out of England, viz., that he should say that we were zealous here as the Scribes and Pharisees were, and as Paul was before his conversion, etc., which he denying, they were proved to his face by a sober, godly woman, whom he had seduced in the ship and drawn to his opinions (but she was after freed again). Among other passages, he told her how he came to his assurance, and that was thus: He had lain under a spirit of bondage and a legal way five years, and could get no assurance, till at length as he was taking a pipe of tobacco the Spirit set home an absolute promise of free grace with such assurance and joy as he never since doubted of his good estate, neither should he, though he should fall into sin. He would not confess nor deny this, but took exceptions at the court for crediting one witness against him, etc., and withal said, that he was still of the same opinion he had been, etc. Upon this, the court committed him for abusing the court with a show of retractation and in-

---

setts, and in 1637 the Court of King's Bench had issued judgment against the MBC. But JW and his colleagues considered this judgment to be spurious, since none of the active governing officials of the MBC in America had been summoned or convicted, and they calculated that Charles I was in no position in 1638 to enforce the court order. For background, see 18 Sept. 1634, 31 May 1636, and 26 June 1637, above.

70. Having been disfranchised in Nov. 1637, Underhill was moving with Wheelwright to Exeter, N.H.

tending no such thing; and the next day he was called again and banished. The Lord's day following, he made a speech in the assembly, showing that, as the Lord was pleased to convert Paul as he was in persecuting, etc., so he might manifest himself to him as he was taking the moderate use of the creature called tobacco[71] . . .

The next Lord's day, the same Capt. Underhill, having been privately dealt with upon suspicion of incontinency with a neighbor's wife[72] and not hearkening to it, was publicly questioned and put under admonition. The matter was for that the woman being young and beautiful, and withal of a jovial spirit and behavior, he did daily frequent her house and was divers times found there alone with her, the door being locked on the inside. He confessed it was ill, because it had an appearance of evil in it; but his excuse was that the woman was in great trouble of mind and sore temptations, and that he resorted to her to comfort her; and that when the door was found locked upon them, they were in private prayer together. But this practice was clearly condemned also by the elders . . .

Mrs. Hutchinson, being removed to the Isle of Aquiday in the Narragansett Bay, after her time was fulfilled that she expected deliverance of a child, was delivered of a monstrous birth. Hereupon the governor wrote to Mr. Clarke,[73] a physician and a preacher to those of the island, to know the certainty thereof, who returned him this answer: Mrs. Hutchinson, six weeks before her delivery, perceived her body to be greatly distempered and her spirits failing and in that regard doubtful of life, she sent to me etc., and not long after (in immoderato fluore

71. Underhill is here perverting the Puritan concept of created order by claiming that tobacco smoking is his means of grace.

72. Mrs. Faber was the wife of a Boston cooper, Joseph Faber, who sold his house and returned to England in 1639—perhaps as a result of this scandal.

73. Dr. John Clarke, a Suffolk man, had come to Boston in 1637 and was disarmed as an Antinomian. He moved to Portsmouth, R.I., and many years later procured Rhode Island's royal charter of 1663 from Charles II.

uterino)[74] it was brought to light, and I was called to see it, where I beheld innumerable distinct bodies in the form of a globe, not much unlike the swims of some fish, so confusedly knit together by so many several strings (which I conceive were the beginning of veins and nerves) so that it was impossible either to number the small round pieces in every lump, much less to discern from whence every string did fetch its original, they were so snarled one within another. The small globes I likewise opened, and perceived the matter of them (setting aside the membrane in which it was involved) to be partly wind and partly water. The governor, not satisfied with this relation, spake after with the said Mr. Clarke, who thus cleared all the doubts: The lumps were twenty-six or twenty-seven, distinct and not joined together; there came no secundine[75] after them; six of them were as great as his fist, and the smallest about the bigness of the top of his thumb. The globes were round things, included in the lumps, about the bigness of a small Indian bean, and like the pearl in a man's eye. The two lumps which differed from the rest were like liver or congealed blood, and had no small globes in them, as the rest had[76] . . .

(10.) [December] 6. Dorothy Talbye was hanged at Boston for murdering her own daughter, a child of three years old.[77] She had been a member of the church of Salem, and of good esteem for godliness, etc.; but, falling at difference with her husband through melancholy or spiritual delusions, she sometimes attempted to kill him and her children and herself by refusing meat, saying it was so revealed to her, etc. After

---

74. In a heavy discharge from the womb.

75. Afterbirth.

76. Drawing upon Clarke's clinical description, Emery Battis argues that Anne Hutchinson had a menopausal pregnancy, and that her fetus aborted into a hydatidiform mole. See Battis, *Saints and Sectaries: Anne Hutchinson and the Antinomian Controversy in the Massachusetts Bay Colony* (Chapel Hill: University of North Carolina Press, 1962), pp. 247–248, 346–347.

77. Dorothy Talby's daughter was named Difficult; her husband's name was John.

much patience, and divers admonitions not prevailing, the church cast her out. Whereupon she grew worse; so as the magistrate caused her to be whipped. Whereupon she was reformed for a time, and carried herself more dutifully to her husband, etc.; but soon after she was so possessed with Satan that he persuaded her (by his delusions, which she listened to as revelations from God) to break the neck of her own child that she might free it from future misery. This she confessed upon her apprehension; yet, at her arraignment she stood mute a good space, till the governor told her she should be pressed to death and then she confessed the indictment. When she was to receive judgment, she would not uncover her face nor stand up but as she was forced, nor give any testimony of her repentance, either then or at her execution. The cloth which should have covered her face she plucked off and put between the rope and her neck. She desired to have been beheaded, giving this reason, that it was less painful and less shameful. After a swing or two, she catched at the ladder. Mr. Peter, her late pastor, and Mr. Wilson went with her to the place of execution but could do no good with her . . .

Those who were gone with Mrs. Hutchinson to Aquiday fell into new errors daily. One Nicholas Easton,[78] a tanner, taught that every of the elect had the Holy Ghost and also the devil indwelling. Another, one Herne,[79] taught that women had no souls, and that Adam was not created in true holiness, etc., for then he could not have lost it.

Those who went to the falls at Pascataquack[80] gathered a church,

---

78. Easton had lived in Ipswich and Newbury, Mass. Banished as an Antinomian, he moved to Portsmouth, R.I., later served as governor of Rhode Island, and converted to Quakerism.

79. Possibly George Hurne, who was laid in irons and whipped for his "insolent & contemptuous carriage" by the Massachusetts General Court in June 1640 (*MR*, 1:296).

80. Exeter, N.H. Note the difference here between the Antinomians who followed Hutchinson to Portsmouth and those who followed Wheelwright to Exeter. Despite their expulsion, Wheelwright and his colleagues still associated themselves with the Massachusetts church system.

and wrote to our church to desire us to dismiss Mr. Wheelwright to them for an officer; but, because he desired it not himself, the elders did not propound it. Soon after came his own letter, with theirs, for his dismission, which thereupon was granted. Others likewise (upon their request) were also dismissed thither . . .

The devil would never cease to disturb our peace, and to raise up instruments one after another. Amongst the rest, there was a woman in Salem, one Oliver his wife,[81] who had suffered somewhat in England for refusing to bow at the name of Jesus, though otherwise she was conformable to all their orders. She was (for ability of speech, and appearance of zeal and devotion) far before Mrs. Hutchinson, and so the fitter instrument to have done hurt but that she was poor and had little acquaintance. She took offence at this, that she might not be admitted to the Lord's supper without giving public satisfaction to the church of her faith, etc., and covenanting or professing to walk with them according to the rule of the gospel. This woman was brought to the court for disturbing the peace in the church, etc., and there she gave such peremptory answers as she was committed till she should find sureties for her good behavior. After she had been in prison three or four days, she made means to[82] the governor, and submitted herself and acknowledged her fault in disturbing the church; whereupon he took her husband's bond for her good behavior and discharged her out of prison. But he found after that she still held her former opinions which were very dangerous, as 1. That the church is the heads of the people, both magistrates and ministers met together, and that these have power to ordain ministers, etc. 2. That all that dwell in the same town and will profess their faith in Christ Jesus ought to be received to the sacraments there; and that she was persuaded that if Paul were at Salem,

81. Mary Oliver; she and her husband Thomas had migrated from Norwich, Norfolk, to Salem in 1637.
82. Got in touch with.

he would call all the inhabitants there saints. 3. That excommunication is no other but when Christians withdraw private communion from one that hath offended.

About five years after, this woman was adjudged to be whipped for reproaching the magistrates. She stood without tying, and bare her punishment with a masculine spirit, glorying in her suffering. But after (when she came to consider the reproach, which would stick by her, etc.) she was much dejected about it. She had a cleft stick put on her tongue half an hour, for reproaching the elders, (6,) 1646.[83]

At Providence also the devil was not idle. For whereas, at their first coming thither, Mr. Williams and the rest did make an order that no man should be molested for his conscience, now men's wives and children and servants claimed liberty hereby to go to all religious meetings, though never so often, or though private upon the week days; and because one Verin refused to let his wife go to Mr. Williams so oft as she was called for, they required to have him censured.[84] But there stood up one Arnold,[85] a witty man of their own company, and withstood it, telling them that when he consented to that order he never intended it should extend to the breach of any ordinance of God, such as the subjection of wives to their husbands, etc., and gave divers solid reasons against it. Some were of opinion that if Verin would not suffer his wife to have her liberty, the church should dispose her to some other man who would use her better. Arnold told them that it was against their own order, for Verin did that he did out of conscience;

83. Aug. 1646. Ezra Stiles, who read Winthrop's journal in 1771 before the second volume was burned, noted that this paragraph was written in different ink—an indication that JW inserted it later.

84. Joshua Verin, a roper, had come to Providence from Salem with his wife Jane. Williams reported to JW (*WP*, 4:31) that he beat his wife so savagely that "with his furious blows she went in danger of life"—a circumstance that JW failed to record.

85. William Arnold arrived in New England in 1635 and came with his son Benedict to Providence in 1636; he was a forebear of the Revolutionary War traitor.

and their order was, that no man should be censured for his conscience.[86]

Another plot the old serpent had against us, by sowing jealousies and differences between us and our friends at Connecticut . . . The ground of all was their shyness of coming under our government, which though we never intended to make them subordinate to us, yet they were very jealous, and therefore in the articles of confederation which we propounded to them, they did so alter the chief article as all would have come to nothing. For whereas the article was, That upon any matter of difference, two, three, or more commissioners of every of the confederate colonies should assemble and have absolute power (the greater number of them) to determine the matter, they would have them only to meet and if they could agree, so; if not, then to report to their several colonies and to return with their advice and so to go on till the matter might be agreed; which, beside that it would have been infinitely tedious and extreme chargeable, it would never have attained the end; for it was very unlikely that all the churches in all the plantations would ever have accorded upon the same propositions[87] . . .

Though we were formerly willing that Agawam (now Springfield)[88]

86. Verin took his wife back to Salem, where she resisted attending Hugh Peter's church services.

87. Around May 1638, representatives from the four Connecticut River towns of Hartford, Windsor, Wethersfield, and Springfield had met to discuss the need for an independent civil government and an alliance with Massachusetts on issues of mutual concern such as Indian relations. They then sent agents to Massachusetts, proposing articles of confederation (*WP*, 4:36–37). The records of this meeting are lost, but it is plain that Connecticut wanted a loose alliance, whereas Massachusetts wanted a tighter union, with some sort of "preeminence" accorded to Massachusetts as the senior partner (*WP*, 4:79–80). By mid-December, when JW seems to have written this account, the Connecticut leaders were drafting their new constitution, the Fundamental Orders, which was adopted by Hartford, Windsor, and Wethersfield in Jan. 1639.

88. This town on the Connecticut River 30 miles N of Hartford had been founded in 1636 by a group from Roxbury, led by William Pynchon. For two years Agawam had joined with the three lower Connecticut River towns, but in March 1638 Pynchon quarreled with Hooker, and in Jan. 1639 the people of Agawam declared their acceptance of the

should have fallen into their government, yet seeing they would not be beholden to us for any thing, we intended to keep it; and accordingly we put it in as an article that the line between us should be, one way, the Pequot River (viz. south and north) and the other way (viz. east and west) the limits of our own grant. And this article we added: That we, etc., should have liberty to pass to and fro upon Connecticut, and they likewise. To these articles all their commissioners offered to consent, but it was thought by our court (because of the new articles) that they should first acquaint their own court with it. And so their commissioners departed.

After this, we understood that they went on to exercise their authority at Agawam. Whereupon the governor wrote to them to desire them to forbear until the line was laid out. After a long time, Mr. Ludlow (in the name of their court) returned answer, which was very harsh; and in fine declared, that they thought it not fit to treat any further before they had advice from the gentlemen of Saybrook, etc. The governor acquainted the council and magistrates with this letter; and, because they had tied our hands (in a manner) from replying, he wrote a private letter to Mr. Haynes wherein he lays open their mistakes (as he called them) and the apparent causes of offence, which they had given us; as by making a treaty of agreement with the Narragansetts and Mohegans without joining us or mentioning us to that end (though we had by letter given them liberty to take us in), and by binding all the Indians (who had received any Pequots) to pay tribute for them all to them at Connecticut, etc. ⟨These and the like miscarriages in point of correspondency were conceived to arise from these two errors in their government: 1. They chose divers scores men who had no learning nor judgment which might fit them for those affairs, though otherwise

---

MBC government, with Pynchon as their chief magistrate. The town's name was changed in 1640 to honor Pynchon's village in Essex.

men holy and religious. 2. By occasion hereof, the main burden for managing of state business fell upon some one or other of their ministers (as the phrase and style of these letters will clearly discover) who, though they were men of singular wisdom and godliness, yet stepping out of their course, their actions wanted that blessing which otherwise might have been expected)[89] . . .

Mo. 1 [March]. A printing house was begun at Cambridge by one Daye, at the charge of Mr. Glover, who died on sea hitherward.[90] The first thing which was printed was the freemen's oath; ⟨the next was an almanac made for New England by Mr. William Peirce, mariner;⟩ the next was the Psalms newly turned into metre[91] . . .

In this year one James Everell,[92] a sober discreet man, and two others saw a great light in the night at Muddy River. When it stood still, it flamed up and was about three yards square; when it ran, it was contracted into the figure of a swine: it ran as swift as an arrow towards Charlestown, and so up and down about two or three hours. They were come down in their lighter about a mile, and when it was over, they found themselves carried quite back against the tide to the place they came from. Divers other credible persons saw the same light[93] after, about the same place.

89. In this cancelled passage JW exhibits considerable animosity toward Thomas Hooker. He eradicated these lines so thoroughly that James Savage had much difficulty in deciphering them; see Savage, 1:344.

90. Stephen Day (1594?–1668) had been a locksmith in England before becoming a printer in Massachusetts. The Rev. Josse (or Joseph) Glover, who died en route to Massachusetts, imported the printing press that Day operated.

91. No copies of the freeman's oath or Peirce's almanac have survived. *The Whole Booke of Psalmes Faithfully Translated into English Metre,* popularly known as the *Bay Psalm Book,* was published in 1640 in an edition of 1700 copies, of which 11 survive; the verse translations from the Hebrew are thought to be the work of Richard Mather, John Cotton, and several other Bay ministers.

92. A shoemaker, admitted to the Boston church in 1634.

93. An ignis fatuus or phosphorescent light, possibly caused by the spontaneous combustion of gases from the Muddy River swamps.

The general court, in the 7th mo. last [September, 1638], gave order to the governor to write to them of Pascataquack[94] to signify to them that we looked at it as an unneighborly part that they should encourage and advance such as we had cast out from us for their offences, before they had inquired of us the cause, etc. (The occasion of this letter was that they had aided Mr. Wheelwright to begin a plantation there, and intended to make Capt. Underhill their governor).[95] Upon this, Capt. Underhill (being chosen governor there) wrote a letter wherein he reviles the governor with reproachful terms and imprecations of vengeance upon us all . . . The general court wrote to all the chief inhabitants of Pascataquack and sent them a copy of his letters (wherein he professeth himself to be an instrument ordained of God for our ruin) to know whether it were with their privity and consent that he sent us such a defiance, etc., and whether they would maintain him in such practices against us, etc.

Those of Pascataquack returned answer to us by two several letters. Those of the plantation[96] disclaimed to have any hand in his miscarriages, etc., and offered to call him to account, etc., whensoever we would send any to inform against him. The others at the river's mouth[97] disclaimed likewise, and showed their indignation against him for his insolences and their readiness to join in any fair course for our satisfaction; only they desired us to have some compassion of him, and not to send any forces against him . . .

[March] 16. There was so violent a wind at S.S.E. and S. as the like was not since we came into this land. It began in the evening, and increased till midnight. It overturned some new, strong houses; but the

---

94. The settlements along the Piscataqua River in New Hampshire.

95. Underhill had been chosen governor at Dover, and Wheelwright had founded a town at Exeter—both towns beyond the northern boundary of the MBC.

96. Dover, N.H.

97. Strawberry Bank, N.H., renamed Portsmouth in 1653.

Lord miraculously preserved old, weak cottages. It tare down fences—people ran out of their houses in the night, etc. There came such a rain withal as raised the waters at Connecticut twenty feet above their meadows, etc.

The Indians near Aquiday being pawwawing[98] in this tempest, the devil came and fetched away five of them. Quere.[99]

At Providence things grew still worse; for a sister of Mrs. Hutchinson, the wife of one Scott,[1] being infected with Anabaptistry and going last year to live at Providence, Mr. Williams was taken (or rather emboldened) by her to make open profession thereof, and accordingly was rebaptized by one Holyman,[2] a poor man late of Salem. Then Mr. Williams rebaptized him and some ten more. They also denied the baptizing of infants, and would have no magistrates.

At Aquiday also Mrs. Hutchinson exercised publicly, and she and her party (some three or four families) would have no magistracy. She sent also an admonition to the church of Boston; but the elders would not read it publicly because she was excommunicated. By these examples we may see how dangerous it is to slight the censures of the church; for it was apparent that God had given them up to strange delusions . . . Mrs. Hutchinson and some of her adherents happened to be at prayer when the earthquake was at Aquiday, etc., and the house being shaken thereby, they were persuaded (and boasted of it) that the Holy Ghost did shake it in coming down upon them, as he did upon the apostles . . .

98. Powwowing, or ceremonial dancing and magic-making.

99. This word seems to be added later, by someone who doubted the accuracy of this story.

1. Catherine Marbury Scott had come to Boston with the Hutchinsons in 1634; her husband Richard Scott was a clothier from Glemsford, Suffolk. She eventually became a Quaker and was flogged by the MBC authorities in the 1650s.

2. Ezekiel Holliman, from Hertfordshire, had lived in Dedham and Salem before moving to Newport, R.I.

[May]. At Aquiday the people grew very tumultuous, and put out Mr. Coddington[3] and the other three magistrates, and chose Mr. William Hutchinson only, a man of a very mild temper and weak parts, and wholly guided by his wife, who had been the beginner of all the former troubles in the country, and still continued to breed disturbance.

[May] 6. The two regiments in the bay were mustered at Boston to the number of one thousand soldiers, able men, and well armed and exercised. They were led, the one by the governor who was general of all, and the other by the deputy who was colonel, etc. The captains, etc., showed themselves very skilful and ready in divers sorts of skirmishes and other military actions, wherein they spent the whole day . . .

The governor received letters from Mr. Cradock, and in them another order from the lords commissioners, to this effect: That, whereas they had received our petition upon their former order,[4] etc., by which they perceived that we were taken with some jealousies and fears of their intentions, etc., they did accept of our answer and did now declare their intentions to be only to regulate all plantations to be subordinate to the said commission; and that they meant to continue our liberties, etc., and therefore did now again peremptorily require the governor to send them our patent by the first ship; and that in the mean time they did give us, by that order, full power to go on in the government of the people until we had a new patent sent us; and withal they added threats of further course to be taken with us, if we failed.

This order being imparted to the next general court, some advised to return answer to it. Others thought fitter to make no answer at all, because being sent in a private letter, and not delivered by a certain

---

3. After his electoral defeat, William Coddington moved from Portsmouth to the south end of Aquidneck and founded the town of Newport.

4. The MBC's address of Sept. 1638 to the Laud Commission, excusing themselves from returning their royal charter to England, as ordered.

messenger as the former order was, they could not proceed upon it because they could not have any proof that it was delivered to the governor; and order was taken that Mr. Cradock's agent, who delivered the letter to the governor, etc., should in his letters to his master make no mention of the letters he delivered to the governor, seeing his master had not laid any charge upon him to that end.

Mr. Haynes, the governor of Connecticut, and Mr. Hooker, etc., came into the bay and stayed near a month. It appeared by them that they were desirous to renew the treaty of confederation with us, and though themselves would not move it, yet by their means it was moved to our general court and accepted; for they were in some doubt of the Dutch, who had lately received a new governor,[5] a more discreet and sober man than the former, and one who did complain much of the injury done to them at Connecticut, and was very forward to hold correspondency with us and very inquisitive how things stood between us and them of Connecticut, which occasioned us the more readily to renew the former treaty, that the Dutch might not take notice of any breach or alienation between us.

[May] 22. The court of elections was; at which time there was a small eclipse of the sun. Mr. Winthrop was chosen governor again, though some laboring had been by some of the elders and others to have changed, not out of any dislike of him (for they all loved and esteemed him), but out of their fear lest it might make way for having a governor for life, which some had propounded as most agreeable to God's institution and the practice of all well ordered states. But neither the governor nor any other attempted the thing; though some jealousies arose which were increased by two occasions. The first was, there being want of assistants,[6] the governor and other magistrates thought fit (in

5. Willem Kieft, who replaced Wouter van Twiller.

6. Only eight assistants were elected in May 1639, which was four fewer than in 1636 (*MR*, 1:256).

the warrant for the court) to propound three, amongst which Mr. Downing, the governor's brother-in-law, was one,[7] which they conceived to be done to strengthen his party, and therefore the people would not choose him. Another occasion of their jealousy was, the court, finding the number of deputies to be much increased by the addition of new plantations, thought fit for the ease both of the country and the court to reduce all towns to two deputies.[8] This occasioned some to fear that the magistrates intended to make themselves stronger and the deputies weaker, and so in time to bring all power into the hands of the magistrates; so as the people in some towns were much displeased with their deputies for yielding to such an order. A petition was brought to the court from the freemen of Roxbury to have the third deputy restored. Whereupon the reasons of the court's proceedings were set down in writing, and all objections answered and sent to such towns as were unsatisfied with this advice, that if any could take away those reasons, or bring us better for what they did desire, we should be ready at the next court to repeal the said order[9] . . .

There fell out at this court another occasion of increasing the people's jealousy of their magistrates, viz.: One of the elders declared his judgment that a governor ought to be for his life, alleging for his authority the practice of all the best commonwealths in Europe, and especially that of Israel by God's own ordinance.[10] But this was opposed

7. Emmanuel Downing had arrived from London in 1638 and settled at Salem. If elected, he would have been the third member of the Winthrop family on the bench of magistrates.

8. This decision of March 1639 is in *MR*, 1:254. In the five years since deputies from the towns had been admitted to the General Court, the number of towns had increased from 11 to 17; if each town sent 3 deputies, there could be 51 town representatives as against 10 magistrates.

9. The effect of the court ruling was to hold the number of deputies to about 35 for most court meetings during the next decade, although the number of towns represented increased to 22 by the time JW died in 1649.

10. The identity of this minister is not known; by calling for a governor for life, he roused suspicions about the Standing Council for Life created in April 1636.

by some other of the elders with much zeal, and so notice was taken of it by the people, not as a matter of dispute but as if there had been some plot to put it in practice, which did occasion the deputies at the next session of this court to deliver in an order drawn to this effect: That, whereas our sovereign lord, King Charles, etc., had by his patent established a governor, deputy and assistants, that therefore no person chosen a counsellor ⟨for life⟩ should have any authority as a magistrate, except he were chosen in the annual elections to one of the said places of magistracy established by the patent. This being thus bluntly tendered, the magistrates advised of it, and drew up another order to this effect: That the standing council should always be chosen out of the magistrates, etc.; and therefore it is now ordered that no such counsellor shall have any power as a magistrate, nor shall do any act as a magistrate, etc., except he be annually chosen, etc., according to the patent; and this order was after passed by vote. That which led those of the council to yield to this desire of the deputies was because it concerned themselves, and they did more study to remove these jealousies out of the people's heads than to preserve any power or dignity to themselves above others. And here may be observed how strictly the people would seem to stick to their patent, where they think it makes for their advantage, but are content to decline it where it will not warrant such liberties as they have taken up without warrant from thence, as appears in their strife for three deputies, etc., when as the patent allows them none at all, but only by inference, etc., voting by proxies, etc.

The governor acquainted the general court, that, in these two last years of his government, he had received from the Indians, in presents, to the value of about £40, and that he had spent about £20 in entertainments of them and in presents to their sachems, etc. The court declared, that the presents were the governor's due, but the tribute was to be paid to the treasurer . . .

[May] *26.* Mr. Hooker being to preach at Cambridge, the governor and many others went to hear him (though the governor did very

seldom go from his own congregation upon the Lord's day). He preached in the afternoon, and having gone on with much strength of voice and intention of spirit about a quarter of an hour, he was at a stand, and told the people that God had deprived him both of his strength and matter, etc., and so went forth, and about half an hour after returned again and went on to very good purpose about two hours . . .

(4.) [June]. We were much afraid this year of a stop in England,[11] by reason of the complaints which had been sent against us, and the great displeasure which the archbishops and others, the commissioners for plantations, had conceived and uttered against us, both for those complaints and also for our not sending home our patent. But the Lord wrought for us beyond all expectation; for ships came to us from England and divers other parts with great store of people and provisions of all sorts . . .

[July]. At Providence matters went after the old manner. Mr. Williams and many of his company, a few months since, were in all haste rebaptized and denied communion with all others, and now he was come to question his second baptism, not being able to derive the authority of it from the apostles otherwise than by the ministers of England (whom he judged to be ill authority), so as he conceived God would raise up some apostolic power. Therefore he bent himself that way, expecting (as was supposed) to become an apostle; and having a little before refused communion with all, save his own wife, now he would preach to and pray with all comers. Whereupon some of his followers left him and returned back from whence they went . . .

[September] 4. At the general court at Boston, one Mr. Nathaniel Eaton, brother to the merchant at Quilipiack, was convented and censured.[12] The occasion was this: He was a schoolmaster and had many

11. An embargo on all shipping to New England.

12. Nathaniel Eaton (1609–1674) of Trinity College, Cambridge, was brother to Theo-

scholars, the sons of gentlemen and others of best note in the country, and had entertained one Nathaniel Briscoe, a gentleman born, to be his usher.[13] He had not been with him above three days but he fell out with him for a very small occasion, and with reproachful terms discharged him, and turned him out of his doors; but it being then about eight of the clock after the Sabbath, he told him he should stay till next morning, and some words growing between them, he struck him and pulled him into his house. Briscoe defended himself and closed with him, and being parted, he came in and went up to his chamber to lodge there. Mr. Eaton caused his man to fetch him a cudgel, which was a walnut tree plant big enough to have killed a horse, and a yard in length, and taking his two men with him, he went up to Briscoe and caused his men to hold him till he had given him two hundred stripes about the head and shoulders, etc., and so kept him under blows (with some two or three short intermissions) about the space of two hours, about which time Mr. Shepherd and some others of the town came in at the outcry, and so he gave over. In this distress Briscoe gat out his knife and struck at the man that held him, but hurt him not. He also fell to prayer (supposing he should have been murdered), and then Mr. Eaton beat him for taking the name of God in vain. After this Mr. Eaton and Mr. Shepherd (who knew not then of these passages) came to the governor and some other of the magistrates, complaining of Briscoe for his insolent speeches, and for crying out murder and drawing his knife, and desired that he might be enjoined to a public acknowledgment, etc. The magistrates answered that they must first hear him speak, and then they would do as they should see cause. Mr. Eaton was displeased at this, but the cause went on notwithstanding, and he was called, and these things laid to his charge in the open court. His

---

philus Eaton of New Haven. In 1637 he had been appointed the first professor or master of Harvard College, and began teaching in 1638.

13. Assistant teacher. Briscoe was the son of a Watertown tanner.

answers were full of pride and disdain, telling the magistrates that they should not need to do any thing herein, for he was intended to leave his employment. And being asked why he used such cruelty to Briscoe his usher, and to other his scholars (for it was testified by another of his ushers and divers of his scholars that he would give them between twenty and thirty stripes at a time, and would not leave till they had confessed what he required), his answer was that he had this rule, that he would not give over correcting till he had subdued the party to his will. Being also questioned about the ill and scant diet of his boarders (for though their friends gave large allowance, yet their diet was ordinarily nothing but porridge and pudding, and that very homely), he put it off to his wife.[14] So the court dismissed him at present, and commanded him to attend again the next day, when in the open court before a great assembly, he made a very solid, wise, eloquent, and serious (seeming) confession, condemning himself in all the particulars, etc. Whereupon, being put aside, the court consulted privately about his sentence, and though many were taken with his confession, and none but had a charitable opinion of it, yet because of the scandal of religion and offence which would be given to such as might intend to send their children hither, they all agreed to censure him and put him from that employment. So, being called in, the governor after a short preface, etc., declared the sentence of the court to this effect, viz.: that he should give Briscoe £30, [be] fined 100 marks,[15] and debarred teaching of children within our jurisdiction. A pause being made, and expectation that (according to his former confession) he would have given glory to God and acknowledged the justice and clemency of the court, he turned away with a discontented look, saying "If sentence be passed,

---

14. Mrs. Eaton confessed to the court that she served the scholars skimpy portions of bad food, though she denied knowing that their hasty pudding had goat's dung in it. See Morison, pp. 232–233.

15. £66 13s. 4d. in sterling.

then it is to no end to speak." Yet the court remitted his fine to £20, and willed Briscoe to take but £20.

The church at Cambridge, taking notice of these proceedings, intended to deal with him. But he soon discovered himself; for ere the church could come to deal with him, he fled to Pascataquack, and being pursued and apprehended by the governor there, he again acknowledged his great sin in flying, etc., and promised (as he was a Christian man) he would return with the messengers. But, because his things he carried with him were aboard a bark there, bound to Virginia, he desired leave to go fetch them, which they assented unto. So he returned to the bark, and presently they set sail and went out of the harbor. Being thus gone, his creditors began to complain; and thereupon it was found that he was run in debt about £1000,[16] and had taken up most of this money upon bills he had charged into England upon his brother's agents, and others whom he had no such relation to. So his estate was seized, and the church proceeded and cast him out. He had been sometimes initiated among the Jesuits,[17] and coming into England, his friends drew him from them, but it was very probable he now intended to return to them again . . .

Mo. 9 [November]. At a general court holden at Boston, great complaint was made of the oppression used in the country in sale of foreign commodities; and Mr. Robert Keaine,[18] who kept a shop in Boston, was notoriously above others observed and complained of; and being con-

16. Incredible as this figure seems, it appears that Eaton did in fact run off with several hundred pounds which he had received as gifts to Harvard College, and that he received at least £500 in cash for worthless bills of exchange. See Morison, pp. 236–238.

17. There is no evidence of this; Eaton had had a standard Puritan training. But after his departure Harvard closed down for a year until Henry Dunster became president in 1640.

18. Robert Keayne (1595–1656), the most successful of the early Boston merchants, had been a member of the Merchant Tailor's Company in London before he emigrated in 1635. One of the few Boston church members to stand out against Anne Hutchinson, Keayne was twice put on public trial himself. Three years after his 1639 appearance before the

vented,[19] he was charged with many particulars; in some for taking above sixpence in the shilling profit; in some above eightpence; and in some small things above two for one; and being hereof convict (as appears by the records) he was fined £200, which came thus to pass: The deputies considered apart of his fine, and set it at £200; the magistrates agreed but to £100. So the court being divided, at length it was agreed that his fine should be £200, but he should pay but £100, and the other should be respited to the further consideration of the next general court. And sure the course was very evil, especial circumstances considered: 1. He being an ancient professor of the gospel: 2. A man of eminent parts: 3. Wealthy, and having but one child: 4. Having come over for conscience' sake, and for the advancement of the gospel here: 5. Having been formerly dealt with and admonished, both by private friends and also by some of the magistrates and elders, and having promised reformation; being a member of a church and commonwealth now in their infancy, and under the curious observation of all churches and civil states in the world. These added much aggravation to his sin in the judgment of all men of understanding. Yet most of the magistrates (though they discerned of the offence clothed with all these circumstances) would have been more moderate in their censure: 1. Because there was no law in force to limit or direct men in point of profit in their trade. 2. Because it is the common practice in all countries for men to make use of advantages for raising the prices of their commodities. 3. Because (though he were chiefly aimed at, yet) he was not alone in this fault. 4. Because all men through the country, in sale of cattle, corn, labor, etc., were guilty of the like excess in prices. 5. Because a certain rule could not be found out for an equal rate between buyer and seller. Lastly, and especially, because the law of God appoints

---

General Court, he was prosecuted by Goody Sherman in the "sow case"; see June 1642 below.

19. Summoned.

no other punishment but double restitution. After the court had censured him, the church of Boston called him also in question, where (as before he had done in the court) he did with tears acknowledge and bewail his covetous and corrupt heart, yet making some excuse for many of the particulars, which were charged upon him, chiefly by being misled by some false principles, as 1. That if a man lost in one commodity, he might help himself in the price of another. 2. That if through want of skill or other occasion his commodity cost him more than the price of the market in England, he might then sell it for more than the price of the market in New England, etc. These things gave occasion to Mr. Cotton, in his public exercise the next lecture day, to lay open the error of such false principles and to give some rules of direction in the case.[20]

Some false principles were these:—

1. That a man might sell as dear as he can, and buy as cheap as he can.

2. If a man lose by casualty[21] of sea, etc., in some of his commodities, he may raise the price of the rest.

3. That he may sell as he bought, though he paid too dear, etc., and though the commodity be fallen, etc.

4. That as a man may take the advantage of his own skill or ability, so he may of another's ignorance or necessity.

5. Where one gives time for payment, he is to take like recompense of one as of another.[22]

The rules for trading were these:—

1. A man may not sell above the current price, i.e., such a price as is usual in the time and place.

---

20. Keayne was John Wilson's brother-in-law, which may help to explain Cotton's zealous pursuit of him.

21. Accident.

22. Cotton is here condemning usury, declaring that it is a false principle to charge interest on a loan.

2. When a man loseth in his commodity for want of skill, etc., he must look at it as his own fault or cross, and therefore must not lay it upon another.

3. Where a man loseth by casualty of sea, or, etc., it is a loss cast upon himself by providence.

4. A man may not ask any more for his commodity than his selling price, as Ephron to Abraham, the land is worth thus much.[23]

The cause being debated by the church, some were earnest to have him excommunicated; but the most thought an admonition would be sufficient . . . So, in the end, the church consented to an admonition.[24]

Being now about church matters, I will here insert another passage in the same church which fell out about the same time. Their old meeting-house being decayed and too small, they sold it away and agreed to build another, which workmen undertook to set up for £600. Three hundred they had for the old, and the rest was to be gathered by voluntary contributions, as other charges were. But there grew a great difference among the brethren where this new one should stand. Some were for the green (which was the governor's first lot, and he had yielded it to the church, etc.); others, viz., the tradesmen especially who dwelt about the market place, desired it might stand still near the market, lest in time it should divert the chief trade from thence. The church referred it to the judgment and determination of ⟨the governor and four others⟩ five of the brethren, who agreed that the fittest place (all things considered) would be near the market; but respited the full determination to another general meeting, thinking it very unsafe to proceed with the discontent of any considerable part of the church.

---

23. Gen. 23:8–16.

24. This censure, together with the court fine, rankled Keayne so deeply that he found it necessary 14 years later to write a 158-page justification of his moral rectitude in the form of a last will and testament. Keayne's extraordinary testament has been edited by Bernard Bailyn as *The Apologia of Robert Keayne: The Self-Portrait of a Puritan Merchant* (New York: Knopf, 1965).

When the church met, the matter was debated to and fro, and grew at length to some earnestness, etc.; but, after Mr. Cotton had cleared it up to them, they all yielded to have it set by the market place; and, though some remained still in their opinion that the green were the fitter place, yet for peace sake they yielded to the rest by keeping silence while it passed[25] . . .

[December] 4. At the general court, etc., the inhabitants of the upper part of Pascataquack, viz. Dover, etc., had written to the governor to offer themselves to come under our government. Answer was returned them that if they sent two or three of their company, with full commission under all their hands to conclude, etc., it was like the court would agree to their propositions. And now at this court, the treaty was brought to a conclusion to this effect: That they should be as Ipswich and Salem, and have courts there, etc., as by the copy of the agreement remaining with the recorder doth appear. This was ratified under our public seal and so delivered to them; only they desired a promise from the court that, if the people did not assent to it (which yet they had no fear of), they might be at liberty, which was granted them.[26]

Those of Exeter sent the like propositions to the court; but not liking (it seems) the agreement which those of Dover had made, they repented themselves and wrote to the court that they intended not to proceed . . .

At Kennebec, the Indians wanting food and there being store in the Plymouth trading house, they conspired to kill the English there for their provisions; and some Indians coming into the house, Mr. Willet,[27]

---

25. The old Boston meetinghouse, built around 1632, was on the S side of King Street. The new building, which opened in 1640, was close by on Cornhill Square at the head of King (now State) Street.

26. This union with Massachusetts was blocked by John Underhill, then governor of Dover, until he was deposed from office early in 1640.

27. Capt. Thomas Willet had previously been in charge of the Plymouth trading post at Castine on the Penobscot when the French seized it in 1635.

the master of the house, being reading in the Bible, his countenance was more solemn than at other times, so as he did not look cheerfully upon them as he was wont to do; whereupon they went out and told their fellows that their purpose was discovered. They asked them how it could be. The others told them that they knew it by Mr. Willet's countenance, and that he had discovered it by a book that he was reading. Whereupon they gave over their design.

The people had long desired a body of laws, and thought their condition very unsafe while so much power rested in the discretion of magistrates. Divers attempts had been made at former courts, and the matter referred to some of the magistrates and some of the elders; but still it came to no effect; for, being committed to the care of many, whatsoever was done by some was still disliked or neglected by others. At last it was referred to Mr. Cotton and Mr. Nathaniel Warde, etc., and each of them framed a model which were presented to this general court, and by them committed to the governor and deputy and some others to consider of, and so prepare it for the court in the 3d month next.[28] Two great reasons there were, which caused most of the magistrates and some of the elders not to be very forward in this matter. One was want of sufficient experience of the nature and disposition of the people, which made them conceive that such laws would be fittest for us which should arise pro re nata[29] upon occasions, etc., and so the laws of England and other states grew, and therefore the fundamental laws of England are called customs, consuetudines. 2. For that it would professedly transgress the limits of our charter, which provide we shall make no laws repugnant to the laws of England, and that we were assured we must do. But to raise up laws by practice and custom had been no transgression; as in our church discipline, and in matters of

28. In May 1640. Ward's draft was preferred to Cotton's, and eventually the MBC approved a formal code of laws, the Body of Liberties, in Dec. 1641.
29. Naturally.

marriage, to make a law that marriages should not be solemnized by ministers is repugnant to the laws of England; but to bring it to a custom by practice for the magistrates to perform it is no law made repugnant, etc. At length (to satisfy the people) it proceeded, and the two models were digested with divers alterations and additions, and abbreviated and sent to every town, (12,)[30] to be considered of first by the magistrates and elders, and then to be published by the constables to all the people, that if any man should think fit that any thing therein ought to be altered he might acquaint some of the deputies therewith against the next court.

By this time there appeared a great change in the church of Boston; for whereas the year before they were all (save five or six) so affected to Mr. Wheelwright and Mrs. Hutchinson, and those new opinions, as they slighted the present governor and the pastor, looking at them as men under a covenant of works and as their greatest enemies; but they bearing all patiently and not withdrawing themselves (as they were strongly solicited to have done), but carrying themselves lovingly and helpfully upon all occasions, the Lord brought about the hearts of all the people to love and esteem them more than ever before, and all breaches were made up and the church was saved from ruin beyond all expectation; which could hardly have been (in human reason) if those two had not been guided by the Lord to that moderation, etc. And the church (to manifest their hearty affection to the governor, upon occasion of some strait he was brought into through his bailiff's unfaithfulness) sent him £200[31] . . .

[December] 3. There were so many lectures now in the country, and

---

30. Feb. 1640. Ward complained to JW about this democratical procedure (*WP*, 4:162–163).

31. JW's unfaithful bailiff was James Luxford, who as steward of his farm at Tenhills on the Mystic River contracted loans in JW's name with various people in England and New England, and also forged bills of exchange, putting JW £2,500 in debt. In Dec. 1639 he was accused of bigamy by the court of assistants, was jailed, pilloried, and in May 1640 had his ears cut off. He then moved to Plymouth.

many poor persons would usually resort to two or three in the week to the great neglect of their affairs and the damage of the public. The assemblies also were (in divers churches) held till night, and sometimes within the night, so as such as dwelt far off could not get home in due season, and many weak bodies could not endure so long in the extremity of the heat or cold, without great trouble and hazard of their health. Whereupon the general court ordered that the elders should be desired to give a meeting to the magistrates and deputies, to consider about the length and frequency of church assemblies, and to make return to the court of their determinations, etc. This was taken in ill part by most of the elders and other of the churches, alleging their tenderness of the church's liberties (as if such a precedent might enthrall them to the civil power, and also raise an ill savour of the people's coldness that would complain of much preaching, etc.,—when as liberty for the ordinances was the main end professed of our coming hither). The magistrates finding how hardly such propositions would be digested, and that if matters should be further pushed, it might make some breach or disturbance at least (for the elders had great power in the people's hearts, which was needful to be upheld, lest the people should break their bonds through abuse of liberty), in this consideration, the magistrates and deputies, which were then met, thought it not fit to enter any dispute or conference with the elders about the number of lectures, or for appointing any certain time for the continuance of the assemblies, but rested satisfied that their church assemblies might ordinarily break up in such season as people that dwell a mile or two off might get home by daylight . . .

(1) [March] 5. Capt. Underhill, being struck with horror and remorse for his offences both against the church and civil state, could have no rest till he had obtained a safe conduct to come and give satisfaction; and accordingly, at a lecture at Boston (it being then the court time), he made a public confession both of his living in adultery with Faber's wife (upon suspicion whereof the church had before admonished him)

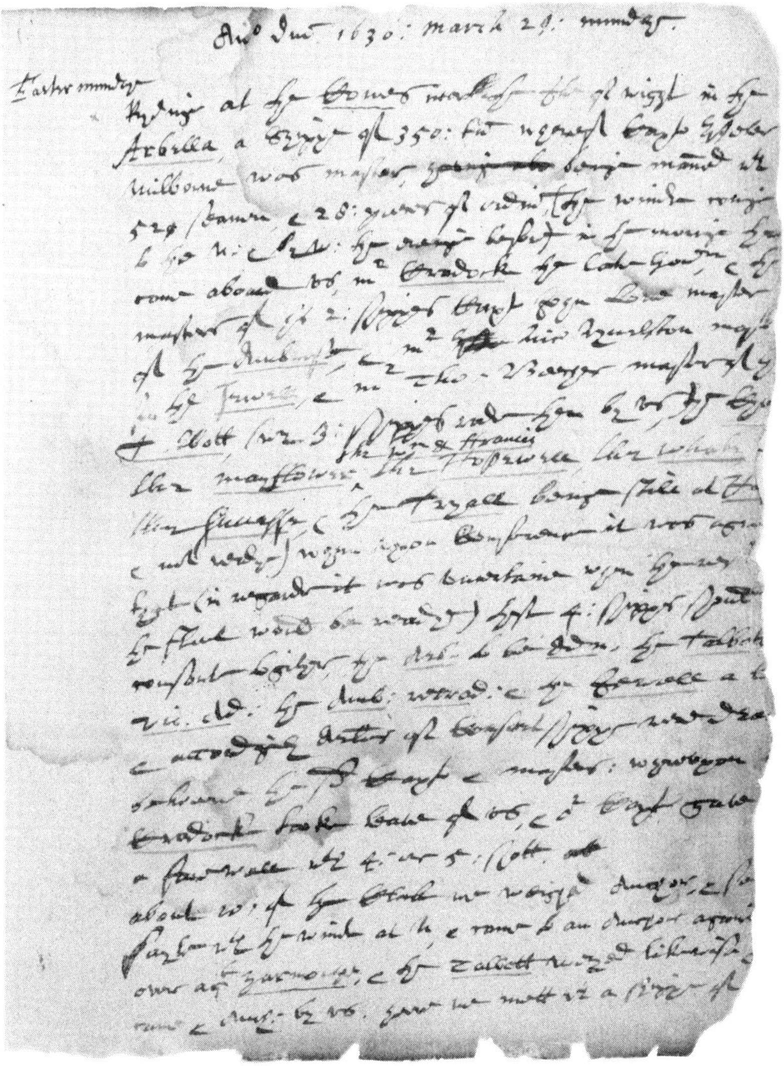

Ano Dni. 1630: march 29: munday.

Easter munday

THE OPENING PAGE OF WINTHROP'S JOURNAL

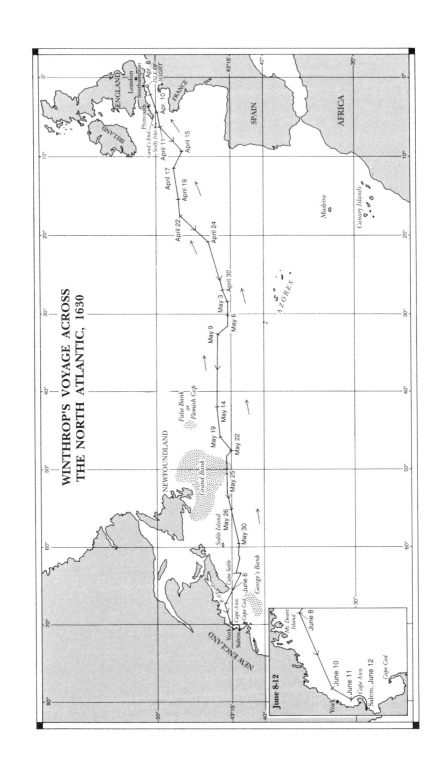

WINTHROP'S VOYAGE ACROSS
THE NORTH ATLANTIC, 1630

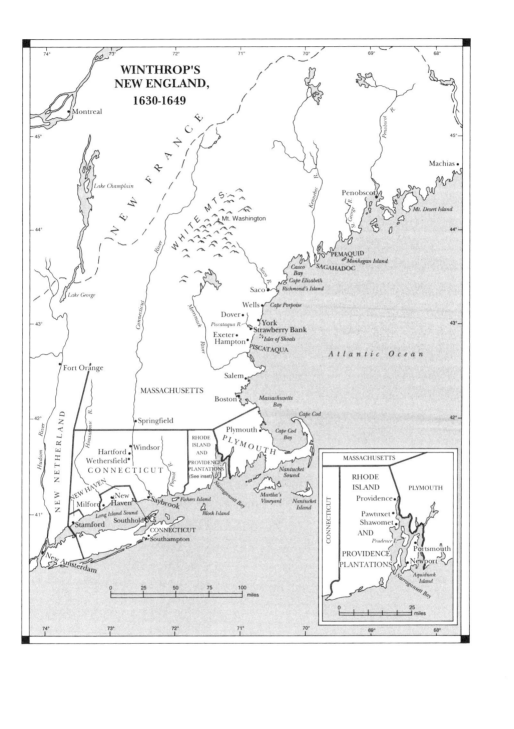

WINTHROP'S
NEW ENGLAND,
1630-1649

Montreal

N E W   F R A N C E

Machias

Lake Champlain

Penobscot

Mt. Desert Island

WHITE MTS.

Mt. Washington

PEMAQUID
Monhegan Island
SAGAHADOC

Casco
Bay
Cape Elizabeth
Richmond's Island

Lake George

Saco
Saco R.

Wells
Cape Porpoise

Dover

Fort Orange

Piscataqua R.
Merrimack River
Connecticut River

York
Strawberry Bank
Isles of Shoals

Exeter
Hampton

PISCATAQUA

Atlantic Ocean

Salem

MASSACHUSETTS

Boston
Massachusetts
Bay

Cape Cod

Springfield

NEW NETHERLAND

Hudson River

Housatonic R.

Plymouth
Cape Cod
Bay

RHODE
ISLAND
AND

PLYMOUTH

Hartford
Windsor

Wethersfield
CONNECTICUT

PROVIDENCE
PLANTATIONS
(See inset)

Nantucket
Sound

NEW HAVEN

Milford
New
Haven

Saybrook
Fishers Island

Narragansett Bay

Murtha's
Vineyard

Nantucket
Island

Pequot R.

Stamford
Southhold

Block Island

CONNECTICUT
Southampton

Long Island Sound

New Amsterdam

0   25   50   75   100
miles

MASSACHUSETTS

RHODE
ISLAND

PLYMOUTH

CONNECTICUT

Providence

Pawtuxet
Shawomet
AND

Prudence I.

PROVIDENCE
PLANTATIONS

Portsmouth
Newport

Aquidneck
Island

Narragansett Bay

0   25
miles

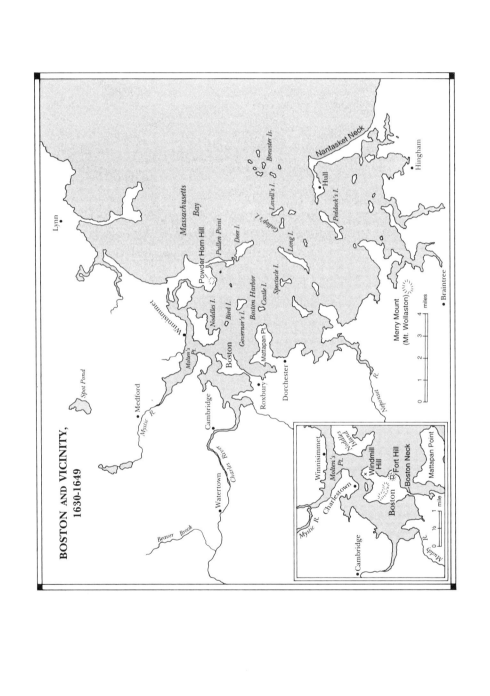

BOSTON AND VICINITY, 1630-1649

Massachusetts Bay

Lynn

Powder Horn Hill

Pullen Point

Deer I.

Noddles I.

Bird I.

Governor's I.

Boston Harbor

Castle I.

Spectacle I.

Nantasket Neck

Breaster Is.

Lovell's I.

Gallop's I.

Long I.

Hull

Peddock's I.

Hingham

Winnisimmet

Molten's Pt.

Boston

Mattapan Pt.

Roxbury

Dorchester

Merry Mount (Mt. Wollaston)

Braintree

0   1   2   3   4
miles

Spot Pond

Medford

Mystic R.

Cambridge

Charles River

Watertown

Beaver Brook

Neponset R.

Winnisimmet

Molten's Pt.

Noddle's Island

Charlestown

Mystic R.

Cambridge

Windmill Hill

Boston

Fort Hill

Boston Neck

Mattapan Point

Muddy R.

0   ½   1 mile

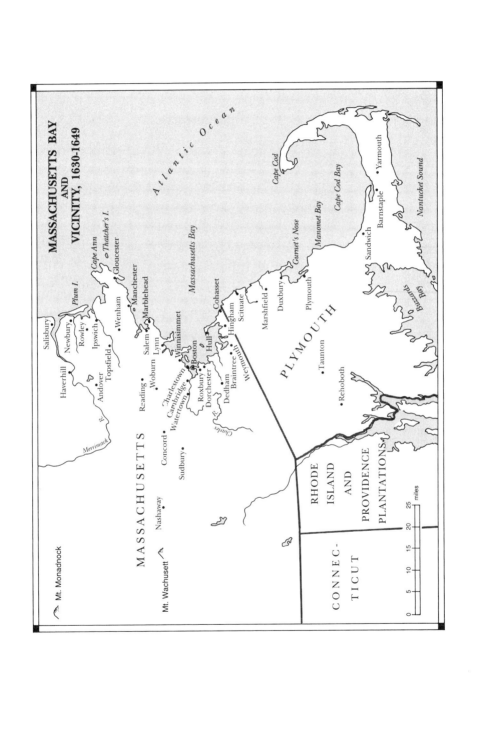

MASSACHUSETTS BAY
AND
VICINITY, 1630-1649

Atlantic Ocean

Cape Ann
Thatcher's I.
Gloucester
Manchester
Plum I.
Salisbury
Newbury
Rowley
Ipswich
Wenham
Marblehead
Haverhill
Andover
Topsfield
Salem
Lynn
Reading
Woburn
Winnisimmet
Charlestown
Cambridge
Watertown
Roxbury
Dorchester
Boston
Hull
Cohasset
Hingham
Scituate
Marshfield
Duxbury
Plymouth
Massachusetts Bay
Garnet's Nose
Manomet Bay
Cape Cod Bay
Cape Cod
Yarmouth
Barnstaple
Sandwich
Nantucket Sound

Merrimack R.

MASSACHUSETTS

Mt. Monadnock

Mt. Wachusett

Nashaway

Concord
Sudbury

Charles R.

Dedham
Braintree
Weymouth

Taunton

Rehoboth

PLYMOUTH

RHODE
ISLAND
AND
PROVIDENCE
PLANTATIONS

Buzzard's Bay

CONNEC-
TICUT

0   5   10   15   20   25
miles

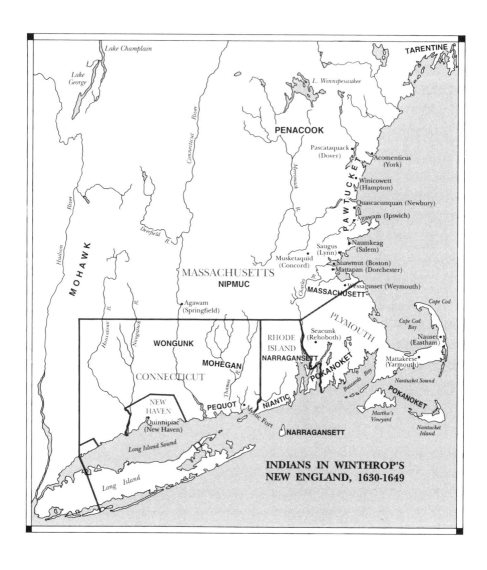

INDIANS IN WINTHROP'S
NEW ENGLAND, 1630-1649

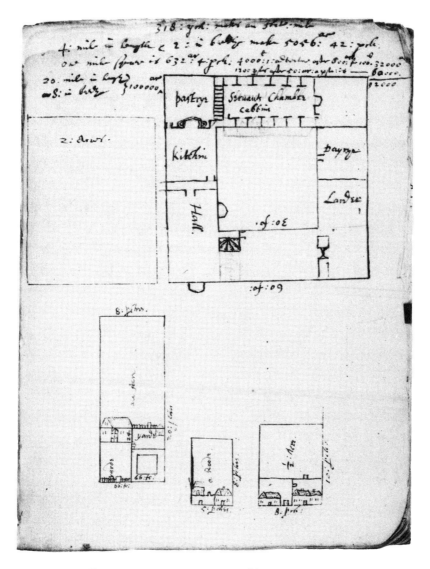

Designs for housing in Massachusetts
by John Winthrop, Jr.

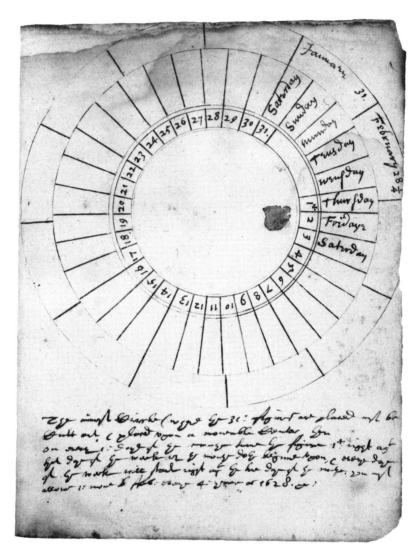

Drawing of a perpetual calendar
by John Winthrop, Jr.

and attempting the like with another woman,[32] and also the injury he had done to our state, etc., and acknowledged the justice of the court in their proceeding against him, etc. Yet all his confessions were mixed with such excuses and extenuations as did not give satisfaction of the truth of his repentance, so as it seemed to be done rather out of policy and to pacify the sting of his conscience than in sincerity. But, however, his offences being so foul and scandalous, the church presently cast him out; which censure he seemed to submit unto, and for the time he stayed in Boston (being four or five days) he was very much dejected, etc.; but being gone back, he soon recovered his spirits again, or at least gave not that proof of a broken heart as he gave hope of at Boston[33] . . .

Our neighbors of Plymouth had procured from [England] this year one Mr. Chancey,[34] a great scholar and a godly man, intending to call him to the office of a teacher; but before the fit time came, he discovered his judgment about baptism, that the children ought to be dipped and not sprinkled; and, he being an active man and very vehement, there arose much trouble about it. The magistrates and the other elders there and the most of the people withstood the receiving of that practice, not for itself so much as for fear of worse consequences, as the annihilating our baptism, etc.[35] Whereupon the church there wrote to all the other churches, both here and at Connecticut, etc., for advice, and sent Mr. Chauncy's arguments. The churches took them into consideration, and returned their several answers, wherein they showed their dissent from

32. Jane Holmes, wife of Robert Holmes of Cambridge.
33. The people in Dover, N.H. dismissed Underhill as their governor after his return.
34. The Rev. Charles Chauncy (1592–1672) of Trinity College, Cambridge, was a proficient Greek and Hebrew scholar. After serving at Plymouth and Scituate, and getting into trouble at both places for his method of baptizing infants, he became president of Harvard College in 1654.
35. According to William Bradford, the Plymouth church members felt that Chauncy's method of baptizing by total immersion "was lawful but in this cold country not so convenient" (Bradford, p. 313).

him and clearly confuted all his arguments, discovering withal some great mistakes of his about the judgment and practice of antiquity. Yet he would not give over his opinion; and the church of Plymouth (though they could not agree to call him to office, yet) being much taken with his able parts, they were very loath to part with him. He did maintain also that the Lord's supper ought to be administered in the evening, and every Lord's day; but that being a matter of no great ill consequence, save some outward inconvenience, there was little stir about it . . .

Many men began to inquire after the southern parts; and the great advantages supposed to be had in Virginia and the West Indies, etc., made this country to be disesteemed of many; and yet those countries (for all their great wealth) have sent hither both this year and formerly for supply of clothes and other necesssaries; and some families have forsaken both Providence and other the Caribbee Islands and Virginia to come live here. And though our people saw what meagre, unhealthful countenances they brought hither, and how fat and well liking they became soon, yet they were so taken with the ease and plenty of those countries, as many of them sold their estates here to transport themselves to Providence; among whom the chief was John Humfrey, Esq., a gentleman of special parts of learning and activity and a godly man, who had been one of the first beginners in the promoting of this plantation and had labored very much therein. He, being brought low in his estate and having many children and being well known to the lords of Providence,[36] and offering himself to their service, was accepted to be the next governor. Whereupon he labored much to draw men to join with him. This was looked at both by the general court and also by the elders as an unwarrantable course; for though it was thought

---

36. The proprietors of the Providence Company who had colonized Providence Island in the Caribbean.

very needful to further plantation of churches in the West Indies, and all were willing to endeavor the same, yet to do it with disparagement of this country (for they gave out that they could not subsist here) caused us to fear that the Lord was not with them in this way. And withal some considerations were propounded to them by the court, which diverted some of them and made others to pause, upon three points especially: 1. How dangerous it was to bring up an ill report upon this good land which God had found out and given to his people, and so to discourage the hearts of their brethren, etc. 2. To leave a place of rest and safety to expose themselves, their wives and children to the danger of a potent enemy, the Spaniard. 3. Their subjection to such governors as those in England shall set over them, etc. Notwithstanding these considerations, divers of them persisted in their resolutions and went about to get some ship or bark to transport them; but they were still crossed by the hand of God . . .

(3.) [May] 13. The court of elections was at Boston, and Thomas Dudley, Esq., was chosen governor.[37] Some trouble there had been in making way for his election, and it was obtained with some difficulty; for many of the elders labored much in it, fearing lest the long continuance of one man in the place should bring it to be for life, and in time hereditary. Beside, this gentleman was a man of approved wisdom and godliness and of much good service to the country, and therefore it was his due to share in such honor and benefit as the country had to bestow. The elders, being met at Boston about this matter, sent some of their company to acquaint the old governor with their desire, which he kindly and thankfully accepted, concurring with them in their motion and expressing his unfeigned desire of more freedom that he might a little intend his private occasions, wherein (they well knew) how

37. Richard Bellingham was elected deputy governor, and JW—after three years as governor—was chosen one of the eight assistants.

much he had lately suffered (for his bailiff, whom he trusted with managing his farm, had engaged him £2500 without his privity) in his outward estate.[38] This they had heard of and were much affected therewith, and all the country in general, and took course (the elders agreeing upon it at that meeting) that supply should be sent in from the several towns by a voluntary contribution for freeing of those engagements; and the court (having no money to bestow, and being yet much indebted) gave his wife three thousand acres of land, and some of the towns sent in liberally, and some others promised but could perform but little, and the most nothing at all. The whole came not to £500 whereof near half came from Boston, and one gentleman of Newbury, Mr. Richard Dummer, himself disbursed £100[39] . . .

Mo. 4 [June]. Divers of the inhabitants of Linne, finding themselves straitened, looked out for a new plantation, and going to Long Island they agreed for a parcel of the isle near the west end, and agreed with the Indians for their right. The Dutch, hearing of this and making claim to that part of the island by a former purchase of the Indians, sent men to take possession of the place, and set up the arms of the Prince of Orange upon a tree. The Lynn men sent ten or twelve men with provisions, etc., who began to build and took down the prince's arms, and in place thereof an Indian had drawn an unhandsome face. The Dutch took this in high displeasure, and sent soldiers and fetched away their men, and imprisoned them a few days and then took an oath of them and so discharged them. Upon this the Lynn men (finding themselves too weak, and having no encouragement to expect aid from

38. At this court James Luxford, JW's bailiff, was bound to the whipping post and his ears were cut off (*MR*, 1:295). JW for his part was stung to discover that some of his neighbors had bargained with Luxford to buy JW's corn at 2s. per bushel under the market price (*WP*, 4:208–209).

39. Dummer had been an opponent of JW in the Antinomian crisis; in 1637 he had been turned out of office and disarmed.

the English) deserted that place, and took another at the east end of the same island;[40] and being now about forty families, they proceeded in their plantation and called one Mr. Pierson,[41] a godly learned man and a member of the church of Boston, to go with them, who with some seven or eight more of the company gathered (9) [November] into a church body at Lynn (before they went), and the whole company entered into a civil combination (with the advice of some of our magistrates) to become a corporation.

Upon this occasion the Dutch governor, one William Kyfte (a discreet man), wrote to our governor complaint of the English usurpations both at Connecticut and now also at Long Island, and of the abuse offered to the Prince's arms, etc., and thereupon excused his imprisoning our men. To which the governor returned answer ⟨in Latin, his letter being in the same,⟩ that our desire had always been to hold peace and good correspondency with all our neighbors; and though we would not maintain any of our countrymen in any unjust action, yet we might not suffer them to be injured, etc. As for our neighbors of Connecticut, etc., he knew they were not under our government, and for those at Long Island, they went voluntarily from us, etc.

This year there came over great store of provisions, both out of England and Ireland, and but few passengers[42] (and those brought very little money) so as now all our money was drained from us, and cattle and all commodities grew very cheap, which enforced us at the next

40. They founded the town of Southampton, about 80 miles E of their first site at Schout's Bay on Long Island.

41. The Rev. Abraham Pierson (1609–1678) had just arrived in Boston from Nottingham, Eng. In 1644 he moved from Southampton to Branford in New Haven Colony, and after Connecticut absorbed New Haven, he migrated in 1667 with most of his Branford congregation to Newark, N.J.

42. The great migration of the 1630s to New England abruptly terminated this year because Charles I summoned Parliament in 1640 for the first time in 11 years, opening the possibility of major political and religious change at home.

general court, in the 8th month [October], to make an order that corn should pass in payments of new debts; Indian at 4s. the bushel; rye at 5s., and wheat at 6s.; and that upon all executions for former debts the creditor might take what goods he pleased (or, if he had no goods, then his lands) to be appraised by three men, one chosen by the creditor, one by the debtor, and the third by the marshal . . .

Mo. 5. [July] 27. Being the second day of the week, the *Mary Rose*, a ship of Bristol of about 200 tons lying before Charlestown, was blown in pieces with her own powder, being 21 barrels; wherein the judgment of God appeared, for the master and company were many of them profane scoffers at us and at the ordinances of religion here; so as, our churches keeping a fast for our native country, etc., they kept aboard at their common service when all the rest of the masters came to our assemblies; likewise the Lord's day following; and a friend of his going aboard next day and asking him why he came not on shore to our meetings, his answer was that he had a family of his own, etc., and they had as good service aboard as we had on shore. Within two hours after this (being about dinner time) the powder took fire (no man knows how) and blew all up, viz. the captain and nine or ten of his men, and some four or five strangers. There was a special providence that there were no more, for many principal men were going aboard at that time, and some were in a boat near the ship, and others were diverted by a sudden shower of rain, and others by other occasions. Some goods were saved, but the whole loss was estimated at £2,000.

This judgment of God upon these scorners of his ordinances and the ways of his servants (for they spake very evil of us, because they found not so good a market for their commodities as they expected, etc.) gives occasion to mention other examples of like kind, which fell out at this and other times, by which it will appear how the Lord hath owned this work and preserved and prospered his people here beyond ordinary ways of providence . . .

One Austin[43] (a man of good estate) came with his family in the year 1638 to Quinipiack, and not finding the country as he expected, he grew discontented, saying that he could not subsist here, and thereupon made off his estate, and with his family and £1000 in his purse, he returned for England in a ship bound for Spain, against the advice of the godly there, who told him he would be taken by the Turks; and it so fell out, for in Spain he embarked himself in a great ship bound for England which carried £200,000 in money, but the ship was taken by the Turks, and Austin and his wife and family were carried to Algiers, and sold there for slaves . . .

Mr. Humfrey, who was now for Providence with his company,[44] raised an ill report of this country, were here kept in spite of all their endeavors and means to have been gone this winter, and his corn and all his hay to the value of £160 were burnt by his own servants, who made a fire in his barn, and by gunpowder which accidentally took fire consumed all;[45] himself having at the court before petitioned for some supply of his want, whereupon the court gave him £250. Soon after also Providence was taken by the Spaniards, and the lords lost all their care and cost to the value of above £60,000.

Mo. 7. [September] 3. Captain Underhill being brought by the blessing of God in this church's censure of excommunication[46] to remorse for his foul sins, obtained by means of the elders and others of the church of Boston a safe conduct under the hand of the governor and one of the council to repair to the church. He came at the time of the court of assistants, and upon the lecture day after sermon the pastor[47]

---

43. We have not identified this New Haven colonist.

44. See pp. 187–188 below.

45. The General Court held Henry Stevens, a servant of John Humfrey, responsible for firing Humfrey's barn, and bound him to serve his master for 21 years in recompense (*MR*, 1:311).

46. See 5 March 1640, above.

47. John Wilson.

called him forth and declared the occasion, and then gave him leave to speak: and indeed it was a spectacle which caused many weeping eyes, though it afforded matter of much rejoicing to behold the power of the Lord Jesus in his own ordinances, when they are dispensed in his own way, holding forth the authority of his regal sceptre in the simplicity of the gospel. He came in his worst clothes (being accustomed to take great pride in his bravery and neatness) without a band,[48] in a foul linen cap pulled close to his eyes; and standing upon a form, he did with many deep sighs and abundance of tears lay open his wicked course, his adultery, his hypocrisy, his persecution of God's people here, and especially his pride (as the root of all, which caused God to give him over to his other sinful courses) and contempt of the magistrates. He justified God and the church and the court in all that had been inflicted on him. He declared what power Satan had of him since the casting out of the church; how his presumptuous laying hold of mercy and pardon, before God gave it, did then fail him when the terrors of God came upon him, so as he could have no rest nor could see any issue but utter despair, which had put him divers times upon resolutions of destroying himself had not the Lord in mercy prevented him, even when his sword was ready to have done the execution. Many fearful temptations he met with beside, and in all these his heart shut up in hardness and impenitency as the bondslave of Satan till the Lord, after a long time and great afflictions, had broken his heart and brought him to humble himself before him night and day with prayers and tears till his strength was wasted; and indeed he appeared as a man worn out with sorrow, and yet he could find no peace, therefore he was now come to seek it in this ordinance of God. He spake well, save that his blubbering, etc., interrupted him, and all along he discovered a broken and melting heart, and gave good exhortations to take heed of such vanities and beginnings of evil as had occasioned his fall; and in the

48. A neck band or collar.

end he earnestly and humbly besought the church to have compassion of him, and to deliver him out of the hands of Satan. So accordingly he was received into the church again; and after he came into the court (for the general court began soon after) and made confession of his sin against them, etc., and desired pardon, which the court freely granted him, so far as concerned their private judgment. But for his adultery they would not pardon that for example's sake, nor would restore him to freedom, though they released his banishment and declared the former law against adultery to be of no force; so as there was no law now to touch his life, for the new law against adultery was made since his fact committed.[49] He confessed also in the congregation, that though he was very familiar with that woman,[50] and had gained her affection, etc., yet she withstood him six months against all his solicitations (which he thought no woman could have resisted) before he could overcome her chastity, but being once overcome, she was wholly at his will. And to make his peace the more sound, he went to her husband (being a cooper) and fell down upon his knees before him in the presence of some of the elders and others, and confessed the wrong he had done him, and besought him to forgive him, which he did very freely, and in testimony thereof he sent the captain's wife[51] a token . . .

[November]. Miantonomi, the sachem of Narragansett, came and was met at Dorchester by Captain Gibbons and a guard of twelve musketeers, and well entertained at Roxbury by the governor; but when we came to parley, he refused to treat with us by our Pequot interpreter, and the governor being as resolute as he, refused to use any other

49. The Court of Assistants in Oct. 1631 and the General Court in March 1638 had ruled that adultery is punishable by death. In Oct. 1640 the General Court abrogated the 1631 law and upheld the 1638 law, apparently as a gesture of conciliation to Underhill, because he had committed adultery before March 1638 and was thus no longer liable to the death penalty.

50. Mrs. Joseph Faber; see 5 March 1640, above.

51. Capt. Underhill's wife was Helena, a Dutch woman who had been admitted to the Boston church in 1633.

interpreter, thinking it a dishonor to us to give so much way to them. Whereupon he came from Roxbury to Boston, departing in a rude manner, without showing any respect or sign of thankfulness to the governor for his entertainment, whereof the governor informed the general court, and would show him no countenance nor admit him to dine at our table, as formerly he had done, till he had acknowledged his failing, etc., which he readily did so soon as he could be made to understand it, and did speak with our committees and us by a Pequot maid who could speak English perfectly. But it was conceived by some of the court that he kept back such things as he accounted secrets of state, and that he would carry home in his breast as an injury the strict terms he was put to, for he told us that when our men came to him they were permitted to use their own fashions, and so he expected the same liberty with us. So as he departed and nothing agreed, only the former articles of peace[52] were read to him and allowed by him with this addition, that if any of his men did set traps in our jurisdiction, etc., they should be liable to satisfy all damages, etc. . . .

[December]. About this time there fell out a thing worthy of observation. Mr. Winthrop the younger, one of the magistrates, having many books in a chamber where there was corn of divers sorts, had among them one wherein the Greek testament, the psalms and the common prayer were bound together. He found the common prayer eaten with mice, every leaf of it, and not any of the two other touched, nor any other of his books, though there were above a thousand[53] . . .

Mo. 8 [October]. We received a letter at the general court from the magistrates of Connecticut and New Haven and of Aquiday, wherein

---

52. See 21 Oct. 1636. Since this treaty was made, Miantonomi had lost value in the English colonists' eyes; he had played a modest role in the Pequot War and was now suspected of organizing a new conspiracy. Consequently the English favored Uncas, the Mohegan chief, over Miantonomi and the Narragansetts.

53. The puritanical mouse was actually not quite so discriminating, for fewer than half of the Anglican Prayer Book leaves are nibbled, and then only at the tips of the lower right-hand corners. JW2's volume is now in the possession of the MHS.

they declared their dislike of such as would have the Indians rooted out as being of the cursed race of Ham, and their desire of our mutual accord in seeking to gain them by justice and kindness, and withal to watch over them to prevent any danger by them, etc. We returned answer of our consent with them in all things propounded, only we refused to include those of Aquiday in our answer, or to have any treaty with them.

Mo. 10 [December]. About the end of this month a fishing ship arrived at Isle of Shoals, and another soon after, and there came no more this season for fishing. They brought us news of the Scots entering into England, and the calling of a parliament, and the hope of a thorough reformation, etc., whereupon some among us began to think of returning back to England.[54] Others despairing of any more supply from thence, and yet not knowing how to live there if they should return, bent their minds wholly to removal to the south parts, supposing they should find better means of subsistence there, and for this end put off their estates here at very low rates. These things, together with the scarcity of money, caused a sudden and very great abatement of the prices of all our own commodities. Corn (Indian) was sold ordinarily at three shillings the bushel, a good cow at seven or eight pounds, and some at £5,—and other things answerable, whereby it came to pass that men could not pay their debts, for no money nor beaver were to be had, and he who last year or but three months before was worth £1000, could not now if he should sell his whole estate raise £200, whereby God taught us the vanity of all outward things, etc.[55] . . .

54. By the fall of 1640 Charles I was completely cornered. He had summoned the Short Parliament in April 1640, dissolved it when he could extract no tax money, and during the summer tried unsuccessfully to fight the Scots, who occupied Newcastle and Durham and compelled him to pay tribute. In order to deal with the Scots, the king was forced to summon a new parliament dominated by his critics—the Long Parliament—which assembled on 3 Nov. 1640 and immediately pressed for fundamental reforms.

55. Throughout the 1630s, the influx of new settlers had brought a constant supply of specie and sustained Massachusetts prices, but the reverse flow of migrants in 1640 shrank the local money supply, so that prices fell steeply. In Oct. 1640 the General Court tried to

[February]. The general fear of want of foreign commodities, now our money was gone and that things were like to go well in England, set us on work to provide shipping of our own, for which end Mr. Peter, being a man of a very public spirit and singular activity for all occasions, procured some to join for building a ship at Salem of 300 tons, and the inhabitants of Boston, stirred up by his example, set upon the building another at Boston of 150 tons. The work was hard to accomplish for want of money, etc., but our shipwrights were content to take such pay as the country could make . . .

The court having found by experience that it would not avail by any law to redress the excessive rates of laborers' and workmen's wages, etc. (for being restrained, they would either remove to other places where they might have more, or else being able to live by planting and other employments of their own, they would not be hired at all), it was therefore referred to the several towns to set down rates among themselves. This took better effect, so that in a voluntary way by the counsel and persuasion of the elders and example of some who led the way, they were brought to more moderation than they could be by compulsion. But it held not long.

Upon the great liberty which the king had left the parliament to in England, some of our friends there wrote to us advice to send over some to solicit for us in the parliament, giving us hope that we might obtain much, etc. But consulting about it, we declined the motion for this consideration, that if we should put ourselves under the protection of the parliament we must then be subject to all such laws as they should make, or at least such as they might impose upon us; in which course though they should intend our good, yet it might prove very

---

protect debtors by ordering that property executed for debt should be valued by three judges, one chosen by the creditor, one by the debtor, and the third by the colony marshal (*MR*, 1:307).

prejudicial to us. But upon this occasion the court of assistants being assembled, and advising with some of the elders about some course to serve the providence of God in making use of present opportunity of a ship of our own being ready bound for England, it was thought fit to send some chosen men in her with commission to negotiate for us, as occasion should be offered, both in furthering the work of reformation of the churches there which was now like to be attempted and to satisfy our countrymen of the true cause why our engagements there have not been satisfied this year, as they were wont to be in all former time since we were here planted; and also to seek out some way by procuring cotton from the West Indies or other means that might be lawful, and not dishonorable to the gospel for our present supply of clothing, etc., for the country was like to afford enough for food, etc. The persons designed hereto were Mr. Peter, pastor of the church at Salem, Mr. Weld the pastor of the church of Roxbury, and Mr. Hibbins of Boston.[56] For this end the governor and near all the rest of the magistrates and some of the elders wrote a letter to the church of Salem, acquainting them with our intentions and desiring them to spare their pastor for that service. But the church, not willing to let their pastor go nor yet to give a plain denial to the magistrates' request, wrote an answer by way of excuse, tendering some reasons of their unsatisfiedness about his going, etc. The agitation of this business was soon about the country, whereby we perceived there would be sinister interpretations made of it, and the ship being suddenly to depart, we gave it over for that season.[57]

56. The General Court had discussed and rejected a proposal to send agents to England in Oct. 1640, but reconsidered in Feb. 1641, when Peter, Weld, and Hibbins were appointed. These agents were instructed to solicit money for Harvard College, supplies for the colony, and funds for evangelizing the Indians. Peter was also to negotiate with the Dutch government over English versus Dutch claims to the Connecticut River valley.

57. The three agents finally sailed on 3 Aug. 1641; see below.

Mo. 2. [April] 13, A negro maid, servant to Mr. Stoughton of Dorchester, being well approved by divers years' experience for sound knowledge and true godliness, was received into the church and baptized[58] . . .

There fell out much trouble about this time at Pascataquack. Mr. Knollys[59] had gathered a church of such as he could get, men very raw for the most part, etc. Afterwards there came amongst them one Mr. Larkham,[60] who had been a minister at Northam near Barnstable in England, a man not savouring the right way of church discipline, but being a man of good parts and wealthy, the people were soon taken with him and the greater part were forward to cast off Mr. Knollys their pastor and to choose him, for they were not willing nor able to maintain two officers, so Mr. Knollys gave place to him, and he being thus chosen did soon discover himself. He received into the church all that offered themselves, though men notoriously scandalous and ignorant, so they would promise amendment, and fell into contention with the people and would take upon him to rule all, even the magistrates (such as they were;) so as there soon grew sharp contention between him and Mr. Knollys, to whom the more religious still adhered, whereupon they were divided into two churches. Mr. Knollys and his company excommunicated Mr. Larkham, and he again laid violent hands upon Mr. Knollys. In this heat it began to grow to a tumult, [and] they marched forth towards Mr. Larkham's, one carrying a bible upon a staff for an ensign, and Mr. Knolles with them armed with a pistol.

---

58. We have not identified this African-American woman.

59. The Rev. Hanserd Knollys (1599?–1691) had come to Massachusetts about 1638; suspected of Antinomianism, he moved to New Hampshire. After his fracas with Larkham, he returned to England and became a popular Baptist preacher in London.

60. The Rev. Thomas Larkham (1602–1669) had been deprived of his vicarage in Devon; he came to Dover, N.H. in 1640, but—like Knollys—returned to England in 1642.

The governor and council gave commission to Mr. Bradstreet, one of our magistrates, Mr. Peter and Mr. Dalton,[61] two of our elders, to go thither and to endeavor to reconcile them.[62] They went accordingly, and finding both sides to be in fault, at length they brought matters to a peaceable end. Mr. Larkham was released of his excommunication and Mr. Knollys was discovered to be an unclean person and to have solicited the chastity of two maids, his servants, and to have used filthy dalliance with them, which he acknowledged before the church there and so was dismissed and removed from Pascataquack. This sin of his was the more notorious because the fact, which was first discovered, was the same night after he had been exhorting the people by reasons and from scripture to proceed against Capt. Underhill for his adultery. And it is very observable how God gave up these two and some others who had held with Mrs. Hutchinson in crying down all evidence from sanctification, etc., to fall into these unclean courses, whereby themselves and their erroneous opinions were laid open to the world . . .

A godly woman of the church of Boston,[63] dwelling sometimes in London, brought with her a parcel of very fine linen of great value which she set her heart too much upon, and had been at charge to have it all newly washed and curiously folded and pressed, and so left it in press in her parlor over night. She had a negro maid went into the room very late and let fall some snuff of the candle upon the linen, so as by the morning all the linen was burned to tinder, and the boards underneath, and some stools and a part of the wainscot burned, and never perceived by any in the house, though some lodged in the cham-

---

61. The Rev. Timothy Dalton (1588–1661) had lived in Watertown and Dedham, Mass., and served as minister of the church in Hampton, N.H. from 1639 to his death.

62. Some of the Dover people opposed to Larkham had petitioned the MBC for help, which was the ground for this intervention.

63. Probably Bridget Peirce, a member of the Boston church from 1634, and the wife of the sea captain William Peirce, who was killed at Providence Island in June 1641; see pp. 187–188 below.

ber over head, and no ceiling between. But it pleased God that the loss of this linen did her much good, both in taking off her heart from worldly comforts and in preparing her for a far greater affliction by the untimely death of her husband, who was slain not long after at Isle of Providence.

Mo. 4. [June] 2. The court of elections, Richard Bellingham, Esq., chosen governor.[64]

The parliament of England setting upon a general reformation both of church and state, the Earl of Strafford being beheaded, and the archbishop (our great enemy) and many others of the great officers and judges, bishops and others, imprisoned and called to account,[65] this caused all men to stay in England in expectation of a new world,[66] so as few coming to us, all foreign commodities grew scarce, and our own of no price. The general court [sent] some chosen men into England, to congratulate the happy success there, and to satisfy our creditors of the true cause why we could not make so current payment now as in former years we had done, and to be ready to make use of any opportunity God should offer for the good of the country here, as also to give any advice, as it should be required, for the settling the right form of church discipline there. The men chosen were Mr. Hugh Peter, pastor of the church in Salem, Mr. Thos. Weld, pastor of the church in Roxbury, and Mr. William Hibbins of Boston. There being no ship

64. John Endecott was chosen deputy governor and JW continued as an assistant.

65. Thomas Wentworth, Earl of Strafford, who had been Charles I's principal advisor, was attainted by Parliament on charges of treason and executed in May 1641. William Laud, Archbishop of Canterbury, was imprisoned in the Tower of London in March 1641, and eventually executed in Jan. 1645.

66. During the first seven months after the Long Parliament convened in Nov. 1640, Charles I not only lost his chief ministers but was forced to agree that the present parliament could be dissolved only with its own consent. Lords and Commons joined in dismantling the king's political innovations of the past eleven years, and in Feb. 1641 the House of Commons began debate on the Root and Branch petition asking for the abolition of Episcopacy in the Church of England. But—as JW indicates here—the opening of the revolutionary crisis was by no means as joyful to him as to his fellow Puritans in England.

which was to return right for England, they went to Newfoundland, intending to get a passage from thence in the fishing fleet. They departed hence the 3d of the 6th month [3 August], and with them went one of the magistrates, Mr. John Winthrop, jun.[67] . . .

A church, being gathered at Providence in the West Indies, wrote to our churches complaining of the persecution of their magistrates and others, and desiring our prayers and help from us, which moved the churches and magistrates more willingly to further those who were already resolved and prepared for that Island.[68] Whereupon two small vessels, each of about 30 tons, with divers families and goods so many as they could bestow, 30 men, 5 women, and 8 children, set sail for the Island and touching at Christophers they heard that a great fleet of Spanish ships was abroad, and that it was feared they had taken Providence,[69] so as the master, Mr. Peirce, a godly man and most expert mariner, advised them to return and offered to bear part of the loss. But they not hearkening to him, he replied, Then am I a dead man. And coming to the Island, they marvelled they saw no colors upon the fort nor any boat coming towards them, whereupon he was counselled to drop an anchor. He liked the advice but yet stood on into the harbor, and after a second advice he still went on; but being come within pistol shot of one fort and hailing, and no answer made, he put his bark a stays,[70] and being upon the deck, which was also full of passengers, women and children, and hearing one cry out, they are traversing a piece at us,[71] he threw himself in at the door of the cuddy,[72] and one

---

67. JW2 helped the Massachusetts agents to solicit money and supplies in England, and to recruit faculty members for Harvard College, but his prime mission was to attract English investment in an ironworks project in Massachusetts. He returned to Boston in Sept. 1643.

68. John Humfrey of Salem had been planning for a year to go to Providence Island as governor; see pp. 172–173 above. He was the leader of this expedition.

69. The Spanish captured Providence Island in May 1641, one month before the New England ships arrived.

70. He turned the ship to windward in order to tack out of the harbor.

71. Shifting a gun around to take aim.

72. The ship's galley, located in the stern.

Samuel Wakeman, a member of the church of Hartford, who was sent with goods to buy cotton, cast himself down by him and presently a great shot took them both. Mr. Peirce died within an hour; the other, having only his thighs tore, lived ten days. Mr. Peirce had read to the company that morning (as it fell in course) that in Genesis the last, Lo I die, but God will surely visit you and bring you back;[73] out of which words he used godly exhortations to them. Then they shot from all parts about thirty great shot, besides small, and tore the sails and shrouds but hurt not the bark nor any person more in it. The other vessel was then a league behind. After this the passengers, being ashamed to return, would have been set on shore at Cape Grace de Dios,[74] or Florida, or Virginia, but the seamen would not, and through the wonderful providence of God they came all safe home the 3d of 7ber [3 September] following. This brought some of them to see their error, and acknowledge it in the open congregation, but others were hardened . . .

[June]. Some of the freemen, without the consent of the magistrates or governor, had chosen Mr. Nathaniel Ward to preach at this court, pretending that it was a part of their liberty. The governor (whose right indeed it is, for till the court be assembled the freemen are but private persons) would not strive about it, for though it did not belong to them, yet if they would have it there was reason to yield it to them. Yet they had no great reason to choose him, though otherwise very able, seeing he had cast off his pastor's place at Ipswich and was now no minister by the received determination of our churches.[75] In his

73. Gen. 50:24.

74. Cape Gracios a Dios, on the Central American Caribbean coast at the present border between Honduras and Nicaragua.

75. Ward had retired from his pastorate at Ipswich in 1636 on the grounds of ill health, but after he returned to England in 1647 he took up another pastorate in Essex at the age of 70, and held it until he died in 1652.

sermon he delivered many useful things, but in a moral and political discourse grounding his propositions much upon the old Roman and Grecian governments, which sure is an error for if religion and the word of God makes men wiser than their neighbors, we may better frame rules of government for ourselves than to receive others upon the bare authority of the wisdom, justice, etc. of those heathen commonwealths. Among other things, he advised the people to keep all their magistrates in an equal rank and not give more honor or power to one than to another, which is easier to advise than to prove, seeing it is against the practice of Israel (where some were rulers of thousands, and some but of tens)[76] and of all nations known or recorded. Another advice he gave, that magistrates should not give private advice and take knowledge of any man's cause before it came to public hearing. This was debated after in the general court, where some of the deputies moved to have it ordered. But it was opposed by some of the magistrates upon these reasons: 1. Because we must then provide lawyers to direct men in their causes.[77] 2. The magistrates must not grant out original process, as now they do, for to what end are they betrusted with this but that they should take notice of the cause of the action, that they might either divert the suit if the cause be unjust, or direct it in a right course if it be good. 3. By this occasion the magistrate hath opportunity to end many differences in a friendly way, without charge to the parties or trouble to the court. 4. It prevents many difficulties and tediousness to the court to understand the cause aright. 5. It is allowed in criminal causes, and why not in civil. 6. Whereas it is objected that such magistrate is in danger to be prejudiced, answer, if the

76. JW is referring to Exod. 18:21.

77. JW, though a lawyer himself, had complained in 1624 that there were too many attorneys in England (*WP,* 1:309), and he much preferred the MBC system where the magistrates were the guardians of the law, and in many cases determined guilt or innocence without recourse to juries.

thing be lawful and useful it must not be laid aside for the temptations which are incident to it, for in the least duties men are exposed to great temptations . . .

Mrs. Hutchinson and those of Aquiday island broached new heresies every year. Divers of them turned professed anabaptists, and would not wear any arms and denied all magistracy among christians and maintained that there were no churches since those founded by the apostles and evangelists, nor could any be, nor any pastors ordained, nor seals administered but by such, and that the church was to want these all the time she continued in the wilderness, as yet she was. Her son Francis[78] and her son-in-law Mr. Collins[79] (who was driven from Barbadoes where he had preached a time and done some good, but so soon as he came to her was infected with her heresies) came to Boston, and were there sent for to come before the governor and council. But they refused to come, except they were brought; so the officer led him,[80] and being come (there were divers of the elders present) he was charged with a letter he had written to some in our jurisdiction, wherein he charged all our churches and ministers to be antichristian, and many other reproachful speeches, terming our king, king of Babylon, and sought to possess the people's hearts with evil thoughts of our government and of our churches, etc. Francis Hutchinson did agree with him in some of these, but not resolutely in all; but he had reviled the church of Boston (being then a member of it) calling her a strumpet. They were both committed to prison . . . At the same court Mr. Collins was fined £100 and Francis Hutchinson £50, and to remain in prison till

78. Francis Hutchinson (1620–1643) went to Rhode Island with his parents after his mother's banishment in 1638. He moved with his mother to Long Island in 1642, and was killed with her in an Indian attack in Sept. 1643.

79. William Collins had preached in Gloucestershire, Barbados, and St. Kitts before coming to New England. Settling at Newport, he married Anne, the daughter of Anne and William Hutchinson, and was murdered by the Indians in 1643.

80. Collins. He and Hutchinson were presented to the Quarter Court of 7 Sept. 1641 (*MR*, 1:336).

they gave security for it. We assessed the fines the higher partly that by occasion thereof they might be the longer kept in from doing harm (for they were kept close prisoners) and also because that family had put the country to so much charge in the synod and other occasions to the value of £500 at least: but after, because the winter drew on and the prison was inconvenient, we abated them to £40 and £20. But they seemed not willing to pay any thing. They refused to come to the church assemblies except they were led, and so they came duly. At last we took their own bonds for their fine, and so dismissed them[81] . . .

[September] 15. A great training at Boston two days. About 1200 men were exercised in most sorts of land service;[82] yet it was observed that there was no man drunk though there was plenty of wine and strong beer in the town, not an oath sworn, no quarrel, nor any hurt done.

The parliament in England falling so readily to reform all public grievances, some of our people being then in London preferred a petition to the Lords' house for redress of that restraint which had been put upon ships and passengers to New England, whereupon an order was made that we should enjoy all our liberties, etc., according to our patent, whereby our patent which had been condemned and called in upon an erroneous judgment in a quo warranto, was now implicitly revived and confirmed. This petition was preferred without warrant from our court.[83]

7. [September] 2. A day of thanksgiving was kept in all our churches for the good success of the parliament in England.

---

81. Collins and Hutchinson were freed in Dec. 1641, without paying any part of their fines (*MR*, 1:340, 344).

82. Infantry drill. In 1641 the MBC militia had no cavalry units. There were about 20 militia companies, one for each town, organized into three regiments corresponding to the three counties of Suffolk, Essex, and Middlesex. They drilled eight days per year.

83. In Feb. 1641, seven months before the MBC agents Weld, Peter, and Hibbins reached England, a group of New England shipmasters and merchants petitioned the House of Lords to remove shipping restraints imposed by the Privy Council in 1634 and 1638; the restraints were ordered abolished on 31 March 1641.

This year men followed the fishing so well, that there was about 300,000 dry fish sent to the market.

The lords and gentlemen that had two patents at Pascataquack, finding no means to govern the people there nor to restrain them from spoiling their timber, etc., agreed to assign their interest to us (reserving the greatest part of the propriety of their lands).[84] So commissioners being sent thither, the whole river agreed to come under our jurisdiction under two propositions. 1. If we took them in upon a voluntary submission, then they would have liberty to choose their own magistrates, etc. 2. If we took them in as being within the line of our patent, they would then submit to be as Ipswich and Salem, etc., and would have such liberties for felling timber, etc., as they had enjoyed, etc. and to have courts there as Ipswich and Salem had. And accordingly at the general court in the 3d month next [May 1642] they sent two deputies, who, being members of the church there, were sworn freemen and order made for giving the oath to others at their own court, the like liberty to other courts for ease of the people[85] . . .

[November] 9. Query, whether the following be fit to be published.

The governor, Mr. Bellingham, was married (I would not mention such ordinary matters in our history, but by occasion of some remarkable accidents). The young gentlewoman[86] was ready to be contracted to a friend of his, who lodged in his house, and by his consent had proceeded so far with her, when on the sudden the governor treated with her, and obtained her for himself. He excused it by the strength

84. In 1633 Lord Brooke and Viscount Saye and Sele had sent colonists to the Piscataqua River. After years of squabbling with the other local settlers, five representatives of Lords Brooke and Saye appeared at the MBC General Court in June 1641 and surrendered governmental jurisdiction over Dover and Portsmouth, N.H. to the MBC (*MR*, 1:324).

85. By this action the MBC pushed its territorial limits northward to incorporate the Piscataqua River settlements in what is now southern New Hampshire.

86. Bellingham's bride was Penelope Pelham, sister of Herbert and William Pelham, who arrived in Massachusetts in 1635 at age 16. She joined the Boston church in 1639.

of his affection, and that she was not absolutely promised to the other gentleman. Two errors more he committed upon it. 1. That he would not have his contract published where he dwelt, contrary to an order of court. 2. That he married himself contrary to the constant practice of the country. The great inquest presented him for breach of the order of court, and at the court following, in the 4th month,[87] the secretary[88] called him to answer the prosecution, not thinking it fit he should sit as a judge, when he was by law to answer as an offender. This he took ill, and said he would not go off the bench, except ⟨I did command him⟩ he were commanded[89] . . .

9. [November] 12. A great tempest of wind and rain from the S.E. all the night, as fierce as an hurricane. It continued very violent at N.W. all the day after. Divers boats and one bark were cast away in the harbor, but (which was a wonder to all) no dwelling house blown down, nor any person killed; and the day after it came to S.E. again, and continued all the night with much wind and rain; and thereupon (it being about the new moon) followed the highest tide which we had seen since our arrival here.

The summer past was very cool and wet, so as much Indian corn never ripened, though some stood till the 20th of this month. It was observed that people who fed upon that corn were extraordinarily infected with worms in their bodies all the year following, which in some was well prevented by leaving their bread and feeding upon salt fish . . .

This year there was discovered a very foul sin committed by three

---

87. June 1642, by which time JW had replaced Bellingham as governor.

88. Increase Nowell.

89. There was no MBC statute that required Bellingham to step down from the magistrates' bench when he faced prosecution in the General Court. But compare JW's action in the Hingham case of May-July 1645, below, when he left the magistrates' bench on being criminally accused, and placed himself beneath the bar throughout the court hearing.

persons, who the year following came under censure for the same. The case was thus: One Daniel Fairfield (an half Dutchman) about forty years of age, and his wife a lusty young woman,[90] dwelling at Salem near a farm of Mr. Humfrey (one of the magistrates) who much neglected his children, leaving them among a company of rude servants, two of them being young girls[91] (the eldest not seven) came oft to this Fairfield's house, and were by him abused very often, especially upon the Lord's days and lecture days, by agitation and effusion of seed, and after by entering the body of the elder, as it seemed; for upon search she was found to have been forced, and in this course he continued about two years. These girls were after put to board and school to one Jenkin Davis of Lynn[92] (who had been servant to Mr. Humfrey), a member of the church there and in good esteem for piety and sobriety. His wife being quick with child and scrupulous of having fellowship with her husband in that condition, he was hurried by the strength of lust to abuse the elder of these girls (being then about 9 years of age), but constantly denied any entrance of her body, and continued this wicked course near a year but with much striving against the temptation, so as he would oft entreat his wife when she went forth to carry the children with her, and put up a bill to the elders to pray for one who was strongly tempted to a foul sin.

There was also one John Hudson,[93] a lusty young man, an household servant to Mr. Humfrey, who working sometimes at the farm, the elder girl being there, and having no woman to lodge with, came to bed to him and then he abused her (she was then about eight years of age),

---

90. Fairfield seems to have settled in Salem about 1639, and later moved to Boston. His wife's name was Elizabeth.

91. John Humfrey's two victimized daughters were Dorcas and Sarah; see *MR*, 2:12–13.

92. Jenkin Davis was a carpenter, who became an MBC freeman in 1637; his wife's name was Sarah. After his conviction and punishment, he repented and was reconciled to the Lynn church.

93. Hudson was an unmarried man, unlike Fairfield and Davis.

and after this he did abuse her many times so as she was grown capable of man's fellowship and took pleasure in it.

All this time the girl never discovered any of this wickedness, nor was there any suspicion thereof till her father was gone into England, which was (8.) 26, 41 [26 Oct. 1641]. Then she told her sister (who was newly married)[94] how Fairfield had abused her, and being brought before the governor and examined, she charged them all three, and declared how they used her from time to time. She also accused two of her own brothers to have used such dalliance with her. (They were so young as they could not use any semination, and so were referred to private correction.) Thus was this family secretly polluted, and brake not out till Mr. Humfrey had left the country, which he had plotted two or three years before against the advice of his best friends.

The offenders, being brought to examination, presently confessed all but entrance of her body; and being committed to prison and the judgment of the case referred to the general court, it was a great question what the kind of this sin was, whether sodomy, or rape, or etc., which caused the court to seek to know the mind of God by the help of all elders of the country, both our own, and Plymouth, and Connecticut, New Haven, etc. They took it into consideration divers months, and at last returned different answers. Most of our own agreed in one, viz., that it was a rape, though she consented, in regard she was unripe and not of understanding fit to give consent, and that before God they were guilty of death; but because there was no express law in the word of God for such a sentence, nor any law made and published in the country, they referred it to the wisdom of the court, etc. They agreed also that penetration must necessarily be concluded (if the body of the child be found to have been opened), though the parties deny it. So also if man and woman be taken in such a manner, (as in bed together, or their naked bodies joined, etc.) as in common intendment

94. Ann Humfrey had married William Palmes of Salem.

the act was committed, it is testimony sufficient, for it is not possible to see further . . .

The help of the elders being presented to the general court, held in the 3 month [May] 1642, the court proceeded against the said offenders (Mr. Winthrop being again chosen governor at this court, and Mr. Thomas Flint[95] of Concord newly elected to be an assistant, so as there were now in all nine magistrates). The court was much divided about the sentence. The foulness of the sin, and their long continuance in it, wrought strongly with many to put them to death (specially Fairfield); but after much dispute (and some remaining doubtful) the court agreed upon another sentence. The only reason that saved their lives was that the sin was not capital by any express law of God, but to be drawn only by proportion; nor was it made capital by any law of our own, so as we had no warrant to put them to death, and we had formerly refrained (by the advice of the elders) upon the same ground in a case of rape of a child under 7 by a boy of about 17.[96]

The sentence against Fairfield was that he should be severely whipped at Boston and at Salem, and confined to Boston neck upon pain of death if he went out, etc.; he should have one nostril slit and seared at Boston and the other at Salem, and to wear an halter about his neck visibly all his life, and to die if he attempted the like upon any person, and £40 to Mr. Humfrey.[97]

Jenkin Davis was to be whipped at Boston and Lynn, to wear an halter, and to pay £40 to Mr. Humfrey.[98]

95. Thomas Flint (d. 1653) had been a deputy from Concord in 1638–1641, and served as assistant from 1642 to his death.

96. In 1641 Jonathan Thing, an apprentice in Hampton, N.H., had been severely whipped and fined £20 for raping a young child named Mary Greenfield. But in June 1642 the General Court ruled that in any future case where a man was found guilty of copulation with a girl under 10 years old, he should be put to death (*MR*, 1:317; 2:21).

97. Fairfield wore a noose around his neck, as a symbol that he deserved to be hanged, until 1652, when the General Court allowed him to take it off.

98. Davis was permitted to take off his halter in 1643.

John Hudson to be whipped at Boston and Lynn, and to pay Mr. Humfrey £20 within two years.[99]

This sentence was accordingly executed. The parties received their punishment very patiently, without any striving or complaining (though they had near 40 stripes) and acknowledged their sins to be greater than their punishment, etc.

As people increased, so sin abounded, and especially the sin of uncleanness, and still the providence of God found them out. One [William] Hackett, a servant in Salem, about 18 or 20 years of age, was found in buggery with a cow upon the Lord's day. He was discovered by a woman, who being detained from the public assembly by some infirmity that day and by occasion looking out at her window, espied him in the very act; but being affrighted at it and dwelling alone, she durst not call to him, but at night made it known so as he was apprehended and brought before the magistrate, to whom he confessed the attempt and some entrance, but denied the completing of the fact. The trial was deferred to the general court, and much scruple there was with many because there was but one witness; but in the end the court agreed that his confession of some entrance was sufficient testimony with the woman (for more cannot be proved by testimony); so the major part condemned him to die. The boy remained stiff in his denial, and seemed not affected with the apprehension of death (for he was noted always to have been a very stupid, idle, and ill-disposed boy, and would never regard the means of instruction, either in the church or family); but after his condemnation, divers of the elders and other christians resorting to him, it pleased the Lord so to bless his own ordinances that his hard heart melted. He freely confessed the full completing this foul fact and attempting the like before, with other wickedness he had been guilty of, and fell into much horror of conscience, and after being shut up in an inner room within the prison, his

99. Dorcas Humfrey was also severely corrected.

keeper (a very godly man) hearing him speaking, drew near the wall and perceiving he was praying, attended carefully to hear one, who but a few days before was so ignorant and blockish, to pray now with such understanding and affection, confessing and bewailing his sins, judging himself for them with their due aggravations, justifying the Lord, appealing to his mercy by the death of his son, and pressing him with strong arguments from the word, etc. When the day of execution came, after he had been at the lecture he went to the place of execution sadly and silently, and being up the ladder he said nothing; but the cow (with which he had committed that abomination) being brought forth and slain before him,[1] he brake out into a loud and doleful complaint against himself, bewailed his sinful course of life, his disobedience to his parents, his slighting and despising their instructions and the instructions of his dame, and other means of grace God had offered him, etc. There is no doubt to be made but the Lord hath received his soul to his mercy; but he was not pleased to afford him that measure of peace and comfort as he might be able to hold out to others, lest sinful men in the love of their lusts should set mercy and repentance at too low a rate, and so miss of it when they vainly expect it.

The general court held in the 10th month [December] . . . continued three weeks, and established 100 laws, which were called the Body of Liberties.[2] They had been composed by Mr. Nathaniel Ward (sometime pastor of the church of Ipswich: he had been a minister in England, and formerly a student and practiser in the course of the common law), and had been revised and altered by the court, and sent forth into every town to be further considered of, and now again in this court they were revised, amended, and presented, and so established for three years, by

1. Massachusetts law here heeded the injunction of Lev. 20:15: "And if a man lie with a beast, he shall surely be put to death: and ye shall slay the beast."

2. The colony leaders had been debating whether and how to construct a law code since 1636. Ward's *Body of Liberties* represented a defeat for JW, since he believed that the magistrates ought to enjoy discretionary power in interpreting the law.

that experience to have them fully amended and established to be perpetual.

At this session Mr. Hathorn,[3] one of the deputies and usually one
of their speakers, made a motion to some other of the deputies of
leaving out two of their ancientest magistrates[4] because they were
grown poor, and spake reproachfully of them under that motion. This
coming to Mr. Cotton his knowledge, he took occasion from his text,
the next lecture day, to confute and sharply (in his mild manner) to
reprove such miscarriage, which he termed a slighting or dishonoring
of parents, and told the country that such as were decayed in their
estates by attending the service of the country ought to be maintained
by the country, and not set aside for their poverty, being otherwise so
well gifted, and approved by long experience to be faithful. This public
reproof gave such a check to the former motion as it was never revived
after. Yet by what followed it appeared, that the fire from which it
brake out was only raked up, not quenched, as will be showed anon.

Mr. Hathorn and some others were very earnest to have some certain
penalty set upon lying, swearing, etc., which the deputy[5] and some
other of the magistrates opposed. This gave occasion to some of the
magistrates to prepare some arguments against the course intended of
bringing all punishments to a certainty. The scope of these reasons was
to make good this proposition, viz. All punishments except such as are
made certain in the law of God, or are not subject to variation by merit
of circumstances, ought to be left arbitrary to the wisdom of the judges.[6]

Reason 1. God hath left a pattern hereof in his word, where so few

3. William Hawthorne (1608?–1681) had been a deputy from Salem since 1635, and
became the first Speaker of the House of Deputies in 1644. He was an ancestor of Nathaniel
Hawthorne.

4. Probably JW and Thomas Dudley.

5. John Endecott.

6. This had been JW's position since he first came to Massachusetts, and he continued
to maintain this position in the face of mounting opposition by the deputies and some of
the magistrates. See 18 May 1642, June 1643, and 14 May 1645, below.

penalties are prescribed and so many referred to the judges; and God himself varieth the punishments of the same offences as the offences vary in their circumstances . . .

Reason 2. All punishments ought to be just, and offences varying so much in their merit by occasion of circumstances, it would be unjust to inflict the same punishment upon the least as upon the greatest.

3. Justice requireth that every cause should be heard before it be judged, which cannot be when the sentence and punishment is determined before hand.

4. Such parts and gifts as the word of God requires in a judge were not so necessary, if all punishments were determined beforehand.

5. God hath not confined all wisdom, etc., to any one generation, that they should set rules for all others to walk by.

6. It is against reason that some men should better judge of the merit of a cause in the bare theory thereof than others (as wise and godly) should be able to discern of it pro re nata.[7]

7. Difference of times, places, etc., may aggravate or extenuate some offences.

8. We must trust God, who can and will provide as wise and righteous judgment for his people in time to come as in the present or forepassed times; and we should not attempt the limiting of his providence and frustrating the gifts of others by determining all punishments, etc. . . .

Mo. 11 [January]. Those of Providence, being all anabaptists, were divided in judgment; some were only against baptizing of infants; others denied all magistracy and churches, etc., of which Gorton,[8] who

---

7. As matters actually are.
8. Samuel Gorton (1592?–1677), a self-educated lay preacher and mystic, was one of the most incendiary characters in early New England. A London clothier who migrated in 1637, he was quickly expelled from Plymouth for his heretical religious views. Proceeding to Rhode Island, he joined William and Anne Hutchinson in a revolt against William Coddington at Portsmouth, but Coddington had him whipped and banished in

had lately been whipped at Aquiday, was their instructer and captain. These, being too strong for the other party, provoked them by injuries, so as they came armed into the field, each against other, but Mr. Williams pacified them for the present. This occasioned the weaker party to write a letter under all their hands to our governor and magistrates, complaining of the wrongs they suffered, and desiring aid or, if not that, counsel from us.[9] We answered them that we could not levy any war, etc. without a general court. For counsel we told them, that except they did submit themselves to some jurisdiction, either Plymouth or ours, we had no calling or warrant to interpose in their contentions, but if they were once subject to any, then they had a calling to protect them. After this answer we heard no more from them for a time.

The frost was so great and continual this winter that all the bay was frozen over, so much and so long as the like by the Indians' relation had not been these 40 years, and it continued from the 18th of this month [January] to the 21st of the 12th month [February]; so as horses and carts went over in many places where ships have sailed. Capt. Gibbons and his wife, with divers on foot by them, came riding from his farm at Pullen point right over to Boston, the 17th of the 12th month, when it had thawed so much as the water was above the ice half a foot in some places; and they passed with loads of wood and six oxen from Muddy River to Boston, and when it thawed it removed great rocks of above a ton or more weight, and brought them on shore . . .

At New Haven there was a sow, which among other pigs had one without hair and some other human resemblances, it had also one eye

---

1640. During the next three years Gorton moved around Narragansett Bay, from Providence to Pawtuxet to Shawomet (later renamed Warwick), R.I. For Gorton's challenge to JW in 1643, see below.

9. Thirteen men from Providence sent this petition for help against Gorton, dated 17 Nov. 1641, to the MBC.

blemished just like one eye of a loose fellow in the town, which occasioned him to be suspected, and being examined before the magistrates he confessed the fact, for which, after they had written to us and some other places for advice, they put him to death[10] . . .

[May] 18. The Court of elections was. Mr. Winthrop was again chosen governor,[11] and Mr. Endecott deputy governor. This being done, Mr. Dudley went away, and though he were chosen an assistant, yet he would not accept it. The court sent a magistrate and two deputies to desire him to come to the court, for as a counsellor he was to assist in the general court. The next day he came, and after some excuse he consented to accept the place . . .

A book was brought into the court, wherein the institution of the standing council was pretended to be a sinful innovation.[12] The governor moved to have the contents of the book examined, and then if there appeared cause to inquire after the author. Whereupon it was found to have been made by Mr. Saltonstall,[13] one of the assistants, and by him sent to Mr. Hawthorne (then a deputy of the court) to be tendered to the court if he should approve of it. This discovery being made, the governor moved again that the matter of the book might be considered, but the court could not agree to it except Mr. Saltonstall were first acquit from any censure concerning the said book. In the end, a day or two after when no further proceeding was otherwise like to be had, it was agreed that in regard the court was not jealous of any

10. George Spencer was the "loose fellow" executed at New Haven; his trial is reported in Charles J. Hoadley, ed., *Records of the Colony and Plantation of New Haven, 1638–1649* (Hartford, 1857), pp. 62–69, 72–73.

11. JW has already reported this May 1642 election on p. 196 above.

12. For the initial formation of the Standing Council, see 7 April 1636, above.

13. Richard Saltonstall, Jr. of Ipswich was 33 years old in 1642 and the youngest of the MBC magistrates. In partnership with Stoughton and Bellingham among the magistrates, he criticized JW for assuming too much political power. Saltonstall's manuscript treatise has not survived.

evil intention in Mr. Saltonstall, etc., and that when he did write and deliver it (as was supposed) there was an order in force, which gave liberty to every freeman to consider and deliver their judgments to the next court about such fundamental laws as were then to be established (whereof one did concern the institution and power of the council), therefore he should be discharged from any censure or further inquiry about the same, which was voted accordingly, although there were some expressions in the book which were very unsound, reproachful and dangerous . . .

This summer five ships more were built, three at Boston, and one at Dorchester, and one at Salem.

A cooper's wife of Hingham,[14] having been long in a sad melancholic distemper near to phrensy, and having formerly attempted to drown her child but prevented by God's gracious providence, did now again take an opportunity, being alone, to carry her child aged three years to a creek near her house, and stripping it of the clothes, threw it into the water and mud. But the tide being low, the little child scrambled out, and taking up its clothes came to its mother who was set down not far off. She carried the child again and threw it in so far as it could not get out; but then it pleased God that a young man, coming that way, saved it. She would give no other reason for it but that she did it to save it from misery, and withal that she was assured she had sinned against the Holy Ghost, and that she could not repent of any sin . . .

One Darby Field, an Irishman living about Pascataquack, being accompanied with two Indians, went to the top of the white hill.[15] He

14. Ann Hett, wife of Thomas Hett, was whipped and imprisoned for attempting to kill her son Eliphalet (*RCA*, 2:126). He lived to maturity, married, and had issue.

15. The White Mountains. Field seems to have ascended the Saco River to its source at the base of the Presidential Range, and then climbed to the summit of Mt. Washington, the highest peak (6,288 feet) in New England. Field is reckoned to be the first European to explore the White Mountains, and Mt. Field in the White Mountain National Forest is named for him.

made his journey in 18 days. His relation at his return was, that it was about one hundred miles from Saco,[16] that after 40 miles travel he did, for the most part, ascend, and within 12 miles of the top was neither tree nor grass, but low savins,[17] which they went upon the top of sometimes, but a continual ascent upon rocks, on a ridge between two valleys filled with snow, out of which came two branches of Saco river, which met at the foot of the hill where was an Indian town of some 200 people. Some of them accompanied him within 8 miles of the top, but durst go no further, telling him that no Indian ever dared to go higher, and that he would die if he went. So they staid there till his return, and his two Indians took courage by his example and went with him. They went divers times through the thick clouds for a good space, and within 4 miles of the top they had no clouds, but very cold. The top of all was plain about 60 feet square. On the north side there was such a precipice as they could scarce discern to the bottom. They had neither cloud nor wind on the top, and moderate heat. All the country about him seemed a level, except here and there a hill rising above the rest, but far beneath them. He saw to the north a great water which he judged to be about 100 miles broad, but could see no land beyond it. The sea by Saco seemed as if it had been within 20 miles. He saw also a sea to the eastward, which he judged to be the gulf of Canada: he saw some great waters in parts to the westward, which he judged to be the great lake which Canada river comes out of.[18] He found there much muscovy glass,[19] they could rive[20] out pieces of 40 feet long and

16. If Field climbed Mt. Washington, he would indeed have traveled about 100 miles from Saco on the Maine coast.

17. Small, bushy evergreen shrubs.

18. Presumably the great waters seen by Field were cloud or fog banks in the mountain valleys, but his "discovery" set off speculation that there existed a fabulous inland sea, a vast breeding ground for beaver.

19. Common mica.

20. Tear or wrench. Mica is readily separated into thin sheets.

7 or 8 broad. They brought some stones which they supposed had been diamonds, but they were most crystal.

Mo. 4. [June] 22. In the time of the general court, in a great tempest of thunder and lightning in the evening, the lightning struck the upper sail of the windmill in Boston by the ferry,[21] and shattered it in many pieces, and the boards upon the sides of the mill rived off, the sacks, etc., in the mill set on fire, and the miller[22] being under the mill upon the ground, chopping a piece of board, was struck dead, but company coming in, found him to breathe so they carried him to an house, and within an hour or two he began to stir and strove with such force as six men could scarce hold him down. The next day he came to his senses, but knew nothing of what had befallen him, but found himself very sore on divers parts of his body. His hair on one side of his head and beard was singed, one of his shoes torn off his foot, but his foot not hurt.

At the same general court there fell out a great business upon a very small occasion. Anno 1636, there was a stray sow in Boston, which was brought to Captain Keayne:[23] he had it cried divers times, and divers came to see it, but none made claim to it for near a year. He kept it in his yard with a sow of his own. Afterwards one Sherman's wife,[24] having lost such a sow, laid claim to it, but came not to see it till Captain Keayne had killed his own sow. After being showed the stray sow, and finding it to have other marks than she had claimed her sow

21. This windmill stood on Copp's Hill (first called Windmill Hill) in Boston's North End; at the foot of this hill was the ferry to Charlestown.

22. Probably John Button (1594?–1681), who operated his mill on Copp's Hill for nearly 50 years.

23. Robert Keayne's unsavory reputation for buying cheap and selling dear hurt him badly in the unfolding of this case; see Nov. 1639, above.

24. Elizabeth Sherman (d. 1667), wife of Richard Sherman, a merchant who migrated from Dedham, Essex to Boston in 1634. She took in boarders, including members of the General Court during court sessions in Boston.

by, she gave out that he had killed her sow. By the instigation of one George Story,[25] a young merchant of London who kept in her house (her husband being then in England) and had been brought before the governor upon complaint of Captain Keayne as living under suspicion, she brought the cause to the inferior court at Boston, where upon a full hearing Capt. Keayne was cleared, and the jury gave him £3 for his cost, and he bringing his action against Story and her for reporting about that he had stolen her sow, recovered £20 damages of either of them. Story upon this searcheth town and country to find matter against Captain Keayne about this stray sow, and petitions in Sherman's name to this general court to have the cause heard again, which was granted, and the best part of seven days were spent in examining of witnesses and debating of the cause; and yet it was not determined, for there being nine magistrates and thirty deputies, no sentence could by law pass without the greater number of both, which neither plaintiff nor defendant had, for there were for the plaintiff two magistrates and fifteen deputies, and for the defendant seven magistrates and eight deputies, the other seven deputies stood doubtful[26] . . . The defendant's lawful possession ought to have been preferred to the plaintiff's doubtful title, but the defendant being of ill report in the country for a hard dealer in his course of trading, and having been formerly censured in the court and in the church also by admonition for such offences, carried many weak minds strongly against him. And the truth is, he was very worthy of blame in that kind, as divers others in the country were also in those times, though they were not detected as he was; yet to give

25. Little is known about Story apart from his prominent role in this case.

26. The case now assumed constitutional significance because of this split between the magistrates who favored Keayne and the deputies who favored Sherman. The MBC had decreed in March 1636 (*MR*, 1:170) that no law, order, or sentence could pass without the consent of the majority of magistrates and the majority of deputies. Hence, although Sherman received a majority of all votes (17–15), the General Court dismissed her charges against Keayne.

every man his due, he was very useful to the country both by his hospitality and otherwise. But one dead fly spoils much good ointment.

There was great expectation in the country, by occasion of Story's clamours against him, that the cause would have passed against the captain, but falling out otherwise gave occasion to many to speak unreverently of the court, especially of the magistrates, and the report went that their negative voice had hindered the course of justice and that these magistrates must be put out, that the power of the negative voice might be taken away. Thereupon it was thought fit by the governor and other of the magistrates to publish a declaration of the true state of the cause, that truth might not be condemned unknown[27] . . .

[July]. The *Mary Rose*, which had been blown up and sunk with all her ordnance, ballast, much lead, and other goods,[28] was now weighed and brought to shore by the industry and diligence of one Edward Bendall of Boston.[29] The court gave the owners above a year's time to recover her and free the harbor, which was much damnified by her; and they having given her over and never attempting to weigh her, Edward Bendall made two great tubs, bigger than a butt,[30] very tight and open at one end, upon which were hanged so many weights as would sink it to the ground (600wt). It was let down, the diver sitting in it, a cord in his hand to give notice when they should draw him up, and another cord to show when they should remove it from place to

27. On 15 July 1642 JW wrote a detailed summary of the Sherman-Keayne case (*WP*, 4:349–352), in which he stated that the magistrates had not exercised a negative voice or veto. A year later, he retracted this statement; see June 1643, below.

28. See 27 July 1640, above.

29. Edward Bendall (d. 1659?) came from Southwark, Surrey, in 1630, and operated docks, warehouses, and lighters in Boston harbor. He joined the Boston church in 1631, and baptized a series of children with Puritan names: Freegrace, Reform, Hopefor, Moremercy, and Restore. He supported Anne Hutchinson and was disarmed in 1638. His ingenious tub was an early example of diving bell salvage, but when he applied to the General Court for a patent in 1649, he was refused (*MR*, 2:273).

30. A large cask twice the capacity of a hogshead, holding from 108 to 140 gallons.

place so he could continue in his tub near half an hour, and fasten ropes to the ordnance and put the lead, etc., into a net or tub. And when the tub was drawn up, one knocked upon the head of it, and thrust a long pole under water which the diver laid hold of, and so was drawn up by it; for they might not draw the open end out of water for endangering him, etc. . . .

One Wequash Cook, an Indian living about Connecticut river's mouth, and keeping much at Saybrook with Mr. Fenwick, attained to good knowledge of the things of God and salvation by Christ, so as he became a preacher to other Indians, and labored much to convert them, but without any effect, for within a short time he fell sick, not without suspicion of poison from them, and died very comfortably . . .

Now came over a book of Mr. Cotton's sermons upon the seven vials. Mr. Humfrey had gotten the notes from some who had took them by characters,[31] and printed them in London ⟨he had 300 copies for it⟩, which was a great wrong to Mr. Cotton, and he was much grieved at it for it had been fit he should have perused and corrected the copy before it had been printed.[32]

Mo. 6 [August]. Mr. Weld, Mr. Peter, and Mr. Hibbins, who were sent the last year into England, had procured £500 which they sent over in linen, woollen, and other useful commodities for the country, which, because the stock might be preserved and returned this year for a further supply, were put off together for about eighty pounds profit, and the principal returned by Mr. Stoughton in the next ship . . .

[September] 6. There came letters from divers Lords of the upper house and some 30 of the House of Commons, and others from the ministers there who stood for the independency of churches, to Mr.

---

31. Shorthand.

32. The pirated edition of *The Powring out of the Seven Vials* was published in London in 1642. A second edition was issued in 1645.

Cotton of Boston, Mr. Hooker of Hartford, and Mr. Davenport of New Haven, to call them, or some of them if all could not, to England to assist in the synod there appointed to consider and advise about the settling of church government.[33] Upon this such of the magistrates and elders as were at hand met together, and were most of them of opinion that it was a call of God, yet Mr. Hooker liked not the business, nor thought it any sufficient call for them to go 3,000 miles to agree with three men (meaning those three ministers who were for independency, and did solicit in the parliament, etc.). Mr. Davenport thought otherwise of it, so as the church there set apart a day to seek the Lord in it, and thereupon came to this conclusion, that seeing the church had no other officer but himself, therefore they might not spare him.

Mr. Cotton apprehended strongly a call of God in it, though he were very averse to a sea voyage. But soon after came other letters out of England, upon the breach between the king and parliament, to advise them to stay till they heard further; so this care came to an end[34] . . .

There fell out a very sad accident at Weymouth. One Richard Sylvester, having three small children, he and his wife going to the assembly upon the Lord's day, left their children at home. The eldest was without doors looking to some cattle; the middle-most, being a son about five years old, seeing his father's fowling piece (being a very great one) stand in the chimney, took it and laid it upon a stool, as he

---

33. Parliament had called for a synod to reform the Church of England in Nov. 1641, and began selecting members for this assembly in the spring of 1642. Some of the reformers wanted a Presbyterian system as in Scotland, while others wanted "Independency" or a national system of gathered Congregational churches as in New England. This second group was trying to recruit Cotton, Hooker, and Davenport.

34. In July 1642, the English Civil War began between adherents of Charles I and his enemies in Parliament. A full year later, in July 1643, the Westminster Assembly of Divines—sponsored by Parliament to reform the Church of England—finally convened. Had Cotton and his New England Congregational colleagues come to Westminster, they would have found themselves in a hopeless minority, for the assembly was totally dominated by Presbyterians.

had seen his father do, and pulled up the cock (the spring being weak) and put down the hammer, then went to the other end and blowed in the mouth of the piece, as he had seen his father also do, and with that stirring the piece, being charged, it went off and shot the child into the mouth and through his head. When the father came home he found his child lie dead, and could not have imagined how he should have been so killed but the youngest child (being but three years old, and could scarce speak) showed him the whole manner of it.

There arrived in a small pinnace one Mr. Bennet,[35] a gentleman of Virginia, with letters from many well disposed people of the upper new farms in Virginia to the elders here, bewailing their sad condition for want of the means of salvation and earnestly entreating a supply of faithful ministers, whom upon experience of their gifts and godliness they might call to office, etc. Upon these letters (which were openly read in Boston upon a lecture day), the elders met and set a day apart to seek God in it, and agreed upon three who might most likely be spared, viz., Mr. Phillips of Watertown, Mr. Tompson of Braintree, and Mr. Miller of Rowley,[36] for these churches had each of them two. But Mr. Phillips being not willing to go, Mr. Knolles,[37] his fellow elder, and Mr. Tompson, with the consent of their churches, were sent away. Mr. Miller did not accept the call. The main argument which prevailed with the churches to dismiss them to that work, and with the court to allow and further it, was the advancement of the kingdom of Christ in those parts. We were so far from fearing any loss by parting with such de-

35. Philip Bennett, from Upper Norfolk County in Virginia, carried to Massachusetts a petition signed by 71 people.

36. The Rev. George Phillips had been at Watertown since 1630; the Rev. William Tomson (1598?–1668) had preached at Acomenticus in Maine before coming to Braintree; and the Rev. John Miller (1604–1663) had lived in Dorchester and Roxbury before coming to Rowley.

37. The Rev. John Knowles (1606–1685) had been ordained by the Watertown church in 1640.

sirable men as we looked at them as seed sown, which would bring us in a plentiful harvest, and we accounted it no small honor that God had put upon his poor churches here, that other parts of the world should seek to us for help in this kind . . .

Mo. 7. [September] 1. There came letters from the court at Connecticut, certifying us that the Indians all over the country had combined themselves to cut off all the English, that the time was appointed after harvest, the manner also, they should go by small companies to the chief men's houses by way of trading, etc., and should kill them in the houses and seize their weapons, and then others should be at hand to prosecute the massacre; and that this was discovered by three several Indians, near about the same time and in the same manner; one to Mr. Eaton of New Haven, another to Mr. Ludlow and the third to Mr. Haynes.[38] Their advice to us was, that it was better to enter into war presently,[39] and if we would send 100 men to the river's mouth of Connecticut, they would meet us with a proportionable number.

Upon these letters, the governor called so many of the magistrates as were near, and being met they sent out summons for a general court, to be kept six days after, and in the mean time, it was thought fit, for our safety and to strike some terror into the Indians, to disarm such as were within our jurisdiction. Accordingly we sent men to Cutshamekin at Braintree, to fetch him and his guns, bows, etc., which was done, and to disarm Passaconamy,[40] who lived by Merrimack . . .

Mo. 7. [September] 8. The general court being assembled, we considered of the letters and other intelligence from Connecticut, and although the thing seemed very probable, yet we thought it not sufficient

38. Theophilus Eaton was governor of New Haven; Roger Ludlow and John Haynes were deputy governor and governor of Connecticut.

39. Immediately.

40. Passaconaway was sachem of the Pennacooks, who lived along the Merrimack River in New Hampshire.

ground for us to begin a war, for it was possible it might be otherwise and that all this might come out of the enmity which had been between Miantonomi and Onkus,[41] who continually sought to discredit each other with the English. Besides we found ourselves in very ill case for war, and if we should begin, we must then be forced to stand continually upon our guard, and to desert our farms and business abroad, and all our trade with the Indians, which things would bring us very low; and besides, if upon this intelligence we should kill any of them or lose any of our own, and it should be found after to have been a false report, we might provoke God's displeasure and blemish our wisdom and integrity before the heathen . . .

According to these considerations, we returned answer to Connecticut, and withal we sent two men with two interpreters, an Englishman and an Indian, to Miantonomi, to let him know what intelligence we had of his drawing the rest of the Indians into a confederation against us, and to desire him to come by such a time to give us satisfaction . . .

When he came, the court was assembled, and before his admission we considered how to treat with him (for we knew him to be a very subtle man). Being called in, and mutual salutations passed, he was set down at the lower end of the table, over against the governor, and had only two or three of his counsellors, and two or three of our neighboring Indians, such as he desired, but would not speak of any business at any time before some of his counsellors were present, alleging that he would have them present, that they might bear witness with him at his return home of all his sayings.

In all his answers he was very deliberate and showed good understanding in the principles of justice and equity, and ingenuity withal. He demanded that his accusers might be brought forth . . . He gave

41. Uncas was sachem of the Mohegan Indians and lived on the Pequot River near Norwich, Conn.

divers reasons why we should hold him free of any such conspiracy, and why we should conceive it was a report raised by Uncas, etc., and therefore offered to meet Uncas at Connecticut, or rather at Boston, and would prove to his face his treachery against the English, etc. We spent the better part of two days in treating with him, and in conclusion he did accommodate himself to us to our satisfaction . . .

When we should go to dinner, there was a table provided for the Indians to dine by themselves, and Miantonomi was left to sit with them. This he was discontented at, and would eat nothing till the governor sent him meat from his table. So at night, and all the time he staid, he sat at the lower end of the magistrate's table. When he departed, we gave him and his counsellors coats and tobacco, and when he came to take his leave of the governor and such of the magistrates as were present, he returned and gave his hand to the governor again, saying that was for the rest of the magistrates who were absent.

The court being adjourned for a few days, there came letters from Connecticut, certifying us of divers insolencies of the Indians, which so confirmed their minds in believing the former report as they were now resolved to make war upon the Indians, and earnestly pressing us to delay no longer to send forth our men to join with them, and that they thought they should be forced to begin before they could hear from us again.[42]

Upon receipt of these letters, the governor assembled such of the magistrates and deputies as were at hand, and divers of the elders also, and in the end concluded, 1. That all these informations might arise from a false ground, and out of the enmity which was between the Narragansett and Monhigen. 2. Being thus doubtful, it was not a sufficient ground for us to war upon them. And accordingly letters were sent back to our brethren at Connecticut, to acquaint them with our

42. The Connecticut General Court was feverishly preparing in Aug.-Sept. 1642 for war; see *CR*, 1:73–75.

opinions, and to dissuade them from going forth, alleging how dishonorable it would be to us all that, while we were upon treaty with the Indians, they should make war upon them. Upon receipt of this our answer, they forbare to enter into war but (it seemed) unwillingly, and as not well pleased with us.

Although we apprehended no danger, yet we continued our military watches till near the end of 8ber [October], and restored the Indians all their arms we had taken from them: for although we saw it was very dangerous to us that they should have guns, etc., yet we saw not in justice how we could take them away, seeing they came lawfully by them (by trade with the French and Dutch for the most part) and used them only for killing of fowl and deer, etc., except they brought themselves into the state of an enemy, therefore we thought it better to trust God with our safety than to save ourselves by unrighteousness . . .

This court also took order that every town should be furnished with powder out of the common store, paying for it in country commodities; likewise for muskets, and for military watches, and alarms, etc. Presently upon this, there arose an alarm in the night upon this occasion. (7.) [September] 19. A man, travelling late from Dorchester to Watertown lost his way, and being benighted and in a swamp about 10 of the clock, hearing some wolves howl and fearing to be devoured of them, he cried out help, help. One that dwelt within hearing, over against Cambridge, hallooed to him. The other still cried out, which caused the man to fear that the Indians had gotten some English man and were torturing him, but not daring to go to him he discharged a piece two or three times. This gave the alarm to Watertown, and so it went as far as Salem and Dorchester, but about one or two of the clock no enemy appearing, etc., all retired but the watch.

At this court also, four of Providence, who could not consort with Gorton and that company and therefore were continually injured and molested by them, came and offered themselves and their lands, etc., to us and were accepted under our government and protection.[43] This we did partly to rescue these men from unjust violence, and partly to draw in the rest in those parts either under ourselves or Plymouth, who now lived under no government but grew very offensive, and the place was likely to be of use to us, especially if we should have occasion of sending out against any Indians of Narragansett and likewise for an outlet into the Narragansett Bay, and seeing it came without our seeking and would be no charge to us, we thought it not wisdom to let it slip[44] . . .

The sudden fall of land and cattle, and the scarcity of foreign commodities, and money, etc., with the thin access of people from England, put many into an unsettled frame of spirit, so as they concluded there would be no subsisting here, and accordingly they began to hasten away, some to the West Indies, others to the Dutch, at Long Island, etc., and others back for England . . . Much disputation there was about liberty of removing for outward advantages, and all ways were sought for an open door to get out at; but it is to be feared many crept out at a broken wall. For such as come together into a wilderness where are nothing but wild beasts and beastlike men, and there confederate together in civil and church estate, whereby they do implicitly at least bind themselves to support each other, and all of them that society, whether civil or sacred, whereof they are members, how they can break from this without free consent, is hard to find, so as may satisfy a tender or good conscience in time of trial. Ask thy conscience, if thou wouldst have plucked up thy stakes and brought thy family 3000 miles,

43. The four men from Providence, R.I. were William Arnold, Robert Cole, William Carpenter, and Benedict Arnold (*MR*, 2:26). Cole had been repeatedly punished for drunkenness when a resident of Massachusetts in the 1630s. Benedict Arnold was an ancestor of the revolutionary soldier and traitor.

44. The MBC was reaching 20 miles beyond its chartered limits in order to get at Samuel Gorton; for the outcome of this policy, see Sept.-Oct. 1643, below.

if thou hadst expected that all or most would have forsaken thee there. Ask again what liberty thou hast towards others which thou likest not to allow others towards thyself; for if one may go, another may, and so the greater part, and so church and commonwealth may be left destitute in a wilderness, exposed to misery and reproach, and all for thy ease and pleasure.[45]

Nine bachelors commenced at Cambridge;[46] they were young men of good hope, and performed their acts so as gave good proof of their proficiency in the tongues and arts. (8.) [October] 5. The general court had settled a government or superintendency over the college, viz., all the magistrates and elders over the six nearest churches and the president, or the greatest part of these. Most of them were now present at this first commencement, and dined at the college with the scholars' ordinary commons, which was done of purpose for the students' encouragement, etc., and it gave good content to all.

At this commencement, complaint was made to the governors of two young men of good quality, lately come out of England, for foul misbehavior in swearing and ribaldry speeches, etc., for which, though they were adulti,[47] they were corrected in the college and sequestered, etc., for a time.

[October] 6. Here came in a French shallop with some 14 men, whereof one was La Tour his lieutenant. They brought letters from La Tour to the governor, full of compliments and desire of assistance from us against Monsieur D'Aulnay.[48] They stayed here about a week and

45. For another eloquent expression of JW's deep and increasing commitment to New England, see his undated letter to JW2 (*WP*, 4:366–367).

46. The first commencement at Harvard College took place on 23 Sept. 1642. Seven of these young men went to England to join the Puritan cause—including JW's talented nephew George Downing (1623–1684); see pp. 285–286 below.

47. Over 18 years old.

48. In 1642 Charles de la Tour and Charles d'Aulnay each claimed to rule Acadia in the name of the French crown; they maintained rival forts on the Bay of Fundy. La Tour, being the weaker, had sent a Protestant envoy to Massachusetts in Nov. 1641, and now he was making a further effort to enlist the support of the MBC against d'Aulnay.

were kindly entertained, and though they were papists yet they came to our church meeting; and the lieutenant seemed to be much affected to find things as he did, and professed he never saw so good order in any place. One of the elders gave him a French testament with Marlorat's notes, which he kindly accepted, and promised to read it[49] . . .

8. *[October] 18.* All the elders met at Ipswich; they took into consideration the book which was committed to them by the general court,[50] and were much different in their judgments about it, but at length they agreed upon this answer . . . They distinguished between a standing council invested with a kind of transcendent authority beyond other magistrates, or else any kind of standing council distinct from other magistrates; the former they seem implicitly to disallow; the latter they approve as necessary for us, not disproportionable to our estate nor of any dangerous consequence for disunion among the magistrates or factions among the people, which were the arguments used by the author against our council. Lastly, they declare their present thoughts about the moulding and perfecting of a council in four rules.

1. That all the magistrates, by their calling and office together with the care of judicature, are to consult for the provision, protection, and universal welfare of the commonwealth.

2. Some select men taken out from the assistants, or other freemen being called thereunto, be in especial to attend by way of council for the provision, protection, and welfare of the commonwealth.

3. This council, as counsellors, have no power of judicature.

4. In cases of instant danger to the commonwealth, in the interim before a general court can be called (which were meet to be done with all speed), what shall be consented unto and concluded by this council

49. By giving La Tour's lieutenant a Biblical commentary written by the Huguenot theologian Augustin Marolet de Pasquier, the MBC leaders were evidently hoping to convert La Tour's party to Protestantism. For the next stage in this diplomatic adventure, see 12 June 1643, below.

50. Richard Saltonstall's critique of the Standing Council; see 18 May 1642, above.

or the major part of them, together with the consent of the magistrates or the major part of them, may stand good and firm till the general court.[51]

9. *[November] 7.* Some of our merchants sent a pinnace to trade with La Tour in St. John's river. He welcomed them very kindly, and wrote to our governor letters very gratulatory for his lieutenant's entertainment, etc., and withal a relation of the state of the controversy between himself and Monsieur D'Aulnay. In their return they met with D'Aulnay at Pemaquid, who wrote also to our governor and sent him a printed copy of the arrest against La Tour,[52] and threatened us that if any of our vessels came to La Tour, he would make prize of them. . . .

The three ministers which were sent to Virginia, viz., Mr. Tompson, Mr. Knowles, and Mr. James from New Haven,[53] departed (8) [October] 7 . . . and had much foul weather, so as with great difficulty and danger they arrived safe in Virginia. Here they found very loving and liberal entertainment, and were bestowed in several places, not by the governor,[54] but by some well disposed people who desired their company . . .

The House of Commons made an order in our favor to this effect, viz. Whereas the plantations in New England have, by the blessing of Almighty God, had good and prosperous success without any charge to this state, and are now likely to prove very happy for the propagation of the gospel in those parts, and very beneficial and commodious for

---

51. The clergy were taking a middle ground between Saltonstall and JW, approving the need for a Standing Council but denying that this council had authority separate from or superior to that of the General Court. Their decision probably pleased Saltonstall and the deputies more than it pleased JW, especially since their second rule opened membership in the Standing Council to non-magistrates.

52. In 1640 d'Aulnay had obtained an order from the French government to arrest La Tour and seize his possessions.

53. Thomas James substituted for John Miller of Rowley; see Sept. 1642, above.

54. Sir William Berkeley, the anti-Puritan royal governor of Virginia, got the Virginia Assembly to ban all nonconformist ministers on 2 March 1643.

this kingdom and nation, the commons now assembled in parliament do ordain that all merchandizes, goods exported, etc., into New England to be spent, used or employed there, or being of the growth of that country, shall be free of all custom, etc., in England and New England, and all other ports, until this house shall take further order[55] . . .

Mo. 3. [May] 10. Our court of elections was held, when Mr. Ezekiel Rogers,[56] pastor of the church in Rowley, preached . . . In his sermon he described how the man ought to be qualified whom they should choose for their governor, yet dissuaded them earnestly from choosing the same man twice together, and expressed his dislike of that with such vehemency as gave offence. But when it came to trial, the former governor, Mr. Winthrop, was chosen again, and two new magistrates, Mr. William Hibbins and Mr. Samuel Simons.[57]

At this court came the commissioners from Plymouth, Connecticut and New Haven. Our court chose a committee to treat with them. These coming to consultation encountered some difficulties, but being all desirous of union and studious of peace, they readily yielded each to other in such things as tended to common utility, etc., so as in some two or three meetings they lovingly accorded upon these ensuing articles, which, being allowed by our court and signed by all the commissioners, were sent to be also ratified by the general courts of other jurisdictions.[58]

---

55. This ordinance of 10 March 1643 was particularly generous because Parliament was casting about for additional sources of revenue to meet the cost of fighting Charles I.

56. Rogers had been minister at Rowley St. Peter, Yorkshire for 17 years before emigrating to Massachusetts in 1638; he and his followers founded Rowley, Mass. in 1639.

57. The May 1643 General Court also altered the oath taken by the governor and magistrates, omitting the pledge to bear allegiance "to our sovereign Lord King Charles," since the king had made war upon Parliament.

58. JW is describing the formation of the United Colonies of New England, generally known as the New England Confederation, the earliest example of intercolonial union

Those of Sir Ferdinando Gorges his province, beyond Pascataquack, were not received nor called into the confederation because they ran a different course from us both in their ministry and civil administration[59] . . .

The Articles of Confederation between the plantations under the government of the Massachusetts, the plantations under the government of New Plymouth, the plantations under the government of Connecticut and the government of New Haven, with the plantations in combination therewith:[60]

Whereas we all came into these parts of America with one and the same end and aim, namely, to advance the kingdom of our Lord Jesus Christ, and to enjoy the liberties of the gospel in purity with peace: and whereas we live encompassed with people of several nations and strange languages, which hereafter may prove injurious to us or our posterity; and for as much as the natives have formerly committed sundry insolences and outrages upon several plantations of the English, and have of late combined themselves against us, and seeing by reason of the sad distractions in England (which they have heard of) and by which they know we are hindered both from that humble way of seek-

---

among the English colonies in America. The articles establishing the New England Confederation were signed on 19 May 1643.

59. The settlements in Rhode Island founded by Roger Williams, by the Antinomians, and by Samuel Gorton were likewise deliberately excluded from the confederation.

60. The New England Confederation was essentially a military alliance against the Indians, the Dutch, and the French, in which the four partners preserved their internal independence while cooperating closely on diplomacy and warfare. The commissioners from the four colonies functioned as ambassadors from independent states, and their presiding officer (clause 7) had no executive authority. The key provision, apparently much debated, was clause 6, which permitted action by the Confederation when only six of the eight commissioners favored it; thus Massachusetts could be committed to action by her three smaller neighbors. Massachusetts was, however, clearly the senior partner. In clause 5, she supplied 43% of the manpower in any fighting, and in clause 6, the commissioners came to Boston for two of every five meetings. JW served as the first president.

ing advice, and reaping those comfortable fruits of protection, which at other times we might well expect; we therefore do conceive it our bounden duty, without delay, to enter into a present consociation amongst ourselves for mutual help and strength in all future concernment, that, as in nation and religion, so in other respects, we be and continue one, according to the tenor and true meaning of the ensuing articles:

1. Wherefore it is fully agreed and concluded between the parties above named that they all be, and henceforth be called by the name of the United Colonies of New England.

2. These united colonies, for themselves and their posterities, do jointly and severally hereby enter into a firm and perpetual league of friendship and amity, for offence and defence, mutual advice and succor upon all just occasions, both for preserving and propagating the truth and liberties of the gospel and for their own mutual safety and welfare.

3. It is further agreed that the plantations which at present are, or hereafter shall be settled within the limits of the Massachusetts shall be forever under the government of the Massachusetts; and that Plymouth, Connecticut, and New Haven shall each of them in all respects have like peculiar jurisdiction and government within their limits . . .

4. It is also by these confederates agreed that the charge of all just wars shall both in men and provisions and all other disbursements be borne by all the parts of this confederation in different proportions, according to their different abilities[61] . . .

5. It is further agreed that if any of these jurisdictions, or any plantation under or in combination with them, be invaded by any enemy

61. Each of the four colonies was expected to contribute to the confederation according to the size of its population; the adult males, aged 16–60, were to be enumerated from time to time.

whatsoever, upon notice and request, the rest of the confederates, without any further notice or expostulation, shall forthwith send aid to the confederate in danger; the Massachusetts one hundred men sufficiently armed and provided for such a service and journey, and each of the rest 45 men so armed and provided;[62] or any less number, if less be required, according to this proportion . . .

6. It is also agreed that for the managing and concluding of all affairs peculiar to and concerning the whole confederation, commissioners shall be chosen by and out of each of these four jurisdictions, viz., two for the Massachusetts, two for Plimouth, two for Connecticut, and two for New Haven, all in church fellowship with us, which shall bring full power from their several general courts respectively to hear, examine, weigh, and determine all affairs of war or peace, leagues, aids, charges, and numbers of men for war and all things of like nature which are the proper concomitants or consequents of such a confederation for amity, offence and defence, not intermeddling with the government of any of the jurisdictions, which by the 3d article is preserved entirely to themselves. But if those eight commissioners when they meet shall not agree, yet it is concluded that any six of the eight agreeing, shall have power to settle and determine the business in question. It is further agreed, that these eight commissioners shall meet once every year (besides extraordinary meetings according to the 5th article) to consider, treat, and conclude of all affairs belonging to this confederation, which meeting shall ever be the first Thursday in 7ber. [September]

7. It is further agreed, that at each meeting of these eight commissioners, whether ordinary or extraordinary, they all, or any six of them agreeing as before, may choose their president out of themselves, whose office and work shall be to take care and direct for order and a comely

62. After a census was taken in each colony, a new ratio was established in Sept. 1643: 150 men from Massachusetts, 30 from Connecticut, 30 from Plymouth, and 25 from New Haven.

carrying on of all proceedings in their present meeting, but he shall be invested with no such power or respect, as by which he shall hinder the propounding or progress of any business, or any way cast the scales otherwise than in the preceding articles is agreed.

8. It is also agreed that the commissioners for this confederation hereafter at their meetings do endeavor to frame and establish agreements and orders in general cases of a civil nature wherein all the plantations are interested for preserving peace amongst themselves, and preventing as much as may be all occasions of war or differences with others . . .

9. And for that the justest wars may be of dangerous consequence, especially to the smaller plantations in these united colonies, it is agreed, that [none of the members] shall at any time hereafter begin, undertake, or engage themselves or this confederation, or any part thereof, in any war whatsoever (sudden exigencies with the necessary consequences thereof excepted) without the consent and agreement of the aforenamed eight commissioners, or at least six of them . . .

11. It is further agreed that if any of the confederates shall hereafter break any of these present articles, or be otherway injurious to any one of the other jurisdictions, such breach of agreement or injury shall be duly considered and ordered by the commissioners for the other jurisdictions, that both peace and this present confederation may be entirely preserved without violation.

12. Lastly, this perpetual confederation and the several articles and agreements thereof being read and seriously considered both by the general court for the Massachusetts and the commissioners for the other three, were subscribed presently by the commissioners, all save those of Plymouth, who for want of sufficient commission from their general court deferred their subscription till the next meeting, and then they subscribed also, and were to be allowed by the general courts of the several jurisdictions, which accordingly was done, and certified at the next meeting held at Boston, (7) [September] 7, 1643.

4. [June] 12. Mr. La Tour[63] arrived here in a ship of 140 tons, and 140 persons. The ship came from Rochelle,[64] the master and his company were protestants. There were two friars and two women sent to wait upon La Tour his lady. They came in with a fair wind, without any notice taken of them. They took a pilot out of one of our boats at sea, and left one of their men in his place. Capt. Gibbons' wife and children passed by the ship as they were going to their farm, but being discovered to La Tour by one of his gentlemen who knew her, La Tour manned out a shallop, which he towed after him to go speak with her. She seeing such a company of strangers making towards her, hastened to get from them, and landed at the Governor's Garden.[65] La Tour landed presently after her, and there found the governor and his wife, and two of his sons, and his son's wife,[66] and after mutual salutations he told the governor the cause of his coming, viz. that this ship being sent him out of France, D'Aulnay his old enemy had so blocked up the river to his fort at St. John's, with two ships and a galliot,[67] as his ship could not get in, whereupon he stole by in the night in his shallop, and was come to crave aid to convey him into his fort. The governor answered that he could say nothing to it till he had conferred with other of the magistrates; so after supper he went with him to Boston in La Tour's boat, having sent his own boat to Boston to carry home Mrs.

63. Charles de la Tour, who had operated since 1635 as the French lieutenant general in Acadia, was in grave difficulty in June 1643. His rival Charles d'Aulnay, who also claimed to govern French Acadia, had razed La Tour's outpost at Cape Sable on the southern tip of Nova Scotia and was now blockading La Tour's fort on the St. John River in present New Brunswick. La Tour's wife (see 17 Sept. 1644, below) had gone to France and obtained for him a new commission, a warship named the *Saint-Clement*, and some soldiers, but La Tour was not strong enough to break d'Aulnay's blockade without help from Massachusetts. Hence this visit.

64. La Rochelle, the French seaport and Huguenot stronghold.

65. Governor's Island, in the middle of Boston harbor, was owned by JW; he had a vineyard and orchard there.

66. JW, his wife Margaret, his sons Adam and Samuel, and Adam's wife Elizabeth were all on the island.

67. A small oared galley.

Gibbons. Divers boats having passed by him had given notice hereof to Boston and Charlestown, the towns betook them to their arms, and three shallops with armed men came forth to meet the governor and to guard him home. But here the Lord gave us occasion to take notice of our weakness, etc., for if La Tour had been ill minded towards us, he had such an opportunity as we hope neither he nor any other shall ever have the like again; for coming by our castle and saluting it, there was none to answer him, for the last court had given order to have the Castle Island deserted, a great part of the work being fallen down, etc., so as he might have taken all the ordnance there. Then, having the governor and his family and Captain Gibbons' wife, etc., in his power, he might have gone and spoiled Boston, and having so many men ready, they might have taken two ships in the harbor and gone away without danger or resistance, but his neglecting this opportunity gave us assurance of his true meaning. So being landed at Boston, the governor with a sufficient guard brought him to his lodging at Captain Gibbons'. This gave further assurance that he intended us no evil, because he voluntarily put his person in our power. The next day the governor called together such of the magistrates as were at hand and some of the deputies, and propounding the cause to them, and La Tour being present and the captain of his ship, etc., he showed his commission, which was fairly engrossed in parchment under the hand and seal of the Vice Admiral of France. Upon this it appeared to us that notwithstanding the news which D'Aulnay had sent to our governor the last year, whereby La Tour was proclaimed a rebel, etc., yet he stood in good terms with the state of France. And accordingly we answered him that we would allow him a free mercate,[68] he might hire any ships which lay in our harbor, etc. This answer he was very well satisfied

68. The opportunity to make any deal he could. In effect, JW and his colleagues were bypassing the newly constituted New England Confederation by permitting La Tour to recruit ships and men in Boston without official sanction from the MBC.

with and took very thankfully; he also desired leave to land his men that they might refresh themselves, which was granted him so they landed in small companies, that our women, etc., might not be affrighted by them. This direction was duly observed.

But the training day at Boston falling out the next week, and La Tour having requested that he might be permitted to exercise his soldiers on shore, he landed 40 men in their arms (they were all shot).[69] They were brought into the field by our train band, consisting of 150, and in the forenoon they only beheld our men exercise. When they had dined (La Tour and his officers with our officers, and his soldiers invited home by the private soldiers), in the afternoon they were permitted to exercise and all ours stood and beheld them. They were very expert in all their postures and motions . . .

Our governor and others in the town entertained La Tour and his gentlemen with much courtesy, both in their houses and at table. La Tour came duly to our church meetings, and always accompanied the governor to and from thence. Those who engrossed the ships,[70] understanding his distress, and the justice of his cause, and the magistrates' permission, were willing to be entertained[71] by him.

But the rumor of these things soon spreading through the country, were diversely apprehended not only by the common sort, but also by the elders, whereof some in their sermons spoke against their entertainment, and the aid permitted them. Divers also wrote to the governor, laying before him great dangers, others charging sin upon the conscience in all these proceedings.[72] Also, the masters and others, who

69. Discharged.
70. Contracted (with La Tour) for the ships.
71. Maintained.
72. Endecott, Thomas Gorges, and Bradstreet all wrote to JW, protesting his support of La Tour (*WP*, 4:394–395, 396, 412–413). But the strongest surviving protest was a letter signed by Saltonstall and six other leaders from Essex County, on 14 July 1643 (*WP*, 4:397–401), the day that La Tour sailed from Boston with four New England ships and 70 New England soldiers.

were to go in the ships, desired advice about their proceedings, etc. whereupon the governor appointed another meeting, to which all the near magistrates and deputies and the elders also were called, and there the matter was debated upon these heads.

1. Whether it were lawful for Christians to aid idolaters, and how far we may hold communion with them?

2. Whether it were safe for our state to suffer him to have aid from us against D'Aulnay? . . .

Argument [against the first question]. By aiding papists, we advance and strengthen popery. Answer. Such aid may as well work to the weakening of popery by winning some of them to the love of the truth, as hath sometimes fallen out, and sometimes by strengthening one part of them against another they may both be the more weakened in the end.

For the 2d question, whether it be safe, etc., the arguments on the negative part were these. 1. Papists are not to be trusted, seeing it is one of their tenets that they are not to keep promise with heretics. Answer. In this case we rely not upon their faith but their interest, it being for their advantage to hold in with us, we may safely trust them . . .

[Another negative argument:] Solomon tells us, that he that meddleth with a strife which belongs not to him, takes a dog by the ear, which is very dangerous.[73] Answer. This is a strife which doth belong to us, both in respect of La Tour seeking aid of us in his distress, and also in respect it so much concerns us to have D'Aulnay subdued or weakened.

[Another negative argument:] It is not safe to permit this aid to go from us, especially without advice of the general court. Answer. For the general court, it could not have been assembled under fourteen days, and such delay might have lost the opportunity of relieving him, or it might have put him upon some dangerous design of surprising

---

73. Prov. 26:17.

our ships, etc. Besides, if the court had been assembled, we knew they would not have given him aid without consent of the commissioners of the other colonies, and for a bare permission, we might do it without the court.

[Another negative argument:] We hear only one party, we should as well hear the other, otherwise we deal not judicially and perhaps may aid a man in an unjust quarrel. Answer. We heard formerly D'Aulnay's allegations against La Tour, and notwithstanding all that, La Tour his cause appears just; for they being both the subjects of the same prince, the ship coming by permission from their prince's authority, D'Aulnay ought to permit him to enter peaceably . . .

The arguments on the affirmative part [to the first question] are these. 1. By the royal law, thou shalt love thy neighbor as thyself. If our neighbor be in distress, we ought to help him without any respect to religion or other quality; but an idolater in distress is our neighbor, as appears by that parable, Luke 10, where it is plainly concluded, that the Samaritan was neighbor to the distressed traveller, and our Saviour bids the lawyer, being a Jew, to do likewise, that is, even to a Samaritan, if in distress.[74] 2. Argument out of Gal. 6. 10. Do good to all, but specially to the household of faith, by which it appears that under all, he includes such as were not believers, and those were heathen idolaters, and if we must do good to such, we must help them in distress. 3. We are exhorted to be like our Heavenly Father in doing good to the just and unjust, that is to all, as occasion is offered. 4. We may hold some kind of communion with idolaters and the Jews were not forbidden to trade with the heathen in Nehemiah's time, so it were not on the Sabbath[75] . . .

To the second question, the arguments on the affirmative part were these. 1. D'Aulnay is a dangerous neighbor to us which, in regard of

74. Luke 10:25–37.
75. See Neh. 13:15–22.

our own safety, lays a necessity upon us of aiding La Tour, and aiding him so as he may subsist and be able to make good his place against his enemy. 2. La Tour being in urgent distress, and therefore as our neighbor to be relieved, if it be well done of us, we may trust in God. 3. It will be no wisdom for D'Aulnay to begin with us, for he knows how much stronger we are than he in men and shipping . . .

The governor by letters informed the rest of the commissioners of the united colonies of what had passed about La Tour, [explaining why] there would have been no need of advice in the case, for . . . we doubted not but we might safely give him such answer as we did, without further trouble to the country or delay to him.[76]

The sow business[77] not being yet digested in the country, . . . the plaintiff (or rather one G. Story her solicitor) being of an unsatisfied spirit, and animated or at least too much countenanced by some of the court, preferred a petition at the court of elections[78] for a new hearing, and this being referred to the committee for petitions, it was returned that the greater part of them did conceive the cause should be heard again, and some others in the court declared themselves of the same judgment, which caused others to be much grieved to see such a spirit in godly men, that neither the judgment of near all the magistrates, nor the concurrence of the elders and their mediation, nor the loss of time and charge, nor the settling of peace in court and country could prevail with them to let such a cause fall (as in ordinary course of justice it ought), as nothing could be found in, by any one testimony, to be of criminal nature, nor could the matter of the suit, with all damages, have amounted to forty shillings. But two things appeared to carry men on in this course as it were in captivity. One was, the deputies stood only

76. As JW's presentation of the debate over La Tour indicates, he was strongly in favor of aiding him. For the next chapter in this story, see 14 July 1643, below.

77. Elizabeth Sherman and George Story, plaintiffs, versus Robert Keayne, defendant. See 22 June 1642, above.

78. In May 1643.

upon this, that their towns were not satisfied in the cause (which by the way shows plainly the democratical spirit which acts our deputies, etc.). The other was, the desire of the name of victory; whereas on the other side the magistrates, etc., were content for peace sake, and upon the elders' advice, to decline that advantage, and to let the cause fall for want of advice to sway it either way.

Now that which made the people so unsatisfied, and unwilling the cause should rest as it stood, was the 20 pounds which the defendant had recovered against the plaintiff in an action of slander for saying he had stolen the sow, etc., and many of them could not distinguish this from the principal cause, as if she had been adjudged to pay 20 pounds for demanding her sow, and yet the defendant never took of this more than 3 pounds, for his charges of witnesses, etc., and offered to remit the whole if she would have acknowledged the wrong she had done him. But he being accounted a rich man, and she a poor woman, this so wrought with the people as being blinded with unreasonable compassion, they could not see or not allow justice her reasonable course. This being found out by some of the court, a motion was made that some who had interest in the defendant would undertake to persuade him to restore the plaintiff the 3 pounds (or whatever it were) he took upon that judgment. This the court were satisfied with, and proceeded no further[79] . . .

The governor had published a writing about the case of the sow,[80] wherein some passages gave offence, which he being willing to remove, so soon as he came into the general court, he spake as followeth: "I

79. In Oct. 1643, Story and Sherman petitioned again, but the General Court refused to reopen the case (*MR*, 2:51).

80. On 15 July 1642 JW had composed "A breaviate of the Case betwene Richard Sheareman pl[aintiff] by petition and Capt. Robert Keaine defen[dan]tt aboute the title to A straye Sowe . . . " (*WP*, 4:349–352). In this breviate, as in his journal, JW challenges Sherman's evidence and upholds Keayne's, and argues that the case was properly dismissed in May-June 1642 because neither party was backed by a majority of magistrates and deputies in the General Court.

understand divers have taken offence at a writing I set forth about the sow business; I desire to remove it, and to begin my year in a reconciled estate with all. The writing is of two parts, the matter and the manner. In the former I had the concurrence of others of my brethren, both magistrates and deputies; but for the other, viz., the manner, that was wholly mine own, so as whatsoever was blameworthy in it I must take it to myself. The matter is point of judgment, which is not at my own disposing. I have examined it over and again by such light as God hath afforded me from the rules of religion, reason, and common practice, and truly I can find no ground to retract any thing in that, therefore I desire I may enjoy my liberty herein, as every of yourselves do and justly may. But for the manner, whatsoever I might allege for my justification before men, I now pass it over: I now set myself before another judgment seat . . . I did arrogate too much to myself and ascribe too little to others. The other particular was the profession I made of maintaining what I wrote before all the world,[81] which though it may modestly be professed (as the case may require), yet I confess it was now not so beseeming me, but was indeed a fruit of the pride of mine own spirit. These are all the Lord hath brought me to consider of, wherein I acknowledge my failings and humbly intreat you will pardon and pass them by; if you please to accept my request, your silence shall be a sufficient testimony thereof unto me, and I hope I shall be more wise and watchful hereafter."

The sow business had started another question about the magistrates' negative vote in the general court. The deputies generally were very earnest to have it taken away; whereupon one of the magistrates wrote a small treatise,[82] wherein he laid down the original of it from the patent,

---

81. In concluding his breviate, JW had written: "That this is the true state of the Case . . . and which we shall not be ashamed (by the Lord's help) to avouch and maintain, before all the world, I do here affirm under my hand" (*WP*, 4:352).

82. JW wrote two treatises supporting the negative voice, and Richard Bellingham wrote a treatise attacking it. See *WP*, 4:359–361, 380–391.

and the establishing of it by order of the general court in 1634,[83] showing thereby how it was fundamental to our government, which if it
were taken away would be a mere democracy. He showed also the
necessity and usefulness of it by many arguments from scripture, reason, and common practice, etc. Yet this would not satisfy, but the
deputies and common people would have it taken away . . . But the
magistrates told them the matter was of great concernment, even to
the very frame of our government; it had been established upon serious
consultation and consent of all the elders; it had been continued without
any inconvenience or apparent mischief these fourteen years, therefore
it would not be safe nor of good report to alter on such a sudden . . .
One of the elders[84] also wrote a small treatise, wherein scholastically
and religiously he handled the question, laying down the several forms
of government both simple and mixt, and the true form of our government, and the unavoidable change into a democracy if the negative
voice were taken away;[85] and answered all objections, and so concluded
for the continuance of it, so as the deputies and the people also, having
their heat moderated by time, and their judgments better informed by
what they had learned about it, let the cause fall[86] . . .

Sacononoco and Pumham, two sachems near Providence, having
under them between 2 and 300 men, finding themselves overborne by
Miantonomi, the sachem of Narragansett, and Gorton and his company,
who had so prevailed with Miantonomi as he forced one of them to

83. JW seems to be referring here to the General Court's order of March 1636 (MR,
1:170), which stipulates that majority consent by both magistrates and deputies is necessary
for the passage of any law, order, or sentence.

84. John Cotton submitted a treatise to the General Court "in the name of himself &
other elders" (MR, 2:46).

85. In one of his treatises defending the negative voice, JW warned that if the deputies
obtained more power, the MBC would become "a mere Democratie," and in JW's view
"a Democratie is, among most Civil nations, accounted the meanest and worst of all forms
of Government" (WP, 4:383).

86. JW was too optimistic here. Strong opposition to magisterial authority continued
into 1645.

join with him in setting his hand or mark to a writing whereby a part of his land was sold to Gorton and his company, they came to our governor and by Benedict Arnold, their interpreter, did desire we would receive them under our government, and brought withal a small present of wampom, about ten fathom. The governor gave them encouragement, but referred them to the court. In the beginning of the court Miantonomi came to Boston,[87] and being demanded in open court, before divers of his own men and Cutshamekin and other Indians, whether he had any interest in the said two sachems as his subjects, he could prove none. Cutshamekin also in his presence affirmed that he had no interest in them, but they were as free sachems as himself. Whereupon it was referred to the governor and some other of the magistrates and deputies to send for the two sachems after the court, and to treat with them about their receiving in to us.[88]

But before this, Gorton and his company (12 in number) sent a writing to our court of four sheets of paper full of reproaches against our magistrates, elders and churches, of familistical and absurd opinions, and therein they justified their purchase of the sachems' land and professed to maintain it to the death.[89] They sent us word also after (as Benedict Arnold reported to us), that if we sent men against them, they were ready to meet us, being assured of victory from God, etc. Whereupon the court sent two of the deputies to speak with them, to see whether they would own that writing which was subscribed by them all. When they came, they with much difficulty came to find out Gorton and two or three more of them, and upon conference they did own and justify the said writing. They spake also with the two sachems,

---

87. Probably in May 1643. Miantonomi's visit is not recorded in the MBC records.

88. Sacononoco and Pumham signed their marks to a treaty of submission to the MBC on 22 June 1643 (*MR*, 2:38, 40).

89. Gorton published this letter, dated 20 Nov. 1642, in his tract, *Simplicities Defence against Seven-Headed Policy* (London, 1646), 9–31. It is easy to see why JW disliked it; on p. 18, Gorton compares himself to Jesus and JW to Pontius Pilate.

as they had commission, and giving them to understand upon what terms they must be received under us, they found them very pliable to all, and opening to them the ten commandments, they received this answer, which I have set down as the commissioners took it in writing from their mouths.[90]

1. Quest. Whether they would worship the true God that made heaven and earth, and not blaspheme him? Ans. We desire to speak reverently of Englishman's God and not to speak evil of him, because we see the Englishman's God doth better for them than other Gods do for others.

2. That they should not swear falsely. Ans. We never knew what swearing or an oath was.

3. Not to do any unnecessary work on the Lord's day within the gates of proper towns. Ans. It is a small thing for us to rest on that day, for we have not much to do any day, and therefore we will forbear on that day.

4. To honor their parents and superiors. Ans. It is our custom so to do, for inferiors to be subject to superiors, for if we complain to the governor of the Massachusetts that we have wrong, if they tell us we lie we shall willingly bear it.

5. Not to kill any man but upon just cause and just authority. Ans. It is good, and we desire so to do.

6. 7. Not to commit fornication, adultery, bestiality, etc. Ans. Though fornication and adultery be committed among us, yet we allow it not, but judge it evil, so the same we judge of stealing.

8. For lying, they say it is an evil, and shall not allow it.

9. Whether you will suffer your children to read God's word, that they may have knowledge of the true God and to worship him in his

---

90. This is the first evidence in JW's journal of interest in teaching or converting the Indians. Heretofore, the MBC had made no missionary effort, and generally relied upon non-Massachusetts settlers such as Roger Williams to act as interpreters and intermediaries.

own way? Ans. As opportunity serveth by the English coming amongst us, we desire to learn their manners.

After the court, the governor, etc., sent for them, and they came to Boston at the day appointed, viz., the 22d of the 4th month [June], and a form of submission being drawn up, and they being by Benedict Arnold, their neighbor, and interpreter (who spake their language readily), made to understand every particular, in the presence of divers of the elders and many others, they freely subscribed the submission, as it here followeth verbatim . . .

"This writing is to testify, That we Pumham, sachem of Shawomock, and Sacononoco, sachem of Patuxet, etc., have, and by these presents do, voluntarily and without any constraint or persuasion, but of our own free motion, put ourselves, our subjects, lands and estates under the government and jurisdiction of the Massachusetts, to be governed and protected by them according to their just laws and orders, so far as we shall be made capable of understanding them: and we do promise for ourselves and our subjects, and all our posterity, to be true and faithful to the said government, and aiding to the maintenance thereof to our best ability, and from time to time to give speedy notice of any conspiracy, attempt, or evil intention of any which we shall know or hear of against the same: and we do promise to be willing, from time to time, to be instructed in the knowledge and worship of God. In witness whereof, etc."[91] . . .

5. [July] 14. In the evening La Tour took ship, the governor and divers of the chief of the town accompanying him to his boat. There went with him four of our ships and a pinnace.[92] He hired them for two months, the chiefest, which had 16 pieces of ordnance, at 200 pounds the month; yet she was of but 100 tons, but very well manned

91. The text printed in *MR*, 2:40 adds the marks of Sacononoco and Pumham, and the signatures of JW and other MBC witnesses.

92. Edward Gibbons and Thomas Hawkins of Boston provided La Tour with these ships.

and fitted for fight, and the rest proportionable. The owners took only his own security for their pay. He entertained also about 70 land soldiers, volunteers, at 40s. per month a man, but he paid them somewhat in hand.

Of the two friars which came in this ship, the one was a very learned acute man. Divers of our elders who had conference with him reported so of him. They came not into the town lest they should give offence but once, being brought by some to see Mr. Cotton and confer with him, and when they came to depart, the chief came to take leave of the governor and the two elders of Boston,[93] and showed himself very thankful for the courtesy they found among us . . .

Three errors the governor, etc., committed in managing this business. 1. In giving La Tour an answer so suddenly (the very next day after his arrival). 2. In not advising with any of the elders, as their manner was in matters of less consequence. 3. In not calling upon God, as they were wont to do in all public affairs before they fell to consultation, etc. . . . . This fault hath been many times found in the governor to be over sudden in his resolutions, for although the course were both warrantable and safe, yet it had beseemed men of wisdom and gravity to have proceeded with more deliberation and further advice.

Those about Ipswich, etc., took great offence at these proceedings, so as three of the magistrates and the elders of Ipswich and Rowley, with Mr. Nathaniel Ward, wrote a letter to the governor and assistants in the bay, and to the elders here, protesting against the proceedings. The governor made answer to this protestation, so did Mr. Dudley and the pastor of Boston . . .

6 [August]. Uncas, being provoked by Sequasson, a sachem of Connecticut who would not be persuaded by the magistrates there to a reconciliation, made war upon him and slew divers of his men and burnt his wigwams; whereupon Miantonomi, being his kinsman, took

93. John Cotton and John Wilson.

offence against Uncas and went with near 1,000 men and set upon Uncas before he could be provided for defence, for he had not then with him above 3 or 400 men. But it pleased God to give Uncas the victory, after he had killed about 30 of the Narragansetts and wounded many more, and among these two of Canonicus' sons and a brother of Miantonomi, who fled, but having on a coat of mail, he was easily overtaken,[94] which two of his captains perceiving, they laid hold on him and carried him to Uncas, hoping thereby to procure their own pardon. But so soon as they came to Uncas, he slew them presently; and Miantonomi standing mute, he demanded of him why he would not speak. If you had taken me, sayeth he, I would have besought you for my life. The news of Miantonomi's captivity coming to Providence, Gorton and his company, who had bought of him the lands belonging to the sachems who were come under our jurisdiction, wrote a letter to Uncas, willing him to deliver their friend Miantonomi, and threatened him with the power of the English if he refused ⟨and they sent their letter in the name of the governor of Massachusetts⟩.[95] Upon this Uncas carries Miantonomi to Hartford to take advice of the magistrates there, and at Miantonomi's earnest entreaty he left him with them, yet as a prisoner. They kept him under guard, but used him very courteously, and so he continued till the commissioners of the United Colonies met at Boston, who taking into serious consideration what was safest and best to be done, were all of opinion that it would not be safe to set him at liberty, neither had we sufficient ground for us to put him to death. In this difficulty we called in five of the most judicious elders (it being in the time of the general assembly of the elders), and propounding the case to them, they all agreed that he ought to be put to death. Upon this concurrence we agreed that, upon the return of the

94. Samuel Gorton had provided his Indian ally Miantonomi with this suit of armor.

95. Since JW cancelled this passage, he probably decided that this particular charge against Gorton was false.

commissioners to Hartford, they should send for Uncas and tell him our determination that Miantonomi should be delivered to him again, and he should put him to death so soon as he came within his own jurisdiction, and that two English should go along with him to see the execution, and that if any Indians should invade him for it we would send men to defend him[96] . . .

The commissioners, at their return to Connecticut, sent for Uncas, and acquainted him therewith, who readily undertook the execution, and taking Miantonomi along with him, in the way between Hartford and Windsor (where Uncas hath some men dwell), Uncas' brother, following after Miantonomi, clave his head with an hatchet, some English being present.[97] And that the Indians might know that the English did approve of it, they sent 12 or 14 musketeers home with Uncas to abide a time with him for his defence, if need should be.

Mo. 6 [August]. About the 20th of this month the ships which went with La Tour came back safe, not one person missing or sick. But the report of their actions was offensive and grievous to us; for when they drew near to La Tour's place, D'Aulnay, having discovered them, set sail with his vessels (being two ships and a pinnace) and stood right home to Port Royal.[98] Ours pursued them but could not fetch them up, but they ran their ships on ground in the harbor and began to fortify themselves: whereupon ours sent a boat to D'Aulnay with the governor's letter and a letter from Captain Hawkins,[99] who by agreement among themselves was commander in chief . . . But [D'Aulnay] refused to come to any terms of peace. Upon this La Tour urged much to have

---

96. The New England Confederation commissioners reached this decision in Sept. 1643. They believed that Miantonomi was plotting a conspiracy against the English, and they also blamed him for selling land at Shawomet to Samuel Gorton.

97. Uncas reportedly then cut out and ate a large piece of Miantonomi's shoulder, exclaiming that "it was the sweetest meat he ever ate."

98. D'Aulnay's fort on the site of Annapolis Royal, Nova Scotia, was on the opposite side of the Bay of Fundy from La Tour's Fort St. Jean in present New Brunswick.

99. Thomas Hawkins (d. 1648) was a Boston shipwright and mariner.

our men to assault him, but they refused. Then he desired that some of ours might be landed with his to do some mischief to D'Aulnay. Captain Hawkins would send none, but gave leave to any that would go; whereupon some 30 of ours went with La Tour's men, and were encountered by D'Aulnay's men who had fortified themselves by his mill, but were beaten out with loss of three of their men, and none slain on our side nor wounded, only three of La Tour's men were wounded. They set the mill on fire and burnt some standing corn, and retired to their ships with one prisoner whom they took in the mill. D'Aulnay shot with his ordnance at their boats as they went aboard, but missed them, nor did our ships make one shot at him again, but set sail and went to La Tour's fort . . .

Mo. 7 [September]. The Indians near the Dutch, having killed 15 men, began to set upon the English who dwelt under the Dutch. They came to Mrs. Hutchinson's[1] in way of friendly neighborhood, as they had been accustomed, and taking their opportunity, killed her and Mr. Collins, her son-in-law (who had been kept prisoner in Boston, as is before related), and all her family, and such [other] families as were at home; in all sixteen, and put their cattle into their houses and there burnt them. These people had cast off ordinances and churches, and now at last their own people, and for larger accommodation had subjected themselves to the Dutch and dwelt scatteringly near a mile asunder . . .

These Indians at the same time set upon the Dutch with an implacable fury, and killed all they could come by, and burnt their houses and killed their cattle without any resistance, so as the governor and such as escaped betook themselves to their fort at Monhaton[2] . . .

[September] 7. Upon the complaint of the English of Patuxet near

---

1. Anne Hutchinson, after the death of her husband William in 1642, had moved from Rhode Island with six of her children to Pelham Bay on Long Island Sound (now in the Bronx, N.Y.), within Dutch territory.
2. Manhattan.

Providence who had submitted to our jurisdiction, and the two Indian sachems there,[3] of the continual injuries offered them by Gorton and his company, the general court sent for them. But they answered our messengers disdainfully, refused to come, but sent two letters full of blasphemy against the churches and magistracy and other provoking terms, slighting all we could do against them.[4] So that having sent three times, and receiving no other answer, we took testimonies against them both of English and Indians, and determined to proceed with them by force . . . And accordingly we sent the next week Captain George Cook, Lieutenant Atherton, and Edward Johnson, with commission and instructions, and with them 40 soldiers.[5]

They came to Providence, and by the way received another letter from Gorton, of the like contents with the former, and told them plainly they were prepared for them, etc. Being come near, they found they had put themselves all into one house, which they had made musket-proof with two flankers.[6] But by the mediation of others of Providence they came to parley, and then offered to refer their cause to arbitrators. We considered of the motion, and agreed that it was neither seasonable nor reasonable, neither safe nor honorable, for us to accept of such a proposition . . . So accordingly we wrote to our commissioners to proceed, which accordingly they did, and approached the house where they had fortified themselves with trenches so near as they might fire the house, which they attempted two or three times, but they within quenched it. At last three of them escaped out and ran away, and the rest yielded and were brought to Boston . . .

3. Saconnoco and Pumham.

4. On 15 Sept. 1643, Randall Holden, one of Samuel Gorton's companions, sent a provocative letter to the "generation of vipers" in Massachusetts, in which he referred to the MBC General Court as "the great and honored Idol General."

5. Cook was captain of the Cambridge militia, Humphrey Atherton was lieutenant of the Dorchester militia, and Johnson was lieutenant of the Woburn militia. Johnson later published *The Wonder-Working Providence of Sions Saviour in New England* (London, 1654), the first Puritan history of New England to appear in print.

6. Fortifications projecting from the corners of their house.

[October] 13. Captain Cook and his company which were sent out against Gorton returned to Boston, and the captives, being nine, were brought to the governor his house in a military order, viz., the soldiers being in two files and after every five or six soldiers a prisoner. So being before his door, the commissioners came in, and after the governor had saluted them he went forth with them, and passing through the files welcomed them home, blessing God for preserving and prospering them, and gave them all thanks for their pains and good carriage. Then having conferred privately with the commissioners, he caused the prisoners to be brought before him in his hall, where was a great assembly, and there laid before them their contemptuous carriage towards us, and their obstinacy against all the fair means and moderation we had used to reform them and bring them to do right to those of ours whom they had wronged, and how the Lord had now justly delivered them into our hands. They pleaded in their excuse that they were not of our jurisdiction, and that though they had now yielded themselves to come and answer before us, yet they yielded not as prisoners. The governor replied, they were brought to him as taken in war. So the governor committed them to the marshall to convey to the common prison, and gave order they should be well provided for both for lodging and diet.

The next Lord's day in the forenoon the prisoners would not come to the meeting, so as the magistrates determined they should be compelled. They agreed to come, so as they might have liberty after sermon to speak, if they had occasion. So in the afternoon they came, and were placed in the fourth seat right before the elders. Mr. Cotton (in his ordinary text) taught then out of Acts 19. of Demetrius pleading for Diana's silver shrines or temples, etc.[7] After sermon Gorton desired

---

7. Acts 19:24–27. Demetrius the silversmith got rich by making shrines for the pagan goddess Diana and protested Paul's teaching that gods made by hand are not gods. Whereas Cotton interpreted Paul as attacking popish saint-worship and worldliness, Gorton saw Demetrius as emblematic of the man-made churches and corrupt ministry of Massachusetts.

leave to speak, which being granted he repeated the points of Mr. Cotton's sermon, and coming to that of the silver shrines, he said that in the church there was nothing now but Christ, so that all our ordinances, ministers, sacraments, etc., were but men's inventions for show and pomp, and no other than those silver shrines of Diana. He said also that if Christ lived eternally, then he died eternally; and it appeared both by his letters and examinations that he held that Christ was incarnate in Adam, and that he was that image of God wherein Adam was created, and that his being born after of the Virgin Mary and suffering, etc., was but a manifestation of his sufferings, etc., in Adam.[8]

When the general court was assembled, Gorton and his company were brought forth upon the lecture day at Boston, and there, before a great assembly, the governor declared the cause and manner of our proceeding against them, and their letters were openly read, and all objections answered. As 1. That they were not within our jurisdiction. To this was answered. 1. That they were either within Plymouth or Mr. Fenwick, and they had yielded their power to us in this cause.[9] 2. If they were under no jurisdiction, then we must either right ourselves and our subjects by force of arms, or else we must sit still under all their reproaches and injuries . . .

After this they were brought before the court severally to be examined (divers of the elders being desired to be present) . . . They

8. While JW saw this extreme christocentrism as lunatic nonsense, Gorton's belief that all human beings are made divine through the miracle of Christ's presence was a theological position widely shared by English radical Puritans in the Baptist, Seeker, and Ranter movements of the 1640s.

9. The MBC was here asserting that Shawomet was either within Plymouth or Connecticut jurisdiction—Plymouth, because the Pilgrims claimed Narragansett Bay as their western boundary; or Connecticut, because the Hartford government was hoping to obtain from George Fenwick, one of the proprietors of Saybrook at the mouth of the Connecticut River, a patent to the territory between Narragansett Bay and the Connecticut River. At the New England Confederation meeting of Sept. 1643, both Connecticut and Plymouth had empowered the MBC to proceed against Gorton (PR, 9:12).

excel the jesuits in the art of equivocation, and regard not how false they speak to all other men's apprehensions, so they keep to the rules of their own meaning. Gorton maintained that the image of God wherein Adam was created was Christ, and so the loss of that image was the death of Christ, and the restoring of it in regeneration was Christ's resurrection, and so the death of him that was born of the Virgin Mary was but a manifestation of the former. In their letters, etc., they condemned all ordinances in the church, calling baptism an abomination, and the Lord's supper the juice of a poor silly grape turned into the blood of Christ by the skill of our magicians, etc.

They were all illiterate men, the ablest of them could not write true English, no not common words, yet they would take upon them the interpretation of the most difficult places of scripture and wrest them any way to serve their own turns . . . The court and the elders spent near a whole day in discovery of Gorton's deep mysteries which he had boasted of in his letters, and to bring him to conviction, but all was in vain. Much pains was also taken with the rest, but to as little effect. They would acknowledge no error or fault in their writings, and yet would seem sometimes to consent with us in the truth.

After all these examinations the court began to consult about their sentence. They were charged to be blasphemous enemies of the true religion of our Lord Jesus Christ, and of all his holy ordinances, and likewise of all civil government among his people, and particularly within this jurisdiction. . . . All the magistrates save three[10] were of opinion that Gorton ought to die, but the greatest number of the deputies dissenting, that vote did not pass. In the end all agreed upon this sentence for seven of them, viz., that they should be dispersed into seven several towns and there kept to work for their living, and wear irons upon one leg, and not to depart the limits of the town, nor by word or writing maintain any of their blasphemous or wicked errors

---

10. Probably Saltonstall, Bellingham, and Bradstreet.

upon pain of death, only with exception for speech with any of the elders, or any other licensed by any magistrate to confer with them; this censure to continue during the pleasure of the court[11] . . .

About a week after, we sent men to fetch so many of their cattle as might defray our charges, both of the soldiers and of the court, which spent many days about them, and for their expenses in prison.[12] It came to in all about 160 pounds. Their arms were all taken from them, and of their guns the court gave one fowling piece to Pumham and another to Sacononoco, and liberty granted them to have powder as being now within our jurisdiction . . .

10. [December] 27. By order of the general court all the magistrates and the teaching elders of the six nearest churches were appointed to be forever governors of the college,[13] and this day they met at Cambridge and considered of the officers of the college, and chose a treasurer, H. Pelham, Esq., being the first in that office.

This day five ships set sail from Boston; three of them were built here, two of 300 tons and the other of 160. One of them was bound for London with many passengers, men of chief rank in the country, and great store of beaver. Their adventure was very great, considering the doubtful estate of the affairs of England, but many prayers of the churches went with them and followed after them . . .

12. [February] 5. Cutshamekin and Agawam and Josias, Chickatabot his heir,[14] came to the governor, and in their own name and the names of all the sachems of Watchusett,[15] and all the Indians from Merrimack

11. On 3 Nov. 1643 Gorton was sentenced to labor in irons at Charlestown, Randall Holden was sent to Salem, five of their companions were assigned to other towns, and three received more minor punishments (*MR*, 2:52–53).

12. The General Court soon discovered that the Gortonists were troublesome prisoners; see 7 March 1644, below.

13. Overseers of Harvard College. The six ministers appointed to this board were from Cambridge, Watertown, Charlestown, Boston, Roxbury, and Dorchester.

14. Three sachems of the Massachusetts Indians. They were performing a ritual of submission to the MBC, as Sacononoco and Pumham had done in June 1643.

15. In present Worcester County, 50 miles W of Boston.

to Tecticutt,[16] tendered themselves to our government and gave the governor a present of 30 fathom of wampom, and offered to come to the next court to make their acknowledgment, etc. The governor received their present to keep it till the court, etc., and if the court and they did agree, then to accept it. We now began to conceive hope that the Lord's time was at hand for opening a door of light and grace to those Indians, and some fruit appeared of our kind dealing with Pumham and Saconococo, protecting them against the Narragansett, and righting them against Gorton, etc., who had taken away their land: for this example gave encouragement to all these Indians to come in and submit to our government, in expectation of the like protection and benefit.

[February] 16. Pesacus, the Narragansett sachem,[17] sent again a message to the governor with another present by Washose, a sachem who came before, and his errand was, that seeing they, at our request, had sitten still this year, that now this next year we would grant their request, and suffer them to fight with Uncas, with many arguments. The governor refused his present, and told him that if they sent us 1000 fathom of wampom and 1000 skins, yet we would not do that which we judged to be unjust, viz. to desert Uncas, but our resolution was, and that they must rest upon, that if they made war upon Uncas the English would all fall upon them . . .

1. [March] 7. The court finding that Gorton and his company did harm in the towns where they were confined, and not knowing what to do with them, at length agreed to set them at liberty, and gave them 14 days to depart out of our jurisdiction in all parts, and no more to come into it upon pain of death.[18] This censure was thought too light

16. Now Taunton; 30 miles S of Boston.

17. The brother of Miantonomi, murdered by Uncas in Sept. 1643. In Oct. 1643 Pesacus had sent a present to JW and asked the MBC not to intervene when he fought Uncas, but JW told him that he would refuse the present unless the Narragansetts kept peace with the Mohegans.

18. After their release, the Gortonists defiantly returned to Shawomet, but soon con-

and favorable, but we knew not how in justice we could inflict any punishment upon them, the sentence of the court being already passed, etc. . . . .

At this court of assistants one James Britton, a man ill affected both to our church discipline and civil government, and one Mary Latham, a proper young woman about 18 years of age, whose father was a godly man and had brought her up well, were condemned to die for adultery[19] upon a law formerly made and published in print. It was thus occasioned and discovered. This woman, being rejected by a young man whom she had an affection unto, vowed she would marry the next that came to her, and accordingly, against her friends' minds, she matched with an ancient man who had neither honesty nor ability, and one whom she had no affection unto.[20] Whereupon, soon after she was married, divers young men solicited her chastity, and drawing her into bad company and giving her wine and other gifts, easily prevailed with her, and among others this Britton. But God smiting him with a deadly palsy and fearful horror of conscience withal, he could not keep secret, but discovered this, and other the like with other women. Upon her examination, she confessed he did attempt the fact but did not commit it, and witness was produced that testified (which they both confessed) that in the evening of a day of humiliation through the country for England, etc., a company met at Britton's and there continued drinking sack, etc., till late in the night, and then Britton and the woman were seen upon the ground together a little from the house. It was reported also that she did frequently abuse her husband, setting a knife to his

---

tinued on to New Amsterdam, where they boarded a ship for England to present their case to the Earl of Warwick's Commissioners for Plantations. For the results of this mission, see 13 Sept. 1646, below.

19. Britton lived in Weymouth, and had been whipped in 1639 for casting aspersions on the ministry. Latham lived across the Plymouth Colony border in Marshfield; she was extradited to Massachusetts in Feb. 1644, since the offense took place in Weymouth.

20. Mary's husband, William Latham, was probably in his 40s in 1644; while hardly "ancient," he was much older than his wife.

breast and threatening to kill him, calling him old rogue and cuckold, and said she would make him wear horns as big as a bull. And yet some of the magistrates thought the evidence not sufficient against her, because there were not two direct witnesses; but the jury cast her,[21] and then she confessed the fact and accused twelve others, whereof two were married men. Five of these were apprehended and committed (the rest were gone), but denying it and there being no other witness against them than the testimony of a condemned person, there could be no proceeding against them. The woman proved very penitent, and had deep apprehension of the foulness of her sin, and at length attained to hope of pardon by the blood of Christ, and was willing to die in satisfaction to justice. The man also was very much cast down for his sins, but was loth to die and petitioned the general court for his life, but they would not grant it.

1. [March] 21. They were both executed, they both died very penitently, especially the woman, who had some comfortable hope of pardon of her sin, and gave good exhortation to all young maids to be obedient to their parents, and to take heed of evil company, etc. . . .

At the same court in the first month [March], upon the motion of the deputies, it was ordered that the court should be divided in their consultations, the magistrates by themselves and the deputies by themselves, what the one agreed upon they should send to the other, and if both agreed, then to pass, etc. This order determined the great contention about the negative voice[22] . . .

---

21. Found her to be guilty. Latham was the last person condemned to death for adultery by a Massachusetts jury. The MBC General Court had twice decreed, in 1631 and 1638, that adultery was punishable by death; and in the Body of Liberties (the Massachusetts law code of 1641) adultery was a capital crime. But the death penalty remained very much in question, because the General Court had pardoned a confessed adulterer, John Underhill; see 3 Sept. 1640, above.

22. The General Court's decision that the magistrates and deputies should divide formally into two houses (*MR,* 2:58–59) was a compromise solution to the two-year dispute over the magistrates' negative voice. The magistrates preserved their veto power, while the deputies strengthened their authority as a constitutional counterweight.

3. [May] 20. A ship coming from Virginia certified us of a great massacre lately committed by the natives upon the English there, to the number of 300 at least, and that an Indian whom they had since taken confessed that they did it because they saw the English took up all their lands from them, and would drive them out of the country, and they took this season for that they understood that they were at war in England, and began to go to war among themselves, for they had seen a fight in the river between a London ship which was for the parliament and a Bristol ship which was for the king. He confessed further that all the Indians within 600 miles were confederate together to root all strangers out of the country.

It was very observable that this massacre came upon them soon after they had driven out the godly ministers we had sent to them,[23] and had made an order that all such as would not conform to the discipline of the church of England should depart the country by a certain day, which the massacre now prevented: and the governor (one Sir Robert Berkeley,[24] a courtier, and very malignant towards the way of our churches here) and council had appointed a fast to be kept through the country upon good Friday (as they call it) for the good success of the king, etc., and the day before, this massacre began in the outparts of the country round about and continued two days, for they killed all by sudden surprisal living amongst them, and as familiar in their houses as those of the family. This massacre was accompanied with a great mortality. Upon these troubles divers godly disposed persons came from thence to New England, and many of the rest were forced to give glory to God in acknowledging, that this evil was sent upon them from God for their reviling the gospel and those faithful ministers he had sent among them . . .

23. See 20 June 1643.

24. Actually Sir William Berkeley, who was royal governor of Virginia in 1642–1652 and 1660–1677.

The general court being assembled, Mr. Endecott was chosen governor and Mr. Winthrop deputy governor[25] . . .

4. [June] 5. Two of our ministers' sons,[26] being students in the college, robbed two dwelling houses in the night of some 15 pounds. Being found out, they were ordered by the governors of the college to be there whipped, which was performed by the president himself[27]—yet they were about 20 years of age; and after they were brought into the court and ordered to two fold satisfaction, or to serve so long for it. We had yet no particular punishment for burglary.

At this court, . . . the great difference was about a commission which the deputies sent up, whereby power was given to seven of the magistrates and three of the deputies and Mr. Ward (some time pastor of Ipswich, and still a preacher) to order all affairs of the commonwealth in the vacancy of the general court,[28] which the magistrates returned with this answer: That they conceived such commission did tend to the overthrow of the foundation of our government, and of the freemen's liberty.

Upon this return, all the deputies came to confer with the magistrates. The exceptions the magistrates took were these. 1. That this court should create general officers which the freemen had reserved to the court of elections. 2. That they should put out four of the magistrates from that power and trust which the freeman had committed to them. 3. At the commission itself, seeing they ought not to accept that power by commission which did belong to them by the patent and by their election.

---

25. JW served as deputy governor for two years, 1644–1646, and then was elected governor for the last three years of his life.

26. James Ward, son of the Rev. Nathaniel Ward, and John Weld, son of the Rev. Thomas Weld, were the culprits.

27. Henry Dunster (1609–1659) was the first president of Harvard College, serving from 1640 to 1654. He resigned over his opinions concerning infant baptism.

28. The 11-member commission proposed by the deputies would take over the administrative function of the magistrates (a 13-member body in 1644) who had heretofore governed the colony between sessions of the General Court.

[The deputies] chiefly stood upon this, that the governor and assistants had no power out of court but what was given them by the general court. To this the magistrates replied that the governor and assistants had power of government before we had any written laws or had kept any courts; and to make a man a governor over a people gives him, by necessary consequence, power to govern that people, otherwise there were no power in any commonwealth to order, dispose, or punish in any case where it might fall out, that there were no positive law declared in. So as these [magistrates] being chosen by the people, by virtue of the patent to govern the people, a chief part whereof consists in counsel, they are the standing council of the commonwealth, and therefore in the vacancy of this court may act in all the affairs thereof without any commission.

Upon this [the deputies] withdrew, and after a few hours came again, and then they tendered a commission for war only, and none of the magistrates to be left out. But the magistrates refused to accept of any commission. [The deputies] then moved that we would consent that nothing might be done till the court met again, which was before agreed to be adjourned to the 28th of (8) [October]. To this was answered, that if occasion required, [the magistrates] must act according to the power and trust committed to them; to which their speaker[29] replied— You will not be obeyed.

4. *[June] 23.* Two days after the court was broken up, Pumham sent two men to Boston to tell us that the Narragansetts had taken and killed six of Uncas' men and five women, and had sent him two hands and a foot to engage him in the war, but he refused to receive them and sent to us for counsel, etc. This occasioned such of the magistrates and deputies as were at hand (advising also with some of the near elders) to meet to consult about calling the court, and agreed, both in regard of this news from the Indians and especially for speedy reconciling the

29. William Hawthorne.

magistrates and deputies, to write to the governor[30] that the court might be called the 28th following, which the governor assented unto.

The court being assembled, they took order for ten men to be sent to Pumham according to his desire, to help him make a fort of palisadoes, etc. . . . The commission also for the serjeant major general was agreed and sealed, and in it he was referred to receive his instructions, etc., from the council of the commonwealth, but who were this council was not agreed. Whereupon the magistrates (all save two) signed a declaration in maintenance of their authority, and to clear the aspersions cast upon them, as if they intended to bring in an arbitrary government, etc.[31] This they sent first to the deputies, with intimation that they intended to publish it, whereupon the deputies sent to desire that it might not be published, and desired a committee might meet to state the difference between us, which was done, and the difference was brought under this question: whether the magistrates are by patent and election of the people the standing council of the commonwealth in the vacancy of the general court, and have power accordingly to act in all cases subject to government, according to the said patent and the laws of this jurisdiction. This difference being thus stated, [the deputies] drew up this following order and sent it to us, viz.

Whereas there is a difference between the governor, assistants, and deputies in this court, concerning the power of the magistrates in the vacancy of the general court,—we therefore (salvo jure)[32] for the peace and safety of this colony do consent, that the governor and assistants shall take order for the welfare of this commonwealth in all sudden

30. Governor Endecott had gone home to Salem when the General Court adjourned on 21 June. JW clearly feels that the magistrates could have handled the Narragansett crisis without reconvening the General Court, had they been permitted as in the past to exercise flexible discretionary authority.

31. The magistrates' declaration (*WP*, 4:467) insists that they alone have executive authority between sessions of the General Court. It was signed by Endecott, JW, and seven assistants. Two assistants were absent, and Bellingham and Saltonstall abstained.

32. Without prejudice to our right.

cases that may happen within our jurisdiction, until the next session of this court when we desire this question may be determined. This we accepted (with the salvo jure).

Upon this agreement the magistrates consented that the declaration should remain with the secretary, and not be published without the consent of the major part of the magistrates, which we intended not to do, except we were necessitated thereto by the deputies' misreport of our proceedings . . .

Anabaptistry increased and spread in the country, which occasioned the magistrates, at the last court, to draw an order for banishing such as continued obstinate after due conviction. This was sent to the elders, who approved of it with some mitigations, and being voted, and sent to the deputies, it was after published[33] . . .

5. [July] 15. Here arrived Monsieur La Tour, who understood by letters from his lady that Monsieur D'Aulnay had prevailed against him in France, and was coming with great strength to subdue him: whereupon he came to desire some aid, if need should be[34] . . .

[July] 23. La Tour having been with the governor at Salem and made known his condition to him, he was moved with compassion towards him, and appointed a meeting of the magistrates and elders at Boston this day.[35] Most of the magistrates and some of the elders were clear in the case that he was to be relieved, both in point of charity as a distressed neighbor, and also in point of prudence as thereby to root out, or at least weaken, an enemy or a dangerous neighbor. But because many of the elders were absent, and three or four of the magistrates dissented, it was agreed the rest of the elders should be called in, and that another meeting should be at Salem the next week.

33. In Nov. 1644 the General Court ordered that any person who obstinately condemned or opposed the baptism of infants be sentenced to banishment (*MR*, 2:85).

34. La Tour's information was correct: d'Aulnay was authorized by the French government to seize La Tour, and he came back to Acadia with reinforcements.

35. Gov. Endecott had been critical of JW's support for La Tour in 1643.

When they were met, the governor propounded the case to them, and it was brought to the two former questions. 1. Whether it were lawful for true christians to aid an antichristian. 2. Whether it were safe for us in point of prudence. After much disputation, some of the magistrates and elders remaining unsatisfied, a third way was propounded, which all assented to, which was this, that a letter should be sent to D'Aulnay to demand satisfaction for the wrongs he had done us and our confederates in taking Penobscot, and our men and goods at Isle Sable, and threatening to make prize of our vessels if they came to Penobscot, etc., declaring withal that although our men which went last year to aid La Tour did it without any commission from us, or any counsel or act of permission of our state, yet if he made it appear to us that they had done him any wrong (which yet we knew not of), we should be ready to do him justice. We sent also in the letter a copy of an order published by the governor and council, whereby we forbade all our people to use any act of hostility, otherwise than in their own defence, towards French or Dutch, etc., till the next general court, etc. In our letter we also mentioned a course of trade our merchants had entered into with La Tour, and our resolution to maintain them in it . . .

Captain Stagg[36] arriving at Boston in a ship of London, of 24 pieces of ordnance, and finding here a ship of Bristol of 100 tons, laden with fish for Bilboa, he placed his ship between Charlestown and the Bristol ship, and moored himself abreast her. Then he called the master of the Bristol ship and showed him his commission, and told him if he would yield, himself and all his should have what belonged to them and their wages to that day, and turning up the half hour glass, set him in his own ship again, requiring to have his answer by that time of half an hour. The master coming aboard acquainted his men with it, and de-

---

36. Capt. Thomas Stagg was a Virginia merchant who sailed as a privateer under a parliamentary commission issued by the lord high admiral, the Earl of Warwick.

manded their resolution. Two or three would have fought, and rather have blown up their ship than have yielded; but the greater part prevailed, so she was quietly taken and all the men save three sent to Boston, and there order was taken by the captain for their diet.

In this half hour's time much people gathered together upon Windmill hill to see the issue, and some who had interest in the ship, especially one Bristol merchant (a very bold malignant person), began to gather company and raise a tumult. But some of the people present laid hold of them and brought them to the deputy governor,[37] who committed the merchant and some others who were strangers to a chamber in an ordinary,[38] with a guard upon them, and others who were town dwellers he committed to prison, and sent the constable to require the people to depart to their houses; and then hearing that the ship was taken, he wrote to the captain to know by what authority he had done it in our harbor, who forthwith repaired to him with his commission, which was to this effect:

Robert, Earl of Warwick, etc., Lord High Admiral of England, etc., to all of whatsoever condition his rank, etc., greeting. Know you that it should be lawful for all men, etc., to set forth ships and to take all vessels in or outward bound to or from Bristol, Barnstable, Dartmouth, etc., in hostility against the king and parliament, and to visit all ships in any port or creek, etc., by force if they should refuse, etc., and they were to have the whole prize to themselves, paying the tenth to the admiral, provided, before they went forth, they should give security to the admiral to observe their commission, and that they should not rob or spoil any of the parliament's friends, and so concludes thus: Captain Stagg has bound himself etc., in £2,000, etc. Dated March, 1644.

Upon sight of this commission, the deputy appointed Captain Stagg to bring or send it to the meeting at Salem; and the tumult being

37. JW.
38. A tavern.

pacified, he took bond, with sureties, of the principal stirrers, to appear at the meeting and to keep the peace in the mean time. The captain brought his commission to Salem, and there it was read and considered. Some of the elders, the last Lord's day, had in their sermons reproved this proceeding, and exhorted the magistrates, etc., to maintain the people's liberties, which were, they said, violated by this act, and that a commission could not supersede a patent. And at this meeting some of the magistrates and some of the elders were of the same opinion, and that the captain should be forced to restore the ship. But the greater part of both were of a different judgment. Their reasons were these.

1. Because this could be no precedent to bar us from opposing any commission or other foreign power that might indeed tend to our hurt and violate our liberty; for the parliament had taught us, that salus populi is suprema lex.[39]

2. The king of England was enraged against us, and all that party and all the popish states in Europe: and if we should now by opposing the parliament cause them to forsake us, we could have no protection or countenance from any, but should lie open as a prey to all men.

3. We might not deny the parliament's power in this case, unless we should deny the foundation of our government by our patent; for the parliament's authority will take place in all peculiar and privileged places where the king's writs or commissions will not be of force, as in the Dutchy of Lancaster, the Cinque ports, and in London itself, the parliament may fetch out any man, even the Lord Mayor himself, and the reason is, because what the parliament doth is done by themselves, for they have their burgesses, etc., there;[40] nor need they fear that the

---

39. The welfare of the people is the supreme law.

40. JW is arguing that Massachusetts is one of these "peculiar and privileged places" because the MBC has special powers of self-government granted in the royal charter of Oct. 1629—equivalent to the liberties granted to the Duchy of Lancaster in northern England, to the Cinque Ports on the SE coast, and to the city of London. But Parliament has authority over all of these privileged places, because they are represented by knights of the shire or by burgesses in the House of Commons.

parliament will do any man wrong: and we have consented to hold our land of the manor of E. Greenwich, and so such as are burgesses or knights for that manor, are our burgesses also.[41] But if we stand upon this plea, we must then renounce our patent and England's protection, which were a great weakness in us, seeing their care hath been to strengthen our liberties and not overthrow them: and if the parliament should hereafter be of a malignant spirit, etc., then if we have strength sufficient, we may make use of salus populi[42] to withstand any authority from thence to our hurt . . .

Upon these and other considerations, it was not thought fit to oppose the parliament's commission, but to suffer the captain to enjoy his prize[43] . . .

[August]. At Stamford an Indian came into a poor man's house, none being at home but the wife and a child in the cradle, and taking up a lathing hammer as if he would have bought it, the woman stooping down to take her child out of the cradle, he struck her with the sharp edge upon the side of her head, wherewith she fell down, and then he gave her two cuts more which pierced into her brains, and so left her for dead, carrying away some clothes which lay at hand. This woman after a short time came to herself and got out to a neighbor's house, and told what had been done to her, and described the Indian by his person and clothes, etc. Whereupon many Indians of those parts were brought before her, and she charged one of them confidently to be the

41. The royal charter of Oct. 1629 had stipulated that the MBC was to hold its territory in New England as of the royal manor of East Greenwich in Kent (*MR*, 1:4), a formula meaning that the MBC's lands in America are not only part of the King's demesne, but also—as JW here points out—that the colonists are represented in Parliament by the members who represent East Greenwich (in this case, the knights of the shire for the county of Kent). Thus the MBC is subject to parliamentary authority. For more on the East Greenwich clause, see note 49 on p. 308.

42. The welfare of the people.

43. The Boston merchants who had put goods aboard the Bristol ship tried to bring suit against Capt. Stagg, but the MBC magistrates persuaded them not to, and wrote to the Earl of Warwick in hopes of parliamentary restitution.

man, whereupon he was put in prison with intent to have put him to death, but he escaped, and the woman recovered, but lost her senses. A good time after the Indians brought another Indian whom they charged to have committed that fact, and he upon examination confessed it, and gave the reason thereof, and brought forth some of the clothes which he had stolen.[44] Upon this the magistrates of New Haven, taking advice of the elders in those parts and some here, did put him to death. The executioner would strike off his head with a falchion,[45] but he had eight blows at it before he could effect it, and the Indian sat upright and stirred not all the time . . .

[September]. At the court of assistants, Thomas Morton was called forth presently after the lecture, that the country might be satisfied of the justice of our proceeding against him.[46] There was laid to his charge his complaint against us at the council board, which he denied. Then we [showed that] Morton had set forth a book against us, and had threatened us, and had prosecuted a quo warranto against us, which he did not deny. [Then] his letter was produced, written [in 1634] to Mr. [William] Jeffery, his old acquaintance and intimate friend, in these words.

My Very Good Gossip,

You shall hereby understand that although, when I was first sent to England to make complaint against Ananias and the brethren,[47] I ef-

---

44. The Indian's name was Busshege. His attack was one of a series of ambushes triggered by Kieft's War in New Netherland. The Indians were aiming to kill Dutchmen, but the English in border towns like Stamford were also vulnerable.

45. A sword with a curving blade.

46. Morton had been deported to England by the MBC (see 30 Sept. 1630, above), and had worked to revoke the MBC charter. One of his letters against the MBC was intercepted (see 4 Aug. 1634, above), and in 1637 he published *The New English Canaan*, attacking the Puritan colonists. Nevertheless, Morton returned to New England in 1643, spending the winter of 1643–1644 at Plymouth. He was arrested by the Massachusetts government around June 1644.

47. Ananias was struck dead for lying (Acts 5:1–5). To Morton, JW is Ananias and his Puritan colleagues are "the brethren."

fected the business but superficially (through the brevity of time), I have at this time taken more deliberation and brought the matter to a better pass. And it is thus brought about, that the king hath taken the business into his own hands. The Massachusetts Patent by order of the council was brought in view; the privileges there granted well scanned upon, and at the council board in public and in the presence of Sir Richard Saltonstall and the rest it was declared, for manifest abuses there discovered, to be void. The king hath reassumed the whole business into his own hands, appointed a committee of the board, and given order for a general governor of the whole territory to be sent over. The commission is passed the privy seal, I did see it, and the same was 1 mo. Maii sent to the Lord Keeper to have it pass the great seal for confirmation; and I now stay to return with the governor, by whom all complainants shall have relief:[48] So that now Jonas being set ashore may safely cry, repent you cruel separatists, repent, there are as yet but forty days.[49] If Jove vouchsafe to thunder, the charter and kingdom of the separatists will fall asunder. Repent you cruel schismatics, repent . . . And as for Ratcliffe,[50] he was comforted by their lordships with the cropping of Mr. Winthrop's ears: which shows what opinion is held amongst them of King Winthrop with all his inventions and his Amsterdam fantastical ordinances, his preachings, marriages, and other abusive ceremonies, which do exemplify his detestation to the church of England, and the contempt of his majesty's authority and wholesome

48. Morton is exaggerating the vigor of the royal attack on the New England Puritans. As of May 1634, when this letter was written, the king had only authorized Archbishop Laud's Commission for Regulating Plantations to supervise the Puritan colonies more closely. This body opened suit for repeal of the MBC charter in 1635 and secured a judgment againt the company in 1637, whereupon Charles I announced his appointment of Sir Ferdinando Gorges as royal governor. But this judgment was invalid, because the MBC officers in America were neither summoned nor convicted, and the king never sent an expeditionary force to New England. See July 1634, June 1635, Sept. 1638, and June 1639, above.

49. Jonah 3:4.

50. Philip Ratcliffe had been banished by the Massachusetts government, and had his ears cropped; see 14 June 1631, above.

laws, which are and will be established in those parts. Resting your loving friend.

Thomas Morton.

Dated 1. mo. Maii, 1634.

Having been kept in prison about a year, in expectation of further evidence out of England, he was again called before the court, and after some debate what to do with him he was fined 100 pounds, and set at liberty. He was a charge to the country, for he had nothing, and we thought not fit to inflict corporal punishment upon him, being old and crazy, but thought better to fine him and give him his liberty, as if it had been to procure his fine, but indeed to leave him opportunity to go out of the jursidiction, as he did soon after, and he went to Acomenticus, and living there poor and despised, he died within two years after . . .

[September] *17.* The lady La Tour[51] arrived here from London in a ship commanded by Captain Bayley. They had been six months from London, having spent their time in trading about Canada, etc. They met with D'Aulnay near Cape Sable and told him they were bound for the Bay, and had stowed the lady and her people under hatches, so he not knowing it was Captain Bayley, whom he earnestly sought for to have taken or sunk him, he wrote by the master to the deputy governor to this effect: That his master the king of France, understanding that the aid La Tour had here the last year was upon the commission he showed from the Vice Admiral of France, gave him in charge not to molest us for it, but to hold all good correspondency with us and all the English, which he professed he was desirous of, so far as might stand with his duty to his master.

Here arrived also Mr. Roger Williams of Providence, and with him

51. Françoise-Marie Jacquelin, madame de La Tour, had been in France trying to plead her husband's cause. Forbidden to return to Acadia, she went to England and paid Capt. John Bayley and Alderman William Berkeley to take her to her husband's Fort St. Jean.

two or three families.[52] He brought with him a letter from divers lords and others of the parliament, the copy whereof ensueth.

Our Much Honoured Friends:

Taking notice, some of us long time, of Mr. Roger Williams his good affections and conscience, and of his sufferings by our common enemies and oppressors of God's people, the prelates, as also of his great industry and travail in his printed Indian labors in your parts, the like whereof we have not seen extant from any part of America,[53] and in which respect it hath pleased both houses of parliament freely to grant unto him and friends with him a free and absolute charter of civil government for those parts of his abode: and withal sorrowfully resenting, that amongst good men (our friends) driven to the ends of the world, exercised with the trials of a wilderness, and who mutually give good testimony each of other as we observe you do of him and he abundantly of you, there should be such a distance; we thought it fit, upon divers considerations, to profess our great desires of both your utmost endeavours of nearer closing, and of ready expressing of those good affections which we perceive you bear each to other, in the actual performance of all friendly offices,

Your true and faithful friends,

Northumberland [and eleven other signatures][54] . . .

52. Williams had been in England in 1643–1644, and had obtained a patent from Parliament creating the colony of Providence Plantations—defeating efforts by Thomas Weld, the MBC agent, to annex the Narragansett Bay region to Massachusetts. Before returning home, Williams also secured a letter of safe conduct from 12 members of Parliament, copied here by JW. This letter was necessary to Williams, since he stood under sentence of banishment in Massachusetts.

53. Williams had just published his *Key into the Language of America* (London, 1643), the first systematic effort by a New England Puritan to interpret the Algonquian language. He also published his famous plea for religious toleration, *The Bloudy Tenent of Persecution for cause of Conscience* (London, 1644)—in answer to *A Short Story of the Rise, reign and ruine of the Antinomians, Familists & Libertines, that infected the Churches of New England* (London, 1644), which was a collection of documents gathered by JW seven years earlier to justify the MBC's persecution of Anne Hutchinson.

54. The MBC dared not quarrel with the 12 men who signed this parliamentary passport.

[October]. While the governor and other of the magistrates were at Boston, a boat sent from Mr. D'Aulnay with ten men arrived at Salem, hearing that the governor dwelt there. There was in her one Marie,[55] supposed to be a friar, but habited like a gentleman. He wrote a letter to our governor by a gentleman of his company to know where he should attend him: and upon our governor's answer to him, he came the next day to Boston, and with letters of credence and commission from Mr. D'Aulnay; he showed us the king of France his commission under the great seal of France, with the privy seal annexed, wherein the proceedings against La Tour were verified, and he condemned as a rebel and traitor, etc., with command for the apprehension of himself and lady, who had fled out of France against special order, under, etc. He complained also of the wrong done by our men the last year in assisting of La Tour etc., and proffered terms of peace and amity. We answered to the 1. That divers of the ships and most of the men were strangers to us, and had no commission from us nor any permission to use any hostility, and we were very sorry when we heard what had been done. This gave him satisfaction. To the other proposition we answered that we could not conclude any league with him without the advice of the commissioners of the united colonies; but if he would set down his propositions in writing, we would consider further of them. Upon these things we discoursed half the day, sometimes with our governor in French, and otherwhile with the rest of the magistrates in Latin. We urged much for a reconciliation with La Tour, and that he would permit his lady to go to her husband. His answer was that if La Tour would voluntarily submit and come in, he would assure him his life and liberty, but if he were taken he were sure to lose his head in France; and for his lady, she was known to be the cause of his contempt

---

They included war leaders, influential peers, members of the Commission for Plantations in the West Indies, and the lord mayor of London.

55. François-Marie de Paris was a Capuchin friar from d'Aulnay's base at Port Royal. The Capuchins in France vigorously supported d'Aulnay, and accused La Tour of heresy.

and rebellion and therefore they could not let her go to him, but if we should send her in any of our vessels he must take her, and if we carried any goods to La Tour he would take them also, but he would give us satisfaction for them. In the end we came to this agreement, which was drawn up in Latin in these words, and signed by the governor and six other magistrates, and Mr. Marie, whereof one copy we kept and the other he carried with him . . .

8 die mensis 8 [8 October], An. Dom. 1644. The governor and the rest of the magistrates do promise to Mr. Marie that they and all the English within the jurisdiction of the Massachusetts aforesaid shall observe and keep firm peace with Mr. D'Aulnay, etc., and all the French under his command in Acadie: and likewise the said Mr. Marie doth promise for Mr. D'Aulnay that he and all his people shall also keep firm peace with the governor and magistrates aforesaid, and with all the inhabitants of the jurisdiction of the Massachusetts aforesaid; and that it shall be lawful for all men, both French and English, to trade each with other: so that if any occasion of offence shall happen, neither party shall attempt any thing against the other in any hostile manner before the wrong be first complained of, and due satisfaction not given. Provided always, the governor and magistrates aforesaid be not bound to restrain their merchants to trade with their ships with any persons, either French or other, wheresoever they dwell: provided also, that the full ratification and conclusion of this agreement be referred to the next meeting of the commissioners of the united colonies of New England, for the continuation or abrogation of the same; and in the mean time to remain firm and inviolate.[56]

By this agreement we were freed from the fear our people were in that Mr. D'Aulnay would take revenge of our small vessels or out

56. This agreement was ratified by the commissioners of the New England Confederation on 2 Sept. 1645.

plantations for the harm he sustained by our means the last year; and also from any further question about that business.

We were now also freed from as great a fear of war with the Narragansetts. For the commissioners, meeting at Hartford, sent for Uncas and some from Narragansett (a sachem and a chief captain were sent), and whereas the Narragansett's plea against Uncas was, that he had put their sachem to death after he had received a ransom for his life,[57] it was clearly proved otherwise. In the end it was agreed by all parties, that there should be peace on all sides till planting time were over the next year;[58] and then neither of them should attempt any hostile act against the other, without first acquainting the English, etc. therewith.[59]

A Continuation of the History of New England[60]

17 (7) [September], 1644. The lady La Tour arrived here in a ship set forth from London by Alderman Berklye and Captain Bayley.[61] The lady being arrived brought her action against them for delaying her so long at sea, whereby she lost the opportunity of relieving her fort, and must be at excessive charges to get thither. The cause was openly heard at a special Court at Boston before all the magistrates, and a jury of principal men impaneled (most merchants and seamen), and the charter party[62] being read and witnesses produced, it appeared to the Court

---

57. The Narragansett sachem Miantonomi had been murdered by Uncas; see Aug. 1643, above.

58. The Narragansetts remained dissatisfied with this settlement, and in the summer of 1645 once more threatened to attack Uncas.

59. This is the last entry selected from the second volume of JW's journal.

60. JW wrote this title on the first page of the third volume, as he had in the second volume.

61. William Berkeley was a London merchant who had freighted the ship *Gillyflower,* commanded by Captain Bayley, that carried Madame de La Tour to Boston.

62. The contract between Madame de La Tour and Bayley and Berkeley for hire of the ship *Gillyflower.*

that they had broken charter party, so as the jury gave her £2000 damages. Whereupon, the cargo of the ship was seized in execution (so much of it as could be found), and being meal and peas and trading stuff, etc., and being appraised by 4 men sworn, etc., it was found to the value of about £1100. The defendants desired liberty till the next year to bring a review, pretending they had evidence in England, etc. It was granted them, and they were offered to have all their goods again (except £100 for defraying the lady's present charges in Boston, for which they should have good security, etc.) so as they would put in security to answer the whole £2000 if they did not reverse the judgment within the year. This they refused, and would give security for no more than what they should receive back. Whereupon the execution proceeded. But the master of the ship ⟨petitioned to⟩ brought his action upon the goods in execution for security for his freight and men's wages (which did amount to near the whole extended).[63] The jury found against him, whereupon at the next General Court he petitioned for redress. A great part of the Court was of opinion that the goods, being his security by charter party, ought not to be taken from him upon the execution, and most of the deputies and the deputy governor[64] and some other of the magistrates voted that way. But the greater part of the magistrate being of the other side he could not be relieved. The Lady was forced to give £700 to 3 ships to carry her home.

It may be of use to mention a private matter or 2 which fell out about this time, because the power and mercy of the Lord did appear in them in extraordinary manner. One of the deacons of Boston Church,

---

63. Elias Pilgrim, as master of the *Gillyflower*, was in charge of the ship and crew; he had contracted with Captain Bayley, who held title to the cargo and commanded the voyage, to sail the ship and deliver her cargo as directed. When the Boston authorities impounded Bayley's cargo, Pilgrim petitioned the Nov. 1644 General Court for his share of this cargo in order to pay the crew's wages.

64. JW.

Jacob Eliot (a man of a very sincere heart and an humble frame of spirit),[65] had a daughter of 8 years of age, which being playing with other children about a cart, the hinder end thereof fell upon the child's head, and an iron sticking out of it struck into the child's head and drive a piece of the scull before it into the brain so as the brains came out, and 7 surgeons (some of the country, very experienced men, and others of the ships which rode in the harbor) being called together for advice, etc., did all conclude that it was the brains (being about half a spoonful at one time and more at other times), and that there was no hope of the child's life except the piece of scull could be drawn out. But one of the ruling elders of the church,[66] an experienced and very skillful surgeon, liked not to take that course but applied only plasters to it. And withal earnest prayers were made by the Church to the Lord for it. And in 6 weeks it pleased God that the piece of scull consumed and so came forth, and the child recovered perfectly, nor did it lose the senses at any time[67] . . .

(8) [October] 30. The General Court assembled again, and all the elders were sent for to reconcile the differences between the magistrates and deputies.[68] When they were come, the first question put to them was that which was stated by consent the last session, viz., whether the magistrates are by patent and election of the people the Standing Council of this commonwealth in the vacancy of the General Court, and have power accordingly to act in all cases subject to government, according to the said patent and the laws of this jurisdiction; and when any necessary occasions call for action from authority, in cases where

65. He was the older brother of the Rev. John Eliot of Roxbury.

66. Probably Thomas Oliver, who was also a physician in Boston.

67. Abigail Eliot was actually five years old at the time of this accident. Cotton Mather, who evidently knew her in old age, recorded that she wore a silver plate "as big as a half crown" over the hole in her skull (*Magnalia Christi Americana* [Hartford, 1820], 2:336).

68. This was a continuation of the quarrel in the June 1644 General Court when the deputies had challenged the magistrates' authority to administer the colony government between court sessions.

there is no particular express law provided, there to be guided by the word of God till the General Court give particular rules in such cases.

The elders, having received the question, withdrew themselves for consultation about it, and the next day sent to know when we would appoint a time that they might attend the Court with their answer. The magistrates and deputies agreed upon an hour, but the deputies came not all, but sent a committee of 4 (which was not well nor respectively,[69] that when all the elders had taken so much pains at their request, some having come 30 miles, they would not vouchsafe their presence to receive their answer). Their answer was affirmative on the magistrates' behalf, in the very words of the question, with some reasons thereof. It was delivered in writing by Mr. Cotton in the name of them all, they being all present and not one dissenting.[70]

Upon the return of this answer, the deputies prepared other questions to be propounded to the elders, and sent them to the magistrates to take view of. Likewise, the magistrates prepared 4 questions and sent them also to the deputies.

The magistrates' questions, with the elders' answers, were:

1. Whether the deputies in the General Court have judicial and magistratical authority?

2. Whether by patent the General Court, consisting of magistrates and deputies (as a General Court), have judicial and magistratical authority?

3. Whether we may warrantably prescribe certain penalties to offences which may probably admit variable degrees of guilt?

4. Whether a judge be bound to pronounce such sentence as a positive law ⟨requires⟩ prescribes, in case it be apparently above or beneath the merit of the offence?

69. Respectfully.

70. This verdict did not settle the issue, however, because the deputies rejected the clergy's position and the General Court took no vote on this troublesome issue in Oct. 1644.

The elders' answer to the 2 first:

1. The patent, in express words, giveth full power and authority, as to the governor and assistants, so to the freemen also assembled in General Court.

2. Whereas there is a 3 fold power of magistratical authority, viz., legislative, judicial, and consultative or directive of the public affairs of the country for provision and protection, the 1 of these, viz., legislative, is expressly given to the freemen jointly with the governor and assistants. Consultative or directive power, etc., is also granted by the patent as the other. But now for power of judicature (if we speak of the constant and usual administration thereof), we do not find that it is granted to the freemen, or deputies in the General Court, either by the patent, or the election of the people, or by any law of the country . . .

To the 3. and 4. questions the elders' answer: . . . In those cases wherein the judge is persuaded in conscience that a crime deserveth a greater punishment than the law inflicteth, he may lawfully pronounce sentence according to the prescript penalty, etc., because he hath no power committed to him by law to go higher. But where the law may seem to the conscience of the judge to inflict a greater penalty than the offence deserveth, it is his part to suspend his sentence till by conference with the lawgivers he find liberty either to inflict the sentence or to mitigate it[71] . . .

Questions propounded to the elders by the deputies:

1. Whether the governor and assistants have any power by patent to dispense justice in the vacancy of the General Court, without some law or order of the same to declare the rule?

The elders' answer was negative.

2. Question: Whether any General Court hath not power by patent

---

71. Again, the deputies rejected this judgment, and the General Court voted that the magistrates had no power to vary from penalties prescribed in the law.

in particular cases to choose any commissioners (either assistants or freemen), exempting all others, to give them commission to set forth their power and places? By "any particular case" we mean in all things and in the choice of all officers.

The elders' answer:

If the terms "all things" intend all cases of constant judicature and counsel, we answer negatively, etc., because then it would follow that the magistrates might be excluded from all cases of constant judicature and counsel which are their principal work; whereby also the end of the people's election would be made frustrate . . .

3. Question: Whether the titles of governor, deputy, and assistants do necessarily imply magistratical authority in the patent?

The elders' answer was affirmative.

4. Question: Whether the magistratical power be not given by the patent to the people or General Court, and by them to the governor, etc.?

The elders' answer: The magistratical power is given to the governor, etc., by the patent. To the people is given by the same patent to design the persons to those places of government. And to the General Court power is given to make laws as the rules of their administration.

Most of the deputies were now well satisfied concerning the authority of the magistrates, etc., but some few leading men (who had drawn on the rest) were still fixed upon their own opinions. So hard a matter it is to draw men (even wise and godly) from the love of the fruit of their own inventions.

There fell out at this Court another occasion of further trouble. The deputy governor having formerly, and from time to time, opposed the deputies' claim of judicial authority, and the prescribing of set penalties in cases which may admit variable degrees of guilt, which occasioned them to suspect that he and some other of the magistrates did affect an arbitrary government, he now wrote a small treatise about these points, showing what arbitrary government was and that our government (in the state it now stood) was not arbitrary, neither in the ground and foundation of it nor in the exercise and administration thereof[72] . . .

At this Court Mr. Saltonstall moved very earnestly that he might be left out at the next election, and pursued his motion after to the towns. It could not appear what should move him to it, only Mr. Bellingham and he held together and joined with the deputies against the rest of the magistrates,[73] but not prevailing, and being oft opposed in public, might put some discouragement upon his spirit to see all differ from him save one. And indeed it occasioned much grief to all the elders, and gave great offence through the country. And such as were acquainted with other states in the world and had not well known the persons would have concluded such a faction here as hath been usual in the Council of England and other states, who walk by politic principles only. But these gentlemen were such as feared God and endeavored to walk by the rules of his word in all their proceedings, so as it might be conceived in charity that they walked according to their judgments and conscience, and where they went aside it was merely for want of light, or their eyes were held through some temptation for a time, that they could not make use of the light they had. For in all these differences and agitations about them they continued in brotherly love, and in the exercise of all friendly offices each to other as occasion required . . .

[(1) March] 26, 1645. Two great fires happened this week, one at Salem, Mr. Downing having built a new house at his farm. He being gone to England, and his wife[74] and family gone to the Church meeting

72. JW's "Discourse on Arbitrary Government," written in July 1644, is printed in *WP*, 4:468–482; it argues belligerently that the magistrates have full executive and judicial authority—a position rejected by the General Court in Nov. 1644.

73. Despite Saltonstall's efforts to step down, he and Bellingham were annually reelected as assistants, 1645–1649. Saltonstall returned to England in 1649 and came back to Massachusetts in the 1660s.

74. Lucy Winthrop Downing (1601–1679) was JW's sister; she had married Emmanuel Downing in 1622 and came with him to Salem, Mass. in 1638.

upon the Lord's day, the chimney took fire and burnt down the house and ⟨much⟩ ∧bedding∧, apparel, and household to the value of £200. The other was at Roxbury this day. Jo. Johnson, the surveyor general of the ammunition, a very industrious and faithful man in his place, having built a fair house in the middest of the town with divers barns and other out houses, it fell on fire in the daytime (no man knowing by what occasion), and there being in it 17 barrels of the country's powder and many arms, all was suddenly burnt and blown up to the value of £4 or £500. Wherein a special providence of God appeared, for he being from home, the people came together to help and many were in the house, no man thinking of the powder, till one of the company put them in mind of it, whereupon they all withdrew, and ⟨presently⟩ ∧soon after∧ the powder took fire and blew up all about it, and shook the houses in Boston and Cambridge, so as men thought it had been an earthquake, and carried great pieces of timber a great way off, and some rags and such light things beyond Boston meeting house . . .

Mr. John Winthrop the younger, coming from England 2 years since, brought with him £1,000 stock and divers workmen to begin an iron-work, and had moved the Court for some encouragement to be given the undertakers, and for the Court to join in carrying on the work here. The business was well approved by the Court as a thing much conducing to the good of the country, but we had no stock in the treasury to give furtherance to it. Only some 2 or 3 private persons joined in it, and the Court granted the adventurers near all their demands, as a monopoly of it for 21 years, liberty to make use of any ∧5∧ places not already granted, and to have 3 miles square in every place to them and their heirs, and freedom from public charges, trainings, etc.[75] . . .

75. JW2 had gone to England in 1641 to gather capital and workmen for a blast furnace and forge. Returning in 1643, he built a furnace at Braintree and produced some pig iron. In 1645 Richard Leader replaced JW2 as manager, moved operations to Lynn, and built a

Mr. Shepard, the pastor of the Church in Cambridge, being at Connecticut when the Commissioners met there for the United Colonies, moved them for some contribution of help towards the maintenance of poor scholars in the college. Whereupon the Commissioners ordered that it should be commended to the deputies of the General Courts and the elders within the several colonies to raise (by way of voluntary contribution) one peck of corn or 12d. in money or other commodity of every family. Which those of Connecticut presently performed[76] . . .

Divers free schools were erected as at Roxbury (for maintenance whereof every inhabitant bound some house or land for a yearly allowance forever) and at Boston (where they made an order to allow forever £50 to the master and an house, and £30 to an usher, who should also teach to read and write and cipher, and Indians' children were to be taught freely, and the charge to be by yearly contribution, either by voluntary allowance, or by rate of such as refused, etc., and this order was confirmed by the General Court). Other towns did the like, providing maintenance by several means[77] . . .

(2) [April] 13. Mr. Hopkins, the governor of Hartford upon Connecticut, came to Boston and brought his wife with him (a godly young woman and of special parts),[78] who was fallen into a sad infirmity, the loss of her understanding and reason, which had been growing upon her divers years by occasion of her giving herself wholly to reading

---

furnace and forge on the Saugus River that produced bar iron and ironware, but at too high a cost. In the 1650s the company promoted by JW2 went bankrupt.

76. The Rev. Thomas Shepard made his appeal for Harvard College to the Commissioners in Sept. 1644.

77. The Roxbury school was founded in 1646. By this date Boston, Cambridge, Charlestown, Dedham, Dorchester, Ipswich, Newbury, and Salem also had schools. In 1647 the General Court ordered that every Massachusetts town of 50 households should appoint a school teacher and that every town of 100 households should set up a grammar school (*MR*, 2:203).

78. Ann Yale Hopkins (d. 1698) was the stepdaughter of Theophilus Eaton, gov. of New Haven, and the wife of Edward Hopkins, gov. of Connecticut. She had come to New England with her husband in 1637.

and writing, and had written many books. Her husband being very loving and tender of her was loath to grieve her, but he saw his error when it was too late, for if she had attended her household affairs and such things as belong to women, and not gone out of her way and calling to meddle in such things as are proper for men, whose minds are stronger, etc., she had kept her wits and might have improved them usefully and honorably in the place God had set her.[79] He brought her to Boston and left her with her brother, one Mr. Yale,[80] a merchant, to try what means might be had here for her, but no help could be had.

[April] 23. The governor and assistants met at Boston to consider what might lawfully be done for saving La Tour and his fort out of the hands of D'Aulnay, who was now before it with all his strength, both of men and vessels.[81] So soon as we were met, word was brought us that a vessel sent by some merchants to carry provisions to La Tour was fallen into the hands of D'Aulnay, who had made prize of her, and turned the men upon an island and kept them there 10 days, and then gave them an old shallop (not above 2 ton) and some provisions to bring them home, but denied them their clothes, etc. (which at first he had promised them), and any gun or compass, whereby it was justly conceived that he intended they should perish either at sea or by the Indians (who were at hand, and chased them next day, etc.). Upon this news we presently dispatched away a vessel to D'Aulnay with letters, wherein we expostulated with him about this act of his, complaining of it as a breach of the articles of our peace, and required the vessel and goods to be restored . . .

79. JW2 tried unsuccessfully to treat Ann Hopkins in 1647 (*WP*, 5:156, 231). She returned to England with her husband in 1652, was provided with nursing care in his will, and outlived him by 41 years.

80. David Yale, a Boston merchant. His son Elihu became the principal benefactor of Yale College.

81. D'Aulnay had captured La Tour's fort on the St. John River on 16 April 1645, a week before this meeting. He did not capture La Tour, who was in Boston trying once again to recruit help, but he imprisoned Madame de La Tour (who soon died) and he hanged a number of La Tour's garrison.

The governor and assistants had used for 10 or 11 years at least to appoint one to preach ⟨at⟩ ∧on∧ the day of election, but about 3 or 4 years since, the deputies challenged it as their right, and accordingly had twice made the choice (the magistrates still professing it to be a mere intrusion, etc). And now at the last General Court in October they had given order to call Mr. Norton to that service (never acquainting the magistrates therewith), and about some 2 months before the time, the governor and divers other of the magistrates (not knowing anything of what the deputies had done) agreed upon Mr. Norris of Salem and gave him notice of it. But at this meeting of the magistrates it grew a question whether of these 2 should be employed, seeing both had been invited and both were prepared. At last it was put to vote, and that determined it upon Mr. Norton. The reason was the unwillingness of the magistrates to have any fresh occasion of contestation with the deputies. But some judged it a failing (especially in one or 2 who had already joined in calling Mr. Norris) and a betraying, or at least weakening, the power of the magistrates, and a ⟨mere usurpation⟩ countenancing of an unjust usurpation, for the deputies could do no such act as an act of Court without the concurrence of the magistrates, and out of Court they had no power at all (but only for regulating their own body). And it was resolved and voted at last Court (according to the elders' advice) that all occurrents out of Court belong to the magistrates to take care of, being the standing council of the commonwealth . . .

The wars in England kept servants from coming to us, so as those we had could not be hired when their times were out but upon unreasonable terms. And we found it very difficult to pay their wages to their content (for money was very scarce). I may upon this occasion report a passage between one of Rowly and his servant: the master, being forced to sell a pair of his oxen to pay his servant his wages, told his servant he could keep him no longer, not knowing how to pay him the next year. The servant answered he would serve him for more of his cattle. But how shall I do (saith the master) when all my cattle are gone? The servant replied: you shall then serve me and so you may have your cattle again . . .

(3) [May] 14. The Court of Elections was held at Boston. ∧Mr.∧ Thomas Dudley was chosen governor, Mr. Winthrop deputy governor again, and Mr. Endecott sergeant major general . . .

This Court fell out a troublesome business which took up much time. The town of Hingham, having one Emes their lieutenant 7 or 8 years, had lately chosen him to be their captain and had presented him to the Standing Council for allowance. But before it was accomplished, the greater part of the town took some light occasion of offence against him, and chose one Allen to be their captain, and presented him to the magistrates (in the time of the last General Court) to be allowed.[82] But the magistrates, considering the injury that would hereby accrue to Eames (who had been their chief commander so many years and had deserved well in his place, and that Allen had no other skill but what he learned from Eames), refused to allow of Allen, but willed both sides to return home and every officer to keep his place until the Court should take further order. Upon their return home the messengers who came for Allen called a private meeting of those of their own party, and told them truly what answer they received from the magistrates, and soon after they appointed a training day (without their lieutenant's knowledge), and being assembled, the lieutenant hearing of it came to them and would have exercised them as he was wont to do. But those of the other party refused to follow him except he would show them some order for it. Another of them professeth he will die at the sword's point if he might not have the choice of his own officers. The tumult continuing, one of the officers required Allen to take the captain's place.

82. Anthony Eames was one of the few Hingham settlers from the west of England, coming from Fordington, Dorset. His rival, Bozoan Allen, like most of the other Hingham settlers, was a Norfolk man and came from King's Lynn; he was a leading critic of J W's political views.

But he not then accepting it, they put it to the vote whether he should be their captain. The vote passing for it, he then told the company it was now past question, and thereupon Allen accepted it and exercised the company 2 or 3 days. Only about $\frac{1}{3}$ part of them followed the lieutenant. He, having denied in the open field that authority had advised him to lay down his place, and putting (in some sort) the lie upon those who had so reported, was the next Lord's day called to answer it before the Church. Whereupon the ⟨Church⟩ pastor, one Mr. Hubbert (brother to 3 of the principal in this sedition),[83] was very forward to have excommunicate the lieutenant presently, but, upon some opposition, it was put off to the next day. Hereupon the lieutenant, and some 3 or 4 more of the chief men of the town, inform 4 of the next magistrates of these proceedings, who sent warrant to the constable to attach some of the principal offenders (viz., 3 of the Hobarts and 2 more). Upon the day [of the next Court] they came to Boston, but their said brother the minister came before them, and fell to expostulate with the said magistrates about the said cause, complaining against the complainants as talebearers, etc., taking it very disdainfully that his brethren should be sent for by a constable, with other high speeches, which were so provoking as some of the magistrates told him that were it not for respect to his ministry they would commit him. So they were bound over (each for other) to the next Court of Assistants. After this 5 other came before the deputy governor[84] when he was alone, and demanded the cause of their sending for, and to know their accusers. The deputy told them so much of the cause as he could remember, and referred them to the secretary for a copy, and for their accusers he told them they knew both the men and the matter. Neither was ∧a judge∧ ⟨he⟩

---

83. The Rev. Peter Hobart (1604–1679) was pastor of the Hingham Church from 1635 to his death. His brother Joshua was the ringleader of opposition to Lieutenant Eames and to the magistrates. Two other brothers, Edmund and Thomas Hobart, were also active in this dispute.

84. JW.

bound to let a criminal offender know his accusers before the day of trial, but only in his own discretion, lest the accuser might be taken off or perverted, etc. Being required to give bond for their appearance, etc., they refused, and upon their second refusal [he] committed them in the open Court.[85]

The General Court falling out before the Court of Assistants, the Hobarts and the 2 which were committed and others of Hingham, about 90 (whereof Mr. Hobart, their minister, was the first), presented a petition to the General Court to this effect: that whereas some of them had been bound over, and others committed by some of the magistrates for words spoken concerning the power of the General Court and their liberties ∧and the liberties of the Churches,∧ etc., they craved that the Court would hear the cause, etc.[86] This was first presented to the deputies, who sent it to the magistrates, desiring their concurrence with them that the cause might be heard, etc. The magistrates, marveling that they would grant such a petition without desiring conference first with themselves whom it so much concerned, returned answer that they were willing the cause should be heard, so as the petitioners would name the magistrates whom they intended, and the matters they would lay to their charge. Thereupon they singled out the deputy governor, and 2 of the petitioners undertook the prosecution[87] . . .

The day appointed being come, the Court assembled in the meeting

85. JW sent two of his Hingham antagonists—John Folsom and John Tower—to jail. This seems to have happened shortly before the May 1645 General Court.

86. The Hingham petition was signed by 81 persons and must have been endorsed by the great majority of the townspeople, since there were only 79 adult males in Hingham in 1647.

87. The Hingham case now turned into the most dramatic power struggle in Massachusetts since the Antinomian controversy of 1637. The Hingham leaders were challenging the MBC magistrates collectively and JW personally. They were articulating two principles that JW had always opposed: (a) local autonomy in town and church affairs, and (b) representative participation in colony government. By staging what was in effect an impeachment trial, the Hingham petitioners hoped to receive overwhelming support from the deputies in the General Court and from the three dissident magistrates: Bellingham, Saltonstall, and Bradstreet. For his part, JW wrote up the Hingham controversy so as to

house at Boston. Divers of the elders were present and a great assembly of people. The deputy governor, coming in with the rest of the magistrates, placed himself beneath within the bar and so sat uncovered. Some question was in the Court about his being in that place (for many both of the Court and the assembly were grieved at it). But the deputy telling them that, being criminally accused, he might not sit as a judge in that cause, and if he were upon the bench it would be a great disadvantage to him, for he could not take that liberty to plead the cause ∧which∧ he ought to be allowed at the bar. Upon this the Court was satisfied . . .

Hereupon the Court proceeded to examine the whole cause. The deputy justified all the particulars laid to his charge, as according to the equity of laws here established, and the custom and laws of England, and our constant practice here these 15 years. And for some speeches he was charged with as spoken to the delinquents when they came before him at his house, when none were present with him but themselves, first he appealed to the judgment of the Court whether delinquents may be received as competent witnesses against a magistrate in such a case? Then, for the words themselves, some he justified, some he explained, so as no advantage could be taken of them, as that he should say that the magistrates could try some criminal causes without a jury, that he knew no law of God or man which required a judge to make known to the party his accusers (or rather witnesses) before the cause came to hearing. But 2 of them charged him to have said that it was against the law of God and man so to do, which had been absurd, for the deputy professed he knew no law against it, only a judge may sometimes in discretion conceal their names, etc., lest they should be tampered with or conveyed out of the way, etc.

Two of the magistrates[88] and many of the deputies were of opinion

---

dramatize his central role, quoting the full text of his "little speech" (see below) in vindication of his position.

88. Probably Bellingham and Saltonstall.

that the magistrates exercised too much power, and that the people's liberty was thereby in danger. And other of the deputies (being ⟨with⟩ about half) and all the rest of the magistrates were of a different judgment, and that authority was overmuch slighted, which if not ⟨timely prevented⟩ timely remedied would endanger the commonwealth and bring us to a mere democracy. By occasion of this difference there was not so orderly carriage at the hearing as was meet, each side striving unseasonably to enforce the evidence and declaring their judgments thereupon, which should have been reserved to a more private debate (as after it was), so as the best part of 2 days was spent in this public agitation, and examination of witnesses, etc. This being ended, a committee was chosen of magistrates and deputies, who stated the case as it appeared upon the whole pleading and evidence, though it cost much time, and with great difficulty did the committee come to accord upon it.[89]

The case being stated and agreed, the magistrates and deputies considered it apart. First the deputies, having spent a whole day and not attaining ∧to∧ any issue, sent up to the magistrates to have their thoughts about it, who, taking it into consideration (the deputy always withdrawing when that matter came into debate), agreed upon those 4 points ∧chiefly∧:[90] 1. That the petition was false and scandalous; 2. That those who were bound over, etc., and others that were parties to the disturbance at Hingham, were all offenders, though in different degrees; 3. That they and the petitioners were to be censured; 4. That the deputy governor ought to be acquit and righted, etc. This being

89. The Hingham case is reported at length in the deputies' minutes (*MR*, 3:19–26), but very briefly in the magistrates' minutes (*MR*, 2:113–114).

90. The magistrates sent down ten resolutions, which JW has here condensed. In a series of close votes, the deputies accepted eight of these resolutions, but the gap between the two houses remained wide. By a vote of 16–12, the deputies agreed that some things in the Hingham petition were false and scandalous, but by a vote of 17–14 they denied that the charges against JW were causeless and unjust (*MR*, 3:19–21).

sent down to the deputies, they spent divers days about it, and made 2 or 3 returns to the magistrates. And though they found the petition false and scandalous ∧and so voted it,∧ yet they would not agree to any censure.[91] The magistrates on the other side were resolved for censure, and for the deputy's full acquittal. The deputies being thus hard held to it and growing weary of the Court (for it began (3) [May] 14, and brake not up, save one week, till (5) [July] 5), were content they should pay the charges of the Court. After, they were drawn to consent to some small fines, but in this they would have drawn in Lieutenant Eames to have been fined deeply, he being neither plaintiff nor defendant but an informer only, and had made good all the points of his information, and no offence found in him other than that which was afore adjudged worthy admonition only. And they would have imposed the charges of the Court upon the whole trained band at Hingham, when it was apparent that divers were innocent and had no hand in any of these proceedings[92]. . . . At last [the deputies and magistrates] came to this agreement, viz., ⟨all⟩ the ∧chief∧ petitioners and the rest of the offenders were severally fined (all their fines not amounting to £50); the rest of the petitioners to bear equal share to £50 more towards the charges of the Court (2 of the principal offenders were the deputies of the town, Joshua Hobart and Bozone Allen; the first was

91. The majority of the deputies differed from the magistrates on the following points. They held (1) that the Hingham militia had not mutinied, because Lieutenant Eames had laid down his place; (2) that Eames was partly to blame for the troubles at Hingham; (3) that the magistrates had exceeded their authority when they confirmed Eames's appointment; (4) that while the Hingham ringleaders deserved punishment, the rest of the petitioners should not be censured; and (5) that JW should also be censured for telling two of the ringleaders "that it was contrary to the law of God and man to know their accusers before the time of trial."

92. The magistrates wanted the Hingham petitioners to pay for the cost of the extended seven-week General Court session, with fines totaling £155. The deputies, on the other hand, were willing to levy only £105 in fines, of which £55 was to be paid by the Hingham militia rather than the petitioners (MR, 3:23–24).

fined £20 and the other £5); Lieutenant Eames to be under admonition; the deputy governor to be legally and publicly acquit of all that was laid to his charge.[93]

According to this agreement, ⟨5⟩ [July] 3, presently after the lecture the magistrates and deputies took their places in the meeting house, and the people being come together, and the deputy governor placing himself within the bar as at the time of ∧the∧ hearing, etc., the governor read the sentence of the Court without speaking any more, for the deputies had (by importunity) obtained a promise of silence from the magistrates. Then was the deputy governor desired by the Court to go up and take his place again upon the bench, which he did accordingly. And the Court being about to rise, he desired leave for a little speech which was to this effect.[94]

I suppose something ⟨will⟩ may be expected from me upon this charge that is befallen me, which moves me to speak ⟨speak less⟩ ∧now to you∧. Yet I intend not to intermeddle in the proceedings of the Court, or with any of the persons concerned therein. Only I bless God that I see an issue of this troublesome business. I also acknowledge the justice of the Court, and for mine own part I am well satisfied. I was publicly charged, and I am publicly and legally acquitted, which is all

93. A clear victory for the magistrates and for JW, although the deputies did succeed in scaling down the fines. Nine of the Hingham ringleaders were fined a total of £46 10s, the other 78 petitioners were fined a total of £53 10s, and Lieutenant Eames was admonished but not fined (*MR*, 2:113–114; 3:25–26, 94, 113).

94. JW's "little speech" is his most eloquent and best remembered statement on political theory. It may usefully be compared with his "Model of Christian Charity" of 1630; see pp. 1–11, above. In both this speech and the "Model," JW makes a distinction between natural law and moral law, but his applications are rather different. Back in 1630, he had emphasized the positive character of moral or Gospel love in arguing that the colonists must bind themselves into a covenanted community. Now in 1645 he emphasizes the negative character of natural or beastlike liberty in urging submission to magisterial authority. The authority of the MBC magistrates rests upon moral or Christian liberty. The magistrates are God's lieutenants; they and the people are in covenant with God; and hence the people must obey God's ordinances and the magistrates' interpretation of these ordinances.

I did expect or desire. And though this be sufficient for my justification before men, ∧yet not so before the Lord∧ who hath seen so much amiss in any dispensations (and even in this affair) as calls me to be humbled. For to be publicly and criminally charged in this Court is matter of humiliation (and I desire to make a right use of it), notwithstanding I be thus acquitted. If her father had spit in her face (saith the Lord ⟨of⟩ concerning Miriam), should she not have been ashamed 7 days? Shame had lain upon her whatever the occasion had been.[95] I am unwilling to stay you from your urgent affairs, yet give me leave (upon this special occasion) to speak a little more to this assembly. It may be of some good use to inform and rectify the judgments of some of the people, and may prevent such distempers as have arisen amongst us. The great questions that have troubled the country are about the authority of the magistrates and the liberty of the people. It is yourselves who have called us to this office, and being called by you we have our authority from God in way of an ordinance, such as hath the image of God eminently stamped upon it, the contempt and violation whereof hath been vindicated with examples of divine vengeance. I entreat you to consider that when you choose magistrates you take them from among yourselves, men subject to like passions as you are. Therefore, when you see infirmities in us, you should reflect upon your own, and that would make you bear the more with us, and not be severe censurers of the failings of your magistrates when you have continual experience of the like infirmities in yourselves and others. We account him a good servant who breaks not his covenant. The covenant between you and us is the oath you have taken of us, which is to this purpose, that we shall govern you and judge your causes ⟨accord⟩ ⟨after⟩ by the rules of God's laws and our own, according to our best skill. When you agree with a workman to build you ∧a∧ ship or house, etc., he undertakes as well for his skill as for his faithfulness,

95. Num. 12:14.

for it is his profession, and you pay him for both. But when you call one to be a magistrate, he doth not profess nor undertake to have sufficient skill for that office, ∧nor can you furnish him with gifts, etc.∧ Therefore you must run the hazard of his skill and ability. But if he fail in faithfulness, which by his oath he is bound unto, that he must answer for. If it fall out that the case be clear to common apprehension and the rule clear also, if he transgress here the error is not in the skill but in the evil of the will; it must be required of him. But if the case be doubtful, or the rule doubtful, to men of such understanding and parts as your magistrates are, if your magistrates should err here your-selves must bear it.

For the other point concerning liberty, ⟨let⟩ I observe a great mistake in the country about that. There is a twofold liberty: natural (I mean as our nature is now corrupt), and civil or federal. The first is common to man with beasts and other creatures. By this, man as he stands in relation to man simply, hath liberty to do what he list. It is a liberty to evil as well as to good. This liberty is incompatible and inconsistent with authority, and cannot endure the least restraint of the most just authority. The exercise and maintaining of this liberty makes men grow more evil, and in time to be worse than brute beasts, omnes sumus licentia deteriores.[96] This is that great enemy of truth and peace, ⟨which all⟩ that wild beast which all the ordinances of God are bent against, to restrain and subdue it.

The other kind of liberty I call civil or federal. It may also be termed moral, in reference to the covenant between God and man in the moral law, and the politic covenants and constitutions amongst men them-selves. This liberty is the proper end and object of authority and cannot subsist without it, and it is a liberty to that only which is good, just,

96. "We all degenerate in the absence of control" (a quotation from Terence, *Heau-tontimorumenos*, III, 1, 74).

and honest. This liberty you are to stand for, with the hazard not only of your goods but of your lives, if need be. Whatsoever crosseth this is not authority, but a distemper thereof. This liberty is maintained and exercised in a way of subjection to authority. It is of the same kind of liberty wherewith Christ hath made us free.[97] The woman's own choice makes such a man her husband, yet being so chosen he is her lord and she is to be subject to him, yet in a way of liberty, not of bondage, and a true wife accounts her subjection her honor and freedom, and would not think her condition safe and free but in her subjection to her husband's authority. Such is the liberty of the church under the authority of Christ her King and ⟨master⟩ husband. His yoke is so easy and sweet to her as a bride's ornaments,[98] and if through frowardness or wantonness, etc., she shake it off at any time, she is at no rest in her spirit until she take it up again. And whether her Lord smiles upon her and embraceth her in his arms, or whether he frowns, or rebukes, or smites her, she apprehends the sweetness of his love in all and is refreshed, supported, and instructed by every such dispensation of his authority over her. On the other side, you know who they are that complain of this yoke and say: let us break their bands, etc.; we will not have this man to rule over us. Even so, brethren, it will be between you and your magistrates. If you stand for your natural corrupt liberties, and will do what is good in your own eyes, you will not endure the least weight of authority, but will murmur and oppose and be always striving to shake off that yoke. But if you will be satisfied to enjoy such civil and lawful liberties, such as Christ allows you, then will you quietly and cheerfully submit unto that authority which is set over you in all the administrations of it for your good; wherein if we fail at any time, we hope we shall be willing (by God's assistance) to hearken to good

97. Gal. 5:1.
98. Eph. 5:22–24; Rev. 21:2; Matt. 11:30.

advice from any of you, or in any other way of God. So shall your liberties be preserved in upholding the honor and power of authority amongst you.

The deputy governor having ended his speech, the Court arose, and the magistrates and deputies retired to attend their other affairs. Many things were observable in the agitation and proceedings about this case . . . Some of the deputies had seriously conceived that the magistrates affected an arbitrary government, and that they had (or sought to have) an unlimited power to do what they pleased without control. This caused them to interpret all the magistrates' actions and speeches (not complying exactly with their own principles) as tending that way, by which occasions their fears and jealousies increased daily . . . All which tended still to weaken the authority of the magistrates and their reputation with the people. Then fell out the Hingham case, which they eagerly laid hold on and pursued to the utmost, for they doubted not but they could now make it appear either that the magistrates had abused their authority, or else that their authority was too great to consist with the people's liberty, and therefore ought to be reduced ⟨into⟩ within narrower bounds . . .

I should have mentioned in the Hingham case what care and pains many of the elders had taken to reconcile the differences which were grown in that Church. Mr. Hobart, the pastor there, being of a presbyterial spirit, did manage all affairs without the Church's advice, which divers of the congregation not liking of, they were divided in 2 parts. Lieutenant Eames, etc., having complained to the magistrates as is before expressed, Mr. Hobart, etc., would have cast him out of the church, pretending that he had told a lie. Whereupon they procured the elders to write to the Church, and so did some of the magistrates also. Whereupon, they stayed proceeding against the lieutenant for a day or 2, but he and some 12 more of them, finding no way of reconciliation, they withdrew from the Church and openly declared it in the congregation.

This course the elders did not approve of; but being present in the Court when their petition against the deputy governor was heard, Mr. Hobart, perceiving the cause was like to go against him and his party, desired the elders to go to Hingham to mediate a reconciliation (which he would never hearken to before). They readily accepted the motion and went to Hingham and spent 2 or 3 days there, and found the pastor and his part in great fault, but could not bring him to any acknowledgment. In their return by water they were kept 24 hours in the boat, and were in great danger by occasion of a tempest which arose in the night, but the Lord preserved them . . .

We understood for certain afterward that Monsieur La Tour's fort was taken by assault and scalado,[99] that Monsieur D'Aulnay lost in the attempt 12 men and had many wounded, and that he had put to death all the men (both French and English) and had taken the Lady, who died within 3 weeks after, and her little child and her gentlewoman were sent into France. La Tour valued his jewels, plate, household, ordnance, and other movables at £10,000. The more was his folly to leave so much substance in so great danger when he might have brought the most of it to Boston, whereby he might have discharged his engagement of more than £2500 to Major Edward Gibbons (who by this loss was more quite undone) and might have had somewhat to have maintained himself and his men. For want whereof his servants were forced to go out of the country, some to the Dutch and others to France, and he himself to lie at other men's charge . . .

The scarcity of good ministers in England and want of employment for our new graduates here occasioned some of them to look abroad. Three honest young men, good scholars and very hopeful, viz., a younger son of Mr. Higginson to England and so to Holland and after to the East Indies; a younger son of Mr. Buckly, a Bachelor of Art, to England; and Mr. George Downing, son to Mr. Emmanuel Downing

---

99. Scaling ladders. D'Aulnay had captured La Tour's Fort St. Jean on 16 April 1645.

of Salem, ∧Bachelor of Art also,∧ about 20 years of age, went in a ship to the West Indyes to instruct the seamen.[1] He went by Newfoundland, and so to Christophers and Barbados and Nevis, and being requested to preach in all those places, he gave such content as he had large offers made to stay with them. But he continued in the ship to England, and being a very able scholar, and of a ready wit and fluent utterance, he was soon taken notice of and called to be a preacher in Sir Thomas Fairfax his army, to Colonel Okye his regiment[2] . . .

Mr. James Smith with his mate [Thomas] Keyser were bound to Guinye to trade for negroes.[3] But when they arrived there they met with some Londoners, with whom they consorted, and the Londoners having been formerly injured by the natives (or at least pretending the same) they invited them aboard one of their ships upon the Lord's day, and such as came they kept prisoners. Then they landed men and a murderer,[4] and assaulted one of their towns and killed many of the people, but the country coming down, they were forced to retire without any booty, divers of their men being wounded with the negroes' arrows, and one killed. Mr. Smith, having taken in wine at Maderas, sailed to Barbados to put off his wine. But his ship and cargo [being] bound over to the said Keysar, his mate, and others of Boston who set out the ship, Keysar refused to let any of the wines go on shore except he might have security for the proceed to be returned on shipboard. So the ship lay a week in the road, and then Keysar, fearing that the

---

1. Francis Higginson, John Bulkeley, and George Downing all settled permanently in England. Downing, who was JW's nephew, graduated from Harvard in 1642, became a chaplain in the parliamentary army, an intelligence officer for Oliver Cromwell in the 1650s, ambassador to the Netherlands for Charles II in the 1660s, and a London real estate developer; Downing Street is named after him.

2. Fairfax was Captain-General of the parliamentary army, and John Okey a commander of dragoons. Okey signed Charles I's death warrant in 1649; at the Restoration he was arrested through the connivance of his former chaplain Downing, and was hanged, drawn, and quartered.

3. Capt. Smith was a member of the Boston Church.

4. A small cannon.

master would use some means by other ships which rode there to deprive him of the cargo, told him plainly that ∧if∧ he would not come aboard and return to Boston (which was the last port they were bound to), he would carry away the ship and leave him behind. Which accordingly he did, and arriv[ed] at Boston about midsummer. A short time after Mr. Smith came, and brought his action against Keysar and the other mariners for bringing away the ship, and by a jury of seamen and merchants recovered 3 or 4 times the value of what he was damnified, and the mate Keysar to lose not only his wages, but he and the rest of the merchants to lose the proceed or interest agreed for their stock and adventure, which was 40 per cent, and all the mariners to lose their wages[5] . . .

For the matter of the Negroes, whereof 2 were brought home in the ship, and near 100 slain by the confession of some of the mariners, the magistrates took order to have those 2 set at liberty, and to be sent home. But for the slaughter committed, they were in great doubt what to do in it, seeing it was in another country, and the Londoners pretended a just revenge. So they called the elders, and desired their advice.[6]

Mr. Israel Stoughton, one of the magistrates, having been in England about merchandise and returned with good advantage, went for England again the last winter with divers other of our best military men and entered into the Parliament's service. Mr. Stoughton was made lieutenant colonel to Colonel Reinsborowe; Mr. Nehemia Bourne, a ship carpenter, was major of his regiment; and Mr. John Leverett, son of one of the elders of the Church of Boston, a captain of a foot

---

5. This case was appealed to the General Court, which decided for Smith and against Keysar in Oct. 1645 (*MR*, 2:129).

6. In Oct. 1645 Richard Saltonstall petitioned the General Court that justice be done on Smith and Keysar for murder and man stealing. The court directed Francis Williams of Strawberry Bank, N.H. to release the Negro slave he had acquired from Smith so that he could be sent back to Guinea (*MR*, 2:136, 168; 3:46), but took no further action against Smith and Keysar.

company; and one William Hudson, ensign of the same company; [Francis] ∧Lisle, surgeon to Earl of Manchester lifeguard.∧[7] These did good service and were well approved. But Mr. Stoughton falling sick and dying at Lincoln, ⟨they⟩ ∧the rest∧ all returned to their wives and families . . .

1 (5) [July]. Many books coming out of England, ∧some∧ in defense of Anabaptism and other errors, and for liberty of conscience as a shelter for their toleration, etc., others in maintenance of the presbyterial government (agreed upon by the Assembly of divines in England) against the Congregational way, which was practiced here, the elders of the Churches through all the United Colonies agreed upon a meeting at Cambridge this day, where they conferred their counsels and examined the writings which some of them had prepared in answer to the said books; which being agreed and perfected were sent over into England to be printed. The several answers were these: Mr. Hooker in answer to Mr. Rutterford, the Scotch minister, about presbyterial government (which being sent in the New Haven ship was lost). While Mr. Hooker lived he could not be persuaded to let another copy go over, but after his death, a copy was sent and returned in print, (3) [May] 48.[8]

A sad business fell out this year in Boston. One of the brethren of the Church there,[9] being in England in the Parliament's service about 2 year, had committed the care of his family and business to another[10]

---

7. Israel Stoughton had military experience fighting in the Pequot War; Nehemiah Bourne had built the ship *Trial* in Boston; John Leverett was a future governor (1673–1679) of the MBC; William Hudson was the son of a Boston baker; and Francis Lisle was a barber surgeon in Boston.

8. In 1644 Samuel Rutherford had published *Due right of Presbyteries*, in which he criticized the Congregationalist system of New England. The manuscript of Thomas Hooker's rejoinder, *A Survey of the Summe of Church-Discipline*, was lost at sea in Jan. 1646; this treatise was published posthumously in London in 1648.

9. William Hudson.

10. Henry Dawson, a Boston laborer. He was excommunicated by the Boston Church on 3 Aug. 1645.

of the same Church (a young man of good esteem for piety and sincerity, but his wife was in England), who in time grew over familiar with his master's wife[11] (a young woman, no member of the Church), so as she would be with him oft in his chamber, etc. And one night 2 of the servants being up perceived him to go up into their dame's chamber, which coming to the magistrates' knowledge they were both sent for and examined (but it was not discovered till about $\frac{1}{4}$ of a year after, her husband being then come home) and confessed not only that he was in the chamber with her in such a suspicious manner, but also that he was in bed with her. But both denied any carnal knowledge. And being tried by a jury upon their lives by our law which makes adultery death, the jury acquitted them of the adultery, but found them guilty of adulterous behavior. ⟨his⟩ This was much against the mind of many, both of the magistrates and elders, who judged them worthy of death. But the jury attending what was spoken by other of the magistrates: 1. That seeing the main evidence against them was their own confession of being in bed together, their whole confession must be taken and not a part of it; 2. The law requires 2 witnesses but here was no witness at all, for although circumstances may amount to a testimony against the person where the fact is evident, yet it is otherwise where no fact is apparent; 3. All that the evidence could evince was but suspicion of adultery, but neither God's law nor ours doth make suspicion of adultery (though never so strong) to be death. Whereupon, the case seeming doubtful to the jury, they judged it safest in case of life to find as they did. So the Court adjudged them to stand upon the ladder at the place of execution with halters about their necks one hour, and then to be whipped, or each of them to pay £20. The husband (although he condemned his wife's immodest behavior yet) was so confident of her innocency in point of adultery as he would have paid the £20 rather than she should have been whipped. But their estate being but mean,

11. Ann Hudson.

she chose rather to submit to the rest of her punishment than that her husband should suffer so much for her folly. So he received her again and they lived lovingly together. All that she had to say for herself upon her trial was the same which she had revealed to her husband as soon as he came home, before the matter had been discovered, viz., that he did indeed come into bed to her, which so soon as she perceived she used the best arguments she could to dissuade him from so foul a sin, so as he lay still and did not touch her, but went away again as he came. And the reason why she did not cry out was because he had been very faithful and helpful to her in her husband's absence, which made her very unwilling to bring him to punishment or disgrace . . .

[October]. At the General Court held at Boston the 1 of this month there was a petition preferred by divers merchants and others about 2 laws: the one forbidding the entertaining of any strangers above 3 weeks, except such as should be allowed by 2 magistrates, etc. (this was made in Mrs. Hutchinson's time); the other for banishing of Anabaptists, made the last year. The petitioners complained to the Court of the offence taken thereat by many godly in England, and that some churches there did thereupon profess to deny to hold communion with such of our churches as should resort thither. Whereupon they entreated the Court that they would please to take the said laws into further consideration, and to provide as far as they might for the indemnity of such of ours as were to go into England. Many of the Court well inclined for these and other considerations to have had the execution of those laws to have been suspended for a season. But many of the elders hearing of it went first to the deputies, and after to the magistrates, and laying before them what advantage it would give to the Anabaptists (who began to increase very fast through the country here and much more in England, where they had gathered divers churches, and taught openly, and had published a confession of their faith), entreated that the law might continue still in force and the exe-

cution of it not suspended, though they disliked not that all lenity and patience should be used for convincing and reclaiming such erroneous persons. Whereupon the Court refused to make any further order about the petition . . .

This year about 20 families (most of them of the Church of Braintree) petitioned the Court for allowance to begin a plantation at the place where Gorton and his company had erected 3 or 4 small houses upon the land of Pumham, the Indian sachem by Narragansett who had submitted himself and country to this jurisdiction.[12] The Court readily granted their petition, promising all encouragement, etc. (for it was of great concernment to all the English in these parts that a strong plantation should be there as a bulwark, etc., against the Narragansetts). But Mr. John Brown, one of the magistrates of Plymouth and then one of their Commissioners for the United Colonies, dwelling at Rehoboth and intending to drive a trade with the Indians in those parts, meeting with some of ours when they went to view the place and to take the bounds of it, forbad them in the name of the government of Plymouth to proceed in the said plantation, telling them that it belonged to Plymouth and that it should be restored to the right owners, meaning Gorton and his company. Whereupon the planters (not willing to run any hazard of contention for place in a country where there was room enough) gave over their purpose, and disposed themselves otherwise. Some removed more southward, and others stayed where they were. This practice of Mr. Brown being complained of to the governor of the Massachusetts, Mr. Dudley, he informed the magistrates of Plymouth thereof by letter, who returned answer that Mr. Brown had no order from their Court to forbid the proceeding, etc., for they should have been glad to have had the place planted by us, though the right of it were (as they conceived) in themselves. The case being after put

12. See 22 June 1643, above.

to the Commissioners for explanation of their said order, they resolved for the Massachusetts[13] . . .

At the last General Court it was ordered that divers farmers belonging to Ipswich and Salem (but so far distant from either town as they could not duly repair to the public ordinances there) should erect a village and have liberty to gather a Church.[14] This was much opposed by those of the town of Ipswich, pleading their interest in the land, etc. But it was answered that when the land was granted to the town, it was not intended only for the benefit of the near inhabitants, or for the maintenance of the officers of that one Church only, but of all the inhabitants and of any other Church which should be there gathered. And a principal motive which led the Court to grant them and other towns such vast bounds was that (when the towns should be increased by their children and servants growing up, etc.) they might have place to erect villages, where they might be planted, and so the land improved to the more common benefit.

15 (10) [December]. There appeared about noon upon the north side of the sun a great ∧part of a∧ circle like a rainbow, with the horns reversed, and upon each side of the sun, E. and west, a bright light. And about a month after were seen 3 suns, about the sun setting; and about a month after that 2 suns at sun rising. The one continued close to the horizon while the other (which was the true sun) arose about half an hour. This was the earliest and sharpest winter we had since we arrived in the country, and it was as vehement cold to the southward as here. Divers of our ships were put from their anchors with the ice and driven on shore, 25 (10) [December], and one ketch carried out to sea and wrecked upon Lovells Island. At New Haven a ship bound for England was forced to be cut out of the ice 3 miles. And in Virginia the ships were frozen up 6 weeks.

13. The New England Confederation commissioners discussed this issue in Sept. 1646 (*PR*, 9:79–80).
14. This was the village of New Meadows, renamed Topsfield in 1648.

At Ipswich there was a calf brought forth with one head and 3 mouths, 3 noses, and 6 eyes. What these prodigies pretended the Lord only knows, which in His due time He will manifest . . .

26 (1) [March]. The governor and Council met at Boston to take order about a rescue which they were informed of to have been committed at Hingham upon the marshal, when he went to levy the fines imposed upon Mr. Hobart, their pastor, and many others who joined with him in the petition against the magistrates, etc. And having taken the information of the marshal and others, they sent out summons for their appearance at another day, at which time Mr. Hobart came not nor sent any excuse, though it were proved that he was at home and that the summons was left at his house. Whereupon he was sent for by attachment directed to the constable, who brought him at the day of the return. And being then charged with joining in the said rescue by animating the offenders and discouraging the officer, questioning the authority of his warrant because it was not in the King's name, and standing upon his allegiance to the crown of England, all the answer he would give was that if he had broken any wholesome law not repugnant to the laws of England he was ready to submit to censure. So he was bound over to the next Court of Assistants.

The Court being at Boston Mr. Hobart appeared, and the marshal's information and other concurrent testimony being read to him, and his answer demanded, he desired to know in what state he stood, and what offence he should be charged with, or what wholesome law of the land, not repugnant to the law of England, he had broken. The Court told him that the matters he was charged with amounted to a seditious practice and derogation and contempt of authority. He still pressed to know what law, etc. He was told that the oath which he had taken was a law to him, and besides, the law of God which we were to judge by in case of defect of an express law. He said that the law of God admitted various interpretations, etc. The matters testified against him were his speeches to the marshal before 30 persons against our authority and government, etc. 1. That we were but as a corporation in England; 2. That by our patent (as he understood it) we could not put any man to death, nor do divers other things which we did; 3. That he knew not wherefore the General Court had fined them, except it were for petitioning, and if they were so waspish (or captious) as they might not be petitioned, etc., and other speeches tending to disparage our authority and proceedings. Accordingly, a bill was drawn up, etc., and the jury found that he seemed to be ill-affected to this government, and that his speeches tended to sedition and contempt of authority. Whereupon, the whole Court (except Mr. Bellingham who judged him to deserve no censure, and desired in open Court to have his dissent recorded) adjudged him to pay £20 fine and to be bound to his good behavior till the next Court of Assistants, and then further if the Court should see cause. At this sentence his spirit rose, and he would know what the good behavior was, and desired the names of the jury and a copy of all the proceedings, which was granted him. And so he was dismissed at present . . .

There fell out a loathsome disease at Boston, which raised a scandal upon the town and country, though without just cause. One of the town ⟨of Rox[illeg.]⟩[15] having gone cooper in a ship ⟨into S[illeg.]⟩, at his return ∧his wife∧ was infected with lues veneria[16] ⟨and infected his wife, and leaving her with child went to sea again; the woman knew all, but knew not what she ailed⟩ ∧which appeared thus: being delivered of a child and nothing then appearing, but the midwife, a skilful woman, finding her body as sound as any other,∧ after her delivery she had a sore breast; whereupon divers neighbors resorting to her, some of them drew her breast, and other suffered their children to draw her, and others let her child suck them (no such ⟨infectious⟩ disease being sus-

15. Probably Roxbury.
16. Plague of Venus, or syphilis.

pected by any), by occasion whereof about 16 persons, men, women, and children, were infected. Whereupon it came at length to be discovered by such in the town as had skill in physic and surgery, but there was not any in the country who had been practiced in that cure. But (see the good providence of God) at that very season there came by accident a young surgeon out of the West Indies who had had experience of the right way of the cure of that disease. He took them in hand, and through the Lord's blessing recovered them all in a short time. And it was observed that although many did eat and drink and lodge in bed with those who were infected and had sores, etc., yet none took it of them but by copulation or sucking. It was very doubtful how this disease came at first. The magistrates examined the husband and wife, but could find no dishonesty in either, nor any probable occasion how they should take it by any other (and the husband was found to be free of it), so as it was concluded by some that the woman was infected by the mixture of so many spirits of men and women as drew her breast (for thence it began). But this is a question to be decided by physicians.

6 (3) [May]. The Court of Elections was at Boston. ∧Mr. Norris of Salem preached.∧ Mr. Winthrop was chosen governor,[17] Mr. Dudley (the last governor) deputy governor, Mr. Endecott sergeant major general, and he and Mr. Pelham Commissioners for the United Colonies. The magistrates and deputies had formerly chosen the Commissioners, but the freemen looking at them as general officers would now choose them themselves, and the rather because some of the deputies had formerly been chosen to that office, which gave offense to our confederates and to many among ourselves.[18] This Court lasted near 3 weeks,

17. JW, who had been deputy governor for the past two years, now resumed the governorship for the remainder of his life; he was reelected in 1647 and 1648.

18. The deputies chose two magistrates, Simon Bradstreet and Thomas Dudley, as alternate commissioners, in case Endecott or Pelham were unable to attend.

and was carried on with much peace and good correspondency, and when the business was near ended the magistrates and deputies met and concluded what remained, and so departed in much love . . .

One Mr. William Vassall,[19] sometimes one of the assistants of the Massachusetts but now of Scituate in Plymouth jurisdiction, a man of a busy and factious spirit, and always opposite to the civil governments of this country and the way of our Churches, had practiced with such as were not members of our Churches to take some course, first by petitioning the Courts of the Massachusetts and of Plymouth, and (if that succeeded not) then to the Parliament of England, that the distinctions which were maintained here both in civil and Church estates might be taken away, and that we might be wholly governed by the laws of England.[20] And accordingly a petition was drawn up to the Parliament, pretending that they being freeborn subjects of England were denied the liberty of subjects both in church and commonwealth, themselves and their children debarred from the seals of the covenant, except they would submit to such a way of entrance and church covenant as their consciences could not admit, and take such a civil oath as would not stand with their oath of allegiance, or else they must be deprived of all power and interest in civil affairs, and were subjected to an arbitrary government and extrajudicial proceedings, etc.[21] And now at this Court at Boston a petition to the same effect, much en-

19. William Vassall (1592–1656), one of the original assistants of the MBC in 1629, came over with JW in 1630 but returned to England in 1631. Coming back with his family in 1635, he settled in Scituate in Plymouth Colony, where he quarreled with the pastor and established a rival church with more liberal admission to membership. In 1645 he seems to have worked with the Hobarts in Hingham (just across the Massachusetts border from Scituate) during their confrontation with JW. He left New England for good in 1646 and died in Barbados.

20. In Nov. 1645 Vassall introduced a bill in the Plymouth General Court that would have permitted toleration for all peaceable persons, including Familists, Papists, Jews, and Turks. Edward Winslow reported to JW that the Plymouth magistrates had much difficulty in blocking this bill (*WP,* 5:55–56).

21. Vassall circulated this petition in Plymouth, and took it to England in 1646. He may also have taken a similar petition from Massachusetts; see 4 Nov. 1646, below.

larged,[22] was delivered into the deputies under the hands of Dr. [Robert] Child, Mr. Thomas Fowle, Mr. Samuel Maverick, Mr. Thomas Burton, Mr. John Smith, Mr. David Yale, and Mr. John Dand[23] in the name of themselves and many others in the country, whereto they pressed to have present answer. But the Court being then near at an end, and the matter being very weighty, they referred the further consideration thereof to the next session. And whereas a law was drawn up and ready to pass for allowing non-freemen equal power with the freemen in all town affairs, and to some freemen of such estate, etc., their votes in election of magistrates, it was thought fit to defer this also to the next session.

(4) [June]. The Narragansetts having broken their covenants with us in 3 days of payment, so as there was now due to us above 1300 fathom of wampum, they now sent us to Boston to the value of 100 fathom (the most in old kettles), excusing themselves by their poverty and by the Niantics and others failing to contribute their parts. But the Commissioners (who were then 2 of them at Boston) refused to accept so small a sum, and rebuking them sharply for breaking their covenants both in their payments [and] other articles, told them that if they were forced to fetch the rest, they could as well fetch this. So they sold their kettles to a brazier in Boston, and left the pay in his hands for us if we would accept it when they should bring the rest[24] . . .

22. This "Remonstrance and humble Petition" was presented to the MBC General Court in May 1646. For the MBC's response to this petition, see 4 Nov. 1646, below.

23. These seven petitioners were known as the Remonstrants because of their "Remonstrance and humble Petition." Their leader, Dr. Child, was a physician and scientist; several of the others were merchants; none was a church member or a freeman. Their contest with the MBC government was the last major political crisis of JW's career, and lasted from May 1646 to June 1647. The Remonstrants were hoping to attract support from everyone dissatisfied with the Massachusetts church-state system, to introduce some of the religious and political ideas being practiced in England in the 1640s, and to place the colony under parliamentary supervision.

24. The Narragansetts sold their kettles and wampum to Henry Shrimpton, a Boston brazier, for £17 19s. 6d.

Mr. Eaton, the governor of New Haven, wrote to the governor of the Bay to desire the advice of the magistrates and elders in a special case which was this: one [William] Plaine of Gilford being discovered to have used some unclean practices, upon examination and testimony it was found that, being a married man, he had committed sodomy with 2 persons in England, and that he had corrupted a great part of the youth of Guilford by masturbation, which he had committed, and provoked others to the like above 100 times. And to some who questioned the lawfulness of such a filthy practice he did insinuate seeds of atheism, questioning whether there were a God, etc. The magistrates and elders (so many as were at hand) did all agree that he ought to die, and gave divers reasons from the word of God, and indeed it was horrendum facinus[25] (and he a monster in human shape), exceeding all human rules and examples that ever had been heard of, and it tended to the frustrating of the ordinance of marriage and the hindering the generation of mankind.

A petition was presented to the Court under many hands for the continuance of the 2 laws against Anabaptists and other heretics, which was done in reference to a petition presented at the former Court concerning the same laws.[26]

A plantation was this year begun at Pequot River by Mr. John Winthrop, junior, [and] Mr. Thomas Peter, a minister (brother to Mr. Peter of Salem), and this Court power was given to them 2 for ordering and governing the plantation till further order, etc., although it was uncertain whether it would fall within our jurisdiction or not, because they of Connecticut challenged it by virtue of a patent from the King which was never showed us.[27] It mattered not much to which jurisdiction it

---

25. A horrible crime.

26. See 1 Oct. 1645, above.

27. This new town of Pequot lay far outside the MBC's chartered boundaries, and Connecticut was granted jurisdiction over it by the New England Confederation in 1647; the town was renamed New London in 1657.

did belong, seeing the Confederation made all as one. But it was of great concernment to have it planted, to be a curb to the Indians, etc.

Monsieur La Tour being returned from Newfoundland, was (by some merchants of Boston) set forth in the same pinnace to the eastward with trading commodities to the value of £400. When he came at Cape Sable (which was in the heart of winter), he conspired with the master (being a stranger) and his own Frenchmen, being 5, to go away with the vessel, and so forced out the other 5 English (himself shooting one of them in the face with a pistol), who through special providence, having wandered up and down 15 days, found some Indians who gave them a shallop and victuals and an Indian pilot. So they arrived safe at Boston in the (3) month [May]. Whereby it appeared (as the Scripture saith) that there is no confidence in an unfaithful or carnal man, though tied with many strong bonds of courtesy, etc.[28] He turned pirate, etc. . . . .

(5) [July]. A daughter of Mrs. Hutchinson was carried away by the Indians near the Dutch, when her mother and others were killed by them; and upon the peace concluded between the Dutch and the same Indians, she was returned to the Dutch governor, who restored her to her friends here. She was about 8 years old when she was taken, and continued with them about 4 years, and she had forgot her own language, and all her friends, and was loath to have come from the Indians.[29]

Great harm was done in corn (especially wheat and barley) in this month by a caterpillar like a black worm about an inch $\frac{1}{2}$ long. They eat up first the blades of the stalk, then they eat up the tassels,[30] where-

---

28. Prov. 25:19. Soon after JW's death, La Tour's fortunes improved dramatically. His rival d'Aulnay died in 1650, La Tour regained the support of the French government, resumed his governorship of Acadia, and married d'Aulnay's widow! He was in possession of Fort St. Jean when he died in 1666.

29. For similar responses to Indian captivity by other Puritan children (especially girls), see Laurel Thatcher Ulrich, *Good Wives: Image and Reality in the Lives of Women in Northern New England, 1650–1750* (New York: Knopf, 1982), ch. 11.

30. JW spelled this word "thathells."

upon the ear withered. It was believed by divers good observations that they fell in a great thunder shower, for divers yards and other bare places, where not one of them was to be seen an hour before, were presently after the shower almost covered with them, besides grass places where they were not so easily discerned. They did the most harm in the southern parts, as Rhode Island, etc., and in the eastern parts in their Indian corn. In divers places the churches kept a day of humiliation, and presently after the caterpillars vanished away . . .

When the time of the synod drew near, it was propounded to the Churches.[31] All the Churches in this jurisdiction sent their messengers except Boston, Salem, Hingham, Concord. Concord would have sent if their elder had been able to come, or if they had had any other whom they had judged fit, etc. Boston and Salem took offence at the order of Court . . . [They] inferred that this synod was appointed by the elders to the intent to make ecclesiastical laws to bind the Churches, and to have the sanction of the civil authority put upon them, whereby men should be forced under penalty to submit to them. Whereupon they concluded that they should betray the liberty of the Churches if they should consent to such a synod. The principal men ⟨To these⟩ who raised these objections were some of Boston who came lately from England, where such a vast liberty was allowed and sought for by all that went under the name of Independents, not only the Anabaptists, Antinomians, Familists, Seekers, etc., but even the most godly and orthodox, as Mr. Goodwin, Mr. Nye, Mr. Burrowes, etc.,[32] who in the Assembly there had stood in opposition to the Presbytery, and also the

31. In May 1646 the MBC General Court had urged the clergy of Massachusetts, Connecticut, Plymouth, and New Haven to meet in a synod in Cambridge on 1 Sept. 1646 and establish a uniform system of church government and discipline (*MR*, 2:155–156).

32. Thomas Goodwin, Philip Nye, and Jeremiah Burroughs were leading spokesmen for the Independents or Congregationalists in the Westminster Assembly. Goodwin and Nye had joined 11 other English clergy in protesting to the MBC General Court, c. June 1645, against the persecution of Anabaptists in Massachusetts (*WP*, 5:23–25).

greater part of the House of Commons, who by their commissioners had sent order to all English plantations in the West Indies and Sumers Islands[33] that all men should enjoy their liberty of conscience, and had by letters intimated the same to us. To these did some other of the Church of Boston adhere, but not above 30 or 40 in all . . .

Two Lord's days this agitation was in Boston, and no conclusion made by reason of the opposite party, so the elders sat down much grieved in spirit, yet told the congregation that they thought it their duty to go notwithstanding, not as sent by the Church but as specially called by the order of Court.[34]

The assembly or synod being met at Cambridge, 1 (7) [September], they wrote letters to the elders and brethren of the Church of Boston, inviting them and pressing them also by argument to send their elders and other messengers. The next day was Boston lecture, to which most of the synod repaired, and Mr. Norton, teacher of the Church of Ipswich, being procured to supply the place, took his text suitable to the occasion, viz., of Moses and Aron meeting in the mount and kissing each other,[35] where he laid down the nature and power of the synod as only consultative, decisive, and declarative, not coactive, etc. He showed also the power of the civil magistrate in calling such assemblies, and the duty of the Churches ⟨to⟩ in yielding obedience to the same. He showed also the great offence and scandal which would be given in refusing, etc.

The next Lord's day the matter was moved again . . . In the end it was agreed by vote of the major part that the elders and 3 of the brethren should be sent as messengers, etc.

The synod brake up and was adjourned to 8 (4) [8 June 1647], having

---

33. The Somers Islands, or Bermuda.

34. John Cotton and John Wilson, the pastor and teacher of the Boston church, were here accepting the General Court as a higher ecclesiastical authority than their own church—a position that Cotton had argued against in his earlier writings.

35. Exod. 4:27. Moses symbolizes the MBC magistrates, and Aaron the clergy.

continued but about 14 days, in regard of winter drawing on, and few of the elders of other colonies were present.[36]

Gorton and ∧2 other of∧ his company, viz., John Greene and Randall Holden, going into England,[37] complained to the Commissioners for Plantations, etc., against us, etc., who gave order that some of ours then in England should be summoned to answer their petition.[38] Whereupon some appeared, but they having no instruction about the case, and the writings sent over to Mr. Weld the year before being either lost or forgotten, so as a full answer could not be given in the particular, and the petitioners being favored by some of the Commissioners, partly for private respects and partly for their adhering to some of their corrupt tenets, and generally out of their dislike of us for our late law for banishing Anabaptists, they seemed to be much offended with us for our rigorous proceeding (as they called it) against them. And thereupon (without sending to us to hear our answer, etc.) they gave them this order following:

By the governor in chief, lord high admiral, and commissioners appointed by Parliament for the English plantations in America.

Whereas we have thought fit to give an order for Mr. Samuel Gorton, Mr. Randall Holden, Mr. John Greene and others, late inhabitants of a tract of land called the Narragansett Bay, near the Massachusetts

36. The synod asked three ministers—John Cotton, Richard Mather, and Ralph Partridge—each to prepare models of church government for submission to the next session in 1647. See 8 June 1647, below.

37. After the MBC released and banished Samuel Gorton and his colleagues in 1644, Gorton, Greene, and Holden went to England, where Gorton published *Simplicities Defence against Seven-Headed Policy* (London, 1646), a vigorous attack upon the Massachusetts government.

38. In 1643 Parliament had established a commission to regulate the English plantations in America, headed by the Earl of Warwick. This body had protected Roger Williams from the MBC in 1644 by granting him a patent for the colony of Rhode Island and Providence Plantations. Now it was protecting Gorton.

Bay in New England, to return with freedom to the said tract of land and there to inhabitate and abide without interruption:[39] These are therefore to pray and require you, and all others whom this may concern, to permit and suffer the said Samuel Gorton etc. with their company, goods, and necessaries carried with them out of England, to land at any port in New England where the ship wherein they do embark themselves shall arrive, and from thence to pass without any of your lets or molestations through any part of the continent of America within your jurisdiction to the said tract of land called Narragansett Bay . . . Hereof you may not fail: And this shall be your warrant: Dated at Westminster this 15 of May 1646.

Nottingham [and eight other signatures][40]

13 (7) [September]. Randall Holden arrived here in a London ship, Captain Wall master, and sent this order to the governor, to desire leave to land, etc. Accordingly the governor answered that he could not give him leave of himself, nor dispense with an order of the General Court, but the Council were to meet within 2 or 3 days and he would impart it unto them, etc., and in the mean time he would not seek after him, etc.

The Council being met, they were of different judgment in the case, so as they agreed to take the advice of such of the elders as were then met at the lecture at Boston (being about 10). The elders also differed.

39. In a separate order, also dated 15 May 1646, the Earl of Warwick and twelve other parliamentary commissioners informed the MBC that they had granted the Gortonists the right to continue to live and govern themselves at Shawomet on Narragansett Bay, where they were "wholly without the bounds of the Massachusettes patent granted by His Majesty." JW copied this order also into his journal, but it has been omitted in this abridged edition.

40. One of the parliamentary commissioners who signed this order was Samuel Vassall, brother of William Vassall who was busily stirring up protests in New England against the MBC government.

Some were very earnest for his commitment till the General Court, etc., but the greater part, both of magistrates and elders, thought it better to give so much respect to the protection which the Parliament had given him (and whereupon he adventured his life, etc.) as to suffer him to pass quietly away, and when the General Court should be assembled (which would be within a month), then to consider further about their repossessing the land they claimed.

20 (7) [September]. Being the Lord's day, and the people ready to go to the assembly after dinner, Monsieur Marie and Monsieur Louis, with Monsieur D'Aulnay his secretary, arrived at Boston in a small pinnace,[41] and Major Gibbons sent 2 of his chief officers to meet them at the waterside, who conducted them to their lodging *sine strepitu*.[42] The public worship being ended, the governor repaired home and sent Major Gibbons with other gentlemen with a guard of musketeers to attend them to the governor's house, who meeting them without his door, carried them into his house where they were entertained with wine and sweetmeats. And after a while he accompanied them to their lodging (being the house of Major Gibbons, where they were entertained that night). The next morning they repaired to the governor and delivered him their commission. Their diet was provided at the ordinary[43] where the magistrates use to diet in court times, and the governor accompanied them always at meals. Their manner was to repair to the governor's house every morning about 8 of the clock, who accompanied them to the place of meeting, and at night either himself or some of the commissioners accompanied them to their lodging. It was the 3d day [Tuesday] at noon before our commissioners could come together. When they were met, they propounded great injuries and dam-

---

41. After d'Aulnay captured La Tour's fort in 1645, the MBC decided in May 1646 to send a delegation to Penobscot to negotiate a peace treaty with him. But in June 1646 d'Aulnay offered to send his agents to Boston instead.

42. Without fanfare.

43. Tavern.

ages sustained by Captain Hawkins and our men in assistance of La Tour, and would have engaged our government therein. We denied that we had any hand, either by commission or permission, in that action; we only gave way to La tour to hire assistance to conduct his ship home according to the request made to us in the commission of the vice-admiral of France . . . Their commissioners alleged damages to the value of £8000, but did not stand upon the value. They would have accepted of very small satisfaction if we would have acknowledged any guilt in our government. In the end they came to this conclusion: we accepted their commissioners' answer in satisfaction of those things we had charged upon Monsieur D'Aulnay, and they accepted our answer for clearing our government of what he had charged upon us, and because we could not free Captain Hawkins and the other voluntaries of what they had done, we were to send a small present to Mr. D'Aulnay in satisfaction of that, and so all injuries and demands to be remitted, and so a final peace to be concluded. Accordingly, we sent Monsieur D'Aulnay by his commissioners a very fair new sedan (worth £40 or £50 where it was made, but of no use for us), sent by the viceroy of Mexico to a lady his sister, and taken in the West Indies by Captain Cromwell and by him given to our governor.[44] This the commissioners very well accepted, and so, the agreement being signed in several instruments by the commissioners of both parts on 28 day of the same month, they took leave and set sail, Major Sedgwick and some other gentlemen accompanying them as far as Castle Island. The Lord's day they were here, the governor acquainting them with our manner, that all men either come to our public meetings or keep themselves quiet in their houses, and finding that the place where they lodged would not be convenient for them that day, invited them home to his house, where they continued private all that day until sunset, and made use of such

---

44. Capt. Thomas Cromwell, an English privateer, had acquired this sedan chair when he looted a Spanish ship; he presented it to JW in June 1646.

books, Latin and French, as he had, and the liberty of a private walk in his garden, and so gave no offence, etc. The 2 first days after their arrival, their pinnace kept up her flag in the main-top, which gave offence both to the Londoners which rode in the harbor and also to our own people, whereupon Monsieur Marie gave order to have it taken down.

There fell a sad affliction upon the country this year, though it more particularly concerned New Haven and those parts. A small ship of about 100 ton set out from New Haven in the middle of the 11th month [January] last (the harbor there being so frozen as they were forced to hew her through the ice near 3 miles). She was laden with pease and some wheat, all in bulk, with about 200 West Indy hides, and store of beaver and plate, so as it was estimated in all at £6000. There were in her about 70 persons, whereof divers were of very precious account, as Mr. Grigson, one of their magistrates, the wife of Mr. Goodeare, another of their magistrates (a right godly woman), Captain Turner, Mr. Lamberton, master of the ship, and some 7 or 8 others, members of the Church there. The ship never went voyage before, and was very crank-sided,[45] so as it was conceived she was overset in a great tempest, which happened soon after she put to sea, for she was never heard of after . . .

(9) *[November]* 4. The General Court began again . . . The business of Gorton, etc., and of the petitioners, Dr. Child, etc., were taken into consideration, and it was thought needful to send some able man into England with commission and instructions to satisfy the Commissioners for Plantations about those complaints. And because it was a matter of so great and general concernment, such of the elders as could be had were sent for to have their advice in the matter. Mr. Hobart of Hingham came with the rest, but the Court being informed that he had an hand in a petition which Mr. Vassall carried into England against the country

45. Easily tipped.

in general,[46] the governor propounded that if any elder present had any such hand, etc., he would withdraw himself. Mr. Hobart sitting still a good space and no man speaking, one of the deputies informed the Court that Mr. Hobart was the man suspected, whereupon he arose and said that he knew nothing of any such petition. The governor replied that seeing he was now named he must needs deliver his mind about him, which was that although they had no proof present about the matter of the petition and therefore his denial was a sufficient clearing, etc., yet in regard he had so much opposed authority and offered such contempt to it, as for which he had been lately bound to his good behavior, he thought he would (in discretion) withdraw himself, etc.; whereupon he went out. Then the governor put the Court in mind of a great miscarriage, in that our secretest counsels were presently known abroad, which could not be but by some among ourselves, and desired them to look at it as a matter of great unfaithfulness, and that our present consultations might be kept in the breast of the Court and not be divulged abroad, as others had been.

Then it was propounded to consideration in what relation we stood to the state of England, whether our government were founded upon our charter or not. If so, then what subjection we owed to that state.[47] The magistrates delivered their minds first that the elders might have the better light for their advice. All agreed that our charter was the foundation of our government and thereupon some thought that we were so subordinate to the Parliament as they might countermand our orders and judgments, etc., and therefore advised that we should petition the Parliament for enlargement of our power, etc. Others con-

46. William Vassall had circulated a petition in Plymouth in Nov. 1645, calling for religious toleration. Hobart may have joined Vassall in this petition, or in a similar petition circulating in Massachusetts.

47. The General Court was responding to the Remonstrants' declaration in May 1646 that the MBC was an English corporation, not a free state, and that the MBC government had no authority to infringe upon the rights of Englishmen living in New England.

ceived otherwise, and that though we owed allegiance and subjection to them, as we had always professed, yet by our charter we had absolute power of government. For thereby we have power to make laws, to erect all sorts of magistracy, to correct, punish, pardon, govern, and rule the people absolutely,[48] and ergo should not need the help of any superior power, either general governor, or, etc., to complete our government. Yet we did owe allegiance and subjection: 1. Because our commonwealth was founded upon the power of that state and so had been always carried on; 2. In regard of the tenure of our lands of the manor of East Greenwich;[49] 3. We depended upon them for protection, etc; 4. For advice and counsel when in great occasions we should crave it; 5. In the continuance of naturalization and free legeance of ourselves and our posterity. Yet we might be still independent in respect of government as Normandy, Gascony, etc., were, though they had dependence upon the crown of France and the Kings of England did homage, etc., yet in point of government they were not dependent upon France.[50]

And for that motion of petitioning, etc., it was answered: 1. That if we receive a new charter that will be (ipso facto) a surrender of the old; 2. The Parliament can grant none now but by way of ordinance,

48. The MBC royal charter of March 1629 granted a "full and absolute power and authoritie to correct, punishe, pardon, governe, and rule all such . . . as shall . . . inhabite within the precinctes and partes of Newe England aforesaid" (*MR*, 1:17).

49. The MBC charter—like other royal grants of land in America—specified that the company's land was part of the royal demesne; the king granted land to the MBC to be held "as of his mannor of Eastgreenewich, in the County of Kent, in free and common Soccage, and not in Capite nor by Knightes Service" (*MR*, 1:4). By placing the MBC under this form of tenure, the king exempted the company from most of the feudal incidents of land tenure (especially the requirement of military service), and guaranteed its members the legal and tenurial rights of Englishmen as though their lands lay within the realm of England. To the crown, the MBC's land had strictly economic value, and the company was directed to pay one-fifth of any gold or silver discovered in Massachusetts (none was discovered).

50. JW is here arguing that the MBC is theoretically dependent on the English government, but independent in practice, just as the medieval English kings who ruled Normandy and Gascony were only nominally dependent on their liege lord, the king of France.

and it may be questioned whether the King will give his royal assent, considering how he hath taken displeasure against us; 3. If we take a charter from the Parliament we can expect no other than such as they have granted to us at Narragansett and to others in other places, wherein they reserve a supreme power in all things.[51]

The Court having delivered their opinions, the elders desired time of consideration, and the next day they presented their advice which was delivered by Mr. Allen, pastor of the Church in Dedham, in divers articles which (upon request) they delivered in writing as followeth: . . .

Concerning the question of our dependence upon England, we conceive:

1. That we have received the power of our government and other privileges derived from thence by our charter . . .

2. We conceive that in point of government we have granted by patent such full and ample power of choosing all officers that shall command and rule over us, of making all laws and rules of our obedience, and of a full and final determination of all cases in the administration of justice, that no appeals or other ways of interrupting our proceedings do lie against us.

3. Concerning our way of answering complaints against us in England, we conceive that it doth not well suit with us, nor are we directly called thereto, to profess and plead our right and power further than in a way of justification of our proceedings questioned from the words of the patent . . .

4. Furthermore, we do not clearly discern but that we may give the

---

51. Roger Williams's Narragansett patent, obtained from the Warwick Commission on 14 March 1644, granted full self-government to the towns of Providence, Portsmouth, and Newport, but conveyed considerably narrower powers than the MBC charter of 1629. It lacked royal approval, and Parliament neither granted title to the land nor surrendered ultimate governmental authority over the Narragansett region.

Earl of Warwick and the rest such titles as the Parliament hath given them without subjecting to them in point of our government.

5. Lastly, we do call the Churches to a solemn seeking of the Lord for the upholding of our state and disappointment of our adversaries.[52]

The Court had made choice of Mr. Edward Winslow (one of the magistrates of Plymouth) as a fit man to be employed in our present affairs in England. But it was now moved by one of the elders to send one of our own magistrates and one of our elders. The motion and the reasons of it were well apprehended, so as the governor and Mr. Norton, teacher of the church in Ipswich, were named and in a manner agreed upon.[53] But upon second thoughts it was let fall, chiefly for these 2 reasons: 1. It was feared, in regard that Mr. Peter had written to the governor to come over and assist in the Parliament's cause, etc.,[54] that if he were there he would be called into the Parliament and so detained; 2. Many were upon the wing, and his departure would occasion more new thoughts and apprehensions, etc.; 3. It was feared what changes his absence might produce, etc.

The governor was very averse to a voyage into England, yet he declared himself ready to accept the service if he should be called to it, though he were then 59 years of age wanting one month, but he was very glad when he saw the mind of the Lord to be otherwise.

The Court conferred with the elders about the petition of Dr. Child, etc., also, for it had given great offence to many godly in the country, both elders and others, and some answers had been made to it and presented to the Court, out of which one entire answer had been framed in way of declaration of the Court's apprehension thereof, ∧and∧ not

---

52. The General Court appointed a day of public humiliation on 24 Dec. 1646 (*MR*, 2:167).

53. The magistrates also tried to persuade Herbert Pelham and Richard Saltonstall, Jr. to serve as agents, but they "utterly refused" (*WP*, 5:120).

54. See Hugh Peter to JW2, 4 Sept. 1646 (*WP*, 5:102).

by way of answer, because it was adjudged a contempt; which declaration was after published.[55]

There was a ship then ready to set sail for England, wherein Mr. Fowle (one of the petitioners) was to go, etc. The Court therefore sent for him and required an account of him about it before his departure, and also Mr. John Smith of Rhode Island, being then in town, and they were both required to find sureties to be responsal, etc.[56] Whereupon they were troubled and desired they might answer presently in regard they were to depart, taking exception also that the rest of the petitioners were not called as well as they. Whereupon Dr. Child, etc., were sent for and all appeared save Mr. Maverick, and the Doctor (being the chief speaker) d[emanded] what should be laid to their charge, seeing it was no offence to prefer a petition, etc. . . . Upon this pressing, one clause in their petition was read to them which was this: our brethren of England's just indignation against us, so as they fly from us as from a pest, etc. whereby they lay a great scandal upon the country, etc. This was so clear as they could not evade it, but quarrelled with the Court with high terms. The Doctor said they did beneath themselves in petitioning to us, etc., and in conclusion appealed to the commissioners in England. The governor told them we could admit no appeal, nor was it allowed by our charter, but by this it appeared what their aim was in their petition. They complained of fear of perpetual slavery, etc., but their intent was to make us slaves to them and such as themselves were. The Court let them know that they did take notice of their contemptuous speeches and behavior, as should further appear in due

55. This "Declaration of the General Court," which JW helped to draft, was circulated in manuscript, not published in print. It contains a point-by-point refutation of Dr. Child's Remonstrance, and argues that the MBC is not arbitrary, and that its laws are in accord with Magna Carta and the English common law.

56. Securities that they would be answerable [to the judgment of the court]; see *MR*, 3:88–89.

time. In conclusion, Mr. Fowle and Mr. Smith were committed to the marshal for want of sureties, and the rest were enjoined to attend the Court when they should be called. So they were dismissed, and Mr. Fowle, etc., found sureties before night and were set at liberty.[57]

A committee was appointed to examine the petition and out of it to draw a charge which was done as followeth:

The Court doth charge Dr. Child etc., with divers false and scandalous passages in a certain paper entitled A Remonstrance and Petition (exhibited by them to this Court in the (3) month [May] last) against the churches of Christ and the civil government here established, derogating from the honor and authority of the same and tending to sedition, as in the particulars following will appear: . . .

They charge us with manifest injury to a great part of the people here, persuading them that the liberties and privileges in our charter belong to all freeborn Englishmen, inhabitants here, whereas they are granted only to such as the governor and company shall think fit to receive into that fellowship . . .

They go about to weaken the authority of our laws and the reverence and esteem of them, and consequently their obedience to them, by persuading the people that, partly through want of the body of English laws, and partly through the insufficiency or ill frame of those we have, they can expect no sure enjoyment of their lives and liberties under them . . .

Their speeches tend to sedition by insinuating into the people's minds that there are many 1000s secretly discontented at the government, etc., whereby those which indeed were so might be emboldened to discover themselves and to attempt some innovation, in confidence of so many 1000s to join with them, and so to kindle a great flame, the foretelling whereof is a chief means to kindle it.

57. Thomas Fowle and John Smith were each ordered to provide £100 in surety, but Fowle forfeited his bond and left for England before sentencing.

They raise a false report and foul slander upon the discipline of our Churches and upon the civil government by inferring that the frame and dispensation thereof are such as godly, sober, peaceable, etc., men cannot live here like Christians . . .

They falsely charge and slander the people of God in affirming that Christian vigilancy is no way exercised towards such as are not in church fellowship, whereas themselves know and have had experience to the contrary . . .

Having thrown all this dirt and shame upon our Churches and government, etc., they endeavor to set it on that it might stick fast, so as all men might undoubtedly be persuaded of the reality thereof, by proclaiming it in their conclusion that our own brethren in England have just indignation against us for the same, which they labor to confirm by the effect thereof, viz. that for these evils amongst us these our own brethren do fly from us as from a pest.

Lastly, by appealing from this government, they disclaimed the jurisdiction thereof before they knew whether the Court would give any sentence against them or not.

Their petition being read and this charge laid upon them in the open Court before a great assembly, they desired time to make answer to it, which was granted. And giving the Court notice that their answer was ready, they assembled again and before all the people caused their answer to be read, which was large and to little purpose . . .

They charge us with breach of our charter and of our oaths of allegiance, whereas our allegiance binds us not to the laws of England any longer than while we live in England, for the laws of the Parliament of England reach no further, nor do the King's writs under the Great Seal go any further[58] . . . They also justify that speech of flying from us as from a pest by the like speeches some of them have heard from

58. The General Court was here claiming a greater degree of autonomy for Massachusetts than ever before.

godly men in England, and by so many going from us, and so few coming to us. But admit all this to be true, yet what calling have these men to publish this to our reproach? And besides, they know well that as some speak evil of us because we conform not to their opinions in allowing liberty to every erroneous judgment, so there are many no less godly and judicious who do approve our practice and continue their good affection to us . . .

I should also have noted the Doctor's logic, who undertook to prove that we were subject to the laws of England. His argument was this: every corporation of England is subject to the laws of England; but this was a corporation of England; ergo, etc. To which it was answered: We must distinguish between corporations within England and corporations of, but not within, England. The first are subject to the laws of England in general yet not to every general law, as the city of London and other corporations have divers customs and bylaws differing from the common and statute laws of England. Again, though plantations be bodies corporate (and so is every city and commonwealth), yet they are ∧also∧ above the rank of an ordinary corporation. And among the Romans, Grecians, and other nations, colonies have been esteemed other than towns, yea, than many cities, for they have been the foundations of great commonwealths. And it was a fruit of much pride and folly in these petitioners to despise the day of small things.

These petitioners persisting thus obstinately and proudly in their evil practice, the Court proceeded to consider of their censure, and agreed that the Doctor (in regard he had no cause to complain, and yet was a leader to the rest and had carried himself proudly, etc., in the Court) should be fined £50, Mr. Smith (being also a stranger) £40, Mr. Maverick (because he had not as yet appealed) £10, and the other 4 £30 each.[59] So being again called before the Court they were exhorted

59. Thomas Fowle, David Yale, Thomas Burton, and John Dand were each fined £30. Collectively the seven Remonstrants were fined £220 in Nov. 1646, whereas the 87 Hingham protesters and petitioners had been fined £100 in July 1645. Another difference

to consider better of their proceedings and take knowledge of their miscarriage, which was great, and that they had transgressed the rule of the apostle [Paul]: study to be quiet and to meddle with your own business.[60] They were offered also, if they would ingenuously acknowledge their miscarriage, etc., it should be freely remitted. But they remaining obstinate, the Court declared their sentence, as is before expressed. Upon which they all appealed to the Parliament, etc., and tended their appeal in writing. The Court received the paper, but refused to accept it or to read it in the Court.

3 of the magistrates, viz. Mr. Bellingham, Mr. Saltonstall, and Mr. Bradstreet, dissented and 2 or 3 of the deputies did the like.[61] So the Court dissolved.

Dr. Child prepared now in all haste to go for England in the ship which was to go about a week after, to prosecute their appeal and to get a petition from the non-freemen to the Parliament, and many high and menacing words were given forth by them against us, which gave occasion to the governor and Council (so many of them as were then assembled to hold the Court of Assistants) to consider what was fit to be done. Neither thought they fit to impart their counsel to such of the magistrates as had declared their dissent, but the rest of them agreed to stay the Doctor for his fine and to search his trunk and Mr. Dand's study, but spake not of it till the evening before the Doctor was to depart. Then it was propounded in Council, and Mr. Bellingham dissented as before (yet the day before he moved for stopping the Doctor, which was conceived to be to feel if there were any such intention) and presently went aside and spake privately with one who we were sure would prevent our purpose if it were possible. Whereupon (whereas

---

between the two cases is that the magistrates and deputies were no longer split as they had been in 1645; the great majority in both houses stood united against the Remonstrants.

60. St. Paul's advice in 1 Thess. 4:11.

61. Actually, five deputies dissented, including Bozoan Allen and Joshua Hobart from Hingham (*MR*, 3:94).

we had agreed to defer it till he had been on shipboard) now perceiving our counsel was discovered, we sent the officers presently to fetch the Doctor and to search his study and Dand's both at one instant; which was done accordingly, and the Doctor was brought and his trunk that was to be carried on shipboard, but there was nothing in that which concerned the business. But at Dand's they found Mr. Smith who catched up some papers, and when the officer took them from him he brake out into these speeches, viz. We hope shortly we shall have commission to search the governor's closet. There were found the copies of 2 petitions and 23 queries which were to be sent to England to the Commissioners for Plantations.[62] The one from Dr. Child and the other 6 petitioners, wherein they declare how they had formerly petitioned our General Court and had been fined for the same and forced to appeal, and that the ministers of our Churches did revile them, etc., as far as the wit or malice of man could, etc., and what affronts, jeers, and despiteful speeches were cast upon them by some of the Court, etc. Then they petition: 1. For settled Churches according to the reformation of England; 2. That the laws of England may be established here and that arbitrary power may be banished; 3. For liberties for English freeholders here as in England, etc; 4. That a general governor or some honorable commissioners be appointed for settling, etc; 5. That the oath of allegiance may be commanded to be taken by all, and other covenants, which the Parliament shall think most convenient, to be as a touchstone to try our affections to the state of England and true restored Protestant religion; 6. To resolve their queries, etc; 7. To take into consideration their Remonstrance and Petition exhibited to the General Court.

Their queries were chiefly about the validity of our patent and how it might be forfeited, and whether such and such acts ∧or speeches∧ in the pulpits or in the Court, etc., were not high treason. The other

62. These petitions and queries have not survived.

petition was from some non-freemen (pretending to be in the name and upon the sighs and tears of many 1000s). They sent their agents up and down the country to get hands to this petition, but of the many 1000s they spake of we could hear but of 25 to the chief petition, and those were (for the most part) either young men, who came over servants and never had any show of religion in them, or fishermen of Marblehead, profane persons, divers of them brought the last year from Newfoundland to fish a season and so to return again. Others were such as a barber of Boston, who being demanded by the governor what moved him to set his hand made answer that the gentlemen were his customers, etc. And these are the men who must be held forth to the Parliament as driven out of England by the bishops, etc., and whose tears and sighs must move compassion.

Dr. Child, being upon this apprehended and brought before the governor and Council, fell into a great passion and gave big words, but being told that if he would behave himself ∧no∧ better, he should be committed to the common prison and clapped in irons, upon this he grew more calm; so he was committed to the marshal, with Smith and Dand, for 2 or 3 days till the ships were gone, for he was very much troubled to be hindered from his voyage and offered to pay his fine, but that would not be accepted for his discharge, seeing we had now new matter and worse against him (for the writings were of his hand).[63] Yet upon tender of sufficient bail he was set at liberty, but confined to his house. The other 2 were committed to prison, yet lodged in the keeper's house and had what diet they pleased, and none of their friends forbidden to come to them.

There was also one Thomas Joye, a young fellow, a carpenter, whom

---

63. The General Court had tried Child for contempt in Nov. 1646, because he presented an obnoxious petition and appealed to England before sentence was passed by the MBC. The discovery of his petitions and queries offered grounds for a second trial on the more serious charge of conspiracy. This trial was postponed until June 1647, in order to delay his return to England as long as possible.

they had employed to get hands to the petition. He was laid hold on and kept in irons about 4 or 5 days and then he humbled himself, confessed what he knew, and blamed himself for meddling in matters belonged not to him and blessed God for these irons upon his legs, hoping they should do him good while he lived. So he was let out upon reasonable bail.[64]

For their trial at the General Court in the (4) 47 [June 1647] and the sentence against them, etc., it is set down at large in the records of that Court with their petitions and queries intended for England and all proceedings.[65]

Mr. Winslow being now to go for England, etc., the Court was troubled how to furnish him with money or beaver (for there was nothing in the treasury, the country being in debt £1000, and what comes in by levies is corn or cattle), but the Lord stirred up the hearts of some few persons to lend £100 to be repaid by the next levy. Next, we went in hand to draw up his commission and instructions, and a Remonstrance and petitions to the commissioners in England, which were as follow:[66]

To the right honorable Robert, Earl of Warwick, Governor in Chief, Lord Admiral, and other the lords and gentlemen, Commissioners for

---

64. After his punishment Joy moved in 1647 from Boston to Hingham, where he built and operated the town mill.

65. There is little surviving information about the Remonstrants' conspiracy trial, held in June 1647. The General Court punished all five defendants savagely. Robert Child was fined £200, John Dand £200, Samuel Maverick £150, John Smith £100, and Thomas Burton £100, for a collective total equivalent to the annual tax laid on the entire colony. Child, Smith, and Burton paid in full; Dand could not pay, and was kept in prison until 1648 when he made a humble submission; and Maverick got his fine lowered to £75 in 1650.

66. The following memorial is the MBC's reply to the parliamentary commissioners' order of 15 May 1646 protecting Samuel Gorton (see p. XXX above). It also addresses the complaints raised by Dr. Child, adopting the title of Dr. Child's "Remonstrance and humble Petition" of May 1646 to the MBC.

Foreign Plantations. The humble Remonstrance and Petition of the Governor and Company of the Massachusetts Bay in New England in America. In way of answer to the Petition and Declaration of Samuel Gorton, etc.

Whereas by virtue of his Majesty's charter granted to your petitioners in the 4th year of His Highness' reign we were incorporated into a body politic with divers liberties and privileges extending to that part of New England where we now inhabit, we do acknowledge (as we have always done, and as in duty we are bound) that although we are removed out of our native country, yet we still have dependence upon that state and owe allegiance and subjection thereunto, according to our charter: And whereas by order from your honors dated May 15, 1646, we find that our answer to the information of the said Gorton, etc., is expected, and something also required of us, which (in all humble submission) we conceive may be prejudicial to the liberties granted us by the said charter and to our well-being in this remote part of the world, . . . therefore, we are bold to represent to your honors our apprehensions, whereupon we have thus presumed to petition you in this behalf.

It appears to us by the said order that we are conceived: 1. To have transgressed our limits by sending soldiers to fetch in Gorton, etc., out of Shawomet in the Narragansett Bay; 2. That we have either exceeded or abused our authority in banishing them out of our jurisdiction when they were in our power. For the 1. we humbly crave (for your better satisfaction) that your honors will be pleased to peruse what we have delivered to the care of Mr. Edward Winslow, our agent or commissioner, and the letters of the said Gorton and his company (according to their own bad English). Thereby it will appear what the men are, and how unworthy your favor; thereby also will appear the wrongs and provocations we received from them, and our long patience towards them, till they became our professed enemies, wrought us disturbance, and attempted our ruin. In which case our charter (as we conceive) gives us full power to deal with them as enemies by force of arms.

For the other particular in your honors' order, viz. the banishment of Gorton, ∧etc.∧, as we are assured upon good grounds that our sentence upon them was less than their deserving, so (as we conceive) we had sufficient authority by our charter to inflict the same, having full and absolute power and authority to punish, pardon, rule, govern, etc., granted us therein.

Now, by occasion of the said order, those of Gorton's company begin to lift up their heads and speak their pleasures of us, threatening the poor Indians also, who (to avoid their tyranny) had submitted themselves and their lands under our protection and government, and some of them brought (by the labor of one of our elders, Mr. John Eliot, who hath obtained to preach to them in their own language) to good forwardness in embracing the gospel of God in Christ Jesus.[67] All which hopeful beginnings are like to be dashed if Gorton, etc., shall be countenanced and upheld against them and us; which also will endanger our peace here at home, for some among ourselves (men of unquiet spirits, affecting rule and innovation)[68] have taken boldness to prefer scandalous and seditious petitions for such liberties as neither our charter, nor reason, or religion will allow, and being called before us in open court to give account of their miscarriage therein, they have threatened us with your honors' authority, and (before they knew whether we would proceed to any sentence against them or not) have refused to answer but appealed to your honors. Their appeals we have not admitted, being assured that they cannot stand with the liberty and power granted us by our charter, nor will be allowed by your honors, who well know it

67. John Eliot began preaching to the Indians in Sept. or Oct. 1646, only two or three months before the date of this memorial.
68. Dr. Child and his fellow Remonstrants.

would be destructive to all government, both in the honor and also in the power of it, if it should be in the liberty of delinquents to evade the sentence of justice and force us by appeal to follow them into England, where the evidence and circumstances of facts cannot be so clearly held forth as in their proper place, besides the insupportable charges we must be at in the prosecution thereof. These considerations are not new to your honors and the High Court of Parliament, the records whereof bear witness of the wisdom and faithfulness of our ancestors in that great Council, who in those times of darkness, when they acknowledged a supremacy in the bishops of Rome in all causes ecclesiastical, yet would not allow appeals to Rome, etc., to remove causes out of the courts in England[69] . . . Our humble petition to your honors (in the next place) is that you will be pleased to continue your favorable aspect upon these poor infant plantations, And this in special, if you shall please to pass by any failings you may have observed in our course, to confirm our liberties granted to us by charter by leaving delinquents to our ⟨justice⟩ just proceedings, and discountenancing our enemies and disturbers of our peace or such as molest our people there upon pretence of injustice. Thus we continue our earnest prayers for your prosperity for ever.

By order of the General Court,

[December, 1646]   Increace Nowell, secretary

John Winthrop, governor.

. . .

(1) [March]. At the Court of Assistants 3 or 4 were sent for who had been very active ⟨in⟩ about the petition to the commissioners in procuring hands to it (it being thought fit to pass by such as, being

---

69. A reference to Magna Carta, which asserted that the Church in England is to be free and hold its liberties inviolate, and also to the Statutes of Praemunire, passed in 1353, 1365, and 1393, which tried to forbid appeals of English ecclesiastical appointments to Rome.

drawn in, had only subscribed the petition), especially Mr. Samuel Maverick and Mr. [William] Clerke of Salem, the keeper of the ordinary there and a church member; these having taken an oath of fidelity to the government and enjoying all liberties of freemen, their offence was far the greater. So they were bound over to answer it at the next General Court.[70]

Mr. Smith and Mr. Dand (giving security to pay their fines assessed upon the former petition within 2 months) were bailed to the General Court.

Dr. Child also was offered his liberty upon bail to the General Court, and to be confined to Boston, but he chose rather to go to prison and so he was committed.[71]

Mr. Burton, one of the petitioners, being in the town meeting when the Court declaration was read, was much moved and spake in high language and would needs have a copy of it, which so soon as he had he went with it (as was undoubtedly believed) to Dr. Child and in the way fell down and lay there in the cold near half an hour, till company was gotten to carry him home in a chair, and after he continued in great pain and lame divers months.

It is observable that this man had gathered some providences about such as were against them, as that Mr. Winslow's horse died as he came riding to Boston, that his brother's son (a child of 8 years old) had killed his own sister (being 10 years of age) with his father's piece, etc., and his great trouble was lest this providence which now befell him should be imputed to their cause . . .

Mention was made before of some beginning to instruct the Indians,

<hr>

70. William Clark was a militia officer as well as the tavern keeper at Salem. He was criticized in 1646 for quarreling with the town constable, and also for keeping a "shuffling board in his house, occasioning misspending of time." He died before May 1647 and thus escaped trial for conspiracy.

71. Robert Child was held in the house of George Munnings, the Boston prison keeper, from about Dec. 1646 to about Sept. 1647, when (having paid £200 of his £250 fine levied at the two trials) he was finally allowed to sail for England.

etc. Mr. John Eliot, teacher of the Church of Roxbury, found such encouragement as he took great pains to get their language, and in a few months could speak of the things of God to their understanding, and God prospered his endeavors so as he kept a constant lecture to them in 2 places, one week at the wigwam of one Wabon, a mere sachem, near Watertown Mill, and the other ∧the next week∧ in the wigwam of Cutshamekin near Dorchester Mill. And for the furtherance of the work of God, divers of the English resorted to his lecture, and the governor and other of the magistrates ∧and elders∧ sometimes, and the Indians began to repair thither from other parts. His manner of proceeding was thus: he would persuade one of the other elder or some magistrate to begin the exercise with prayer in English. Then he took a text and read it first in the Indian language and after in English. Then he preached to them in Indian about an hour (but first I should have spoke of the catechizing their children, who were soon brought to answer him some short questions, whereupon he gave every of them an apple or a cake). Then he demanded of some of the chief if they understood him. If they answered, yea, then he asked of them if they had any questions to propound, and they had usually 2 or 3 or more questions which he did resolve. At one time (when the governor was there and about 200 people, Indian and English, in one wigwam of Cutshamekin's) an old man asked him if God would receive such an old man as he was; to whom he answered by opening the parable of the workmen that were hired into the vineyard,[72] and when he had opened it he asked the old man if he did believe it, who answered he did and was ready to weep. A 2 question was, what was the reason that when all Englishmen did know God, yet some of them were poor. His answer was: 1. That God knows it is better for his children to be good than to be rich; he knows withal that if some of them had riches they would abuse them and wax proud and wanton, etc.; therefore he gives

72. Matt. 20:1–16.

them no more riches than may be needful for them that they may be kept from pride, etc., depended upon him; 2. He would hereby have men know that he hath better blessings to bestow upon good men than riches, etc., and that their best portion is in heaven, etc. A 3 question was if a man had 2 wives (which was ordinary with them), seeing he must put away one, which he should put away. To this it was answered that by the law of God the 1 is the true wife and the other is no wife, but if such a case fell out they should then repair to the magistrates and they would direct them what to do, for it might be that the 1 wife might be an adulteress, etc., and then she was to be put away. When all their questions were resolved, he concluded with prayer in the Indian language.

The Indians were usually very attentive and kept their children so quiet as caused no disturbance. Some of them began to be seriously affected and to understand the things of God and they were generally ready to reform whatsoever they were told to be against the word of God, as their sorcery (which they call pawwawing), their whoredoms, etc., idleness, etc.[73] The Indians grew very inquisitive after knowledge both in things divine and also human, so as one of them meeting with an honest plain Englishman would needs know of him what were the first beginnings, which we call principles, of a commonwealth? The Englishman being far short in the knowledge of such matters, yet ashamed that an Indian should find an Englishman ignorant of anything, bethought himself what answer to give him, at last resolved upon this, viz. that the 1. principle of a commonwealth was salt, for (saith he) by means of salt we can keep our flesh and fish to have it ready

---

73. In Nov. 1646 the General Court decided to provide land for Indians who wanted to live in an orderly way among the English, to fine those Indians who performed "outward worship to their false gods, or to the devill" within MBC jurisdiction, and to appoint two ministers to preach to the Indians. Eliot was the only minister who stepped forward; he received £10 for his Indian labors in May 1647, and the promise of £20 annually thereafter.

when we need it, whereas you lose much for want of it and are sometimes ready to starve. A 2. principle is iron, for therewith we fell trees,
build houses, till our land, etc. A 3. is ships, by which we carry forth
such commodities as we have to spare and fetch in such as we need,
as cloth, wine, etc. Alas (saith the Indian), then I fear we shall never
be a commonwealth, for we can neither make salt, nor iron, nor
ships . . .

One of Windsor arraigned and executed at Hartford for a
witch[74] . . .

[May] 26. The Court of Elections was at Boston. Great laboring
there had been by the friends of the petitioners to have one chosen
governor who favored their cause, and some new magistrates to have
been chosen of their side, but the mind of the country appeared clearly,
for the old governor was chosen again with 2 or 300 votes more than
any other, and no one new magistrate was chosen but only Captain
Robert Bridges.[75]

Captain Weld of Roxbury being dead, the young men of the town
agreed together to choose one George Denyson, a young soldier come
lately out of the wars in England; which the ancient and chief men of
the town understanding, they came together at the time appointed and
chose one Mr. Pricharde, a godly man ∧and one∧ of the chief in the
town, passing by their lieutenant, fearing least the young Dennison
would have carried it from him. Whereupon much discontent and murmuring arose in the town. The young men were over strongly bent to
have their will, although their election was void in law (George Den-

---

74. This was Alice Young, New England's first known convicted witch, who was hanged at Windsor, Conn. (not Hartford) on 26 May 1647. Her husband John sold his land
in Windsor and moved away.

75. Bridges had been the speaker of the deputies in Nov. 1646, when the Remonstrants
were first condemned, so he was probably no supporter of Dr. Child. But the General
Court did make one concession advocated by the Remonstrants: they gave non-freemen
the liberty to serve on juries, and to vote for town officers and assessment of taxes.

nison not being then a freeman) and the ancient men over voted them above 20, and the lieutenant was discontented because he was neglected, etc. The cause coming to the Court and all parties being heard, Mr. Prichard was allowed, and the young men were pacified, and the lieutenant.[76]

4 (4) [June]. Canonicus the great sachem of Narragansett died, a very old man.

8 (4). The synod began again at Cambridge.[77] The next day Mr. Ezekiel Rogers of Rowley preached in the forenoon, and the magistrates and deputies were present, and in the afternoon Mr. Eliot preached to the Indians in their own language before all the Assembly. Mr. Rogers in his sermon took occasion to speak of the petitioners (then in question before the Court) and exhorted the Court to do justice upon them, yet with desire of favor to such as had been drawn in, etc., and should submit. He reproved also the practice of private members making speeches in the Church Assemblies to the disturbance and hindrance of the ordinances; also he call[ed] for the reviving the ancient practice in England of children asking their parents' blessing upon their knees, etc. Also, he reproved the great oppression in the country, etc., and other things amiss, as long hair, etc. Divers were offended at his zeal in some of these passages.

Mr. Bradford, the governor of Plymouth, was there as a messenger of the Church of Plymouth, but the sickness (mentioned here in the next leaf) prevailed so as divers of the members of the synod were taken with it, whereupon they were forced to break up on the sudden.

The success of Mr. Eliot's labors in preaching to the Indians appears

76. JW is obviously relieved that this quarrel in Roxbury did not blow up into another Hingham militia case. Lt. Isaac Johnson, who was bypassed in 1647, was eventually promoted to captain of the Roxbury militia in 1667; he was killed in King Philip's War.

77. This synod had first convened in Sept. 1646; see above. The second session of June 1647 was soon disrupted by the "epidemical sickness" described by JW, whereupon the synod met again for its final and most important session on 15 Aug. 1648; see below.

in a small book set forth by Mr. Shepard and by other observations in the country.[78]

19 (1), 1646 [March 1647]. One Captain [Venner] Dobson in a ship of 80 ton, double manned and fitted for a man-of-war, was set forth from Boston to trade to the eastward. Their testimonial[79] was for the Gulf of Canada, but being taken with foul weather ∧and having lost their boat∧, they put into harbor at Cape Sable, and there shooting off 5 or 6 pieces of ordnance the Indians came aboard them and traded some skins. And withal Mr. D'Aulnay had notice and presently sent away 20 men overland (being about 30 miles from Port Royal), who lurking in the woods for their advantage, providence offered them a very fair one, for the master and merchant and most of the company went on shore (leaving but 6 men aboard) and carried no weapons with them, which the French perceiving, they came upon them and bound them and carried the master to the ship side, who commanded the men aboard to yield up the ship. The French being possessed of the ship carried her to Port Royal, and left some of their company to conduct the rest by land. When they came there they were all imprisoned and examined apart upon oath, and having confessed that they had traded, etc., the ship and cargo (being worth in all £1000) was kept as confiscate, and the men were put into 2 old shallops and sent home and arrived at Boston 6 (3) [May] 47. The merchants complained to the Court for redress, and offered to set forth a good ship to deal with some of D'Aulnay's vessels, but the Court thought it not safe nor expedient for us to begin a war with the French, nor could we charge any manifest wrong upon D'Aulnay, seeing we had told him that if ours did trade within his liberties they should do it at their own peril,[80]

---

78. Two tracts were published in London describing Eliot's mission work: an anonymous pamphlet, probably by Thomas Shepard, entitled *The Day-Breaking, If Not the Sun-Rising of the Gospell With the Indians in New-England* (1647), followed by Thomas Shepard's *The Clear Sun-Shine of the Gospel Breaking Forth upon the Indians in New England* (1648).

79. Warrant.

80. See 8 Oct. 1644 and 20 Sept. 1646, above.

and though we judged it an injury to restrain the natives and others from trading, etc. (they being a free people), yet, it being a common practice of all ∧civil∧ nations, his seizure of our ship would be accounted lawful and our letters of reprisal unjust. And besides, there appeared an overruling providence in it, otherwise he could not have seized a ship so well fitted, nor could wise men have lost her so foolishly . . .

(4) [June]. An epidemical sickness was through the country among Indians and English, French and Dutch. It took them like a cold, and a light fever with it. Such as bled or used cooling drinks died; those who took comfortable things for most part recovered, and that in few days. Wherein a special providence of God appeared, for not a family nor but few persons escaping it, had it brought all so weak as it did some and continued so long, our hay and corn had been lost for want of help, but such was the mercy of God to his people as few died, not above 40 or 50 in the Massachusetts and near as many at Connecticut. But that which made the stroke more sensible and grievous both to them and to all the country was the death of that faithful servant of the Lord, Mr. Thomas Hooker, pastor of the Church in Hartford, who for piety, prudence, wisdom, zeal, learning, and what else might make him serviceable in the place and time he lived in, ⟨was⟩ might be compared with men of greatest note. He shall need no other praise; the fruit of his labors in both Englands shall preserve an honorable ∧and happy∧ remembrance of him forever.[81]

14 (4) [June]. In this sickness the governor's wife, daughter of Sir John Tindale, knight, left this world for a better, being about 56 years of age: a woman of singular virtue, prudence, modesty, and piety, and specially beloved and honored of all the country[82] . . .

---

81. Hooker died on 7 July 1647.
82. Margaret Winthrop died on 14 June 1647. JW may also have contracted the disease, for he was very ill in Aug. 1647 (*WP*, 5:175–176).

The General Court made an order that all elections of governor, etc., should be by papers delivered in to the deputies before the Court as it was before permitted.[83] This was disliked by the freemen, and divers of the near towns petitioned for the repeal of it as an infringement of their liberty, for when they consented to send their deputies with full power, etc., they reserved to themselves matter of election. Upon these petitions the said order was repealed and it was referred to the next Court of Elections to consider of a meet way for ordering elections to the satisfaction of the petitioners and the rest of the freemen. But that Court being full of business and breaking up suddenly, it was put off further[84] . . .

It pleased the Lord to open to us a trade with Barbados and other islands in the West Indies, which as it provided gainful, so the commodities we had in exchange there for our cattle and provisions, as sugar, cotton, tobacco, and indigo, were a good help to discharge our engagements in England.[85] And this summer there was so great a drought as their potatoes and corn, etc., were burnt up, and divers London ships which rode there were so short of provision as if our vessels had not supplied them they could not have returned home, which was an observable providence, that whereas many of the London seamen were wont to despise New England as a poor, barren country, should now be relieved by our plenty . . .

4 (6) [August]. There was a great marriage to be solemnized at Boston. The bridegroom being of Hingham, Mr. Hobart's church, he

83. On 11 Nov. 1647 the General Court directed the freemen to cast their ballots for governor and magistrates in their respective towns, with the sealed ballots carried to the court of elections. Previously, the freemen had come personally to the court of elections, or sent proxies.

84. The General Court records do not indicate that the order of 11 Nov. 1647 was repealed. No further changes in the electoral procedure were introduced during JW's lifetime.

85. By 1647 the Barbados planters had discovered how to cultivate sugar cane; converting most of their land to this immensely profitable cash crop, they imported slave labor from Africa and provisions from Britain and New England.

was procured to preach and came to Boston to that end, but the magistrates hearing of it sent to him to forbear. The reasons were: 1. For that his spirit had been discovered to be averse to our ecclesiastical and civil government, and he was a bold man and would speak his mind; 2. We were not willing to bring in the English custom of ministers performing the solemnity of marriage, which sermons at such times might induce, but if any minister were present and would bestow a word of exhortation, etc., it was permitted.[86]

The new governor of the Dutch, called Peter Stevesant, being arrived at the Monados [Manhattan], sent his secretary to Boston with letters to the governor with tender of all courtesy and good correspondency, but withal ⟨complaining⟩ taking notice of the differences between them and Connecticut, and offering to prepare for a hearing and determination in Europe; in which letter he lays claim to all between Connecticut and Delaware. The Commissioners being then assembled at Boston, the governor acquainted them with the letter and it was put to consideration what answer to return. Some advised that, seeing he made profession of much good will and desire of all neighborly correspondency, we should seek to gain upon him by courtesy, and therefore to accept his offer and to tender him a visit at his own home or ∧a meeting∧ at any of our towns where he should choose. But the Commissioners of those parts thought otherwise, supposing it would be more to their advantage to stand upon terms of distance, etc.; and answer was returned accordingly, only taking notice of his offer and showing our readiness to give him a meeting in time and place convenient. So matters continued as they were.

26, (7) [September]. But it happened that a Dutch ship from Holland being in the harbor at New Haven (where they had traded about a

---

86. Marriage in Puritan New England was a civil ceremony. The first marriage solemnized by a clergyman in Massachusetts took place in 1686, after the annulment of the MBC charter.

month) was surprised by the Dutch governor and carried to the Manhattan. The manner was thus: the merchants of New Haven had bought a ship at the Manhattan, which was to be delivered at New Haven. In her the Dutch governor put a company of soldiers, who being under decks when the ship came into New Haven, took their opportunity afterward upon the Lord's day to seize the Dutch ship, and having the wind fair carried her away.[87] The governor of New Haven complained of the injury to the Dutch governor and made a protest, etc. The Dutch governor justified the act by examples of the like in Europe, etc., but especially by claiming the place and so all along the seacoast to Cape Cod. He pretended to seize the ship as forfeit to the West India Company by trading in their limits without leave or recognition. It fell out at the same time that 3 of the Dutch governor's servants fled from him and came to New Haven, and being pursued were there apprehended and put in prison. The Dutch governor writes to have them delivered to him, but directs his letter to New Haven in New Netherlands. Upon this the governor of New Haven refuseth to deliver them and writes back to the Dutch, maintaining their right to the place, both by patent from King James and also by purchase from the natives and by quiet possession and improvement many years. He wrote also to the governor of the Massachusetts, acquainting him with all that had passed and desired advice. These letters coming to Boston about the time of the General Court, he acquainted the Court with them, and a letter was drawn and sent (as from the Court) to this purpose, to the Dutch governor, viz. that we were very sorry for the difference which was fallen out between him and our confederates of New Haven; that we might not withhold assistance from them in case of any injurious violence offered to them; that we accounted their title to the place they

87. This ship, the *Sint Beninjo*, belonged to two Dutch merchants, Samuel Goodhouse and William Westerhouse, who lived in New Haven. Eventually these merchants and the New Haven government were forced to acquiesce in Stuyvesant's seizure.

possessed to be as good as the Dutch had to the Manhattan; that we would willingly interpose for a friendly reconciliation; and that we would write to New Haven to persuade the delivery of the fugitives, etc. We wrote also to the governor of New Haven to the same purpose. But this notwithstanding, they detained the fugitives still, nor would send our letter to the Dutch governor. Whereupon he made proclamation of free liberty for all servants, etc., of New Haven within his jurisdiction.

This course not prevailing, about the end of winter he wrote privately to the fugitives, and the minister of their Church wrote also, whereby he gave such assurance to the fugitives both of pardon of what was past and satisfaction otherwise, as they made an escape and returned home.[88]

(1) [March]. After this the Dutch governor writes to our governor in Dutch, complaining of injuries from the governor of New Haven (calling him the pretended governor, etc.), particularly for wronging his reputation by slanderous reports . . . The governor of New Haven, Mr. Theophilus Eaton, he writes also about the same time, complaining of the Dutch governor, and informing of Indian intelligence of the Dutch his animating the natives to war upon the English, and of the excessive customs and other ill usage of our vessels arriving there, propounding withal a prohibition of all trade with the Dutch until satisfaction were given. These letters being imparted, 15 (1) [15 March 1648], to the General Court at Boston, they thought the matter more weighty and general to the concernment of all the country than that anything should then be determined about it, and more fit for the Commissioners first to consider of, etc., and returned answer to New Haven accordingly.[89]

88. The fugitive Dutch servants were ready to return to New Netherland, since they had been arrested for drunkenness in New Haven.

89. See 28 May 1648, below.

About this time we had intelligence of an observable hand of God against the Dutch at New Netherlands, which though it were sadly to be lamented in regard of the calamity, yet there appeared in it so much of God in favor to his poor people here, and displeasure towards such as have opposed and injured them, as is not to be passed by without due observation and acknowledgment. The late governor Mr. William Kieft (a sober and prudent man), though he abstained from outward force, yet had continually molested the colonies of Hartford and New Haven and used menacings ∧and protests∧ against them upon all occasions, and had burnt down a trading house which New Haven had built upon Delaware River, and went for Holland in a ship of 400 ton, well manned and richly laden, to the value (as was supposed) of £20,000, and carried away with him 2 of our people under censure (the one condemned for rape), though we pursued them, etc. But in their passage in the (8th) month [October] the ship, mistaking the channel, was carried into Severn and cast away upon the coast of Wales near Swansea, the governor and 80 other persons drowned, and some 20 saved.[90]

Complaint had been made to the Commissioners of the colonies at their last meeting by Pumham and Sacononoco against the Gortonists (who were now returned to Shawomet and had named it Warwick) for eating up all their corn with their cattle, etc., so as the poor Indians were in danger to be starved, etc. Upon their further complaints to us, the General Court in the (1) month [March] sent 3 messengers to demand satisfaction for the Indians and for other wrongs to some English there, and to command them to depart the place as belonging to us, etc. They used our messengers with more respect than formerly, but gave no satisfaction, bearing themselves upon their charter, etc. We

90. Kieft sailed from New Amsterdam on the *Princess* on 16 Aug. 1647 and was drowned when the ship was wrecked in the Bristol Channel on 27 Sept.

could do no more at present, but we procured the Indians some corn in the meantime.[91]

In the agitation of this matter ⟨at⟩ ∧in∧ the General Court some moved to have an order (upon refusal of satisfaction, etc.) to send forces presently against them, but others thought better to forbear any resolution until the return of our messengers, and the rather because we expected our agent out of England shortly, by whom we should know more of the success of our petition to the Parliament, etc.,[92] it being very probable that their charter would be called in as illegal, etc. and this counsel prevailed.

It may be now seasonable to set down what success it pleased the Lord to give Mr. Winslow, our agent, with the Parliament.

Mr. Winslow set sail from Boston about the middle of December 1646, and carried such commission, instructions, etc., as are before mentioned. Upon his arrival in England and delivery of his letters to the Earl of Warwick, Sir Henry Vane, etc., from the governor, he had a day appointed for audience before the Committee;[93] and Gorton and other of his company appeared also, to justify their petition and information which they had formerly exhibited against the Court, etc., for making war upon them and keeping them prisoners, etc. But after that our agent had showed the 2 letters they wrote to us from Shawomet, and the testimony of the Court and some of the elders concerning their blasphemous heresies and other miscarriages, it pleased the Lord to bring about the hearts of the Committee so as they discerned of Gorton, etc., what they were, and of the justice of our proceedings against them. Only they were not satisfied in this, that they were not within our

91. Trouble continued between the Gortonists and their Indian neighbors in 1648. This time the Gortonists appealed to the New England Confederation commissioners, who on 10 Sept. warned the Indians to commit no further outrages against the English.

92. See 4 Dec. 1646, above.

93. While waiting for his hearing before the Warwick Commission, Winslow wrote a pamphlet, *Hypocrisie Unmasked* (London, 1647), to rebut Samuel Gorton's tract of 1646, *Simplicities Defence against Seven-Headed Policy.*

jurisdiction, etc., to which our agent pleaded 2 things: 1. That they were within the jurisdiction of Plymouth or Connecticut, and so the order of the Commissioners of the United Colonies had left them to us; 2. The Indians (upon whose land they dwelt) had subjected themselves and their land to our government. Whereupon, the Committee made this order following: . . .

After our hearty commendations, etc.

By our letter of May 15, 1646, we communicated to you our reception of a complaint from Mr. Gorton and Mr. Holden, etc., touching some proceedings tried against them by your government. We also imparted to you our resolutions for their residing upon Shawomet and the other parts of that tract of land which is mentioned in a charter of civil incorporation heretofore granted them by us,[94] praying and requiring you to permit the same accordingly, without extending your jurisdiction to any part thereof or disquieting them in their civil peace or otherwise interrupting them in their possession until we should receive your answer to the same in point of title, and thereupon give further order. We have since received a Petition and Remonstrance from you by your commissioner, Mr. Winslow, and though we have not yet entered into a particular consideration of the matter, yet we do in the general take notice of your respect, as well to the Parliament's authority, as your own just privileges, and find cause to be further confirmed in our former opinion and knowledge of your prudence and faithfulness to God and His cause. And perceiving by your petition that some persons[95] do take advantage from our said letter to decline and question your jurisdiction and to pretend a general liberty to appeal hither, upon their being called in question before you for matters proper to your cognizance, we thought it necessary (for preventing of further inconveniences in this

---

94. Roger Williams's patent for the colony of Rhode Island and Providence Plantations, issued by the Warwick Commission on 14 March 1644.

95. The Remonstrants.

kind) hereby to declare that we intended not thereby to encourage any appeals from your justice, nor to restrain the bounds of your jurisdiction to a narrower compass than is held forth by your letters patents, but to leave you with all that freedom and latitude that may in any respect be duly claimed by you, knowing that the limiting of you in that kind may be very prejudicial (if not destructive) to the government and public peace of the colony. For your further satisfaction wherein, you may remember that our said resolution took ⟨place⟩ ∧rise∧ from an admittance that the Narragansett Bay (the thing in question) was wholly without the bounds of your patent, the examination whereof will in the next place come before us. In the meantime we have received advertisement that the place is within the patent of New Plymouth, and that the grounds of your proceedings against the complainants was a joint authority from the 4 governments of Massachusetts, Plymouth, Connecticut, and New Haven, which if it falls in upon proof will much alter the state of the question. And we declare, that we shall for the future be very ready to give our encouragement and assistance in all your endeavors for settling of your peace and government, and the advancement of the gospel of Jesus Christ, to whose blessing we commend your persons and affairs.

Your very loving friends,

From the Committee of Lords and
Commons, etc., 25 May, 1647.

Warwick,
Governor and Admiral
[and eleven other signatures].[96]

The Committee having thus declared themselves to have an honorable regard of us, and care to promote the welfare of the 4 United

---

96. With this order, the Warwick Commission rejected the appeal of Dr. Child and the Remonstrants. But the status of the Gortonists at Warwick, R.I. remained unsettled. On 22 July 1647, the Warwick Commission directed that the Gortonists should be left undisturbed, even if Warwick lay within Plymouth jurisdiction.

Colonies, . . . our agent proceeded to have the charter (which they had lately granted to those of Rhode Island and Providence) to be called in as lying within the patent of Plymouth or Connecticut.[97]

10 (3) [May]. The Court of Elections was at Boston. Mr. Symmes, pastor of Charlestown, preached. Mr. Winthrop was chosen governor again[98] and Mr. Dudley deputy governor, Mr. Endecott sergeant major, and he and Mr. Bradstreet Commissioners, etc.

(3) [May]. Here arrived 3 ships from London ∧in one day∧. By the passengers we understood, as also by letters from Mr. Winslow, etc., how the hopes and endeavors of Dr. Child and other the petitioners, etc., had been blasted by the special providence of the Lord who still wrought for us.

Dr. Child had a brother, a major of a regiment in Kent, who being set on by his brother and William Vassall (who went from Scituate to petition against the country, etc.), set out a pamphlet,[99] wherein he published their petition exhibited to our General Court and other proceedings of the Court. This was answered by Mr. Winslow in a book entitled *The Salamander*[1] (pointing therein at Mr. Vassall, a man never at rest but when he was in the fire of contention), wherein he cleared the justice of our proceedings. As for those who went over to procure us trouble, God met with them all. Mr. Vassall, finding no entertainment for his petitions, went to Barbados.

---

97. JW was too optimistic here. Edward Winslow tried but failed to call in Roger Williams's patent, and in the 1650s Gorton's town of Warwick was incorporated into the colony of Rhode Island.

98. JW does not mention that on 20 Dec. 1647 he was married to his fourth wife, Martha Coytemore, widow of Capt. Thomas Coytemore. In Dec. 1648 Martha bore him a son named Joshua (JW's sixteenth child), who died at age two.

99. Major John Child published *New-Englands Jonas Cast up at London* (London, 1647) on behalf of his brother. This pamphlet described the MBC's brutal persecution of the Remonstrants, and presented documents that William Vassall had brought to England in 1646 and supplied to John Child.

1. *New-Englands Salamander Discovered* (London, 1647), a point-by-point refutation of John Child's tract, which Winslow claimed was really the work of Vassall.

Dr. Child preferred a petition to the Committee against us and put in Mr. Thomas Fowle his name among others, but he hearing of it protested against it (for God had brought him very low both in his estate and in his reputation since he joined in the first petition). After this, the Doctor meeting with Mr. Willoughby[2] upon the Exchange[3] (this Mr. Willoughby dwelt at Charlestown, but his father was a colonel of the City), and falling in talk about New England, the Doctor railed against the people, saying they were a company of rogues and knaves. Mr. Willoughby answered that he who spake so, etc., was a knave; whereupon the Doctor gave him a box on the ear. Mr. Willoughby was ready to have closed with him, etc., but being upon the Exchange he was stayed, but presently arrested him. And when the Doctor saw the danger he was in, he employed some friends to make his peace, who ordered him to give £5 to the poor of New England (for Mr. Willoughby would have nothing of him) and to give Mr. Willoughby open satisfaction in the full Exchange, and to give it under his hand never to speak evil of New England men after, nor to occasion any trouble to the country or to any of the people; all which he gladly performed, and besides God had so blasted his estate as he was quite broken, etc.[4]

Samuel Gorton arrived here.[5] The Court being informed of it made an order that he should be apprehended, etc., but he sending us the Earl of Warwick's letter desiring only that he might have liberty to pass home, the Court recalled their former order and gave him a week's liberty to provide for his departure. This was much opposed by some, but the most considered that it being only at the Earl's request (no

2. Francis Willoughby, a Charlestown merchant, had served as a deputy in the General Court in 1646 when the Remonstrants' case was first tried.

3. The Royal Exchange, built in London by Sir Thomas Gresham in 1566 as a place where merchants could meet and conduct business.

4. Robert Child led a more satisfactory life after leaving New England than JW indicates. He pursued chemical and alchemical experiments, mixed with the leading scientists of the day, published a treatise on husbandry, and died in Ireland in 1654.

5. He arrived in May 1648.

command), it could be no prejudice to our liberty, and our commissioner being still attending the Parliament, it might much have disadvantaged our cause and his expedition if the Earl should have heard that we had denied him so small a request. Yet it was carried only by a casting voice . . .

Mr. Eaton having again moved the governor to know the mind of the Court touching the Dutch governor's proceedings, the Court appointed a committee to consider of it (after the Court was adjourned), and withal to consider of the Articles of Confederation, and some of the Commissioners' orders, for there was some murmuring among the people about the inequality of some articles, as that we bearing more than half the charge upon all occasions, etc., should yet have no more Commissioners than the smallest of the other; and that all charges should be levied by the poll, considering how great a part of our people were laborers and craftsmen, and of theirs the most were farmers and well stocked, etc.[6]

28 (3) [May]. Soon after the Court was adjourned, the governor received 2 letters from the Dutch governor, holding forth much assurance of his sincere affection to a firm peace and neighborly compliance with all the English, and that upon these grounds: 1. Our unity in the true religion; 2. The ancient league between the 2 nations; 3. The community in danger, in respect of the common enemy, both Spaniards and Indians; 4. The reconciling former differences and preventing future; 5. The benefit of a mutual league, both offensive and defensive, against a common enemy; and offered to meet Mr. Bradford, the governor of Plymouth, and Mr. Winthrop, the governor of the Massachu-

6. The May 1648 General Court appointed a committee headed by JW to propose revisions in the Articles of Confederation among Massachusetts, Plymouth, Connecticut, and New Haven. This committee complained that the Confederation was interfering in the internal affairs of the MBC, and that Massachusetts was overtaxed and underrepresented. The Confederation commissioners considered these grievances in Sept. 1648, but refused to make any major changes in the Articles.

setts, at Connecticut a[t] such time as we should appoint, and to refer all to us.[7]

There was some reason why the Dutch governor's spirit should begin to fall, both in regard of the weakness the state of Holland (especially the West India Company) were fallen into (which was not the least occasion of their late peace with Spain),[8] and also in respect of the doubts which he was fallen into at this time, both from his own unruly people and also of the neighbor Indians, for neither would his people be restrained from furnishing the Indians with guns, powder, etc., nor would the Indians endure to be without that trade; and the great loss the company had sustained by late wreck of 3 ships, and the old governor and many principal men with him, made him doubtful of any great supply from Holland . . .

At this Court one Margaret Jones of Charlestown was indicted and found guilty of witchcraft and hanged for it.[9] The evidence against her was: 1. that she was found to have such a malignant touch as many persons (men, women, and children) whom she stroked or touched with any affection of displeasure or, etc., were taken with deafness, or vomiting, or other violent pains, or sickness; 2. she practicing physic, and her medicines being such things as (by her own confession) were harmless, as aniseed, licorice, etc., yet had extraordinary violent effects; 3. she would use to tell such as would not make use of her physic that they would never be healed, and accordingly their diseases and hurts continued with relapses against the ordinary course and beyond the apprehension of all physicians and surgeons; 4. some things which she foretold came to pass accordingly; other things she could tell of (as

7. Stuyvesant eventually met with the New England Confederation commissioners at Hartford in Sept. 1650, after JW's death.

8. The Dutch had been at war with Spain since 1621; they reached a peace settlement at Munster in Jan. 1648, in one of the treaties that closed the Thirty Years' War in Europe.

9. Jones was hanged on Lecture day, 14 June 1648, at Boston—one of four women executed for witchcraft in New England in 1647–1648.

secret speeches, etc.) which she had no ordinary means to come to the knowledge of; 5. she had (upon search) an apparent teat ⟨as⟩ in her secret parts as fresh as if it had been newly sucked, and after it had been searched, upon a second search that was withered, and another began on the opposite side; 6. in the prison in the clear daylight there was seen in her arms, she sitting on the floor and her clothes up, etc., a little child which ran from her into another room, and the officer following it, it was vanished; the like child was seen in 2 other places to which she had relation, and one maid that saw it fell sick upon it, and was cured by the said Margaret who used means to be employed to that end. Her behavior at her trial was very intemperate, lying notoriously, and railing upon the jury and witnesses, etc., and in the like distemper she died. The same day and hour she was executed there was a very great tempest at Connecticut, which blew down many trees, etc. . . .

28 (5) [July]. The *Wellcome* of Boston, about 300 ton, riding before Charlestown, having in her 80 horses and 120 ton of ballast, in calm weather fell a rolling and continued so about 12 hours, so as though they brought a great weight to the one side yet she would heel to the other, and so deep as they feared her foundering. It was then the time of the County Court at Boston, and the magistrates hearing of it, and withal that one [Thomas] Jones (the husband of the witch lately executed) had desired to have passage in her to Barbados, they sent the officer presently with a warrant to apprehend him, one of them saying that the ship would stand still as soon as he was in prison. And as the officer went and was passing over the ferry, one said to him, you can tame men sometimes, can't you tame this ship? The officer answer, I have that here that (it may be) will tame her and make her be quiet, and with that showed his warrant, and at the same instant she began to stop and presently stayed, and after he was put in prison moved no more.

There appeared over the harbor at New Haven in the evening the form of the keel of a ship with 3 masts, to which were suddenly added all the tackling and sails, and presently after upon the top of the poop a man standing with one hand akimbo under his left side, and ∧in∧ his right hand a sword stretched out towards the sea. Then from the side of the ship which was from the town arose a great smoke which covered all the ship, and in that smoke she vanished away. But some saw her keel sink into the water. This was seen by many, men and women, and it continued about $\frac{1}{4}$ of an hour[10] . . .

15 (6) [August]. The synod met at Cambridge by adjournment from the (4) last [June 1647].[11] Mr. Allen of Dedham preached out of Acts 15,[12] a very godly, learned and particular handling of near all the doctrines and applications concerning that subject, with a clear discovery and refutation of such errors, objections, and scruples as had been raised about it by some young heads in the country.

It fell out about the middest of his ⟨sentence⟩ ∧sermon∧ there came a snake into the seat where many of the elders sat behind the preacher. It came in at the door where people stood thick upon the stairs; divers of the elders shifted from it, but Mr. Tompson, one of the elders of Braintree, (a man of much faith), trod upon the head of it and so held it with his foot and stale[13] with a small pair of grains[14] until it was killed. This being so remarkable and nothing falling out but by divine providence, it is out of doubt the Lord discovered somewhat of his mind in it: the serpent is the devil, the synod the representation of the Churches of Christ in New England. The devil had formerly and lately attempted their disturbance and dissolution, but their faith in the seed of the woman overcame him and crushed his head.[15]

10. This apparition was of the New Haven ship lost at sea in Jan. 1646.
11. The Cambridge synod convened on 15 Aug. 1648 for its third and most important session. It had previously convened on 1 Sept. 1646 and 8 June 1647; see above.
12. Acts 15:22–27, on the origin and efficacy of church synods.
13. A handle, as of a pitchfork.
14. The prongs of Tompson's pitchfork.
15. Gen. 3:15, a principal text of covenant theologians.

The synod went on comfortably and intended only the framing of a confession of faith, etc., and a form of church discipline (not entertaining any other business). For the first, they wholly agreed with that which the Assembly in England had lately set forth;[16] for the other, viz. for discipline, they drew it by itself according to the general practice of our Churches.[17] So they ended in less than 14 days.

(6) *[August]*. This month, when our first harvest was near had in, the pigeons came again all over the country, but did no harm (harvest being just in), but proved a great blessing, it being incredible what multitudes of them were killed daily. It was ordinary for one man to kill 8 or 10 dozen in half a day, yea, 5 or 6 dozen at one shoot, and some 7 or 8. Thus the Lord showed us that he could make the same creature which formerly had been a great chastisement now to become a great blessing.

About the middest of this summer there arose a fly out of the ground about the bigness of the top of a man's little finger of brown color. They filled the woods from Connecticut to Sudbury with a great noise, and eat up the young sprouts of the trees but meddled not with the corn. They were also between Plymouth and Braintree, but came no further. If the Lord had not stopped them they had spoiled all our orchards, for they did some few . . .

(9) *[November]* 8. One Bezaliell Payton of the Church of Boston,

16. The Westminster Assembly had completed a Confession of Faith in Dec. 1646 which was adopted by Parliament in June 1648. By approving this Confession, the New England clergy asserted their doctrinal unity with the Puritans at home.

17. The Cambridge Platform of Church Discipline, drawn up by Richard Mather, spelled out the distinctive features of the Congregational system practiced in the orthodox New England churches in the late 1640s—a system far more uniform than the mix of Presbyterians, Independents, and radical sects to be found in Puritan England at this date. Published under the title *A Platform of Church Discipline* at Cambridge in 1649, it affirmed the autonomy of each local church, limited in membership to visible saints; it spelled out the duties and powers of pastors, teachers, elders, and deacons; it provided for communion and close consultation among the churches; and it recognized the right of the civil magistrates to interfere in matters of doctrine and practice.

coming from Barbados in a vessel of 60 ton, was taken with a great storm of wind and rain at east in the night between Cape Cod and the Bay, so as he was forced to put out 2 anchors, but the storm increasing they were put from their anchors, and seeing no way but death before their eyes they commended themselves to the Lord who delivered them marvelously, for they were carried among Conyhassat[18] rocks, yet touched none of them, and put on shore upon a beach. And presently there came a mighty sea which lifted their vessel over the beach into a smooth water, and after the storm was over they used means and gat her safe out.

The like example of the blessing of prayer fell out not long after in saving a small open vessel of ours, wherein was one Richard Collecut of the Church of Dorchester, who being eastward about trading was carried by a violent storm among the rocks where they could find no place to get out, so they went to prayer and presently there came a great sea and heaved their vessel over into the open sea in a place between 2 rocks.

11 (11) [January]. About 8 persons were drowned this winter . . . 2 were the children of one of the Church of Boston. While their parents were at the lecture, the boy (being about 7 years of age) having a small staff in his hand ran down upon the ice towards a boat he saw, and the ice breaking he fell in, but his staff kept him up till his sister about 14 years old ran down to save her brother (though there were 4 men at hand and called to her not to go, being themselves hasting to save him) and so drowned herself and him also, being past recovery ere the men could come at them, and could easily reach ground with their feet. The parents had no more sons, and confessed they had been too indulgent towards him and had set their hearts over much upon him.

This puts me in mind of another child, very strangely drowned a little before winter. The parents were also members of the Church of

18. Cohasset.

Boston. The father had undertaken to maintain the mill dam, and being at work upon it (with some help he had hired) in the afternoon of the last day of the week, night came upon them before they had finished what they intended, and his conscience began to put him in mind of the Lord's day and he was troubled, yet went on and wrought an hour within night. The next day after evening exercise and after they had supped, the mother put 2 children to bed in the room where themselves did lie and they went out to visit a neighbor. When they returned they continued about an hour in the room and missed not the child, but then the mother going to the bed and not finding her youngest child (a daughter about 5 years of age), after much search she found it drowned in a well in her cellar; which was very observable, as by a special hand of God, that the child should go out of that room into another in the dark and there fall down at a trap door or go down the stairs and so into the well in the further end of the cellar, the top of the well and the water being even with the ground. But the father freely in the open congregation did acknowledge it the righteous hand of God for his profaning His holy day against the checks of his own conscience.[19]

19. This is the final entry in the journal. JW fell ill in Feb. 1649, and on 14 March Adam Winthrop reported to JW2 that their father had been in bed for over a month and was now "very low, weaker than ever I knew him," and too ill to write. He died on 26 March.

Abbreviations

Bradford	William Bradford, *Of Plymouth Plantation, 1620–1647,* ed. Samuel Eliot Morison (New York: Knopf, 1952)
CR	*Public Records of the Colony of Connecticut,* ed. J. Hammond Trumbull (Hartford: Lockwood & Brainard, 1850–1877); 10 vols.
Hall	David D. Hall, *The Antinomian Controversy, 1636–1638,* 2d ed. (Durham, N.C.: Duke University Press, 1990)
JW	John Winthrop
JW2	John Winthrop, Jr.
MBC	The Massachusetts Bay Company
MHS	The Massachusetts Historical Society
Morison	Samuel Eliot Morison, *The Founding of Harvard College* (Cambridge, Mass.: Harvard University Press, 1935)
MR	*Records of the Governor and Company of the Massachusetts Bay in New England, 1628–1686,* ed. Nathaniel B. Shurtleff (Boston: William White, 1853–1854); 5 vols. in 6
PR	*Records of the Colony of New Plymouth in New England,* ed. Nathaniel B. Shurtleff et al. (Boston: William White, 1855–1861); 12 vols.
RCA	*Records of the Court of Assistants of the Colony of the Massachusetts Bay, 1630–1692,* ed. John Noble and John F. Cronin (Boston: County of Suffolk, 1901–1928); 3 vols.
Savage	John Winthrop, *The History of New England from 1630 to 1649. By John Winthrop, Esq. First Governour of the Colony of the Massachusetts Bay. From his Original Manuscripts,* transcribed and edited by James Savage, 2d ed. (Boston: Little, Brown, 1853); 2 vols.
WP	*Winthrop Papers, 1498–1654* (Boston: Massachusetts Historical Society, 1929–); multivolume series in progress

Suggested Further Reading

❧

David Grayson Allen, *In English Ways: The Movement of Societies and The Transferal of English Local Law and Custom to Massachusetts Bay in the Seventeenth Century* (Chapel Hill: University of North Carolina Press, 1981).

Virginia Dejohn Anderson, *New England's Generation: The Great Migration and the Formation of Society and Culture in the Seventeenth Century* (New York: Cambridge University Press, 1991).

Emery Battis, *Saints and Sectaries: Anne Hutchinson and the Antinomian Controversy in the Massachusetts Bay Colony* (Chapel Hill: University of North Carolina Press, 1962).

Sacvan Bercovitch, *The Puritan Origins of the American Self* (New Haven: Yale University Press, 1975).

Charles Lloyd Cohen, *God's Caress: The Psychology of Puritan Religious Experience* (New York: Oxford University Press, 1986).

David Cressy, *Coming Over: Migration and Communication between England and New England in the Seventeenth Century* (New York: Cambridge University Press, 1987).

William Cronon, *Changes in the Land: Indians, Colonists, and the Ecology of New England* (New York: Hill and Wang, 1983).

Hugh J. Dawson, "John Winthrop's Rite of Passage: The Origins of the 'Christian Charitie' Discourse," *Early American Literature* 26 (1991): 219–231.

John Demos, *A Little Commonwealth: Family Life in Plymouth Colony* (New York: Oxford University Press, 1970).

Richard S. Dunn, *Puritans and Yankees: The Winthrop Dynasty of New England, 1630–1717* (Princeton: Princeton University Press, 1962).

Philip J. Greven, Jr., *Four Generations: Population, Land, and Family in Colonial Andover, Massachusetts* (Ithaca: Cornell University Press, 1970).

Philip F. Gura, *A Glimpse of Sion's Glory: Puritan Radicalism in New England, 1620–1660* (Middletown, Conn.: Wesleyan University Press, 1984).

David D. Hall, *Worlds of Wonder, Days of Judgment: Popular Religious Belief in Early New England* (New York: Knopf, 1989).

George Lee Haskins, *Law and Authority in Early Massachusetts: A Study in Tradition and Design* (New York: Macmillan, 1960).

Francis Jennings, *The Invasion of America: Indians, Colonialism, and the Cant of Conquest* (Chapel Hill: University of North Carolina Press, 1975).

Patrick M. Malone, *The Skulking Way of War: Technology and Tactics Among the New England Indians* (Lanham, Md.: Madison Books, 1991).

Perry Miller, *Orthodoxy in Massachusetts, 1630–1650: A Genetic Study* (Cambridge, Mass.: Harvard University Press, 1933).

Edmund S. Morgan, *The Puritan Dilemma: The Story of John Winthrop* (Boston: Little, Brown, 1958).

James G. Moseley, *John Winthrop's World: History as a Story; the Story as History* (Madison: University of Wisconsin Press, 1992).

Darrett B. Rutman, *Winthrop's Boston: A Portrait of a Puritan Town, 1630–1649* (Chapel Hill: University of North Carolina Press, 1965).

Neal Salisbury, *Manitou and Providence: Indians, Europeans, and the Making of New England, 1500–1643* (New York: Oxford University Press, 1982).

Lee Schweninger, *John Winthrop* (Boston: Twayne, 1990).

Roger Thompson, *Mobility and Migration: East Anglian Founders of New England, 1629–1640* (Amherst: University of Massachusetts Press, 1994).

Laurel Thatcher Ulrich, *Good Wives: Image and Reality in the Lives of Women in Northern New England, 1650–1750* (New York: Knopf, 1982).

Index

Personal names are generally given in the form found in the text. Page references to notes with biographical information are set in boldface type.

[LEARNING CENTER]
[COUNTY JUNIOR COLLEGE]
[TEXAS]